The Documentary History of
the Supreme Court of
the United States, 1789–1800

Volume One
Part 2
Commentaries on Appointments
and Proceedings

The Documentary History of the Supreme Court of the United States, 1789–1800

Volume One
Part 2
Commentaries on Appointments and Proceedings

Maeva Marcus, *Editor*
James R. Perry, *Editor*
James M. Buchanan, *Associate Editor*
Christine R. Jordan, *Associate Editor*
Stephen L. Tull, *Assistant Editor*
Sandra F. VanBurkleo, *Assistant Editor*
Sarah E. Blank, *Assistant Editor*
Nancy L. Matthews, *Assistant Editor*
Marc Pachter, *Illustrations Editor*

COLUMBIA UNIVERSITY PRESS
NEW YORK 1985

The Press gratefully acknowledges the assistance of DeWitt Wallace and of The William Nelson Cromwell Foundation in the publishing of this volume.

Library of Congress Cataloging in Publication Data
Main entry under title:

The Documentary history of the Supreme Court of the United States, 1789–1800.

Includes index.
Contents: v. 1. pt. 1. Appointments and proceedings.
pt. 2. Commentaries on appointments and proceedings.
1. United States. Supreme Court—History—Sources.
I. Marcus, Maeva, 1941– . II. Perry, James R.,
1950–   III. United States. Supreme Court.
KF8742.A45D66 1985   347.73'2609   85-3794
ISBN 0-231-08868-x (v. 1, pt. 2) 347.3073509
0-231-04552-2 (v. 1)

Columbia University Press
New York   Guildford, Surrey

Printed in the United States of America

Clothbound editions of Columbia University Press Books are Smyth-sewn and printed on permanent and durable acid-free paper

Contents

Part 2

List of Illustrations

The Documentary History of
the Supreme Court of
the United States, 1789–1800

Volume One
Part 2
Commentaries on Appointments
and Proceedings

Commentaries

This section includes documents that illuminate topics presented in the preceding part of this volume. The letters, newspaper items, diary and journal entries, and autobiographical reminiscences published here relate to the appointment of justices, the appointment of clerks, the Court's record-keeping, and the bar of the Court.

Particularly noteworthy is the extent of documentation on competition for appointment to the bench. Thus, for example, in the summer of 1789, before George Washington made his initial nominations, numerous letters were written debating whether John Lowell or William Cushing, both of Massachusetts, should be appointed to the federal high court. If William Cushing were to be appointed to the Supreme Court, then the office he held as chief justice of the Supreme Judicial Court of Massachusetts might be filled by someone unfriendly to the new federal government. Another frequently noted concern was the effect on John Lowell's reputation if he were passed by for promotion to the Supreme Court. A second topic that is discussed in detail is the interim appointment and eventual Senate rejection of John Rutledge as chief justice in 1795. The publication here of an extensive selection of documents provides a far clearer picture of that event than has been available heretofore.

Two editorial concerns should be mentioned. First, as in other sections of this volume, documents have been extracted and parts of documents abstracted in the interest of brevity and, therefore, greater coverage. Abstracts, like other editorial interventions, appear in italics and within brackets. Second, when pseudonymous letters or newspaper articles are published in part or in full, the identity of the writer is given—where it is known—in the source note to the document.

Letter from an Anonymous Correspondent —————————
Independent Chronicle
July 12, 1788 Philadelphia, Pennsylvania

" . . . No other persons are talked of among the knowing ones to execute the new government, than the great American Fabius,[1] and his Excellency Governour Hancock. _ [2] The former will undoubtedly be President-General _ and as the latter will have the next highest number of votes, he will unquestionably be Vice-President. Mr. Adams[3] will undoubtedly be Chief Justice of the Federal Judiciary. At the southward, the same sentiments prevail."

(Boston) July 24, 1788. Date and place are those given for the letter.
   Reprinted in the *Maryland Journal* (Baltimore), August 5, 1788.
   1. George Washington.

2. John Hancock (1737-1793), governor of Massachusetts. A Boston merchant before the revolution, Hancock was the first signer of the Declaration of Independence and served as president of the Continental Congress from May 24, 1775, until his resignation on October 29, 1777. He remained in Congress through 1780, when he became governor of Massachusetts, which office he resigned in 1785 because of poor health. Hancock was a member of the Confederation Congress in 1785 and 1786. He returned to the governor's chair of Massachusetts in 1787 and presided over the state convention to ratify the Constitution in 1788. Hancock died in 1793 in the midst of his ninth term as governor. *DAB; BDAC.*

3. John Adams (1735-1826), second president of the United States, was admitted to the Boston bar in 1758 and to the bar of the Massachusetts Superior Court of Judicature in 1761. Adams first came to public notice in 1765 with his opposition to the Stamp Act and with the first of his constitutional writings. Between August and October, 1765, "A Dissertation on the Canon and the Feudal Law" appeared in the *Boston Gazette* before its subsequent publication in pamphlet form. He represented several patriots in important cases that drew him closer to the patriotic cause, but his dedication to upholding the law also led him to defend the British soldiers charged in the 1770 Boston Massacre. He declined an appointment as advocate general to the Court of Admiralty and instead continued his patriotic associations. At the first two Continental Congresses, Adams led the battle to declare independence. He also continued to write on constitutional issues. In October, 1775, Adams was appointed chief justice of the Superior Court of Judicature of Massachusetts, but he never sat on the bench because of the pressure of his other state and national commitments. He resigned the post in February, 1777. From 1778 to 1788, Adams represented the United States in France, Holland, and England, as well as at the negotiations for the Treaty of Paris in 1783. Shortly after his return to Massachusetts in 1788, Adams was elected vice president. *DAB;* Superior Court of Judicature [Record], 1760-1762, MBSufC; *PJA,* 1:103-6, 249.

"Spectator" to John W. Allen
Massachusetts Gazette
July 29, 1788 Boston, Massachusetts

Mr. ALLEN,

I find it has been proposed in some of the Southern States, to place the great American Fabius,[1] and the illustrious Hancock, in the two first offices of the new government; this will undoubtedly be the case. Little has been said concerning the men who are to preside as Judges of the Supreme Federal Court. They ought to be men of wisdom and integrity; for the lives and fortunes of the people, in a great measure, depend upon their administration. Mr. Adams has been mentioned as the Chief Justice— give me leave to add two more, who must meet the approbation of all good men— I mean our present worthy Chief Justice Cushing,[2] and the learned Judge Dana.[3] These are men of tried abilities; and are such as to merit the confidence of a great and enlightened people.

SPECTATOR.

(Boston) July 29, 1788. Date and place are those of the newspaper.

John W. Allen was the publisher of the *Massachusetts Gazette.* Clarence S. Brigham, *History and Bibliography of American Newspapers, 1690-1820,* 2 vols. (Worcester, Mass.: American Antiquarian Society, 1947), 1:316.

1. George Washington.

2. William Cushing, chief justice of the Supreme Judicial Court of Massachusetts.

3. Francis Dana (1743-1811) was appointed an associate justice of the Massachusetts Supreme Judicial Court in 1785. Dana gained admission to the bar in 1767 following legal studies with his uncle Edmund Trowbridge, considered one of the best lawyers in Massachusetts. Dana served in the Continental Congress and also in a diplomatic capacity in France and Russia. When he returned to Massachusetts, he was elected to the Confederation Congress and then to the Constitutional Convention but did not attend the latter because of ill health. Dana actively supported ratification of the Constitution in the Massachusetts convention in January, 1788. In 1792 he became chief justice of the Massachusetts Supreme Judicial Court and served until 1806. Clifford K. Shipton, *Sibley's Harvard Graduates,* vol. 15, *1761-1763* (Boston: Massachusetts Historical Society, 1970), pp. 204-17; *DAB.*

Abigail Smith to John Quincy Adams ————————————
August 20, 1788   Jamaica, New York

. . . Coll^n Lee from Virginia a nephew of the Mr Lee's —[1] and a Member of Congress told me the other day that it was his opinion, and the opinion of others, and, he spoke as a Southern Man; — that the offices of Vice President and Chief justice, would lay between my Father and Mr Jay, that he wished my Father might be appointed to the latter and accept of it — for he esteemed it next to the Presidentship — the most respectable under the new Government and that it was esteemed of more importance than the Vice Presidents. I wish our Dear Father to Consider well — as he no doubt will, before he decides[2] against accepting it . . .

ARS (MHi, Adams Manuscript Trust).

Abigail (Adams) Smith (1765-1813), the only surviving daughter of John and Abigail Adams, had married Colonel William Stephen Smith in London on June 12, 1786. Her husband, son of a New York merchant, had been appointed secretary of the American legation in London in 1785, where he met John Adams and his family. Stewart Mitchell, ed., *New Letters of Abigail Adams, 1788-1801* (1947; reprint ed., Westport, Conn.: Greenwood Press, 1973), p. 3n.

John Quincy Adams (1767-1848), sixth president of the United States and eldest son of John and Abigail Adams, had accompanied his father to Europe in 1778 on the first of John Adams's diplomatic missions. John Quincy Adams spent several years in Europe as a secretary to his father and to Francis Dana. He returned to America to attend Harvard, graduated in 1787, and spent the next year studying law in Newburyport with Theophilus Parsons. John Q. Adams gained admission to the bar in 1790, but he resumed his diplomatic career in 1794 when President Washington appointed him minister to the Netherlands. John Q. Adams remained in Europe until September, 1801. *DAB.*

1. Colonel Henry Lee (1756-1818) served in the Confederation Congress from 1785 to 1788. Lee also was elected to the Virginia House of Delegates in 1785, and in 1788 he voted for ratification of the Constitution in the Virginia convention. Lee was a lifelong federalist as well as a friend and admirer of George Washington.

Henry Lee's only surviving uncle on his father's side was "Squire" Richard Lee (ca. 1726-1795); but Abigail (Adams) Smith's reference to "the Mr Lee's" is probably to the brothers Arthur Lee (1740-1792) and William Lee (1739-1795), whom she may have known from their diplomatic service abroad during the Revolutionary War. They were first cousins of Colonel Henry Lee's father. *DAB* entries for Arthur Lee, William Lee, and Henry Lee; Edmund Jennings Lee, *Lee of Virginia, 1642-1892* (1895; reprint ed., Baltimore: Genealogical Publishing, 1974), p. 287.

2. Abigail Smith seems to have written "decided" and then changed the terminal "d" to an "s."

John Brown Cutting to Thomas Jefferson
October 5, 1788   London, England

. . . By the letter of an intelligent correspondent in Philadelphia I understand Mr Adams is much mention'd for Vice-President; he having intimated that the office of Chief-Justice wou'd not be acceptable to him. In the most perfect confidence I mention such rumours to you . . .

ARS (DLC, Thomas Jefferson Papers).

John Brown Cutting (ca. 1755-1831), a Revolutionary War veteran, met John Adams while studying law in London in 1787. That same year, Cutting traveled to Paris, where he met Thomas Jefferson. Cutting later acted as an attorney in England for American seamen who had been impressed into the British navy. "Index of Deaths in *Massachusetts Centinel* and *Columbian Centinel,* 1784-1840," 12 vols., typescript (Worcester, Mass.: American Antiquarian Society, 1952); *PTJ,* 12:138-39, 124; *PAH,* 19:517n.

Thomas Jefferson (1743-1826), later third president of the United States, was serving at this time as minister to France. He had met John Brown Cutting in 1787 when the latter brought a letter of introduction from John Adams. When Cutting returned to London, he continued to correspond with Jefferson. In 1789 Jefferson returned to the United States. He assumed his duties as the first secretary of state early the next year; he resigned that office at the end of 1793. *DAB; PTJ,* 12:138-39, 124, 321.

Robert Ballard to George Washington
January 1, 1789   Baltimore, Maryland

Baltimore   January 1st 1789

Sir,

I flatter myself the period is not far distant when we shall see the new Government in motion, and your Excellency elected president of the United States by the unanimous voice of their grateful Citizens. I entreat your forgiveness in thus early soliciting an appointment under the new Constitution. I have been urged to the measure by a sad reverse of Fortune, and emboldened by the Idea of your disposition to relieve the sufferings of the unfortunate soldier.

My Attachment and Love for my Country have been uniformly ardent and sincere, and though I presume not to claim equal distinction with many other Officers who had the Honor of serving under your Excellency's Command, yet I humbly hope even my services will not be wholly forgotten— Early in the late glorious Struggle for Peace, Liberty and Safety, sacraficing as well pecuniary as other Considerations, I stepped forth a Volenteer to oppose the Depredations of Lord Dunmore, near Williamsburg; after which I received an appointment to command a Company in the First Regiment raised in Virginia, which I speedily recruited and marched to Camp_ resigning at the same time the Clerkship of Mecklenburg County, /a lucrative place which I purchased of John Tabb Esq[r] the then Clerk/ after serving five years.

During the infatuation which generally prevailed in this Town for purchasing Lots, I was unfortunately drawn in to speculate to my distruction, and by one ill-fated step, I lost all I had acquired, which hath left me, with a Wife and a number of small Children, destitute of the means of a comfortable support._ Thus circumstanced, Sir, if I might venture to name the Office I should prefer, I would solicit the Clerkship of the Federal Court, as I flatter myself my past Experience would enable me to discharge its Duties with propriety. If I should be so fortunate as to meet your Excellency's Patronage on this occasion, [*letters inked out*] I shall consider it the happiest Event of my Life, and my Children may live to thank their generous Benefactor. I fear your Excellency will think me premature in thus early addressing you on this subject_ but I trust my necesstous situation will plead my excuse.

I will no further obtrude on your Excellency's Time than to add the anxious hope that my true Federal principles will have some Influence with the Friends of the Federal Constitution, and that I am with the greatest Deference

Your Excellency's   Most Ob[t]hum Serv[t]

Robert Ballard

ARS (DLC, George Washington Papers). Addressed "Mount Vernon," which was George Washington's estate in Fairfax County, Virginia.

Robert Ballard (ca. 1742-1793) was a native of Mecklenburg County, Virginia, where he purchased the clerkship of the county prior to the Revolutionary War. After service in the war, Ballard moved to Baltimore. On August 4, 1789, the Senate confirmed President Washington's nomination of Ballard as surveyor of the port of Baltimore; on March 8, 1792, Ballard became inspector for that port. *PMad,* 2:98; John C. Fitzpatrick, ed., *The Writings of George Washington,* vol. 33 (Washington, D.C.: Government Printing Office, 1940), p. 60; Katherine B. Elliott, comp., *Early Wills, 1765-1800: Mecklenburg County, Virginia* (South Hill, Va., 1963), p. 12; *SEJ,* 1:14, 111.

Benjamin Rush to Tench Coxe

January 31, 1789 Philadelphia, Pennsylvania

be very great. M[r] Wilson

. . . I forsee the Scramble for Offices, will ~~furnish~~ [*word inked out*] ~~for~~ must be supported in the place ~~to~~ which his friends have assigned for him.[1] He assures

&

me that he has 60,000 acres of good land ~~paid~~ in good Situations, <u>paid for</u> in Pennsylnia. This property_ must extricate him under the operation of the new goverment in a few years. If none but men of <u>clear</u> estates_ or if none but

cash

men whose ~~estates at present~~ [*words inked out*] exceeds the <u>present</u> value their estates,

of th[ose?] are to fill the appointments of the new Goverment, one half the Union cannot be represented. _ Even the United States, if sold at public vendue would not bring the amount of her debts, & yet her resources are suffi-

globe.

cient to purchase half the globle. _ I wish you would circulate these facts, & sentiments in New York. _ ...

ARS (PHi, Tench Coxe Papers).

Benjamin Rush (1745-1813), a prominent Philadelphia physician and patriot, joined James Wilson in leading the campaign for ratification of the Constitution in Pennsylvania. *DAB.*

Tench Coxe (1755-1824), a Philadelphia merchant. Coxe and James Wilson both were strong supporters of the federal Constitution, and while Wilson and Benjamin Rush led the fight for Pennsylvania's ratification of the Constitution, Coxe was busy contributing newspaper articles to the cause. On May 10, 1790, Coxe was appointed assistant secretary of the treasury. He became commissioner of the revenue in 1792 and served until December, 1797. *DAB;* Jacob E. Cooke, *Tench Coxe and the Early Republic* (Chapel Hill: University of North Carolina Press, 1978), pp. 111-19, 152.

1. James Wilson's friends probably wanted him to be appointed to the Supreme Court. See *Federal Gazette* under date of February 21, 1789; Benjamin Rush to Tench Coxe, February 26, 1789; *Federal Gazette* under date of March 9, 1789; Frederick Muhlenberg to Benjamin Rush, March 21, 1789: all of these preceded Wilson's application to George Washington for the office on April 21, 1789.

Federal Gazette ———————————————————————————
February 21, 1789   Philadelphia, Pennsylvania

... It is truly agreeable, says a correspondent, to see how much a spirit of union and accommodation pervades the United States. The southern states give a President and the eastern states a Vice-President: upon these generous and just principles Pennsylvania humbly puts in her claim to furnish a CHIEF-JUSTICE for the United States.[1] Her situation and her active federal spirit and conduct, by which she has vanquished all opposition to the new government, entitle her to this distinguished honor.

(Philadelphia) February 21, 1789. Date and place are from headline.

This item also appeared in the *Massachusetts Centinel* (Boston), March 7, 1789.

1. See the *Federal Gazette* under date of March 9, 1789, which suggests James Wilson for chief justice.

Benjamin Rush to Tench Coxe ——————————————————————
February 26, 1789   Philadelphia, Pennsylvania

&

... J_____n[1] is indefatigable _ [*letters inked out*] confident _ & [*letters inked*

more   than ever.

out] But ^ unpopular ^ in the highest degree. His appointment would be an

very disagreeable to some of the best men in the

insult upon _ the State of[2] Pennsylvania. ...

^

ARS (PHi, Tench Coxe Papers). Addressed "new-york." Postmarked "26   FE."

1. Probably James Wilson.

2. "State of" has been crossed out less completely than the rest of this passage. Benjamin Rush may have intended these two words to remain part of the sentence; the sense of the sentence requires their inclusion.

George Washington to Robert Ballard
March 2, 1789   Mount Vernon, Fairfax County, Virginia

To Col? Robt Ballard
Baltimore

Sir,

I have been duly favored with your letter dated   ,[1] and have to give you the same reply in substance, which I have given to all other applications of a similar nature.

Should it become indispensable for me to occupy the office, in which your letter has presupposed me, I shall endeavor to enter upon it as free from all kinds of prejudices, as I shall certainly be from all pre-engagements of every possible description. —

As my sole object would be to adhere strictly to justice and my country's good, so I should wish to be in a predicament which would allow me to weigh with the utmost impartiality the pretentions of the different Candidates for appointments. — [2]

This being my general manner of thinking, you will be pleased to consider this answer as in no sort intended to affect your particular claims, on the one side or the other. I request, in all personal considerations, you will be persuaded that

I am,   With great regard,   Sir,   Your Most Obedient Servt

(Signed)   George Washington

Mount Vernon
March 2nd 1789

Lb (DLC, George Washington Papers); Df (DNA, RG 59, Miscellaneous Letters).

1. See Robert Ballard to George Washington, January 1, 1789.

2. In draft, "appointments" interlined above "Offices."

Jared Ingersoll to John Langdon
March 3, 1789   Philadelphia, Pennsylvania

Philadelphia   March the 3^d 1789

Dear Sir

I know your time is precious, I will intrude but for a moment, just to recommend to your recollection Mr Ezekiel Forman,[1] in case you should have occasion to appoint a Sheriff or other ministerial Officer to your Federal Court[2]

For further particulars relative to this Gentleman I beg leave to refer you to my letter of yesterday to Doc[r] Johnson[3]

I am   D sir   With great regard   Your obed[t]   hum. serv[t]

Jared Ingersoll

ARS (NhHi, Langdon-Elwyn Family Papers). Addressed "New-York." Postmarked "6   MR."

Jared Ingersoll (1749-1822), an eminent Philadelphia lawyer, had graduated from Yale in 1766 before entering the Middle Temple. Admitted to the Philadelphia bar in 1773, Ingersoll established a reputation as a brilliant lawyer. In 1787 he was a member of the Constitutional Convention. Two years later, he was serving on the Philadelphia Common Council, and in 1790 he became attorney general of Pennsylvania. He held the latter office until 1799, and then served briefly (1800-1801) as United States attorney for the district of Pennsylvania. *DAB.*

John Langdon (1741-1819), a merchant in Portsmouth, New Hampshire, represented his state in the Continental and Confederation Congresses and also at the Constitutional Convention. Langdon was elected to the Senate and served from 1789 to 1801. *DAB.*

1. Ezekiel Forman (1736-1795), who was living in Philadelphia in 1789, previously had served as sheriff of Kent County, Maryland, in 1776 and on Maryland's Council of Safety in 1777. Anne Spottswood Dandridge, comp., *The Forman Genealogy* (Cleveland: Forman-Basset-Hatch, 1903), p. 98.

2. Jared Ingersoll probably is referring to the Supreme Court. No other federal court had yet been created by Congress. Even had Ingersoll anticipated the creation of lower federal courts in each state, it is unlikely that he would have written to John Langdon, who was from New Hampshire, on behalf of a Philadelphia applicant for office.

3. This letter has not been found. "Doc[r] Johnson" is probably William Samuel Johnson (1727-1819), senator from Connecticut. A distinguished jurist, Johnson received an honorary doctorate in law from Oxford in 1766. He had known Jared Ingersoll's father well when the Ingersoll family lived in Connecticut. *DAB.*

Robert Ballard to James Madison ─────────────────────────

March 5, 1789   Baltimore, Maryland

... Sir to be as brief as possible I am very depended, indeed, poor— and want the aid of friends, to Assist me in obtaining an Office under the new Government, that will yield a support to a large family, that have been brought up to ease. At a time when my Country wanted the assistance of its Citizens, I turned out a Volenteer to oppose Lord Dunmore near Williamsburg; and afterwards appointed to a Company in the first Regiment raised in Virginia, which I speedily recruited and marched to Camp, sacrificing as well pecuniary as other considerations.— Under these impressions I place faith in the gratitude of my Countrymen to give a return of service.

The Office that I at present contemplate, is the Clerkship of the Federal Court, as I flatter myself my long experience in that business, would enable me to execute its duties with propriety— having injoyed the Office of Clerk

to Mecklenburg County Court, several years, after serving five years appren-
tiship, which Office I relinquished when I went into the Army. It will $_\wedge^{be}$ very
important to me if I am so happy as to meet your patronage and Interest on
this occasion. As it is my intention to be in New York very soon, I will not
comment any further on my necessitous situation, only to thank you to present
my repects to Mr Lee,[1] and will esteem myself greatly obliged for his friendship
and Interest on this my day of Trial—. I have not the Honor of being acquainted with M^{r}Lee— but am on terms of friendly intimacy with Col^{l}Henry
Lee his Brother, from whom I received the other day a pleasing letter on
this $_\wedge^{business}$ letter. . . .

ARS (DLC, James Madison Papers).

   James Madison (1751-1836), later fourth president of the United States, was elected to the
First Congress as a congressman from Virginia. The first discovered connection between James
Madison and Robert Ballard is the mention of Ballard's name in an expense account of Madison
in 1780. *DAB; PMad,* 2:97-98.

   1. Richard Bland Lee (1761-1827), brother of Henry Lee and future United States attorney
general Charles Lee, was a planter in Loudoun County, Virginia, and served as a congressman
from 1789 to 1795. *DAB.*

Federal Gazette ————————————————————————————
March 9, 1789   Philadelphia, Pennsylvania

   It is with singular pleasure we hear that James Wilson, esq. of this state, is
destined by the voice of many thousand federalists, to fill the station of CHIEF
JUSTICE of the UNITED STATES. This worthy citizen devoted himself to the
cause of American freedom in 1774, and has shared in every toil and danger
of the revolution. His hand, his heart, his tongue and his pen, have ever been
at the command of his country. To his laborious investigations into the principles and forms of every species of government that has ever existed in the
world— and to his powerful reasonings in the late federal convention, the
United States are indebted for many of the perfections of the new constitution.

   The office allotted for that distinguished patriot and legislator by his grateful
countrymen, will require an uncommon share of *legal* and *political* abilities and
information. A new system of federal jurisprudence must be formed; a new
region in the administration of justice must be explored, in which genius alone
can supply the defect of precedent; and who so equal to those great and original undertakings as that favorite son of Pennsylvania, James Wilson, esq.

(Philadelphia) March 9, 1789. Date and place are from headline.

   This item also appeared in the *Vermont Gazette* (Bennington), April 6, 1789, and in the *Georgia
Gazette* (Savannah), April 16, 1789. A summary appeared in the *New-York Journal,* April 2, 1789.
The first paragraph was published in the *Massachusetts Centinel* (Boston), March 25, 1789.

Tench Coxe to Joseph Clay —————————————————
March 20, 1789   Philadelphia, Pennsylvania

... The present Appearance of Things holds out no other power ~~to~~ of Appointment, than that of the President — The Senate have an Negative in his Nominations, but cannot officially bring forward a single Name   The friends of the Constitution will be very careful to prevent the least Deviation from that mode made as things now Stand[;?] If however the Law should enable the President to nominate alone in Certain lesser Departments inferior to general Civil officers, tis likely the President will have this business solely, but a Question will arise whether the first appointments will be made in the present Mode pointed out by the Constitution   You will observe that another Change may take place. The Heads of Department may have Nominations & even Appointments under the Constitution   The board of Treasury — or Financier the Commander in Chief when there is one — the Sec^y of War — of Foreign or Domestic Affairs — The Judges — the Board of Customs &c^a will perhaps have many of the State Officers on the fed^l Establishment to Appoint. The Shape this great Business will Take is at present quite uncertain — ...

ALbS (PHi, Tench Coxe Papers). Addressed "Savannah in   Georgia."
    Probably Joseph Clay (1741-1804), a Georgia merchant. Clay served in the Continental Congress and was paymaster general of the Continental Army for the Southern Department. He was a business partner and cousin of Joseph Habersham, the brother of Major John Habersham, who is mentioned in an unpublished part of this letter. His vast mercantile dealings may have brought him into contact with Tench Coxe. *DAB* entries for Joseph Clay and Joseph Habersham.

Frederick Muhlenberg to Benjamin Rush —————————————
March 21, 1789   New York, New York

[*Frederick Muhlenberg briefly describes rumors that his impending election as speaker by the House of Representatives*[1] *will deprive other Pennsylvanians of filling important federal offices.*] I presume the true Apprehension is either that I am not adequate to the Task, and the Honour too great for me, or that it may injure Mr Wilson Election to fill the first jud[i]cial Seat on the Continent. In either Case I have only to lament th[e] Want of Candour & confidential Comunication of my friends, for I do declare to You upon my Honour, & with the utmost Sincerity, that I never did nor do I this Moment wish the Appointment, for Reasons best known to myself, & yet I should not conceive myself justifiable totally to decline it, Nor is there a Man in the U. States who entertains a more favourable Opinion of Mr Wilson than myself. In Point of Abilities I do not know his equal nor any one so well calculated for the Duties of that important Station. From my personal Regard for him I would sooner forego any Advantage than be in any Manner the Means of injuring him or his Views. — ...

ARS (PHi, Gratz Collection). Addressed "Philadª." Readings in brackets are supplied because of damage to the document.

Frederick Muhlenberg (1750-1801) of Pennsylvania was the first speaker of the House of Representatives. He entered politics in 1779 to fill an unexpired term in the Continental Congress. He later served as speaker of the Pennsylvania General Assembly and presided over the state convention to ratify the Constitution. Muhlenberg was a congressman until 1797 and served as speaker, 1789-1791 and 1793-1795. *BDAC; DAB.*

1. Frederick Muhlenberg was elected speaker on April 1, 1789. *FFC,* 3:7.

Ezekiel Forman to John Langdon
March 23, 1789   Philadelphia, Pennsylvania

Philadelphia   23ᵈ March 1789

Sir

I have some reasons to expect, that Mʳ Ingersoll of this City mentioned my Name to you in favor of my being appointed to the Office of High-Sheriff to our Federal Court.[1] Altho' unacquainted, I consider it my duty to lay my desires before you, and to solicit your interest in the business, provided it shall appear to you right and proper, otherwise I can not, nor ought not to expect. I am Sir

with very great respect,   Your Most Obedient   And Most Humble Servᵗ

EzekˡForman

Honorable
John Langdon Esquire.

ARS (NhHi, Langdon-Elwyn Family Papers). Endorsed "Letter not answᵈ."

1. Presumably, Ezekiel Forman is referring to the Supreme Court. See note to Jared Ingersoll to John Langdon, March 3, 1789.

New-York Journal
April 16, 1789   New York, New York

. . . A correspondent, who has read a paragraph in a l[a]te Philadelphia paper, in which it is asserted, that it is the wish of some thousands of federalists, that JAMES WILSON, Esq should be appointed to the office of *chief justice* of the *Un[i]ted States,*[1] is confident, that it is the opinion of *many thousands* of Federalists, throughou[t] the United States, that he is not the proper person for that high and important off[i]ce, b[e]ing convinced that there are characters in the other states of the union, as well as in that of P[e]nnsylvania, who are more deserving of it, on account of their abilities, and from their principles and manners being more republican than those of Mr. Wilson.— South-Carolina presents a Burke—[2] Virginia a Pendleton—[3] Maryla[n]d an Harrison—

New-York a Jay_ Connecticut an Elsworth, or a Johnson_ [4] and Massachusetts a Cushing, either of w[h]om has better qualifications, and therefore mo[r]e justly entitled to the office of chief justice of the United States, than Mr. Wilson. . . .

(New York) April 16, 1789. Date and place are from headline. The letters in brackets have been supplied because their imprint is missing in the newspaper itself.

1. See the *Federal Gazette* item published under date of March 9, 1789, which was summarized by the *New-York Journal* on April 2, 1789.

2. Aedanus Burke (1743-1802) was an associate judge of the South Carolina Court of Common Pleas and General Sessions and a congressman in the First Congress. Burke, born in Ireland, studied law in Virginia and settled in South Carolina in the mid-1770s. In 1778 he became associate judge on the Court of Common Pleas and General Sessions and served on that bench until 1799 when he was elected chancellor of the Court of Equity. He held that office until his death. *DAB.*

3. Edmund Pendleton (1721-1803), Virginia jurist and political leader. At the age of fourteen, Pendleton had been apprenticed to the clerk of Caroline County, Virginia. He read law on his own and was admitted to the Caroline County bar in 1741. Ten years later, he became one of the justices of the peace of that county. Pendleton was prominent in Virginia's revolutionary events, and in 1779 he became "First Judge" of the Virginia High Court of Chancery, by virtue of which office he also served as presiding judge of the Virginia Court of Appeals. After the Virginia legislature in December, 1788, elected Pendleton one of the judges of the new, fully separate Court of Appeals, he resigned from the Court of Chancery on March 2, 1789, and spent the rest of his life as presiding judge of the Court of Appeals. *DAB;* David John Mays, *Edmund Pendleton, 1721-1803: A Biography,* 2 vols. (Cambridge: Harvard University Press, 1952), 1:12, 23-29; 2:164-65, 273-74.

4. William Samuel Johnson (1727-1819) read law under the direction of William Smith and started his practice in Stratford, Connecticut, in 1749. He began a distinguished career as a lawyer and received an honorary doctorate in law from Oxford in 1766. He was made a judge of the Superior Court in 1772. Johnson played a leading role at the Constitutional Convention. Elected as a senator to the First Congress, he resigned in 1791 to concentrate on his duties as president of Columbia College, a post he had held since 1787. He retired from the presidency of Columbia in 1800. *DAB;* Elizabeth P. McCaughey, *From Loyalist to Founding Father: The Political Odyssey of William Samuel Johnson* (New York: Columbia University Press, 1980), pp. 29-31, 149.

James Wilson to George Washington ———————————
April 21, 1789   Philadelphia, Pennsylvania

Dear Sir

A Delicacy arising from your Situation and Character as well as my own has hitherto prevented me from mentioning to your Excellency a Subject of much Importance to me. Perhaps I should not even now have broke Silence but for one Consideration. A Regard to the Dignity of the Government, over which you preside, will naturally lead you to take Care that its Honours be, in no Event, exposed to affected Indifference or Contempt. For this Reason you may well expect that, before you nominate any Gentleman to an Employment (especially one of high Trust) you should have it in your Power to preclude him, in Case of Disappointment, from pretending that the Nomination was made without his Knowledge or Consent. Under this View I commit myself to your Excellency without Reserve and inform you that my Aim rises to the important Office of Chief Justice of the United States.

But how shall I now proceed? Shall I enumerate Reasons in Justification of my high Pretensions? I have not yet employed my Pen in my own Praise_ When I make those high Pretensions, and offer them to so good a Judge, can I say, that they are altogether without Foundation? Your Excellency must relieve me from the Dilemma. You will think and act properly on the Occasion without my saying any Thing on either Side of the Question.

I have the Honour to be with the greatest Esteem and Attachment, dear Sir, Your Excellency's most obedient and very humble Servant

James Wilson

Philadelphia   21st April 1789

His Excellency the President of the United States

ARS (DLC, George Washington Papers).

Benjamin Rush to John Adams ——————————————————
April 22, 1789   Philadelphia, Pennsylvania

... Your influence in the Senate over which you have been called to preside, will give you great weight (without a vote) in determining upon the most suitable Characters to fill the first offices in goverment. Pennsylvania looks up with anxious Solicitude for the ~~the appointment~~ commission of Chief Justice for Mr Wilson. It was from an expectation of this honor being conferred upon him, that he was left out of the Senate, and house of representatives. His Abilities & knowledge in framing the constitution, & his zeal in promoting its establishment, have exposed him to a most virulent persecution from the antifederalists in this state. With those our president general Mifflin[1] has joined. You know the man_ and therefore I shall make no comments upon his conduct, further than that he has detatched himself from all the genius [or virtue?] _ ~~and~~ [&c &c?] of the State, and ~~[merely p?]~~ placed himself at the head of a few men who are in our city what your Col. Sims's & Balchs are in Boston.[2] Should MrWilson be left to sink under this opposition, I shall for ever deplore the ingratitude of republics.

Much will be said of the deranged state of his Affairs. But where will you find an American landholder free from embarrassments?_ Our funding System has reduced all our wealthy men to the utmost distress, & has thrown ~~mu~~ a great part of their ~~wealth~~ property into the hands of quartermasters_ ~~Lon~~ Amsterdam Jews, & London brokers. Mr Wilson has an immense & valuable estate in lands_ much more than enō to discharge all his engagements, provided

Congress does not by funding <u>alienated</u> certificates, put an extinguisher upon
all the hopes of America from _∧ agriculture_ manufactures_ & commerce.
industry in
Under all the disappointments which he has met with, he has preserved a fair
character, & a dignified line of Conduct. His principles are the counterpart of
your own, upon the subject of goverment, & his influence in a high station
will always be in favor of a vigorous_ ballanced, and triple powered Consti-
tution._ To ~~this~~ the facts, I have mentioned, I shall only add that <u>you</u> ~~have~~ had not
a more zealous friend, ~~than~~ nor Massachus[u?]ts a firmer advocate in the late election of vice president in this state, than Mr Wilson. . . .

ARS (MHi, Adams Manuscript Trust).
   1. Thomas Mifflin (1744-1800), president of the Supreme Executive Council of Pennsylvania.
Mifflin and James Wilson had been political allies during the Revolutionary War, and Mifflin had
commanded the forces which tried to defend Wilson and Wilson's home during a riot in 1779.
Both men served in the Pennsylvania delegation to the Constitutional Convention in 1787. Mifflin
became president of the Supreme Executive Council in 1788; the appointments he made while
serving in this office seem to have alienated his former political friends, including James Wilson.
In 1790 James Wilson and Wilson's allies declined to support Mifflin's candidacy for governor
under the new state constitution, but Mifflin won the election and served three successive terms
through 1799. *DAB;* Kenneth R. Rossman, *Thomas Mifflin and the Politics of the American Revolution*
(Chapel Hill: University of North Carolina Press, 1952), pp. 16, 185-93; Charles Page Smith,
James Wilson: Founding Father, 1742-1798 (Chapel Hill: University of North Carolina Press, 1956),
pp. 133-37.
   2. This passage probably refers to two Bostonians, both of whom were allied with Governor
John Hancock. Colonel Andrew Symmes, Jr. (1734-1797), a Boston merchant, had served on the
Committee of Correspondence, Safety, and Inspection, 1779-1780. Following the Revolutionary
War, Symmes served as aide-de-camp to Governor Hancock (1784, 1787-1790). Nathaniel Balch
(1735-1808), a Boston hatter and former Son of Liberty, was a close personal friend of Governor
Hancock. Oliver Ayer Roberts, *History of the Military Company of the Massachusetts,* vol. 2 (Boston:
Alfred Mudge & Son, 1897), p. 103; Boston Records Commissioners, *Boston Births, 1700-1800,*
vol. 24 (Boston, 1894), p. 220; *Index of Deaths in Massachusetts;* William M. Fowler, Jr., *The Baron
of Beacon Hill: A Biography of John Hancock* (Boston: Houghton Mifflin, 1980), pp. 254, 336.

Thomas McKean to George Washington ——————
April 27, 1789 Philadelphia, Pennsylvania

Philadelphia.   April 27th 1789.

Sir,
   I have an ambition to take a share in Your Excellency's administration, and
know of no line in which I can render so good service as in the judicial department. Having expressed this, it will, I trust, not be deemed indelicate in
me to give a short account of myself & my studies.
   I was born in Chester county in this State, and, having been instructed for
seven years in the latin and greek languages, and the arts & sciences usually
taught in the schools, I commenced the study of the law at the age of sixteen

Governor Thomas McKean and His Son, Thomas McKean, Jr., by Charles Willson Peale (1741-1827). Oil on canvas, 1787. Courtesy Philadelphia Museum of Art. Bequest of Phebe Warren McKean Downs.

in Newcastle; at the age of twenty I was admitted to the bar in the courts of common pleas and also in the supreme court of Delaware and soon after in the supreme courts of Pennsylvania & New-Jersey. From that time to the present, the law has been my principal study and my only profession. It is true I have gone thro' the rotine of office, have been annually elected for seventeen years a member of Assembly for Newcastle-county; was a member of Congress, first at New-York in 1765, and from 1774 until the day I had assurance that the preliminaries of peace were signed: But these employments added to & enlarged my legal knowledge.

Among the Learned, I early in life received the degree of Master of Arts from the College of Philadelphia, and have since been honored with the degree of Doctor of Laws by two other Colleges & one University: I am also a Trustee of three incorporated seminaries of learning, and a member of several societies for the promoting the arts & useful knowledge.

My official rank may probably be known to you, I shall therefore only mention, that I have been Speaker of the Delaware Assembly both before and since the Revolution, and sometime President of Congress: In 1766 I first took a seat on the Bench at Newcastle, having before been in the commission of the peace & a Justice of the common pleas for that county, and had influence enough to have justice administered upon unstamped paper. When the Stamp-Act was repealed I returned to the Bar, & there remained until 1777, when I was appointed Chief Justice of the supreme court of Pennsylvania; which station I have now held near[1] twelve years, having been twice chosen by an unanimous ballot. These honors & offices were confered unsollicited by me, and most of them without my previous knowledge.

My character must be left to the World. I have lived in troublesome times, in an unsettled & tumultuous government: A good Judge cannot be very popular, but I believe, that my integrity has never been called in question, and it is certain, that no judgment of the supreme court of Pennsylvania since the Revolution has been reversed, or altered in a single Iotta. A book of reports, by Counsellor Dallas,[2] is now in the press here and will be abroad in about two months, from which some judgement may be formed in the other States of our decisions. I will only add, that I am by habit and inclination the man of business.[3]

Your Excellency will be pleased to excuse this particular self-detail, when it shall be considered, that if you think fit to advance me to this station, my reputation will become in a degree your interest, and my pretensions should be known.

Having lost by depreciated[4] Congress-money upwards of six thousand pounds of my own acquiring /for I have been the maker of my own fortune/ I have a wish to recover in some honorable way[5] at least a part of it, for the sake of eight promising children; however, tho' not affluent[6] I am still above the fear of want, and I owe no man any thing but good-will.

This having been a sudden resolution, I have not dropped the least hint of it to any person whomsoever. With respect to the Senators, I am personally known to most of them, and flatter myself not to my disadvantage; but in this opinion I may be mistaken, for the politics of some of them did not co-incide with mine. However I mean not to trouble them.

For this freedom I must trust to Your great goodness. It is /tho' I am not three years younger than Your Excellency,/ my first essay of the kind. If you shall approve of this overture, I promise you to execute the Trust with assiduity & fidelity and according to the best of my abilities; the only return that I can make, and that, I know, you wish for. There is but one thing more I have to say, and that is, if you should make a single Enemy, or loose a single friend by gratifying my desire, I most sincerely beg you will never spend a thought on the subject; for I profess myself to be, with the utmost attachment and regard,

Sir, Your Excellency's, most[7] obedient & most humble serv!

Tho M:Kean

His Excellency George Washington Esquire.

ARS (DLC, George Washington Papers); ADfS (PHi, Hampton Carson Collection).

Thomas McKean (1734-1817), chief justice of Pennsylvania. McKean's legal career began in New Castle County, Delaware, where he studied law with his cousin and became a prothonotary's clerk. In 1752 McKean was appointed deputy prothonotary and recorder of probate for the same county. He first gained admission to the bar in Delaware at age twenty. Thereafter McKean played a leading role in Delaware politics, supported the revolutionary movement, and represented Delaware in the Continental and Confederation Congresses. McKean was active in Pennsylvania affairs during the mid-1770s and established a home in Philadelphia during that period. In 1777 he was commissioned chief justice of that state. McKean supported ratification of the Constitution in the

Pennsylvania convention, but broke ranks with the federalists in 1792 over foreign policy. McKean remained on the bench until 1799. In that year, he won election as governor and served in that capacity until 1808. *DAB; BDAC.*

1. In draft, "for" crossed out and replaced with "near."

2. Alexander James Dallas, *Reports of Cases Ruled and Adjudged in the Courts of Pennsylvania, Before and Since the Revolution* (Philadelphia: T. Bradford, 1790).

3. In draft, this paragraph follows the next one.

4. In draft, "the receipt of" crossed out before "depreciated."

5. In draft, "by some preferment" crossed out in favor of "in some honorable way."

6. In draft, "tho' I will not think of it without rendering an adequate service, for" crossed out and replaced with "however, tho' not affluent."

7. In draft, "devoted" crossed out and replaced with "most."

Arthur Lee to [Francis Lightfoot Lee] ——————
May 9, 1789 [New York, New York?]

... Wilson is an avowd Candidate for the Cheif Justice ship— Jay is the whispered one— [*Arthur Lee then writes about the political maneuvering for national office. He mentions that Robert Morris[1] is working for the appointment of James Wilson as chief justice and that James Madison will support this effort.*]

AL (ViU, Lee Family Papers). Place suggested by evidence in letter.

This letter, written from New York, has no salutation or cover, but it opens with the words "I am sorry my dear Brother . . ." Arthur Lee had three brothers living in 1789: Francis Lightfoot Lee, William Lee, and Richard Henry Lee. In May, 1789, Richard Henry Lee also was in New York, as a senator from Virginia. William Lee's whereabouts in May, 1789, are not known for certain, but he was probably in New York as well. He was definitely in New York in June, 1789, to receive medical treatment for a serious eye problem.

After comparing this letter of May 9 with a similar one of August 29, 1789, also written by Arthur Lee, it appears that both were probably written to Francis Lightfoot Lee. Both letters begin with a greeting to his "dear Brother" and close with love to "M⁣ʳˢ Lee." The August 29 letter mentions that Richard Henry and William are in New York and closes with "Our B⁣ʳˢ desire their love to Menokin," which was Francis Lightfoot Lee's home in Virginia.

The letter of May 9 also contains a greeting to "Mrs. Lee" and her little girls. Since Francis Lightfoot Lee and his wife had no children, this probably refers to the wife and children of William Lee. Apparently William Lee had left home by May, 1789, and had entrusted his wife and children to the care of his brother. This seems confirmed by the fact that in September, 1789, they were staying at Menokin and awaiting word of William's recovery. Arthur Lee to [Francis Lightfoot Lee], August 29, 1789, Arthur Lee Papers, MH-H; James Curtis Ballagh, ed., *The Letters of Richard Henry Lee,* 2 vols. (1911-1914; reprint ed., New York: Da Capo Press, 1970), 2:492-94, 500-501.

Arthur Lee (1740-1792) was born in Virginia. Arthur Lee studied medicine in Edinburgh and law at Lincoln's Inn and the Middle Temple. He held diplomatic posts in England and France and served in the Confederation Congress before being appointed in 1785 to the treasury board. Lee remained on the board until George Washington's inauguration in 1789. During these years, Lee was living in New York City. An anti-federalist, he was an unsuccessful candidate for Congress in 1789, and, following Washington's inauguration, Lee remained in New York to seek a position in the federal government. *DAB;* Louis W. Potts, *Arthur Lee: A Virtuous Revolutionary* (Baton Rouge: Louisiana State University Press, 1981), pp. 273-77.

Francis Lightfoot Lee (1734-1797) was born at the Lee ancestral home, "Stratford," in West-moreland County, Virginia. After his marriage in 1769 to Rebecca Tayloe he moved to the plan-tation, "Menokin," in Richmond County. He served in the House of Burgesses from 1758 to 1776 and had an important role in fostering revolutionary sentiment in Virginia. He was a signer of the Declaration of Independence and served in the Continental Congress from 1775 to 1779. After his return to Virginia, he was involved in state politics for a short while before retiring to the country for the rest of his life. *DAB.*

1. Robert Morris (1734-1806), best known as "financier of the Revolution," was a senator from Pennsylvania. Morris and James Wilson had first become friends and political allies in No-vember, 1775, when they were elected to the Pennsylvania delegation of the Continental Con-gress. *DAB;* Smith, *James Wilson,* pp. 73, 202.

Arthur Lee previously had referred to Morris's support for Wilson in a letter to Charles Lee (Arthur Lee's cousin) on May 8, 1789. Lee-Ludwell Papers, ViHi.

George Washington to Thomas McKean
May 9, 1789 New York, New York

New York   May 9ᵗʰ 1789

Sir,

I have duly received your letter of the 27ᵗʰ of April; and as the contents are of such a nature as do not require a particular answer, I shall only acknowledge the receipt of it;＿ observing, at the same time, that the resolution which I have formed, and from which I never wish to depart, will always leave me at full liberty to act upon every subject which may come before me, without the embarrassments of any previous engagement.

With great esteem and regard,   I am, Sir,   Your most Obedᵗ Huᵇˡᵉ Servᵗ

GᵒWashington

The Honᵇˡᵉ
Thomas MᶜKean.

RS (PHi, Hampton Carson Collection). Addressed "Philadelphia." Postmarked "N-York   May 11."

George Washington to James Wilson
May 9, 1789 New York, New York

New York   May 9 1789

Dear Sir,

The new and busy scenes in which I have been constantly engaged since the receipt of your letter of the 21ᵗ Ultᵒ will, I trust, apologize for my not having acknowledged it at an earlier period＿

To you, my dear Sir, and others who know me, I presume it will be un-necessary for me to say that I have entered upon my office without the constraint of a single <u>engagement</u> and that I never wish to depart from that line of conduct which will always leave me at full libe[te?]rty to act in the manner which is befitting an impartial[1] & disinterested Magistrate._

I am Dear Sir, with very great esteem & regard Y.ʳ most Obed. H[ˡᵉ?][2] Ser.ᵗ

Hon.ᵇˡᵉ James Wilson_

C (DNA, RG 59, Miscellaneous Letters); Lb (DLC, George Washington Papers).
1. The "m" was written over an "n."
2. "H[ˡᵉ?]" left out in letterbook.

John Adams to Benjamin Rush
May 17, 1789 New York, New York

. . . My Situation, at the head of the Senate, where I was placed by the People at large, not as the Members were by their Legislatures, instead of giving me an influence as you Suppose will prevent me, from having any._[1] M.ʳ Wilson, I have long known esteemed and respected: but, if I had a Vote, I could not promise to give it for him to be Chief Justice._ All Things considered, that have ever come to my Knowledge I feel myself inclined to wish, because I am fully convinced that Services, Hazards, Abilities and Popularity, all properly weighed, the Ballance, is in favour of M.ʳ Jay._ one of the Judges, I wish M.ʳ Wilson to be: and the difference is not great between the first and the other Judges.

You say I had not a firmer Friend in the late Election. I must protest against this mode of reasoning. I am not obliged to vote for a Man because he voted for me, had my office been ever so lucrative or ever so important._ . . .

Now my Friend We start fair_ Never must I again hear a Selfish Motive urged to me, to induce my Vote or Influence in publick affairs. . . .

ARS (Photostat in DLC, Benjamin Rush Papers); ALbS (MHi, Adams Manuscript Trust).
1. See Benjamin Rush to John Adams, April 22, 1789.

Anthony Wayne to James Wilson
May 20, 1789 [Richmond, Georgia]

. . . [Congratulating Wilson upon the adoption of and organization of the Federal Constitution] a business in which you took so early, so conspicuous and so effectual a part, and permit me to add that it was to a display of the perfect knowledge you entertained and the plain elucidation you gave of the component parts of that system, which caused it to be approved by the Convention of Pennsylvania, it being the first that met, and the first in consequence in the Union and perhaps its present operation may justly be attributed to the happy

turning of the scale in [*word obliterated*] that State. I therefore hope and trust
that I may with propriety venture to congratulate you upon an appointment,
so generally acknowledged, due to your professional and other merits, i.e., the
Chief Justiceship of the United States of America. . . .

Tr (Typescript in PSC-Hi, Konkle Manuscripts). Place mentioned in Smith, *James Wilson,* p. 408
note 20. The crossed-out words are reproduced where they appear in the typescript.

    Anthony Wayne (1745-1796) was born in Chester County, Pennsylvania, where he later ran
a tannery. Wayne was an early supporter of the revolutionary movement in Chester County and
went on to distinguished military service during the war, from which he emerged as a brigadier
general. After the war, Wayne represented Chester County in the Pennsylvania General Assembly,
where he opposed the state's radical faction. In 1787 at the Pennsylvania ratifying convention, he
favored the adoption of the federal Constitution. Wayne became major general of the American
army in 1791 and won his most noted military victory in 1794 against the Wabash Indians at
Fallen Timbers (near present-day Toledo, Ohio). *DAB.*

Arthur Lee to George Washington ————————————————
May 21, 1789 [New York, New York?]

May 21ˢᵗ 1789

Sir

    It is not without great apprehension of presuming too much on the favor
you have always shown me, that I offer you my Services, as a Judge of the
Supreme Court which is now establishing.

    The having been calld to the bar in Westminster hall after five years study
at the Temple, & having practisd the Law there for some time— are the
grounds, Sir, on which I presume to ask your protection.

    I quitted the line of the Law in England, where much was to be expected
from the pursuit of it, & with the fairest prospects; the moment my Country
calld upon me, to aid in supporting he[r] violated rights. With what fidelity I
dischargd the trust She reposd in me; the records of the Office of foreign
affairs will shew.

    To return to the profession I ha[d] chosen, in a station, not unbecoming
those in which I have acted, is my most earnest desire. It woud be an additional satisfaction to be distinguis[hed] by your appointment, Sir, & to assist in
distributing equal justice to a well governd People.

    I have the honor to b[e] with the highest respect, Sir. Yʳ most Obedᵗ
Servᵗ

Arthur L[ee]

President general.

ARS (DLC, George Washington Papers). Arthur Lee was probably still in the New York area;
see Arthur Lee to William Lee, May 9, 1789. The margin of this page has been damaged; therefore, conjectural readings are supplied in brackets.

Arthur Lee (1740-1792) by William Russell Birch (1755-1834). Enamel on ivory, 1795. Courtesy Historical Society of Pennsylvania.

Gustavus Scott to ?
May 22, 1789 Cambridge, Maryland

... If the number of Judges for the united States should be no more than six I think I ought not to expect to be one of the Number: whatever professional Knowledge I may have attained I am not generally known. [*Scott then expresses his interest in an appointment to the federal judiciary at the state level.*[1]]

ARS (DLC, James Madison Papers).

    Gustavus Scott (1753-1800), born in Virginia, may have attended King's College in Aberdeen, Scotland, before entering the Middle Temple in 1767. Scott was admitted to the English bar in 1772 and then returned to America where he established a successful practice on Maryland's eastern shore. He supported Revolutionary War efforts, served in the Maryland General Assembly, and also was elected to the Confederation Congress. He shared with George Washington an interest in promoting navigation on the Potomac, and in 1794 Washington appointed him one of the commissioners for the District of Columbia. *DAB* under Gustavus Scott and George Washington.

    1. See also Gustavus Scott to George Washington, August 30, 1789.

Robert Ballard to George Washington
May 30, 1789 Baltimore, Maryland

To the President of the United States of America—

    The Humble petition of Robert Ballard Citizen of Baltimore Town, State of Maryland.

Permit me sir, to renew an application I ventured to make to your Excellency at an early period, which your goodness was then pleased to receive without displeasure.[1] I pray also to be permitted to mention a few circumstances, some of which, perhaps may serve to bring me to your remembrance.

I enjoyed in Virginia the Clerkship of Mecklenburg County (a Lucrative Office) when the invasion of Lord Dunmore induced me to take up Arms against Great Britain. Soon after this, I recruited my Company, raised for that occasion, and joined the army under your Excellencys Command.

It was my fortune to be on the heights of Haarlem — the White Plains — the celebrated retreat through Jersey, and the memorable enterprize of Trenton — Here I received Orders from Lord Sterling major General for the day to march the captured Troops off the field. I was next at Brandywine — and shared in the defence of Fort Mifflin till the last day of that Seige, as well as in all the hardships of the Winter at Valey Forge.

But to shorten a detail which must trespass upon the most precious moments, I shall only add, that, when I returned to private life I married a Miss Plowman of this place, and thought of no other reward for my services. I was now happy, but this did not preserve me from misfortunes. These came upon me and I gave up whatever I possessed to my Creditors. My Wife too who has a fortune of £ 1600. in her own right, gave that up also. This last sacrafice, satisfied my principles but exposed me to the bitterest distress.

Thus circumstanced I throw myself upon your goodness. Should your Excellency think my small talents competent to the duties of Clerk of the Federal Court, or any other Office that does not require great abilities, it will be my constant endeavour to deserve your good opinion, and discharge whatever trust you may be pleased to assign to me, with deligence and fidelity.

I pray more over your Excellency to pardon me for not presenting this Petition in Person, which I am told is the practice. At this moment it is wholly out of my power to go to New York without adding to the disagreeable situation of my family. I cast myself therefore upon your humanity and benevolence, and beg leave to subscribe myself

Your Excellencys Most Obed! Very humble Serv!

Robert Ballard

Balt 30th May 1789

ARS (DLC, George Washington Papers).
1. See Robert Ballard to George Washington, January 1, 1789.

Benjamin Rush to John Adams ————————————————
June 4, 1789 Philadelphia, Pennsylvania

highly respect
...I [words inked out] Mr Jay, [letters inked out] but supposed, he would have [bee?] been continued in his present office. —[1] After stating the abilities — Sac-

to hear t

rifices & services of Mr Wilson＿ could it be offensive ˄ that he ~~was your friend~~
~~before~~ opposed the narrow views of those people who wished to ε render your

to

or ˄ dishonour you by the manner in which it was conducted?＿

election abortive? ˄ In this he acted a manly part, and I have a right to say,

by

that he was less influenced by personal regard, than ˄ genuine＿ federal＿ and
republican principles.＿ Letters from new York & maryland (which I saw)
strongly urged him to an opposite Conduct. But he felt＿ what you have ex-

had

pressed, and could his advice have prevailed fully, you would have ˄ ten, instead of eight votes from Pennsylvania.＿ . . .

ARS (MHi, Adams Manuscript Trust).

1. John Adams, in his letter to Benjamin Rush of May 17, 1789 (q.v.), had mentioned his
preference for John Jay as first chief justice. At this time, Jay was secretary for foreign affairs,
having assumed the duties of that post on December 21, 1784. After the creation of the Department of State on September 15, 1789, he was appointed *ad interim* secretary of state by President Washington and served in that capacity until Thomas Jefferson assumed the duties of that
office on March 22, 1790. See "Appointments to the Bench," headnote to "John Jay: Appointment as Chief Justice in 1789"; *Stat.,* 1:28.

Letter from an Anonymous Correspondent ─────────
State Gazette of North-Carolina
June 5, 1789   New York, New York

. . . "The appointment of the Judges is also a matter of great expectation. We
are told your state[1] expect to furnish a chief. What your[2] reasons are for this
expectation I shall not now enquire; but this I can tell you,[3] that some of you[4]
think more highly of the man you[5] propose[6] than the people of other states
do. Perhaps you will make a like remark respecting our popular character;[7]
but remember he is yet but in the morning of life, and has not been long
enough above the horizon to have extended his rays so far as one that has
reached if not passed his zenith."

(Edenton) July 9, 1789. Date and place are those given for the letter. Printed under a Philadelphia
headline dated June 10, 1789.

This letter had been printed earlier in the *Massachusetts Centinel* (Boston) on June 17, 1789;
but the Boston printing altered the text as noted.

1. Pennsylvania (see source note above). The *Massachusetts Centinel* printing read "Pennsylvania" instead of "your state."

2. In *Massachusetts Centinel,* "their."

3. In *Massachusetts Centinel,* "you" was left out.

4. In *Massachusetts Centinel,* "them."

5. In *Massachusetts Centinel,* "they."

6. James Wilson.

7. The author probably is referring to Alexander Hamilton. In the previous paragraph discussing candidates for secretary of the treasury, Hamilton is mentioned as being so popular with
New Yorkers that no office is thought too high for him.

Samuel Barrett to George Washington ——————————————
June 18, 1789   Boston, Massachusetts

Boston   18 June 1789

May it please your Excellency,

When a Person who is an intire Stranger introduces himself to another who is in every Respect his equal there is an Awkwardness in the Business, wh^h it is extremely difficult to get over, but when he does it to one in every Respect incomparably his superior, the Embarrasment is proportionably encreased & higher Reasons are necessary in his Justification: Of my Apology your Excellency will judge, as it will appear in the following Detail.

Having lost all my little Capital with the extensive Capital & Business of the mercantile House into which on leaving the University, I was, on Prospect very flattering in Point of Property, thô very [word illegible] in every other View, introduced by my Father, & of which I was a Partner when the late War commenced; in Consequence of our early & decided Attachment to the Cause of our Country & liberal Advances of Money & Credit given to public Paper (to the Amount of many thousand Pounds) previous to any Depretiation & in Order to prevent it;_ also, of the Tender made us in Payment of very large Sums of solid Debts in depreciated Paper_ of the Failure of some Capital & many small Debtors by the Operation of War;_ of a great Part of our Merchandize being carried away by the British Army, & the Residue either sold to Government for the Use of our Army, or the Produce of Sales deposited in Government Securities;_ and being thus through the Period of the War, deprived of our Trading Stock, & at the same Time supporting three Families at inhanced Expenses & paying heavy Taxes as Persons of Property, while that Property was so rapidly melting in our Hands; we found ourselves at the Close of the War in the last Stage of Declension from Affluence and Independence to absolute Poverty.

Thus situated I made every Effort to recover my Business, when the Peace commenced, but failed of Success. & indeed such a Series of Misfortunes opposed me, that every Exertion to meliorate my Situation made it worse; untill at length I gave over the Pursuit_ & sought my Support (having happily the Confidence of Government & of many respectable Individuals) in public Employments_ and now scantily support, that I may the better educate, a numerous young Family, giving them barely necessaries & Schooling, from the pitiful Fees arising from the Offices of a Justice of the Peace & a Judge of the Court of Common Pleas for the County of Suffolk.

But these Employments not being sufficient thereto, even with the most rigid Oeconomy I have been advised to make Application for some Appointment under the Fœderal Government

That I might conduct this Application with Propriety & Sucess I wrote to several Gentlemen in New York for Advice, & among other respectable Friends to Major General Knox, whose Letter I now take the Liberty to inclose, with one from his Excellency Governor Hancock.

When the Judicial Arrangements are formed some Person will be necessary to keep the Records; and it would be, thô a laborious, yet perhaps the most suitable Office for me; as it might be conducted without Interference, with my present Employments; & be, thô a moderate Appointment in itself, yet an agreable Addition to my Support.

Should such Appointment be made, permit me to sollicit the Grant of it, or your Excellencys Recommendation to those in whose Gift it may be.

If any Thing more Suitable or beneficial presents itself to you, your Patronage & good Offices will lay me under the highest Obligations — it is immaterial to me in what Line I act, if it be but reputable & [i?] can perform the Part assigned me to Acceptance.

With the Candor inseperable from your Mind, your Excellency will excuse this Application & Detention from more important Concerns, and if you can consistently confer such Office as I could sustain with Propriety & to the public Advantage, I shall from Motives of Gratitude, Honor, Patriotism, & even Interest endeavour to do Credit to your Patronage & the Recommendation of my [*words missing*]

I can with Pleasure refer for such Information as may be necessary to his Excellency the Vice President & to all the Gentlemen of both Houses of the Federal Government from Massachusetts; and to the honorable Mess[rs] Johnson, Sherman, Sturgis, Wadsworth & Trumbull from Connecticut.[1] And by particular Desire of Major General Lincoln[2] & can with perfect Satisfaction refer your Excellency to him —

I have the honor to be, May it please your Excellency Your Excellencys most obedient & most humble Servant

Samuel Barrett

His Excellency
The President.
of the United States

ARS (DLC, George Washington Papers). Addressed "New York." This letter is damaged where it was folded. Therefore, certain readings are conjectural; these have been placed in brackets. A letter from Henry Knox to Samuel Barrett was enclosed with this letter. Knox, writing on May 24, 1789, from New York, advised Barrett as to how to apply for an appointment. Barrett had asked for this advice in a letter to Knox on May 11, 1789.

Before the revolution, Samuel Barrett (1739-1798) had been an unsuccessful Boston merchant. He apparently served as a law clerk to Peter Oliver, who was a judge on the Massachusetts Superior Court of Judicature. In 1774 Barrett received an appointment as a justice of the peace from the provincial government; in 1780 he was reappointed to that post by the state. Ruined financially by the Revolutionary War, Barrett sought judicial appointments in Massachusetts. In 1787 he was appointed to the Quorum of the Court of General Sessions and in 1789 to the bench of the Court of Common Pleas for Suffolk County. Clifford K. Shipton, *Sibley's Harvard Graduates,* vol. 14, *1756-1760* (Boston: Massachusetts Historical Society, 1968), pp. 135-42; *DAB* under Peter Oliver.

1. No definite connection has been found linking Samuel Barrett to Connecticut's Senator William S. Johnson and Connecticut's Congressmen Roger Sherman, Jonathan Sturges, Jeremiah Wadsworth, and Jonathan Trumbull.

2. Benjamin Lincoln (1733-1810), a Revolutionary War general, commanded the Massachusetts troops that put down Shays's Rebellion in 1787. Lieutenant governor of Massachusetts in 1788, Lincoln worked for ratification of the Constitution in the state convention. In 1789 he was named collector of the port of Boston and served until his retirement in 1809. *DAB*.

Samuel Barrett to William Cushing ⸻
June 20, 1789 Boston, Massachusetts

Boston   20 June 1789

Hon^d & Dear Sir

It being suggested to me that your Honor will probably be appointed Chief Justice of the Fœderal Court, & presuming that the Officers of that Court will be appointed by the Judges, I take the Liberty to propose to your Consideration my Wish to be one of the Clerks of ~~of~~ that Court or if your Brother[1] should chuse to be thus appointed, to succeed him in the office he now sustains — those which I hold being far incompetent to my necessary Subsistance —

Excuse an application apparently so premature, as when it may be seasonable, it may be impossible for me to know it untill it may be too late —

Your Patronage & good Offices will lay me & my Family under the highest Obligations

I am   Hon^d & Dear Sir   Your most hum^e Servant

Samuel Barrett

[Ho]n^[le?] Judge Cushing —

ARS (MHi, William Cushing Papers). Addressed to "York" in the District of Maine, Massachusetts. Because some of the writing in the lower left-hand corner of this letter is missing, a conjectural reading has been supplied in brackets.

1. Charles Cushing (1734-1810), brother of William Cushing, was one of the clerks of the Supreme Judicial Court of Massachusetts. Clifford K. Shipton, *Sibley's Harvard Graduates,* vol. 12, *1746-1750* (Boston: Massachusetts Historical Society, 1962), pp. 563-69.

Joseph Jones to James Madison ⸻
June 24, 1789 Richmond, Virginia

. . . Virg^a ought to have one of her Citizens in the Superior Court but we have very few fit for it ~~who are capable of acting~~ — of our Judges — Pendleton,[1] Wythe,[2] Blair, would either of them answer well — the first will I fear be unable to execute his present office long the others are qualified and able if they would act[.?] among the Lawyers I know of none but Randolph —[3] it is of the first consequence to have your Supreme court of able Lawyers & respectable characters. . . .

ARS (DLC, James Madison Papers).

Joseph Jones (1727-1805), a lawyer in Fredricksburg, Virginia, uncle of James Monroe, and close friend of James Madison. Admitted to the Inner Temple (1749) and the Middle Temple (1751), Jones was called to the bar in England in 1751. Three years later, he was appointed deputy attorney for the king in Virginia. Jones was a participant in revolutionary activities at the county, state, and national levels. In 1778 he was appointed a judge of the Virginia General Court but resigned in 1780 to attend the Continental Congress. He was reappointed to the bench of the General Court on November 19, 1789, where he served until his death. *DAB.*

1. Edmund Pendleton.

2. George Wythe (1726-1806), born in Elizabeth City County, Virginia, read law with Stephen Dewey in Prince George County and gained admission to the bar at age twenty. In 1754 he served briefly as Virginia's attorney general. After the revolution began, Wythe served in Congress for one year before returning to Virginia where he worked with Thomas Jefferson and Edmund Pendleton to revise the laws of Virginia. In 1778 Wythe became one of three judges for the Virginia Court of Chancery. Ten years later, following a reorganization of the state's judiciary, he was appointed sole chancellor, an office he held until 1801. Appointed to a chair at the College of William and Mary in 1779, Wythe was the first law professor in the United States. Wythe attended Virginia's ratifying convention and supported adoption of the Constitution. *DAB.*

3. Edmund Randolph (1753-1813) came from a long line of Virginia jurists. After reading law with his father, Edmund Randolph practiced for only a brief time before his appointment as Virginia's first attorney general in 1776. Subsequently he served in the Continental Congress, the Annapolis Convention, and the Constitutional Convention. In 1786 he was elected governor of Virginia. In 1789 he was practicing law in Williamsburg, and in September of that year President Washington appointed Randolph United States attorney general. *DAB;* John J. Reardon, *Edmund Randolph: A Biography* (New York: Macmillan, 1975), pp. 27, 172; *SEJ,* 1:32-33.

Francis Dana to John Adams —————————————————
June 26, 1789   York, District of Maine, Massachusetts

[*Dana reminds Adams of a conversation between them at Cambridge, where Dana had requested that he be considered for a federal office because of the burden of his duties as associate justice of the Supreme Judicial Court of Massachusetts and because of his poor health. He offers himself as a candidate for the position of federal district court judge for Massachusetts.*] A place in the Supreme Federal Court wou'd be more honourable, but on account of the extent of their circuits, and of their sitting twice a year at the seat of the Federal Government, that wou'd expose me to all the difficulties arising from my present office: but for the consideration of which, I wou'd not quit it for any other in the gift of the United States, or of this State.

[*Dana then mentions that he has heard from Theophilus Parsons[1] that if John Lowell[2] becomes the district court judge, Parsons hopes to become the federal attorney for Massachusetts. Dana extols the professional merits of both men and hints that he too would appoint Parsons as federal attorney.*]

I have supposed from the above conversation between us (however it may savour of vanity in me) that you might think of your friend[3] for one of the Supreme Federal Judges. M͏ʳ Lowell has already been in that capacity;[4] and if

John Lowell by Edward Savage
(1761-1817). Oil on canvas, date
unknown. Courtesy Mead Art
Museum, Amherst College.

the reasons I have given against accepting that office, did not exist, I shou'd
not choose to stand a candidate for it against him. Perhaps there may be no
impropriety in both appointments, as every State must have a district Judge
and, I think, Massachusetts, exteris paribus may be entitled to one Judge of
the six of the Supreme Federal Court.[5] . . .

ARS (MHi, Adams Manuscript Trust). Endorsed "ans[d] July 10, 1789."

1. Theophilus Parsons (1750-1813) read law with Theophilus Bradbury in Falmouth (now
Portland, Maine) and began his legal career there in 1774. At the outbreak of the Revolutionary
War, Parsons returned to Byfield, Massachusetts, where he had been born. There he had the
opportunity to study law with Edmund Trowbridge, one of Massachusetts's most learned attorneys
and judges. Parsons then resumed his legal career in neighboring Newburyport and also began
writing about constitutional issues. He played a key role in Massachusetts's ratification of the federal Constitution. In 1789 Parsons was serving in the state legislature representing Newburyport.
DAB.

2. John Lowell (1743-1802) graduated from Harvard in 1760, where he won acclaim for his
oratorical skills. He then studied law with Oxenbridge Thacher and began to practice as a lawyer
in 1763. Lowell quickly became the leading lawyer of his native Newburyport. In 1777 he moved
to Boston where his legal practice continued to thrive. Three years later Lowell, along with John
Adams and James Bowdoin, played an important role in the adoption of the Massachusetts constitution. At this time, Lowell was appointed a justice of the peace and quorum for Suffolk County.
He served one term in the Confederation Congress, and in December, 1782, he was elected by
the Congress to the Court of Appeals in Cases of Capture. Lowell supported adoption of the
federal Constitution. On September 26, 1789, he was appointed United States judge for the district of Massachusetts. Shipton, *Sibley's Harvard Graduates,* 14:650-61; *DAB* under John Lowell and
James Bowdoin; *SEJ,* 1:30.

3. I.e., Francis Dana.

4. In December, 1782, the Confederation Congress had elected John Lowell a judge of the
Court of Appeals in Cases of Capture, a court created by the Continental Congress to hear prize
cases appealed from state admiralty courts. Shipton, *Sibley's Harvard Graduates,* 14:657.

5. The phrase "exteris paribus" can be translated as "different things being equal." In the present context, Francis Dana probably means that Massachusetts, as one of the larger states (and therefore "different" among "equals"), deserves to have one of its residents appointed as an associate justice.

William Bradford, Jr., to Elias Boudinot
June 30, 1789 Philadelphia, Pennsylvania

[*Bradford reports that* "the Gentlemen of the bar here" *would like to recommend Edward Shippen*[1] *to be district court judge for Pennsylvania.*] This idea of recommending him you will be pleased to keep to yourself: but if you can learn who is in contemplation for that post besides Mr Hopkinson,[2] it will oblige me to communicate. Mr H. the district Judge, with an appeal to Mr Wilson as ~~chief~~ one of the circuit Judges, will not be very pleasant to the Gentlemen of the bar in this State. __[3] . . .

ARS (PHi, John W. Wallace Collection). Addressed "New York."

William Bradford, Jr. (1755-1795), Elias Boudinot's son-in-law, was attorney general of Pennsylvania from 1780 to 1790. In August, 1791, Bradford was appointed a justice of the Supreme Court of Pennsylvania, and in January, 1794, he succeeded Edmund Randolph as attorney general of the United States. *DAB.*

Elias Boudinot (1740-1821) had been president of the Confederation Congress in 1782 and 1783. Boudinot served as a congressman from New Jersey from 1789 to 1795. *BDAC.*

1. Edward Shippen (1729-1806) had been one of the leaders of the pre-revolutionary Pennsylvania bar. Shippen, who studied law at the Middle Temple, was admitted to the English bar on February 9, 1750, and to the Supreme Court of Pennsylvania bar on September 25, 1750. Prior to the war, he was a judge of the Court of Vice Admiralty (1752-1776), member of Philadelphia's Common Council (1755-1756), clerk of the Common Council, clerk of the City Court, prothonotary of the Supreme Court of Pennsylvania (1762-1776), and member of the provincial Council (1770-1775). A moderate loyalist, Shippen nonetheless was able to resume his judicial career after the war. He served as president of the Court of Common Pleas of Philadelphia County (1784-1791), president of the Court of Quarter Sessions and General Gaol Delivery (1785-1786), and as judge of the High Court of Errors and Appeals (1784-1791), then the highest appellate court in Pennsylvania. Appointed to the bench of the Supreme Court of Pennsylvania in 1791, he became chief judge in 1799 and sat in that capacity until his resignation in 1805. *DAB.*

2. Francis Hopkinson (1737-1791) was educated at the College of Philadelphia before studying law with Benjamin Chew, attorney general of Pennsylvania. Hopkinson gained admission to the Supreme Court of Pennsylvania bar in 1761. Before devoting himself to his legal practice, however, Hopkinson turned his attention to musical and literary interests. In 1779 he became a judge of Pennsylvania's admiralty court, a post he held for ten years. In September, 1789, he was appointed United States judge for the district of Pennsylvania. *DAB; SEJ,* 1:29, 31.

3. William Bradford, Jr., may have been concerned about an appeal from Francis Hopkinson to James Wilson because of the friendship that existed between the two. In a letter written on September 21, 1789, Edward Tilghman, an eminent Philadelphia lawyer, wrote to George Read, a senator from Delaware, to support the nomination of Edward Shippen for district court judge. Commenting on the qualifications of Francis Hopkinson, Tilghman wrote that "To you I may in confidence say that the other. (F. H) is not competent__ I say this not from my own Experience but from the Voice of the Bar without Exception that I know of, unless Mr Wilson may be of another Opinion, w^h I rather suspect to be the Case from their Intimacy & Friendship__" (Richard S. Rodney Collection, DeHi).

John Adams to Francis Dana ————————————————————————
July 10, 1789 [New York, New York]

[*Adams discusses possible appointments to both the state and lower federal benches should
William Cushing or John Lowell be appointed to sit on the Supreme Court.*] I will
say to you that another person has been mentioned for one of the judges of
the supreme court and that is chief Justice Cushing. For my own part I only
wish that the best and ablest men may be brought into the public service, such
as have the clearest and fairest reputations, are known to the people and have
acquired weight and consequence in their estimation. . . . If the President
should consult me, I shall give him every information in my power, with the
utmost impartiality. With regard to yourself, I have no scruple to say, that any
places in the judicial system would be honored by your acceptance of them in
my humble opinion. Reserving always however, the chief Justices office for
Mr Jay.[1] . . .

ALbS (MHi, Adams Manuscript Trust). Addressed "Cambridge" in Massachusetts. Dated by the
endorsement on the letter from Francis Dana to John Adams of June 26, 1789 (q.v.). Place determined by evidence in letter.
  1. The day before this letter was written, Richard Platt wrote from New York to Winthrop
Sargent: "I mention to you in a whisper, that Hamilton is thought to be the man for Financier
& Jay for Chief Justice_" (Winthrop Sargent Papers, MHi).

Cyrus Griffin to George Washington ————————————————
July 10, 1789 New York, New York

N York.
  Mr Cyrus Griffin, presiding Judge of the Court of appeals and late president
of Congress; having devoted the greater part of his life to the study of Laws,
and particularly the Law of Nations & the Interpretation of Treaties, from duty
and Inclination takes the liberty to offer his farther Services to the union, either
in the diplomatic line or as one of the Judges of the Supreme Court.
  To recommend him upon this important business, he can appeal to certain
resolutions of Congress, to his Colleagues in office, and to the Gentlemen of
the Bar who attended the Continental Court of Admiralty; and whilst a Member and president of Congress he can with like propriety appeal to many
Gentlemen who are now engaged in the federal Legislature, and even to those
Citizens of N. York who had an opportunity of observing and understanding
his public and private demeanor.
  if better Characters should be unwilling to act, and since the underwritten
has invariably pursued the destiny of the Confederation[,?][1] could he be so
happy and experience the good fortune to be honored with the President's

Cyrus Griffin by Lawrence Sully
(1769-1804). Watercolor? on
ivory, 1799. Courtesy Historical
Society of Pennsylvania.

nomination, he flatters himself that the advice and Consent of the Senate will
not be wanting to his appointment.

Cyrus Griffin

July 10th 1789.

ARS (DLC, George Washington Papers).
    Cyrus Griffin (1748-1810) studied law at the University of Edinburgh and the Middle Temple
from 1766 to 1774. Griffin began his career in public service in the Virginia House of Delegates
in 1777 and was elected to the Continental Congress in 1778. Congress named him one of the
three judges of the Court of Appeals in Cases of Capture. Griffin was the last president of the
Confederation Congress. In national politics Griffin was a federalist, and President Washington,
in recognition of Griffin's skills, appointed him United States judge for the district of Virginia in
1789. Henry S. Rorer, "Cyrus Griffin: Virginia's First Federal Judge," *Washington and Lee Law
Review* 21 (1964): 201-7.
    1. The margin of this page is missing, and this comma is conjectural.

Paine Wingate to Timothy Pickering ———————————
July 11, 1789 New York, New York

. . . What you mention respecting Mr Wilson[1] I believe to be very just &
true— The apointment of those high offices in government will depend very
much on the President and who they will be, I have hardly heard conjectured.
It will be a satisfaction to me to have some knowledge of the characters,

^{to}
ef ∧ whose appointment I may be called to give an assent or dissent in Senate
& on this account I am oblidged to you for your information— . . .

ARS (MHi, Timothy Pickering Papers).

Paine Wingate (1739-1838), Timothy Pickering's brother-in-law, was a senator from New
Hampshire. Wingate, who had served one term in the Confederation Congress, stayed in the
Senate until the expiration of his term in 1793 and then won election to the House of Repre-
sentatives. After one term in the House, he returned to state service in the New Hampshire
legislature and in 1798 became a judge of the Superior Court from which he resigned in 1809.
DAB.

Timothy Pickering (1745-1829) had been a lawyer and prominent citizen in Salem, Massachusetts, at the outbreak of the Revolutionary War. Pickering's interest in military science and his
organizational skills brought him to General Washington's notice, and during the war he served
as an adjutant-general, as a member of the Board of War, and as quartermaster-general. After the
war, Pickering moved first to Philadelphia and then to Pennsylvania's Wyoming Valley. He represented Luzerne County in the state ratifying convention in 1788, where he supported adoption
of the Constitution. He also represented the county in the state constitutional convention, 1789-
1790. In 1790 President Washington sent him on a mission to the Seneca Indians and in August,
1791, appointed him postmaster general. In January, 1795, Pickering became secretary of war.
After Edmund Randolph's resignation as secretary of state in August, 1795, Pickering replaced
him. John Adams maintained Pickering in the latter post until May 10, 1800, when the president
belatedly discovered that Pickering had been intriguing behind his back with Alexander Hamilton.
DAB.

1. No letter from Timothy Pickering to Paine Wingate which discusses James Wilson has been
found.

John Miller to George Washington ——————————————
July 13, 1789   Philadelphia, Pennsylvania

Philadelphia   13th July 1789.

Honored Sir

I make bold to address you, just to remind your Excellency of a Memorial
I took the liberty to forward on the 25th ultimo—[1] I was not of ability to go
into the Field in time of our Struggle for liberty, however, Sir, I contributed
all in my power by placing Money in the Funds for the Support of our Armey,
the Interest of which, (and other heavy Losses since) not being paid of late,
render me an object of your Excellencies great Compassion and Indulgance.

I have many years been a Servant to the Publick, and am now out of all
Employ; would therefore most humbly beseech your Excellency would gra-
ciously be pleased to appoint me one of the Assistant Justices, or an Officer
in the Revenue. My abilities are but small, but I trust shall ever be faithful
and honest. —

I have the happyness to be acquainted with the honorable Frederick A.
Muhlenberg, Speaker of the House of Representatives, and the Worthy and
Revd John C. Kunsie Minister of the German Lutheran Church in New York
&c^a and with your Excellency too if I was present; in great expectation of your
gracious favour in granting my humble Request now in time of real need, I
beg leave to subscribe myself

Your Excellencies   most ob.t & very hble Serv.t

John Miller

His Excellency the President of y.e United States.

ARS (DLC, George Washington Papers). Postmarked "13   JY."
    John Miller, who had been a miller in Chester County, Pennsylvania, served as a justice of the peace in that county before moving to Philadelphia, where he was commissioned a judge of the City Court in November, 1779. William Henry Egle, ed., *Pennsylvania Archives,* 3d ser., vol. 11 (Harrisburg: William Stanley Ray, 1897), p. 498; John B. Linn and William Henry Egle, eds., *Pennsylvania Archives,* 2d ser., vol. 9 (Harrisburg: Clarence M. Busch, 1896), pp. 698-99; John B. Linn and William Henry Egle, eds., *Pennsylvania Archives,* 2d ser., vol. 2 (Harrisburg: Clarence M. Busch, 1896), p. 611; William Henry Egle, ed., *Pennsylvania Archives,* 3d ser., vol. 10 (Harrisburg: Clarence M. Busch, 1896), pp. 493-94.
    1. In his memorial of June 25, John Miller had requested employment in Philadelphia in any department of the government. George Washington Papers, DLC.

Benjamin Lincoln to Henry Knox
July 18, 1789   Boston, Massachusetts

Boston   18.º July 1789

My dear sir
    The hour will soon arrive when the President must make his nominations for filling up the seats in the judiciary department— The eyes of the people here are much fixed on M.rLowell for one of the judges of the supreme bench— You have I know very much the ear of the President and you perfectly know M.rLowell whose feelings are such on the occasion that, although
                                                                            yet,
he has the highest sense of the worth & merit of the President, ^ it would be a great relief to him if he could be freed from a personal application   at this you will not wonder when you consider the importance of the office and that when ever it shall be filled with real dignity it must be by persons of great natural & acquired abilities so that when a gentleman comes forward and tenders his own services it is saying I possess the qualifications necessary to the important trust this you know all men of delicacy would avoid if possible— If you think of him as I do you will as a lover of the general interest recommend him to the President for the office mentioned He may be assured should M.r Lowell be appointed to it sir he would think it too flattering and honorable for him to refuse If a direct application should at last be indispensable on the part of M.rLowell pray let me know it by the first opp.y
    I am my dear sir   with real esteem   your affectionate   friend

BLincoln

Hon Gen Knox

ARS (MHi, Henry Knox Papers). Endorsed "answered 26.th July   1789."
    Major general Henry Knox (1750-1806), a Boston bookseller before the Revolutionary War, won renown for his command of the artillery during that conflict. After the war, Knox served on a commission to negotiate with the Penobscot Indians and on March 8, 1785, was elected secretary of war by the Confederation Congress. President Washington appointed him to the same position

in his first cabinet on September 11, 1789. Knox retired to private life in 1794 and moved to an inherited estate in Maine in 1796. *DAB; SEJ,* 1:25.

Benjamin Lincoln to George Washington ——————————
July 18, 1789   Boston, Masachusetts

Boston   July 18ᵗʰ 1789 —

I consider, my dear General, that not only the happiness of the people under the new government but that the very existence of it depend, in a great measure upon the characters and abilities of those who may be employed in the judiciary and executive branches of government. — Under this government I hope yet to live and to leave in its arms a large and extensive family   I cannot therefore be an inattentive spectator while the important business of organization is before your Excellency nor be silent where there is but a possibility of my doing the least good[.] As your Excellency cannot be personally acquainted with all who ought to come forward and aid in the administration but must rely, in some degree, on the information of Gentlemen in the different States for the character of those who may be ~~filled~~ commissioned to fill the several departments which may be erected in perfecting the general system I therefore beg leave to mention to your Excellency that the common voice of the people here points out Mʳ Lowell as a gentleman well qualified to fill one of the seats upon the bench of the supreme court. — The purity of his mind, the strength and promptitude of his judgment, and his knowledge of the law united with his having held a similar office under the old confederation have directed their views to this gentleman —

I am very apprehensive that h[e] has not by anyway communicated his wish to your Excellency. If he has not the ommission may originate in the extreem delicacy of the measure[.] It is an office which to fill with honour and dignity requires an honest heart, a clear head, and a perfect knowledge of law in its extensive relations the truth of which he so fully realises that he is restrained from making a tender of his services as it would evince his belief that he enjoys the great and necessary qualifications to fill the office — To this a gentleman of Mʳ Lowe[ll's] nice feelings would be brought with great reluctance

I hope the above hints will be acceptable — If they do good my intentions wi[ll] be perfectly answered — If they do not my apolog[y] for making them is the rectitude of my intentions.

I have the honour of being   with the highest esteem   My dear General your Excellen[cy's]   most obedient and humbl[e]   servant

BLincoln

His Excellency the
President of the
United States —

ARS (DLC, George Washington Papers). One page is missing part of the margin; conjectural readings are in brackets.

Edmund Randolph to James Madison ——————————
July 19, 1789 Williamsburg, Virginia

. . . I have received from Col? Griffin[1] a letter, dated July 10. 1789,[2] in which is this passage. "I had yesterday morning a long conversation with our worthy president on the subject of officers of the judiciary and the customs. He appears very anxious to know whether any of the gentlemen, who are now in the judiciary department in the state of Virginia, would prefer the continental establishment; and mentioned M: Pendleton, M: Wythe, Mr. Lyons[3] and M: Blair; and ask'd me, whether you had ever intimated a wish to serve in that or any other line under the federal government. May I ask the favor of you to sound M: W. & M: B. on the subject. I have written to M: Marshall[4] relative to the wishes of M: P. and M: L." So far as this paragraph respects myself, I do not choose to make a direct answer to Col? G, but thro' your medium, and I hope you will not find it inconvenient to communicate with him on the subject. The following is a candid exposition of my situation—

When I quitted my practice, I had arranged my affairs in such a manner, [*letters inked out*] as amply to justify the measure, which I then adopted. The most important debt, which I owed, had arisen from a purchase of Fry's land; to which I had opposed for payment a tract, containing twice its quantity in Charlotte. This I cannot sell to answer my purpose, and thus do and must encounter some difficulty. From these circumstances I was led <u>partially</u> to resume my profession— Since that time, the apprehension with respect to my bosom companion grows stronger; and the disorder itself, from cirumstances suggested in a former letter, will probably make a large demand for money. I have lately too discovered a debt, due from my uncle's estate of about 800£, which somewhat alarms me— These pressures must be baffled <u>by some</u> vigorous exertions. If the sale of that portion of property, which I always allotted for the first and third of these exigencies could be effected, my ordinary income would suffice for the second. But a fourth of its value cannot be had; and no extent of practice, which any lawyer possesses, or into which I could return, would supply the necessary aid on this emergency. Unless I were to be in Richmond, or to be 3/4 of the year without my family

300£ would be the utmost produce of the most earnest endeavours. To neither of these conditions can I submit. I had therefore once thought of a seat on our appeals; tho' there are obstacles to a real wish to succeed of a very particular cast.

Col? Gs letter has, however, called me to reflect upon a different destination. It would bring with it many conveniences ~~with man~~ in reference to the complaint of my wife, if a northern journey should be deemed necessary for her. But these would be counterbalanced by the load of calumny, which would be in regard to
poured upon me. I am aware, [~~those with?~~] those, whose irritation against the new gov: is not to be allayed, as I could not assuage them, so I can ot

them
exasperate ∧ to a greater degree, than they already are. But for any emolument
or honor whatsoever, I would not hazard the esteem of the virtuous, who
know my conduct on the great federal topic, and I flatter myself, acknowledge
its consistency, and, above all things, its purity. Yes, my dear friend, its purity.
For it has been insinuated (and in defiance of truth) that my espousal of the
constitution had alienated even its friends from me, who would not elect me
to the house of representatives. The insinuation has been carried so far as to
apply it to the disposal of offices under the government. My ~~real wish~~ sincere
desire then would be to have it in my power to refuse, and actually to refuse
an office. But as the tender of a post could not be made on such ground, I
commit myself to you, and leave you to represent this business to Col° Griffin,
as you please, if you think, that there is no impropriety in my inlisting under
federal banners. And yet I ought to add, that nothing definitive can be said,
until I learn the changes, which the bill has undergone. . . .

AR (DLC, James Madison Papers).
  1. Samuel Griffin (1746-1810), a Williamsburg lawyer and brother of Cyrus Griffin, served as
a representative in Congress from 1789 to 1795. Samuel Griffin, who was a close friend of Edmund Randolph, had resigned from the Virginia House of Delegates in 1788 so that Randolph
(who had resigned the governor's chair) could be elected to Griffin's seat. *PGW, Diary*, 3:277;
"Extracts from the Register of Farnham Parish, Richmond County, Virginia," *Virginia Magazine
of History and Biography* 7 (1899-1900): 55; Reardon, *Edmund Randolph*, p. 168.
  2. Letter not found.
  3. Peter Lyons (ca. 1734-1809) had been born in Ireland, studied law with his uncle James
Power in Virginia, and was admitted to the bar in 1756. Lyons was practicing law successfully—
mainly in the county courts—when he was elected to his first judicial post in 1779 as a judge of
the Virginia General Court. When Virginia reorganized its Court of Appeals in 1788, Lyons was
elected to the bench of that court where he served until his death. David J. Mays, "Peter Lyons,"
Proceedings of the Virginia State Bar Association 37 (1926): 418-19.
  4. Letter not found.

Elbridge Gerry's Recommendations for Offices in Massachusetts [before July 20, 1789?]

Applications for Office from Massachusetts

. . .

In the Judiciary

. . . Roxbury
The Honble John Lowell for an associate Judge is mentioned by a number of Gentlemen, he having been a
Judge of appeals under the former Congress of great
abilities & Integrity: he undoubtedly expects an appointment but from delicacy has made no application for it

AR (DLC, George Washington Papers).
  John Lowell, in his letter to Elbridge Gerry of July 20, 1789 (q.v.), referred to a letter Elbridge
Gerry had sent to Lowell (not found) wherein Gerry had probably discussed the nomination of
Lowell to the Supreme Court. Lowell mentioned "the Part you have taken in the Business referred

to" which may mean Gerry's mention of Lowell as a candidate for the federal judiciary in this document to help George Washington decide on appointments in Massachusetts. Hence, the tentative dating for this letter is before July 20, 1789. This assumption is suppqrted by a letter to Gerry from James Sullivan, whom Gerry also had suggested in this list for the office of federal district judge for Massachusetts. Writing on July 25, 1789, in response to a letter from Gerry of July 19, Sullivan thanked him for his efforts to support Sullivan as a "Candidate" (Miscellaneous Manuscripts Collection, DLC). Sullivan may be referring to the fact that Gerry had mentioned his name in this list to Washington.

Elbridge Gerry (1744-1814), a merchant in Marblehead, Massachusetts, served in the Continental and Confederation Congresses but is best known for his refusal to sign the Constitution as a delegate to the Constitutional Convention in 1787. Gerry served as a congressman from 1789 to 1793. He later accompanied John Marshall and Charles Cotesworth Pinckney as an envoy to France in 1797. *DAB*.

John Lowell to Elbridge Gerry
July 20, 1789   Roxbury, Massachusetts

. . . I received your kind Favour[1] the Day on which I was called <s>to</s> ^on^ a Tour to the Eastward, since which Commencement & our Court have prevented my paying that Attention to it which its very friendly Contents called for, the Part you have taken in the Business referred to, is the most perfect Evidence of your Friendship & Esteem both which I assure give me great Pleasure not a new one indeed for I had not the smallest Doubt of them before _ [2] It is so awkward a Business to me to write or speak on personal Subjects that I have on this Occasion totally omitted to correspond with any Person on the Subject, there are some Employments of an executive Nature in which a Man need not trespass the Bounds of Modesty to avow himself a Candidate for them _ but when superiour Discernment Knowledge & Integrity are the necessary Qualifications for an Office it is only the latter that a Man would chuse to say that he possessed _ if it is considered however as necessary that the President should be informed that such an Appointment would be considered as highly honorary & not declined & this by a personal Application I will not resist the Opinions of my Friends as to that Matter, I have however always determined that if it should be thought proper for me to come forward on the Business, that I owe such Respect to my very worthy & respectable Friend the Vice President that I should immediately open on it to him & have no Hesitation to commit myself there _ I have been lately informed that our worthy Friend Gen[l] L. has in a Letter to the President brought this Subject to his View[3] which may perhaps prevent the Necessity of my doing more _ you mentioned the Ch. Justice.[4] as being talked of for an associate Judge _ I respect & esteem him, but he fills already with Dignity an[5] important Office who may succeed in the Caprice of Appointments is uncertain, it ^is^ certain the Friend you wish to serve must be more than left, [<s>to a druudg</s>?] to drudge at the Bar _ but if the public Peace or Good will be promoted, be it so _ I shall be happy under my Vine, my Figtrees will not grow tall enough to give me Shade _ you will perceive the Labour I have taken to express myself, at last awkwardly, on the Business in which your Friendship has engaged you & which so much deserves my Gratitude— ...

ARS (MHi, Gerry II Collection). Endorsed "ans^d   1st Augt 1789." This letter not found.
  1. Letter not found.
  2. See source note to Elbridge Gerry's Recommendations for Offices in Massachusetts, [before July 20, 1789?].
  3. See Benjamin Lincoln to George Washington, July 18, 1789.
  4. William Cushing.
  5. The word "an" is written over "th."

Edmund Randolph to James Madison
July 21, 1789 Williamsburg, Virginia

July 21. 1789.

Since writing the inclosed,[1] I thought it adviseable to postpone sending it, until the mail of today should arrive; hoping that if there was any ground for the paragraph referred to in my letter, I might possibly hear something of it by you. Col^o Parker[2] came to town last night, and confirms in some measure what that letter says; for he has himself made the communication to me— I confide every thing to you in this business; for it would counteract some capital measures, which I contemplate for the next session, were it divulged, that I would go into office, and yet not have it offered to me.

AR (DLC, James Madison Papers).
  1. This brief note is a postscript to Edmund Randolph's letter to James Madison of July 19, 1789.
  2. Colonel Josiah Parker (1751-1810) was a congressman from Virginia. An anti-federalist, he served in Congress from 1789 to 1801. *DAB*.

Richard Morris to George Washington
July 23, 1789 New York, New York

New York July 23^d 1789.
Sir/

If I should be thought Qualified for and worthy of Employment in the Judicial department of the General Government— I shall be happy to Serve my country in any Office which I can Accept consistant with my Own Reputation—

you will Excuse this Lyberty it is from an Intimation, that you was desirous to know every person who wished to be Employed in the Gen^ll Goverment—

with the Highest Sentiments of Respect and   Real Esteem _   I am Sir
your   most Obedient   Humble Servant.

Ri^dMorris

George Washington Esqr

ARS (DLC, George Washington Papers).
   Richard Morris (1730-1810), a member of the distinguished Morris family of New York, grad-
uated from Yale in 1748 and four years later gained admission to the bar in New York. From
1762 to 1775, Morris was a judge of the colonial vice admiralty court with jurisdiction over New
York, New Jersey, and Connecticut. He was a lukewarm supporter of the revolutionary cause but
was widely respected for his knowledge of jurisprudence and his integrity; in 1779 he succeeded
John Jay as chief justice of the New York Supreme Court of Judicature. Morris retired in 1790.
DAB; PJJ, 1:403n.

Edmund Randolph to James Madison ——————
July 23, 1789 Williamsburg, Virginia

. . . In my letter of yesterday,[1] I gave you a faithful narrative of my situation.
On further reflection I feel the propriety of the communication more strongly.
More confidentially therefore do I repose myself on you. Col° Parker seems
to think (but I am persuaded upon grounds, in no respect tenable,) that the
president expects applications from those, who are willing to become servants
of the U.S. It is too outrageous, to be believed, and even when believed,
cannot be submitted to by men of real merit. . . .

AR (DLC, James Madison Papers).
   1. Edmund Randolph's letter of July 19 and its postscript of July 21 (qq.v.) were probably
mailed July 22.

Henry Knox to Benjamin Lincoln ——————
July 26, 1789 New York, New York

. . . I received your favor of the 18th by the post of thursday last _
                                                        favorable
Mr Lowells character has been placed before the President in the [*letters inked
out*] manner to which it was justly entitled. _ ~~It is~~ Whether a personal application would be in any degree necessary I cannot say, _ That would in my
mind depend almost entirely on the opinion of the gentleman himself _ Certain it is if he should think it necessary to offer himself for public employment
                                             to himself & the
the circumstance in any event would be known only ~~to the~~ President ~~and
himself~~

~~I know the opinion of the Senators here to be highly favorable to Mr Lowell~~
The house of representatives will take up the Judicial bill tomorrow _ ~~If~~

~~they discuss and get through it in fourteen days~~ It will not probably be ready for the Presidents signature before the 10th of next month, so that if M[r] Lowell should think proper to write there will be ample time for it . . .

ADfS (MHi, Henry Knox Papers).

William Tudor to John Adams ─────────────────────
July 27, 1789 Boston, Massachusetts

. . . Our Profession are waiting with some Impatience for the Judicial Appointments. M[r] Dana & M[r] Lowell are supposed to be the Candidates for the Supreme Bench. Neither I believe (indeed the latter I know would not, accept the District. A certain Probate Judge is supposed to have taken great Pains to obtain this Post.[1] . . .

ARS (MHi, Adams Manuscript Trust).
    William Tudor (1750-1819), a close friend and correspondent of John Adams, was a Boston lawyer and justice of the peace. Tudor's friendship with Adams dated back to 1769 when Tudor began his law studies in Adams's office. Tudor was admitted to the bar in 1772 and served as a judge advocate in the continental army. Clifford K. Shipton, *Sibley's Harvard Graduates,* vol. 17, *1768-1771* (Boston: Massachusetts Historical Society, 1975), pp. 252-65.
    1. Probably James Sullivan (1744-1808), a political ally of John Hancock and a judge of probate for Suffolk County from 1788 to 1790. In 1790 Sullivan, who had served on the Superior Court of Judicature of Massachusetts from 1776 to 1782, was appointed attorney general for the state of Massachusetts. For evidence of the efforts being made on Sullivan's behalf to obtain for him a post as district judge, see note to Elbridge Gerry's Recommendations for Offices in Massachusetts, [before July 20, 1789?]. *DAB; William T. Davis, *Professional and Industrial History of Suffolk County,* vol. 1, *History of the Bench and Bar* (Boston: Boston History, 1894), p. 91.

Fisher Ames to John Lowell ─────────────────────
July 28, 1789 New York, New York

. . . It is certain that Chief Justice Cushing has been recommended to the Pres[t] But by whom, or by what influence the nomination will be supported I am not able to discover. I am sure that the Senators, and I believe all the Rep[s] of our state would not wish his appointment. I would not affect reserve upon this subject— because I am sure that you cannot be a stranger to my wishes nor will I claim any merit with you by declaring what they are. Judge Cushing's merit is not to be disputed, nor parted with from the bench where he presides at present. I am informed that the pres[t] asks information in regard to his intended appointments— and I am very positive, that the Mass[tts] delegation will express their wishes and reasons in favour of another appointment than that which has been proposed to him— Those reasons have such intrinsic authority, and will be so maintained as to create a strong probability of their prevailing with the excellent pres[t] who regards nothing else. His mode of conducting the executive business is very secret. He does not ask the advice of the Senators individually, in order to determine beforehand whom it will be proper to nominate to office The revenue officers will be appointed very soon and I understand that ~~the~~ some of the Senate are disgusted that he

leaves— or is likely to leave ^to the Senate^ ,the ~~Job~~ power of rejecting the person nom-
inated ^and nothing more^ . They expected to act more in quality of an executive council. We are, therefore, left to conjecture what nominations he will make. I am sure that he will endeavour to procure the service of those who are but disposed and most able to serve the public. I think that my wishes exactly coincide, as to the Sup. Judge for Mass^tts^, with his. . . .

ARS (PWacD, Sol Feinstone Collection). Addressed "Boston."

Fisher Ames (1758-1808), a lawyer in Dedham, Massachusetts, was a gifted writer and orator, whose career in public service began in 1781. Ames, who supported ratification of the Constitution in Massachusetts, served as a congressman from 1789 to 1797. He was a federalist and in 1796 delivered a dramatic and influential speech on the floor of the House of Representatives in favor of the Jay Treaty. He retired at the end of that term to his farm in Dedham but maintained an active interest in both local and national affairs. *DAB.*

Francis Dana to John Adams ————————————
July 31, 1789 Cambridge, Massachusetts

. . . I was sincere when I told ^you^ that I did not wish for an appointment upon the Sup. Federal Bench.[1] Our Chief Justice[2] or Lowell wou'd be worthy Members of that Court. yet I doubt whether the former wou'd accept of a Seat there, on account of their distant employment at certain times. His abilities are equal to that station. Jay wou'd give universal satisfaction, but I have thought he wou'd rather prefer his present office. [*Immediately preceding and just following this passage, Francis Dana mentions the impact that William Cushing's appointment to the Supreme Court would have on the Supreme Judicial Court of Massachusetts because of the political situation in that state.*]

ARS (MHi, Adams Manuscript Trust).
  1. See Francis Dana to John Adams, June 26, 1789.
  2. William Cushing.

Christopher Gore to Rufus King ————————————
August 6, 1789 Boston, Massachusetts

. . . The appointments to the Judicial seats will soon be made— We flatter ourselves in Massachusetts that one of the Supreme court will be taken from this state— the general expectation is, that our friend Lowell, will be appointed an associate judge— and no doubt was ever entertain'd of this event— till we heard that our Chief Justice[1] was in nomination__ Shoud the Chf Justice be appointed, we shall lose an excellent man; whose talents are peculiarly fitted for the place he fills, without rendering any great service to the United States, and a very good man will be extremely mortified__ The Chf Justice, now 56 yrs of age, cannot long be an active member of the court, and he has new habits, and new modes of legal decision _{to acquire} __ on these grounds, I much doubt if he woud be an acquisition to the Union, or at least so great an acquisition to the govt as Lowell__ but in addition to all the consequences, which will be apparent, in your mind, to taking him from our state bench__ Lowell's situation, from such neglect of him, will be intolerable__ Having held a similar rank, under the old confederation,[2] which commission is superseded only by the adoption of the new government; the neglect to appoint him to the supreme court, will imply a conviction, in the mind of him, who appoints, that he had _{been} tried & found wanting__ this certainly will be disgraceful to a very good and able man__ from a regard to the happiness & welfare of this state, and a wish that the just expectations of a valuable part of the Community shoud not be disappointed__ and that an honorable & good man shoud not be extremely mortified I request your attention & influence in this appointment__ and I am sure if you see no just reason, on national grounds, for preferring Cushing to Lowell, you will endeavor that the latter shall not be disgraced__ . . .

ARS (NHi, Rufus King Papers).

Christopher Gore (1758-1827) was a Boston lawyer and a representative to the Massachusetts General Court. Gore had graduated from Harvard in 1776 and then served a two-year apprenticeship with John Lowell. He was admitted to the bar in 1778. Ten years later, Gore supported adoption of the federal Constitution in the Massachusetts ratifying convention. In the fall of 1789, he resigned his seat in the state legislature following his appointment as United States attorney for the district of Massachusetts, a post he held until 1796. Helen R. Pinkney, *Christopher Gore, Federalist of Massachusetts, 1758-1827* (Waltham, Mass.: Gore Place Society, 1969), pp. 3, 8, 14-15, 22, 31-32, 51, 146.

Rufus King (1755-1827), formerly a lawyer in Newburyport, Massachusetts, served with great distinction in the Confederation Congress and the Constitutional Convention. In 1786 King married Mary Alsop of New York City, and in 1788 he moved to that city and abandoned his law practice. King was elected a senator from New York in 1789 and again in 1795. He resigned in 1796 to become minister plenipotentiary to Great Britain, serving in that post until 1803. King was a staunch and articulate federalist. *DAB; BDAC.*

1. William Cushing.
2. See note to Francis Dana to John Adams, June 26, 1789.

John Lowell to John Adams ──────────────────

August 7, 1789 Roxbury, Massachusetts

. . . Although I have had frequent Occassions to sollicit in Favour of my Friends, (or such other Characters) as I have thought might be usefully employed in public Business, my early Habits, which in all Cases influence our Sentiments, have been such that I have never conversed or written on any such Subject when immediately affecting myself, thô I have been of Opinion that Custom & the Expectation of the World, having created different Ideas even in Persons of the greatest real Delicacy of Mind, that this Habit might lead me into an unnecessary Reserve, & be only false Delicacy; but I have been obliged to combat it with great Efforts;— I have always entertained such an Idea of your Friendship, & had such a Confidence in the Rectitude of your Sentiments, that I can say with much Sincerity that there is no Person to whom I should with more Freedom commit myself in such a Case than to you.— the general Voice, not only of my Circle of Friends & Acquaintance, but of others [have?] so frequently & freely informed me, that in the Arrangement of Appointments under the new Constitution, it was probable I should be thought of to sustain the important & honble Office of an Associate Judge, that I supposed it would not be necessary for me to interfere in the Business, or on that Occasion break thrô the Habit I have explained to you, and that if I should be thought capable of doing Service to my Country in that Line, I should not have Occasion to trouble my Friends on that Subject; but as I have received Letters from two of our Friends at New York[1] which have drawn me out farther than I before thought necessary, I could not omit opening myself to you, for I should feel guilty of not using that Confidence which I really possess;— The Appointment is so important in its Nature to our Country that I dare not assume a Confidance in my own Qualifications for it, I am too much concerned to judge impartially, and I have a Sense of Reputation & I flatter myself of Rectitude too great to wish if it was in my [*letters inked out*] Power that my own Judgment should decide that Point; all I intend is to mention those Circumstances to you which in Case your own Opinion coincides with the Partiality of my Friends might have their Weight when compared with those that may attend other Candidates as I am so far advanced in my professional Line that I find my young Bretheren & Children pressing fast on my Heels, & many of them possessing so much real Merit & having ⌃Warmth & Vigour of Imagination, to be found only in youth & so necessary with other Qualities to the shining Part of our Profession, that I see very plainly my Situation among them will soon be less agreable than it has been— I have sustained a Commission under Congress, which has been repeatedly executed in Philadelphia & New York within the Knowledge & Observation of most of the leading Characters in the Union; & I have acquired a personal Acquaintance with many of them;[2] If the Confederation (too rotten, I confess to have been thoroughly repaired) had been amended by additional Powers given to Congress, respecting Trade Revenue &c this Commission would without doubt have drawn to it Cognizance of these Matters: the new Court will take up specifically the Powers of that Commission, extended it is true & rendered more important; the Gentlemen, who were with me in it have been taken out of Office, by very honble Appointments; one of them having two Years since been ⌃President of Congress, which vacated his Comn; the other is now a

Senator.[4] I am the only one whom the new Appointments will discharge & supercede, this will undoubtedly produce a Question in the Minds of those who have been acquainted with these Facts, respecting the Cause of my being omitted; I can avoid seeing the Gentlemen at a Distance; but so universal has been the prevailing Opinion in this State & New hampshire, that I should be reappointed, that I must meet the Question & Condolence of most with whom I shall converse; If however the Defect of Qualifications is the real Cause, however painful it may be, it is so just, that it ought to be acquiesced in without a Murmur._ A Gentleman of our State,[5] of whose Merit no Man entertains a greater Idea, I have heard has been proposed to fill this Office. that he will fill it honourably there can be no Question; whether he wishes or would incline to to exchange his present Office for it I know not, but I conceive he will not feel himself neglected, or hurt if it should not be proposed to him; he now holds in the State a very respectable Com^n, perhaps as respectable as any in it, & he receives the Satisfaction of knowing that he possesses the Esteem of all whose Esteem he would wish for, the Enemies of our ˰ Peace alone would rejoice at his Removal; ˰ how far & how long he
local   the Friends of it would be satisfied
that he was still doing good [6]
would be able to get thro the Fatigues of an Associate Judge, which if the proposed Arrangement takes place will call him far from Home, at the most inclement Seasons of the Year I cannot tell; But my dear Sir who will take his Place in Massachusetts? [*Lowell continues by describing the adverse effect that William Cushing's appointment to the Supreme Court would have on Lowell's future and on the Supreme Judicial Court of Massachusetts because of the political situation in that state.*] I have great Reason to suppose that among the good Men who ~~would~~ may promote the Appointment of so respectable a Character as our Ch. J.. some will be found of another Class who wish to give Pain & Dishonor to me, I have been told that some of this Description have been already suggesting the Measure._ I am ashamed of being so long on this Subject you will however by it have the fullest Evidence of my entire Confidence._ [you?] I have only intended to suggest some Things, which perhaps might not have occurred to you without; I have an Interest in the happy Establishment of this Government, far superiour, after all, to any personal Event in this Business, which my Family & Country claim & which I would not have receive a Detriment to avoid my own Humiliation_ ...

ARS (MHi, Adams Manuscript Trust).

1. May refer to letter from Fisher Ames to John Lowell on July 28 (q.v.) and to letter from Elbridge Gerry to John Lowell on August 1. The latter has not been found but was mentioned in the endorsement to the letter from Lowell to Gerry on July 20 (q.v.).

2. See Francis Dana to John Adams, June 26, 1789, note concerning John Lowell's service on the Court of Appeals in Cases of Capture.

3. John Lowell inserted this interlineation without a caret; we have supplied a caret for clarification.

4. John Lowell is referring to Cyrus Griffin and George Read. All three had served together on the Court of Appeals in Cases of Capture. Griffin left the court in 1787 and returned to

Congress where, on January 22, 1788, he became its president. Read served as a senator from Delaware from 1789 to 1793. Henry J. Bourguignon, *The First Federal Court: The Federal Appellate Prize Court of the American Revolution, 1775-1787* (Philadelphia: American Philosophical Society, 1977), pp. 120, 118; *DAB* entry for Cyrus Griffin; *BDAC* entry for George Read.

    5. William Cushing, chief justice of the Supreme Judicial Court.

    6. Lowell interlined this phrase without a caret; we have supplied a caret for clarification.

Jonathan Jackson to John Lowell ——————————————
August 8, 1789   New York, New York

[*Jackson begins with a lengthy discussion of the process of appointment by nomination of the president.*] such efforts will be made for you I think at least a district appointment will be offered you _ perhaps more _ perhaps not _

    . . . I doubt if at the present stage of matters any thing of importance could be derived from your personal attendance here_

    As a general rule it may be laid down perhaps that the most deserving are least apt to push themselves into veiw _ those who are not to be marked for such false delicacy started first & many of them will derive advantages from it_ . . .

ARS (MHi, Lee Family Papers). Addressed "Boston." Postmarked "N-York   Aug 9."

    Jonathan Jackson (1743-1810), a Massachusetts merchant, had been John Lowell's roommate at Harvard, and they remained close friends for the rest of their lives. Jackson served in the Continental Congress. In 1789 he went to New York to seek appointment as a collector of revenue for Massachusetts. When he met his friend Benjamin Lincoln, who desired the same post, Jackson went to President Washington to urge that Lincoln get the appointment. Washington, when he learned of Jackson's sacrifice, appointed Jackson marshal of the federal court for the district of Massachusetts. Shipton, *Sibley's Harvard Graduates,* 15:56-67.

John Lowell to Elbridge Gerry ——————————————
August 8, 1789   Roxbury, Massachusetts

Roxbury   Augt 8th 1789

My dear Sir

    I rec^d your Favour[1] by the last Post, if I had rec^d it four Days sooner, it would have probably prevented a Measure, which still may be best; being strongly influenced by your Opinion, which I know proceeded from the most real Friendship; & being shaken in my own, by that of several Friends here, who concurred with you & having been informed the the. V. P. in other Cases had pointed out the same Thing as proper, _ I had written a Letter to the President,[2] which as my Friend Mr Ames had before thought not best, I inclosed to him, as I presumed the Tenor of it would appear unexceptionable

& mentioned your Friendship & Opinion, as with the other Reasons inducing me to do it tho reluctantly; I have written to him now, if he has not del^d it to avoid it till he converses with you, as you now think with me on the
                    tho I confess I have Doubts about³ it _
Subject, _ I rather think Mr Bowdoin has written to the V. Presid^t on the Subject _ ⁴ my Friendship for Gen! L.⁵ I presume may have made the Lt Govr.⁶ cold at least to me, thô I esteem him & have till his new Connections
                                                    Gentleman,⁷
been on a very friendly footing with him _ the other ^ with the least Reason, for I never meant to offend him, I am satisfied by his Conduct has placed me in the Number of his Enemies & therefore I [*letters inked out*] cannot think in any Event of attempting an Interest from the Quarter you hint_ but this Solicitude is a very striking Instance of your continued Friendship & affords me a pleasing Satisfaction_ for whereever I may be placed, my Judgment & my Pride receive an high Gratification, in looking round a Circle & seeing ~~that~~
                                                                    them
who they are whose Partiality have given me a Right to call ^ my particular Friends;_ I hope things will be so managed as to make all reasonable People ~~hap~~ contented & happy under the Government of the Union_ I have always had the fullest Confidence it was your sincere Wish & that you would do everything to effect it_ Mrs Lowell joins me in the Wish that Mrs Gerry your lovely little Ones & amiable Circle of Friends may enjoy every Blessing_

I am with Esteem & Regard   your sincere Friend &   Servt

                                                            JLowell

ARS (MHi, Gerry II Collection). Addressed "New York." Endorsed "ans^d [*August*] 15th 1789."

1. Probably a letter dated August 1, which Elbridge Gerry sent to John Lowell, according to the endorsement on Lowell's letter to Gerry on July 20 (q.v.). Letter of August 1 not found.

2. No letter found from John Lowell to George Washington in late July or early August.

3. The word "about" is written over the word "that."

4. See James Bowdoin to John Adams, August 10, 1789. James Bowdoin (1726-1790), a Boston merchant, began his career in public service in 1753 when he was elected to the Massachusetts General Court. Over the next thirty-five years, Bowdoin served Massachusetts with distinction, particularly at the Massachusetts convention to adopt a state constitution in 1779 and as governor from 1785 to 1787. While governor, Bowdoin sought legal advice from John Lowell about Shays's Rebellion. Both men had served in the state constitutional convention and both strongly supported the adoption of the federal Constitution. *DAB;* Shipton, *Sibley's Harvard Graduates,* 14:658-59.

5. Benjamin Lincoln.

6. Samuel Adams (1722-1803) was lieutenant governor of Massachusetts from 1789 to 1793. Adams had been the leader of the pre-war revolutionary movement in Massachusetts. Like John Hancock, Adams was a reluctant supporter of the federal Constitution in 1788. In 1789 Adams replaced Benjamin Lincoln as lieutenant governor. Adams became governor following Hancock's death in 1793 and served in the statehouse through 1797. *DAB* entries for Samuel Adams and Benjamin Lincoln.

7. Probably someone mentioned in Elbridge Gerry's letter to John Lowell of August 1, which has not been found. The identity of this person is unknown.

George Washington to James Madison ————————
August 9, 1789 New York, New York

. . . I have had some conversation with Mr Jay respecting his views to Office, which I will communicate to you at our first interview — and this, if <u>perfectly</u> convenient and agreeable to you, may be this afternoon as I shall be at home, and <u>expect</u> no Comp^y. . . .

ARS (DLC, James Madison Papers).

James Bowdoin to John Adams ————————————
August 10, 1789 Boston, Massachusetts

[*Bowdoin discusses the efforts "of some intriguing Individuals" to get themselves appointed to the Supreme Judicial Court of Massachusetts by promoting the appointment of the state's Chief Justice William Cushing to the supreme federal bench.*]

I have a high regard for Judge Cushing and think the public Good necessarily Connected with his Continuance in the Office of Chief Justice; which he holds with great dignity to himself, and advantage to ye Commonwealth.

As you wish the peace and happiness of ye Commonwealth, you will permit me, with ye Friends of good government, to hope, you will use your influence with his Excellency the President of the United States, for preventing the Evil, that will arise from the removal of Mr Cushing from the Office of Chief Justice: especially as there is a Gentleman here, every way qualified, who 'tis Said, has been recommended to ye President, for the federal Bench. — I mean the hon^{ble} John Lowell Esqr, who was one of ye Admiralty Judges under the late federal Constitution; and with whose person and character you are perfectly well acquainted. . . .

ARS (MHi, Adams Manuscript Trust).

Stephen Higginson to John Adams ————————————
August 10, 1789 Boston, Massachusetts

. . . I shall now take the liberty of stating to you, some of the Evils which are here thought inevitable, should Mr Cushing, Our present chief Justice, be removed to the federal Bench; a measure, which several Letters by the last post inform us, would probably be taken. you know, & every One acknowleges, his Abilities & many good qualities; which render him a proper person for the Office referred to, & which make him of the highest importance to this commonwealth in his present Station. [*Higginson then describes how the appointment of William Cushing to the Supreme Court would have an adverse impact on the Mas-*

sachusetts supreme bench by allowing the popular party to appoint its own supporters.]
They certainly wish much to derange that Bench, & to place on it some men
of very opposite Characters; & They sometime since intimated that it would
happen ere long. But as no One conceived it in any degree probable, & every
One supposed that M.ʳ Lowell would be the man; no measures have been taken
to guard against it; & perhaps no information of this kind before given to
you.—

 I hope you may not consider this communication as improper or ill timed,
    you
I assure ‸ that it's made upon public principles only. Though your particular
friends, & the best men in this State are much alarmed at the Idea of such a
change; yet it may happen, from various causes, that none of them may write
to you upon this Subject.— M.ʳ Cushing is in the highest estimation with every
good man here, & but for the particular circumstances of the Case, they would
wish him to be removed, if he desired it; which is doubted however by many.
But as M.ʳ Lowell is considered as equally qualified for the place with M.ʳ C:,
& from the Offices he before held [*letters inked out*] has been viewed as the
                   as
only fair Candidate— &, as such great injury is considered ‸ inevitable to the
State from the removal of M.ʳ Cushing, those who are the common friends of
both the Gentlemen, & the best friends to Government, & to those who administer it, would be much pleased at the appointment of the former, but
would lament exceedingly that of the latter— ...

ARS (MHi, Adams Manuscript Trust). Endorsed "ansᵈ Septʳ 21."
 Stephen Higginson (1743-1828), a prosperous Boston merchant, had served in the Confederation Congress. Higginson was a business partner of Jonathan Jackson, who was a close friend
of John Lowell. A bitter opponent of John Hancock, Higginson was often consulted by federalist
leaders. *DAB*.

Hugh Williamson to James Iredell ────────────────
August 12, 1789 New York, New York

... The N. C: Debates[1] are considerably read in this place especially by congress Members. some of whom, who formerly had little Knowledge of the
Citizens of N: C, have lately been very minute in their Enquiries concerning
M.ʳ Iredell. By the Way I have lately been asked by a Senator whether I
thought you would accept of a Judges Place[2] under the new Gov.ᵗ if it required
your moving out of the State as we are not in the Union. To this as you may
suppose I reply'd that I was not prepared to answer, the Question being so
complicated. As[,] How far the Removal. What the allowance &c. ...

ARS (Nc-Ar, Charles E. Johnson Collection). Addressed "Edenton." Endorsed "Ansᵈ Aug. 29ᵗʰ
1789."
 Hugh Williamson (1735-1819), a noted scientist, physician, and statesman, was born and raised
in Pennsylvania. Williamson studied theology in Connecticut and medicine in Europe and then

embarked on a mercantile career in Edenton, North Carolina, during the Revolutionary War. He served as surgeon general to North Carolina state troops during the war and began his elected political career in 1782 when he represented Edenton in the North Carolina House of Commons. That year he was also elected to the Confederation Congress. He served in the House of Commons again in 1785, and in 1787 he attended the Confederation Congress and the Constitutional Convention. He worked with James Iredell for the ratification of the Constitution in North Carolina. Williamson was elected to the House of Representatives in 1789 and 1791. In 1793 he retired to New York City and spent the rest of his life engaged in scientific and literary activities. *DAB.*

1. James Iredell was the leading proponent of the Constitution at North Carolina's first ratifying convention. In June, 1789, almost a year after that convention failed to adopt the Constitution, Iredell and William R. Davie published at their own expense *Proceedings and debates of the Convention of North-Carolina, convened at Hillsborough, on Monday the 21st day of July, 1788, for the purpose of deliberating and determining on the Constitution recommended by the general Convention at Philadelphia, the 17th day of September, 1787. To which is prefixed the said Constitution* (Edenton: Hodge & Wills, 1789).

2. Most likely referring to a position as a justice of the Supreme Court. North Carolina was not yet a member of the union; thus no district judge would have been appointed.

Fisher Ames to George Richards Minot ————————
August 13, 1789   New York, New York

... I never said that I thought Mr. L.[1] should not accept as District Judge. I say he ought. I have my fears whether he will be asked to do it. If the Chief Justice[2] should be Associate Judge, possibly Dana may be District Judge. Our excellent friend, Mr. L. merits every thing in that line. He has my fervent wishes in his favor. ...

Pr (Printed in *Ames,* 1:66-68). The date line as printed reads "August 12, 1789._ Thursday." The events described by Fisher Ames did take place on Thursday, which in fact fell on August 13, 1789.

George Richards Minot (1758-1802) was the clerk of the Massachusetts House of Representatives. Minot, who had studied law with William Tudor, also served as secretary of the state convention to ratify the Constitution. Minot later became a judge of the Boston municipal court and a probate judge of Suffolk County, but is best remembered for his works on Massachusetts history. James Freeman, "Character of the Hon. George Richards Minot, Esq. Judge of Probate in the County of Suffolk, and Judge of the Municipal Court in Boston: extracted from an Elogy delivered a few days after his death," *Collections of the Massachusetts Historical Society,* 1st ser., vol. 8 (1802): 86-96; *DAB.*

1. John Lowell.
2. William Cushing.

Cyrus Griffin to George Washington ————————
August 14, 1789   [Elizabeth Town, New Jersey]

Understanding it as the wish of the president that every Candidate for public business should make known his pretensions, I took the freedom, Sir, the other week to offer my slender Services to the general Government, either in the diplomatic or as one of the Judges of the Supreme Court.[1]

if I have done wrong in that proceeding it has followed from misinformation concerning the manner, and from an ardent desire to continue in the employment of the union, particularly as the Government is now Constituted.

I am Sir, with every Sentiment of the highest respect and Consideration your most obedient Servant

Cyrus Griffin

Elizabeth Town
August 14th 1789.

ARS (DLC, George Washington Papers). Cyrus Griffin wrote this from "Elizabeth Town." This is probably Elizabeth Town, New Jersey (present-day Elizabeth), which was a day's ride from New York City. On August 18, George Washington replied to Griffin (q.v.), who by that time was in New York City.

1. See Cyrus Griffin to George Washington, July 10, 1789.

Robert Morris to Francis Hopkinson ————————
August 15, 1789 New York, New York

. . . By the By. will not he[1] have some appointments to make should all things go to our Wishes.[2] . . .

ARS (PHi, Hopkinson Papers). Addressed "Philad[a]."

1. James Wilson.

2. Robert Morris may be referring to the hope that James Wilson would be appointed chief justice of the United States and then be able to fill offices in the Court's discretion.

James Fairlie to Philip Schuyler ————————————
August 16, 1789 Albany, New York

. . . I had it in contemplation, some time ago, to apply for the Clerkship of the Federal court, which I mentioned to M[r] Hamilton[1] requesting his Interest, he candidly told me that however he might be disposed to serve me, he had engaged all his Interest on that head to another person;[2] for which Reason, added to, my opinion that the person who is generally supposed to be most likely to fill the office of Chief Justice[3] (in whose gift it will be), will have relations enough of his own to give it to.— I have thought it most adviseable to desist applying for it . . .

ARS (NN, John and Philip Schuyler Papers).

James Fairlie (1757-1830) resided in Albany in 1789, where he was a clerk in Chancery and a clerk of the Circuit and the Court of Oyer and Terminer of the Supreme Court of Judicature of New York. John Schuyler, *Institution of the Society of the Cincinnati* (New York: Douglas Taylor, 1886), p. 199; [Robert] Hodge, [Thomas] Allen, and [Samuel] Campbell, *The New-York Directory, and Register, for the Year 1789* (New York, 1789).

Philip Schuyler (1733-1804), one of the largest landowners in the state of New York, had rendered distinguished military service during the French and Indian War. During the Revolutionary War, Schuyler saw active duty and served in the Continental Congress. He became an ardent federalist and a senator from New York in the First Congress. *DAB*.

1. James Fairlie probably means Alexander Hamilton, who was the son-in-law of Philip Schuyler. Hamilton's influence in the federal government would have made him a desirable ally for an aspiring applicant for office. Fairlie may have approached Hamilton as a fellow New-Yorker. Both men also were active in the Society of the Cincinnati in New York. *DAB* entry for Alexander Hamilton; *PAH*, 3:635-37.

2. It is not known who this person is.

3. Probably John Jay.

George Washington to Cyrus Griffin

August 18, 1789 New York, New York

To Cyrus Griffin Esquire
  New-York._

Sir,

I think it expedient to acknowledge the receipt of your two notes, dated the 10ᵗʰ of July and the 14ᵗʰ of August, for the purpose of assuring you that there was certainly nothing improper in the tenor of them._ But it will be an instance of Justice to inform you, at the same time, that, without considering myself at liberty to give either encouragement or discouragement to the wishes of Gentlemen who have offered themselves as Candidates for offices, I have invariably avoided giving any sentiment or opinion; for the purpose of reserving myself unembarrassed with promises until all the Candidates are known and the occasion, when decision shall become necessary on my part._

In the mean time, I pray you to be persuaded that in all personal and private considerations, I am, with great esteem Sir, Your Most Obedient and Most Humble Servant

                    (Signed) George Washington

New York
August 18ᵗʰ 1789

Lb (DLC, George Washington Papers); Df (DNA, RG 59, Miscellaneous Letters) with interlineations in hand of George Washington.

George Washington to James Madison

[August 20-September 11, 1789] [New York, New York]

... What can I do with Art L_[1] he has applied to be nominated one of the Associate Judges_[2] but I cannot bring my mind to adopt the request_ The opinion entertained of him by those with whom I am most conversant is unpropitious and yet few men have received more marks of public favor & confidence than he has. _ These contradictions are embarrassing. _ [3] . . .

ARS (PPRF). Marked "Confidential." The dating of this letter can be approximated from internal evidence. George Washington mentions that William Barton had turned down the nomination to be a judge of the Western Territory and asks James Madison for advice on other potential candidates. The Senate had consented to Barton's nomination on August 20. Washington next nominated George Turner, and the Senate consented on September 11. *SEJ*, 1:18, 25. Place determined by evidence in letter; contemporary George Washington letters are also from New York. George Washington Papers, DLC.

1. Arthur Lee.
2. See Arthur Lee to George Washington, May 21, 1789.
3. George Washington did not nominate Arthur Lee to a seat on the Supreme Court. Lee had held a number of positions of public trust, but his career had been marred by controversy. In November, 1775, the Continental Congress asked him to become its confidential correspondent in London; and in October, 1776, he was appointed one of three commissioners to France. Diplomatic missions took Lee to Spain and Berlin, before he returned to Paris. He distrusted his fellow commissioners—particularly Silas Deane—and succeeded in prompting Deane's recall in December, 1777. On Deane's return to America, he attacked Lee's performance in France; his charges were countered by Lee's supporters in Congress. In September, 1779, Congress ended the debate by recalling Arthur Lee, who returned to Virginia. He was elected to the Confederation Congress, where he served from 1781 to 1784. His time there was an unhappy and frustrating one for him. In 1785 Congress appointed him to the treasury board on which he served until its demise in 1789. Lee was an opponent of the federal Constitution. *DAB*. In a letter to Patrick Henry on September 27, 1789, Richard Henry Lee, the brother of Arthur Lee, suggested that Arthur's "opposition to the Constitution [*was the*] cause for rejecting his abilities, and long public services from this system. . . . " Richard Henry Lee Papers, DLC.

Christopher Gore to Rufus King —————————————————
August 22, 1789   Boston, Massachusetts

. . . if Cushing shou'd be appointed an associate judge _ I do most truly hope, that Lowell will be constituted district judge _ [1] . . .

ARS (NHi, Rufus King Papers).
1. Compared with his strong advocacy of an appointment to the Supreme Court for John Lowell in his letter of August 6, 1789 (q.v.), this letter seems to suggest that Christopher Gore expected William Cushing to receive the nomination.

Thomas Rodney to George Washington —————————————
[on or before August 25, 1789]
[Poplar Grove, Kent County, Delaware?]

. . . Providence having blessed me with Competence among the rural scenes of Retirement I am not solicitous to return again into the busy scenes of the world, but I hope your Excellency will excuse me while I intrude so far on the busy moments of your arduous station as to mention a worthy friend or two. When you are filling that important Court which is to have a supreme Controle over the lives and property of the Citizens of America I hope the merits of M.ʳ M.ᶜKean the present Chief Justice of Pensylvania will recommend him to your Notice; His firm and Uniform Patriotism— his Extensive legal knowledge, and his love of Justice has rendered him highly respected both in Dalaware and Pensylvania and I doubt not will have much greater weight with your Excellency than any thing I can say.

ADf (DeHi, H. F. Brown Collection). Date and place suggested by the fact that this is a draft of Thomas Rodney's letter of August 25, 1789 (q.v.).
   Thomas Rodney (1744-1811), younger brother of Caesar Rodney, was a prominent citizen of Kent County, Delaware. Thomas Rodney, a justice of the peace, commanded Kent County militia during the Revolutionary War. He was also a judge of the state admiralty court from 1778 to 1785. In 1786 and 1787 Rodney was elected to represent Kent County in the Delaware General Assembly. He did not hold office again until December, 1802, when he was appointed an associate justice of the state Supreme Court. *DAB*.

Thomas Rodney to George Washington —————————
August 25, 1789 Poplar Grove, Kent County, Delaware

. . . Being content with Rural retirement, whatever I may have merited in the Revolution I do not come forward to solicit any thing for myself but beg leave when you are filling up the Supreme Court, to recommend to your attention the Chief Justice of Pensylvania whose merits in the revolution are too well known to you for me to ad any thing on that head. . . .

ARS (DLC, George Washington Papers). Addressed "New York." Written at Poplar Grove, a Rodney family estate in Kent County, Delaware. Hazel Wright Reynolds, *Flower of Caroon Manor* (Baltimore: Gateway Press, 1982), pp. 19-21. This is the recipient's copy of the letter drafted on or before August 25, 1789 (q.v.).

Thomas Rodney to Henry Knox —————————
August [25-31], 1789 Poplar Grove, Kent County, Delaware

                                           Dalaware— Poplar-Grove Aug.ˢᵗ 1789.
D.ʳ Sir
   I am happy to hear that you still retain your old station of secret.ʸ of war— your advice I am persuaded will at all Times have great weight with the President and therefore permit me to mention to you that I took the liberty in a letter to his excellency of recommending to his attention the Chief Justice of Pensylvania when he is filling up the Supreme Court,[1] and of recommending col: John Parke[2] to some office that would him[3] a gent[m's?] support; If it is agreable to you to favour these recommendations as oportunity serves your

good offices will be considered and Esteemed by the person advantaged by
them as well as by
    your Most Obedient   And very Huṁ. Serv!

Thomas Rodney

P. S. Col. Pake was the first person from Dalaware that joined that army at
Boston—

ARS (MHi, Henry Knox Papers). Addressed "New-York." This letter has been dated from
Thomas Rodney's mention of his letter to George Washington of August 25.
    1. Thomas Rodney recommended Thomas McKean to George Washington in his letter of
August 25, 1789 (q.v.).
    2. John Parke (1754-1789), a native of Delaware, served on General Washington's staff during
the Revolutionary War, and afterwards worked as a writer and poet. Charles E. Green, *The Story
of Delaware in the Revolution* (Wilmington, Delaware, 1975), pp. 272-73.
    3. Thomas Rodney apparently left out a word such as "give."

James Iredell to Hugh Williamson
August 29, 1789   [Edenton, North Carolina?]

. . . I had the pleasure to receive your obliging favour of the 12 Aug. . . . I
consider myself deeply indebted to the gentlemen who did me the honour to
propose the question as to my being ˄one of the Judges, & doubt not I am prin-
cipally to attribute any favorable opinion entertained of me in this respect to
your partial & friendly representation of me. I cannot but say, if it should be
possible that I could be appointed tho' not now living under the Union, that
it is a situation which would be very agreeable to me, [*word crossed out*] ~~as I
do not~~ [know?] ~~the Salary will~~ provided the salary was such (as I doubt not it
will be) as would be a sufficient compensation for my devoting my whole time
to the duties of the appointment, which I would with pleasure do as my inclination [for a?] long [time?] would direct me sooner to ~~that kind of life than
any other, & I believe I should be better qualified for it than for any other
employment~~ such kind of employment than any other. The necessity of my
removing out of the State (tho' extremely painful to me) I should not consider
as an insuperable objection pro˄vided it was not required of me to remove
        any where to the Southward of this State or very far to the Northward.
~~further to South Carolina or Georgia for I should not chuse to carry my
Family further to the Southward.~~ I take the liberty, in consequence of your
very kind intimation, to mention this, though I can by no means flatter myself
that when I am so little personally known so high & dignified an appointment
could take place in my favour. . . .

ADf (Nc-Ar, Charles E. Johnson Collection). James Iredell probably wrote this draft at his home
in Edenton, North Carolina.

Gustavus Scott to George Washington ——————————
August 30, 1789 Cambridge, Maryland

[*Scott acknowledges the receipt of a letter from George Washington that had been written in response to the application of Scott for an appointment in the federal judiciary.*[1]] however anxious of success I may be . . . it was my fixed Determination to stand in the way of no Gentleman who appeared to deserve a preference; & that I have constantly mentioned Mr Judge Harrison as one whom I conceived to stand in this point of view. As I am persuaded from my own personal Knowledge of this Gentleman, that no man can render his Country more essential service, I shoud hold my self highly culpable did I not make the Acknowledgement: & I wish to God there were hundreds more to whom I cou'd do the same. . . .

ARS (DLC, George Washington Papers).
    1. Gustavus Scott to George Washington, March 10, 1789, and George Washington to Gustavus Scott, March 21, 1789. George Washington Papers, DLC.

"Civis" to George Washington ——————————————
September 1, 1789 [Annapolis, Maryland]

Sir.

When any Citizen presumes to offer his sentiments to you, his Love for his Country and its Glory should be his apology— upon this Principle the writer hopes to be heard, and altho' his opinion may be useless that the freedom will be excused.—

He[1] has been a constant and warm Stickler for the new Government, and is happy to think it is now out of the reach of its Enemies—

He does not fully understand the Judiciary Sy[ste]m and has some fears as to its operation and Extent, yet he [*phrase missing*] He has no doubt but the best men will be appoi[nted] [*phrase missing*] this most important Department— We have, however [*phrase missing*]ed that the <u>Chief</u> will not be a <u>native</u> of America—[2]

This opinion may have arisen from the great abili[*phrase missing*] man, and from their fears;— he can venture to s[uggest that?] [*word missing*]-tenths of the best Friends to America will ever be aver[se to a Foreign?] President, a Foreign Judge, and Foreign Amba[ssadors.?]

He considers judge Harrison's Character [*phrase missing*] Celebrious commander Cyrus and is fully [*phrase missing*] manners, and the satisfaction and ease tha[t?] [*phrase missing*][r?]ers in the General Court that he is the best man in the Union for the head of the Judiciary— best calculated to inspire confidence and love among our People.—

He is aware that from the retired Habits of Col. Harrison, that he is not so well known throughout america as many men of high Characters who perhaps are not near so perfect; but he has this pleasure, that altho' when out of the Chair of Justice he returns home the most recluse Citizen unknown to all but his Neighbours & friends, that his Virtues and abilities are not hidden from the impartial President of the United States He knows him well, and if he considers him, "take him all in all" the properest Character to Suit the Genius of the people of America, to fill the office with dignity, and faithfully execute the Law he will be nominated by your Excellency—

If this appointment takes place the State of Maryland will lose the best man in it, there is no one who can represent him as a Judge and perhaps the Citizens would have cause to regret the removal, but the Writer is one of those men who always will wave local considerations for the good of the whole.—

In [*letters missing*]ing in his mind, the several Characters in America [*phrase missing*] as among the first, and that next to Mᵣ Harrison [*phrase missing*] [s]atisfy all Parties— The writer begs you will excuse his [*phrase missing*] [h]is name, He is a very young man and diffidence [*phrase missing*] propriety, of the Signature of

Civis

[Septe]mber 1, 1789.

United States,
New-york.

ARS (DLC, George Washington Papers). Addressed "New-york." Postmarked "ANNAPOL[IS]." Place in title derived from postmark. This document has been torn, and text is missing; conjectural readings have been supplied in brackets.

1. I.e., "Civis."
2. "Civis" probably means James Wilson, who was born in the shire of Fife, Scotland.

Samuel Chase to George Washington ——————————
September 3, 1789 Baltimore, Maryland

Baltimore   3ʳᵈ Septᵣ 1789.

My Dear Sir/

I beg You to be assured, that no Person more sincerely rejoiced in your unanimous Election as President of the united States, than Myself; and that my personal Respect for, and attachment to your private and public Character have been uniformly manifested, ever since I had the Honour to be known to You. I have always esteemed it honorable to execute a public Office in a free Government; but heretofore my profession furnished ample Support for Myself, and a numerous Family. If, Sir, You should think Me capable, and proper to discharge the Duty of one of the five associate Judges, and should be pleased to put Me in Nomination to the Senate, I shall be highly gratified; and will exert Myself to execute so honorable and important a Station with Integrety, fidelity, and Diligence; and I flatter Myself, that You will never have Occasion to regret the Confidence reposed in Me. I have communicated my wishes to no person, because from your good Opinion, and Confidence alone do I wish for the Appointment. _ If my Desires do not meet your approbation I beg they may remain within your own Breast, for I do not wish to afford my political ~~Enemies~~ Enemies (for I never had any private ones) an opportunity to mortify and insult Me. _ In a public, or private Station You may depend on my attachment, and affection to Yourself, and that my Endeavours shall not be wanting to render your Administration as easy and happy as possible; and that I will support the present Government, agreeably to my late solemn Engagement. _

I pray my most respectful Compliments to M⁅ʳˢ⁆ Washington, and I am, Dear Sir,

with the Greatest respect & Esteem,   Your affectionate and   obedient Servant

Sam⁅!⁆ Chase

ALS (PHi, Gratz Collection).

Jonathan Trumbull to Ephraim Kirby —————————
September 5, 1789 New York, New York

New York   5ᵗʰ Sepʳ 1789

Sir _

I have received your favor of the 28ᵗʰ ulto _ Having a good opinion of your Abilities to perfor[m] the work you mention, I shall not be backward in giving any Aid which may fall within my power to forward your wishes in the appointment you look to _ but the Judicial Bill being not yet passed _ & whenever it does _ the Appointment of the Clerks being committed to the Judges _ who are not yet designated _ it is not in my power to point you to the person who may gratify your wishes _ When the Judicial Appointments are made known _ Should it fall in my way to give you any aid I shall not be wanting in any thing proper for me to do towards your success _ [1]

I am   Sir   Your most Obe⁅ᵗ⁆Serv⁅ᵗ⁆ _

Jon⁅ᵃ⁆ Trumbull

ARS (NcD, Ephraim Kirby Papers). Addressed "Litchfield   Connecticut." Postmarked "N-York   Sep 6."

Jonathan Trumbull (1740-1809), son of a Connecticut governor of the same name and brother of the painter John Trumbull, served as a congressman from Connecticut from 1789 to 1795. In 1794 Trumbull was elected to the Senate and served as a senator from 1795 until June 10, 1796, when he resigned to become deputy governor of Connecticut. Following the death of Governor Oliver Wolcott in December, 1797, Trumbull became governor of Connecticut and was reelected annually to that post until his death. *DAB* under Jonathan Trumbull (1740-1809) and John Trumbull (1756-1843); *BDAC*.

Ephraim Kirby (1757-1804), a lawyer in Litchfield, Connecticut, began his practice in 1779 and also read law in the office of Reynold Marvin at the close of the Revolutionary War. In 1789 Kirby published the first full volume of state law reports in America, *Reports of Cases Adjudged in the Superior Court of the State of Connecticut From the Year 1785 to May 1788 with some Determinations in the Supreme Court of Errors.* Kirby was elected in 1791 to the first of his fourteen terms in the state legislature. Alan V. Briceland, "Ephraim Kirby: Pioneer of American Law Reporting, 1789," *American Journal of Legal History* 16 (1972): 298, 311; *DAB.*

1. Ephraim Kirby's letter to Jonathan Trumbull of August 28 has not been found. It is uncertain whether Kirby wanted to be clerk of the United States Supreme Court or clerk of the federal district or circuit court for Connecticut.

Henry Knox to Thomas Rodney
September 7, 1789 New York, New York

New-York 7th September 1789

Dear Sir

I have the honor to acknowledge the receipt of your favor in which you mention the purport of a letter written by you to the President of the United States, respecting the honorable Judge McKean and Colonel John Parks[1]

I am persuaded the President has a full knowledge of these[2] ~~merits of these~~ Gentlemen, and that he will in all his appoinments evince the most[3] perfect ~~regard~~ impartiality & regard to merit—

I shall not flatter myself that my opinion would be of any importance in this case but if it should be otherwise I should be happy in the opportunity of giving it in concurrence of of yours recommendations—

I am Sir with great respect Your most obedient humble Servant

HK

Colonel Thomas Rodney
Poplar Grove Delaware—

ADfS (MHi, Henry Knox Papers). Addressed "Poplar Grove Delaware."
1. See Thomas Rodney to George Washington, August 25, 1789, and Thomas Rodney to Henry Knox, August [25-31], 1789.
2. Henry Knox altered the word "the" so that it read "these."
3. Henry Knox wrote a "p" and then changed it to an "m."

Matthew Ridley to John Jay
September 7, 1789 Susquehanna, Maryland

... I forgot when with you to mention MrSaml Chase— I wish if it should lay in your Power to save him that you would— He has a large Family— has met with many hard Rubs, and I believe at this Time feels heavily the weight of his Family from the difficulty of making such a provision for them as he might heretofore have reasonably expected— He has on many Occasions been a useful Man in our public Affairs— I have never had any Conversation with him but am led to believe he would willingly accept the appointment of one of the Supreme Judges— He gets rather too much advanced in Life for the drudgery of the Law— If a Judge should be taken out of this State I know no Man more proper— His Abilities[1] as a Lawyer, or Integrity in the profession I have never heard question'd— His uprightness as a Judge in this state (of the Criminal Court) has been much approved— Added to this I am informed that Mr Harrison, who would in all probability be the Person prefered to any other in this state, is satisfied with his present Office of Judge of our General Court— ...

ARS (MHi, Ridley Papers). Matthew Ridley probably was writing from Havre-de-Grace, Maryland, formerly called Susquehanna Lower Ferry. Maryland Writers' Program, Works Project Administration, *Maryland: A Guide to the Old Line State* (New York: Oxford University Press, 1940), p. 323. This letter is addressed "New-York." Postmarked "H, D. Grace. Septe[mber] 7th." Endorsed "ansd 12 Sep. 1789." John Jay's answer of September 12 has not been found.

Matthew Ridley (1749-1789) had become friends with John Jay in 1782 when Jay was in France negotiating the Treaty of Paris and Ridley was Maryland's agent to negotiate loans and purchase supplies in France, Spain, and Holland. In 1787 Ridley married Catherine Livingston, the sister of John Jay's wife. *PJJ*, 2:122, 12; Herbert E. Klingelhofer, ed., "Matthew Ridley's Diary During the Peace Negotiations of 1782," *William and Mary Quarterly*, 3d ser., 20 (1963): 98n.

1. The first letter of this word has been written over a lowercase "a."

Abraham Baldwin to Joel Barlow ——————————
September 13, 1789 New York, New York

... The judiciary is not yet finished, I have formerly given you the outlines of it. John Rutledge or Jay will probably be Chief Justice. ...

AR (CtY, Abraham Baldwin Papers).

At this time, Abraham Baldwin (1754-1807) was a Georgia congressman. Baldwin had been born in Connecticut and educated as a lawyer there before moving to Georgia by 1784. He served Georgia in the Confederation Congress and the Constitutional Convention. He sat in the House of Representatives from 1789 to 1799. In the latter year he was elected to the Senate and served until his death in 1807. *DAB*.

Joel Barlow (1754-1812), who was Abraham Baldwin's brother-in-law, had earlier tried his hand at a number of professions including law. He finally achieved success as a poet with the publication of *The Vision of Columbus* (Hartford: Hudson and Goodwin, 1787). This poem brought him to the attention of many prominent Americans. In 1788 Barlow left for France, where he was employed as an agent for the Scioto Company, a group of American land speculators. Barlow spent the next seventeen years abroad as a writer, diplomat, and shipping agent. From 1795 to 1797 Barlow was United States consul to Algiers. *DAB* entries for Joel Barlow and Abraham Baldwin.

Abraham Baldwin by Robert Fulton (1765-1815). Pencil on paper, date unknown. Courtesy National Portrait Gallery, Smithsonian Institution.

Paine Wingate to Timothy Pickering
September 14, 1789 New York, New York

... The Secretary of State is not yet nominated. The reason of that I conclude is that Mr Jay is designed for Chief Justice[1] when the birth is provided, if the emoluments should be better than the place he now holds— It is suspected that Mr Morris[2] has the ear of the President as much or more than any man.

How it is or where the influence lies I can not say, nor do I care if that influence is not abused. . . .

ARS (MHi, Timothy Pickering Papers).

1. Erkuries Beatty, in a letter to Josiah Harmar on September 13, 1789, also mentioned the popular supposition that John Jay would be offered the position of chief justice. Josiah Harmar Papers, MiU-C.

2. Robert Morris was earlier mentioned as a supporter of James Wilson for chief justice; see Arthur Lee to [Francis Lightfoot Lee], May 9, 1789.

Fisher Ames to Caleb Strong
September 15, 1789 New York, New York

. . . The Judicial is passing rapidly We are yet in the dark whether our friend, L.[1] will be promoted to the Bench. The pres[t] is profoundly secret in his movements_ . . .

ARS (CtHC, Thompson's Collection of Autograph Letters). Addressed "Northampton To be left at Post Office in Springfield." Postmarked "N-York Sep 15."

Caleb Strong (1745-1819), a Massachusetts lawyer, was a senator in the First Congress, was reelected in 1793, and served until 1796. Admitted to the bar in 1772, Strong served as county attorney for Northampton County from 1776 to 1800. He also sat in both houses of the Massachusetts General Court and in the Constitutional Convention of 1787. *DAB*.

1. John Lowell.

Samuel A. Otis to John Langdon
September [16-22], 1789 New York, New York

. . . The *Keeper of the Tower*[1] is waiting to see which Salary is best, that of Lord Chief Justice or Secretary of State.[2] . . .

Pr (Printed in Alfred Langdon Elwyn, ed., *Letters by Washington, Adams, Jefferson, and Others, Written During and After the Revolution to John Langdon, New Hampshire* (Philadelphia: Henry B. Ashmead, 1880), pp. 92-94). The dating can be deduced from a reference to "An Act for allowing Compensation to the Members of the Senate and House of Representatives of the United States, and to the Officers of both Houses." Samuel A. Otis mentions that the bill, passed by both houses of Congress, has been with the president and not signed for "several days." The bill was signed by the vice president in the Senate on September 14. Two days later the committee on enrolled bills reported the delivery of the bill to the president who signed it on September 22. *SLJ*, 1:80-81, 85; *Stat.*, 1:70.

Samuel Allyne Otis (1740-1814), a Massachusetts merchant. Otis was appointed the first secretary of the United States Senate in 1789 and served for twenty-five years until his death in 1814. He previously had held both appointive and elective office in Massachusetts and had served in the Confederation Congress. Shipton, *Sibley's Harvard Graduates*, 14:471-80.

1. John Jay.

2. A similar comment was made in a letter from Samuel A. Otis to Caleb Strong, September, 1789. Stephen Strong Collection, DLC.

John Adams to William Tudor ————————————————
September 18, 1789 New York, New York

... how the President will decide, on the judiciary Appointments I know not. _ There is no system nor Harmony among the Men from Massachusetts_ one recommends one, and another another. Dont you be chagrin'd, mortified humiliated nor vexed let it go as it will. ...

ARS (MHi, Tudor Papers). Addressed Boston. Postmarked "N-York   Sep 23."

Hugh Williamson to George Washington ————————————
September 19, 1789 New York, New York

New York   19th Septr 1789

Sir

I took the Liberty some Time ago to mention a Citizen of North Carolina as a Gentleman ~~as a Gentleman~~ who might discharge the Duties of a Judge with Honour to himself and Satisfaction to the Public.

Mr James Iredell, who is Brother in Law to Governour Johnston,[1] is the Gentleman to whom I referred. At the Beginning of the late Revolution he held an Office under the Crown, he resigned it immediately and in Order to cut off the Bridge he accepted of a Judge's Gown in the superior Court. That Office he quitted after some Time and was afterwards for some Years Attorney for the State. He is in the first Practice as a Lawyer, his Abilities and learning are extensive and he seems generally to be measured as the Standard of Integrity; his private Life is amiable and without Reproach; his Diligence is great and I believe there is not a man in the State who does not think him entitled to any Degree of public Trust.

If you should at any Time be disposed to make further Enquiries concerning Mr Iredell, he is well known to Major Butler[2] and, probably to some other Members of Congress. I have the Honour to be with the utmost Consideration
   Sir   Your most obed'servant

HuWilliamson

The President of the United States.

ARS (DLC, George Washington Papers).
   1. Samuel Johnston had been the governor of North Carolina.
   2. Pierce Butler (1744-1822), son of an Irish peer, lived in South Carolina following his marriage in 1771 to Mary Middleton of that state. Butler, a wealthy planter, served in the state legislature, 1778-1782 and 1784-1789. He formed an enduring friendship with James Iredell and his family during the Revolutionary War, when Butler was a refugee in Edenton, North Carolina. Butler represented South Carolina in the Constitutional Convention and in 1789 was elected to the Senate, where he served until October, 1796. *DAB; PJI,* 2:213-15.

Rufus King to Caleb Strong ————————————————————
September 20, 1789   New York, New York

... You are quite as able to guess [of?] the judiciary appointments as I am; the Mass. Gentlemen say that the probability stands thus _ Ch. J. Cushing, or Mr Lowell associate Judge _ ...

I hope that Mr Jay will be ch. Justice, and the probability in that case is that Mr Jefferson will be secretary of State _ ...

ARS (CtHC, Thompson's Collection of Autograph Letters).

John Adams to Stephen Higginson ————————————————
September 21, 1789   New York, New York

... Your favor of August 10th was duly received and immediately communicated with several other letters on the same subject to the President. His determination which will be made on the best principles and from the purest motives, as well as the most universal information, for he receives letters and makes enquiries from all quarters, we shall soon know. Altho' it is most probable to me that Mr Lowell will be the judge, yet if it should be otherwise, I apprehend your fears of an appoinment to the place of C Justice of the State are not founded _ ... It would have an happy effect if all the judges of the national supreme Court, could be taken from the chief Justices of the several states. The superiority of the national government would in this way be decidedly acknowledged. All the judges of the states would look up to the national bench as their ultimate object. _ As there is great danger of collisions between the national and state judiciaries, if the state judges are men possesed of larger portions of the people's confidence than the national judges, the latter will become unpopular. This however is a subject which cannot be very accurately asscertained. It is easy to determine who a C Justice is but not so easy to say who has most of the public confidence. The morals of the nation and perfection of the constitution: The national character, public credit, private confidence, public liberty, private property: every thing that is sacred, prescious or dear, depends so much upon these judges, that the President will choose I presume with caution. In Massachusetts happily there are several among whom he cannot make a wrong choice. The majority of the Senators and representatives from that state have recommended Lowell. ...

ALbS (MHi, Adams Manuscript Trust). Addressed "Boston."

Samuel Hodgdon to Timothy Pickering —————————————
September 21, 1789   Philadelphia, Pennsylvania

... Jay is expected to be Chief Justice ... Wilson a subordinate ...

Tr (Typescript in PSC-Hi, Konkle Manuscripts).

Samuel Hodgdon (1745-1824) began his military career as an artillery officer under General Henry Knox. In 1777 he started to work in the department of the Commissary of Military Stores. Hodgdon was appointed commissary-general of military stores in 1781 and served in that capacity during the Washington and Adams administrations. In April, 1794, Hodgdon also was appointed to the newly created position of superintendant of military stores. He was removed from both posts in 1801, following Thomas Jefferson's election as president. Daughters of the American Revolution, *Lineage Book*, vol. 25 (Washington, D.C., 1908), p. 341; Erna Risch, *Quartermaster Support of the Army: A History of the Corps, 1775-1939* (Washington, D.C.: Office of the Quartermaster General, Quartermaster Historian's Office, 1962), pp. 77, 83, 93, 100, 123-24.

Robert Morris to James Wilson —————————————————
September 21, 1789   New York, New York

... I confirm to you my Idea that you will be nominated to the Bench, but I still doubt not to the first Seat. ...

Tr (Typescript in PSC-Hi, Konkle Manuscripts).

Matthew Ridley to John Jay —————————————————
September 22, 1789   Susquehanna, Maryland

... What I wrote you about Mᵣ Chase, was from Information I did not doubt, or I would not have mentioned it—:[1] I have since seen him— He would be very glad to serve in the Line I mentioned to you. Or if arrangements will not permit of that; then in the Office of Attorney General— He reckons much on your Friendship & nothing but his embarrased situation I believe prevents him writing you— His Spirits are much broken; & all Things considered I am not surprized at it. Like an Old wounded weather-beaten soldier, he wishes for repose— Altho I have taken the Liberty of writing you on this Subject, I would wish you on this & every other occasion of recommendation, of which I am rather inclined to be sparing, to consider me as writing under an impression, and with a full expectation & desire, that you should act with the strictest propriety; and that I would by no means have you to commit a Reputation, which independant of any Connection; I do sincerely assure you, has ever been [*words inked out*] highly respected by me— ...

ARS (MHi, Ridley Papers). Endorsed "anᵈ 8 Octᵣ 1789."

1. See Matthew Ridley to John Jay, September 7, 1789, in which Ridley recommends Samuel Chase's appointment to the Supreme Court.

Theodore Sedgwick to John Jay
September 23, 1789 Springfield, Massachusetts

... Convinced that you will do honor to the supreme national court by presiding in it, you will pardon the freedom of suggesting to you the interest of a friend of mine— Mr John Tucker of Boston one of the Clerks of the supreme court of this state, posseses equal to any man I have ever known, all the requisite abilities & qualifications of such an officer. It would afford me the most sincere pleasure that he may find employment for those talents in the national government. Sensible how very disagreable applications of this kind must be to men who have the power to confer offices, I should not have addressed you on the subject, had I not the most perfect reliance on your candor, and the vanity to beleive that you will not suppose me influenced by any improper motives— Mr King knows I beleive Mr Tucker[1] and all who know him have the same opinion of his honor— of his capacity for bussiness and of his fidelity in the execution of it. ...

ARS (MHi, Sedgwick III Collection). Addressed "New York." Endorsed "and 8 Octr 1789." John Jay's letter of October 8 has not been found.

Theodore Sedgwick (1746-1813) read law with Mark Hopkins and in 1766 was admitted to the Berkshire County bar in Massachusetts. A prominent attorney, Sedgwick was a Massachusetts congressman from 1789 through 1796, when he was elected to the Senate to complete the term of Caleb Strong. When Sedgwick's Senate term expired in 1799, he returned to the House of Representatives. He retired from Congress in 1801 and in 1802 was appointed to the Supreme Judicial Court of Massachusetts, where he served until his death. *DAB*.

1. Rufus King probably was acquainted with John Tucker from his school days. Although King was born in Maine, he was sent at age twelve to Dummer Academy in Byfield, Massachusetts, where Tucker was a student. In addition, both Tucker and King graduated from Harvard: Tucker in 1774, King in 1777. King then returned to the area around Byfield, studying law in nearby Newburyport. John Tucker's family lived in the neighboring town of Newbury. *DAB* entry for Rufus King; for information on John Tucker, see introduction to "The Clerks and Their Record."

George Washington to James Madison
[before September 24, 1789] [New York, New York]

My solicitude for drawing the first characters of the Union in to the Judiciary, is such that, my cogitations on this subject last night (after I parted with you) have almost determined me /as well for the reason Just mentioned, as to silence the clamours, or more properly, soften the disappointmen[t] of smaller characters— to nominate Mr Blair and Colo Pendleton as Associate & District Judges.— And Mr E. Randolph for the Attorney General trusting to their acceptance.*

*Mr Randolph, in this character, I would prefer to any person[1] I am acquainted of not superior abilities, from habits of intimacy with him

Mr Pendleton could not I fear discharge, and in that case I am sure would not undertake, to execute the duties of an Associate under the present form of the Act. But he may be able to fulfil those of the District— The Salary I believe is greater than what he now has;[2] and he would see or it might be explained to him, the reason of his being prefered to the District Court rather than to the Supreme Bench; though I have no objection to nominating him to the latter, if it is conceived that his health is competent, and his mental faculties unimpaired, by age.

His acceptance of the first would depend in a great measure, I presume, upon the light in which the District Judges are considered— that is, whether superior in Rank to any State Judges.

I am very troublesome, but you must excuse me.— Ascribe it to friendship and confidence, and you will do Justice to my motives.— Remember the Attorney and Marshall for Kentucky, and forget no[t] to give their Christian names.—

Yours ever

GW

ARS (DLC, James Madison Papers). Place determined by evidence in letter. This document may have been trimmed and has been reinforced along the margin; therefore, a conjectural reading has been supplied in brackets.

1. In the original manuscript, the word "person" appears at the end of a line next to the right margin. Washington may have intended to indicate the end of a thought at this point.

2. Since March 7, 1789, Edmund Pendleton had been serving as judge of the newly reconstituted Virginia Court of Appeals. No salary provisions were contained in the reconstituting act, but an act of November 19, 1789, provided that the judges of the Court of Appeals should receive the same amount as those of the General Court. Under the salary act of November 6, 1781, the General Court judges were to receive £300 annually. By 1789, at 6 shillings par value in Virginia currency of the dollar, this £300 would have been worth approximately $1,000. (We are indebted to John J. McCusker for this calculation.) The United States judge for the district of Virginia was to receive $1,800 per annum. Mays, *Edmund Pendleton*, 2:275; William Waller Hening, *The Statutes at Large; Being a Collection of all the Laws of Virginia, From the First Session of the Legislature, in the year 1619*, 13 vols. (Philadelphia and Richmond, 1809-1823), 10:498, 12:766, 13:24; *Stat.*, 1:72.

Paine Wingate to John Langdon

September 24, 1789 New York, New York

... I have but a minute to write, but thinking I may gratify your curiosity I shall improve ^the moment it to inform you that this day ^the President nominated several of the Judicial officers which tomorrow the Senate are to act upon. Mr Jay to be Chief Justice— Jno Rutledge of S.^o Carolina— Willm Cushing Mass.^a— James Wilson Pennsylvania— Robert Harrison Maryland & Jno Blair Vir.^a— to be associate Judges—[1] ... I suppose there is not a doubt but the nominations will be approved of.— I will defer saying any thing about the candidates who were mentiond to the President until I shall see you which I hope to have the pleasure of shortly. ...

ARS (PHi, Dreer Collection).

1. Other individuals also reported the nomination of one or more justices: Thomas Fitzsimmons to Benjamin Rush, September 25, 1789 (Elsie and Philip Sang Collection of Signers of the Constitution of the United States, NjR) [Benjamin Rush has been identified as the recipient of this letter by Kenneth R. Bowling, "The Biddle Sale of Rush Papers and Other Letters from Pennsylvania Members of The First Federal Congress to Their Constituents," *Manuscripts* 24 (Summer, 1972): 180.]; Robert Morris to Richard Peters, September 25, 1789 (Richard Peters Papers, PHi), in which Morris calls the associate justices "Puisne Judges"; Tristram Dalton to Caleb Strong, September 26, 1789 (Stephen Strong Collection, MNF); Seth Johnson to Andrew Craigie, September 26, 1789 (Andrew Craigie Papers, MWA), in which Johnson calls the associate justices "Circuit Judges"; Samuel Meredith to Peggy Meredith, September 26, 1789 (Samuel Meredith Papers, PPL), where Meredith comments that those "nominated by the President ^are^ of the first Characters in the United States, and will do great honor to his Choice＿."

Newspapers that reported the nominations include the *Massachusetts Centinel* (Boston), September 30, 1789, and the *Pennsylvania Mercury* (Philadelphia), October 3, 1789.

Robert Morris to Mary Morris ————————————————
September 25, 1789   New York, New York

. . . Mʳ Jay is Nominated by the President as Chief Justice, Mʳ Wilson as one of the Puisne Judges, MʳHopkinson District Judge Mʳ WᵐLewis[1] Attorney for the District & Clement Biddle[2] Marshall＿ send for MʳWilson & Mʳ Hopkinson the Moment you Receive this & tell them, altho it is probable they may hear of ~~it befo~~ their Nominations before you see them. I am too much engaged in pursuit of permanent Residence[3] to write to either of them. . . .

AR[S?] (CSmH, Robert Morris File). This document has been damaged where the signature should appear. Addressed "Philadel[phia]." Sent "by Mʳ Richard [*name obliterated*]."

Mary (White) Morris (1749–1827), wife of Robert Morris. Charles Henry Hart, "Mary White — Mrs. Robert Morris," *Pennsylvania Magazine of History and Biography* 2 (1878): 157–84.

1. William Lewis (1751-1819) read law with Nicholas Waln of West Chester and Philadelphia and was admitted to the bar in 1773. Lewis became a leader of the bar, gaining fame as defense counsel in treason cases stemming from the revolution and later disturbances in Pennsylvania. Lewis's political career began in 1787 in the Pennsylvania legislature. He served one more term in 1789 and also was elected to the state constitutional convention. He was appointed United States attorney for the district of Pennsylvania on October 6, 1789. On July 20, 1791, Lewis became United States judge for the district of Pennsylvania, a post he resigned in April, 1792, in order to return to private practice. In 1799 he was defense counsel in the famous trial of John Fries. *DAB*.

2. Clement Biddle (1740-1814) was a Philadelphia merchant who had been active in public affairs since 1765. During the Revolutionary War, Biddle fought in the New Jersey and Philadelphia campaigns of 1776 and 1777. He also served as commissary-general for continental troops and as a quartermaster-general for the Pennsylvania militia. Biddle in 1788 was appointed a justice of the Philadelphia Court of Common Pleas. *DAB*.

3. During September, 1789, the Senate was discussing a bill to establish a permanent residence for the nation's capital. Senator Robert Morris was very interested in these proceedings and at first proposed establishing a capital on the Falls of the Delaware River at Trenton, very close to some property he owned in Bucks County, Pennsylvania, named Morrisville. He later withdrew his support from this plan and advocated locating a capital at Germantown near Philadelphia. No bill passed in this session of Congress. When it became clear that a permanent residence would

not be established near Philadelphia, Morris fought for making Philadelphia a temporary capital. The bill establishing the capital on the Potomac River and making Philadelphia a temporary capital was signed on July 16, 1790. Eleanor Young, *Robert Morris: Forgotten Patriot* (New York: Macmillan, 1950), pp. 182-84; Ellis Paxon Oberholtzer, *Robert Morris: Patriot and Financier* (New York: Macmillan, 1903), pp. 291-97; *FFC,* 1:181, 191, 418.

Ralph Izard to Edward Rutledge
September 26, 1789 New York, New York

... I am just returned from the Senate where the following Officers have been approved of— Mr. Jay Chief Justice: Judges of the Supreme Court J. Rutledge, Cushing, Wilson, Harrison, and Blair. Edmund Randolph Attorney General, Major Pinckney[1] is appointed District Judge for South Carolina.[2] The Judges both of the Supreme Court and the District Courts are chosen from among the most eminent and distinguished characters in America, and I do not believe that any Judiciary in the world is better filled. The President asked me before the nominations were made, whether I thought your Brother John, Genl. Pinckney,[3] or yourself would accept of a Judge in the Supreme Court. I told him that I was not authorized to say you would not, but intimated that the office of Chief Justice would be most suitable to either of you: That however was engaged. ... I hope it may suit your Brother to accept, if it should be only for two or three years; as it is of the first importance that the Judiciary should be highly respectable. The Office of District Judge I hope will be agreeable to Major Pinckney. If either of them should refuse to accept, let me know of it by the first opportunity, and tell me whom you wish to be appointed that will accept. The President will not nominate any but the most eminent: and if none in South Carolina of that description will accept, he will be obliged to have recourse to some other state. ...

Pr (Printed in *American Historical Review* 14 (July 1909): 777).

Ralph Izard (1742-1804) spent most of the Revolutionary War years in France in diplomatic service. He returned to South Carolina where in 1782 he was elected to the Confederation Congress. Izard served in the Senate from 1789 to 1795. *DAB.*

Edward Rutledge (1749-1800), a Charleston attorney, was the brother of John Rutledge. Edward Rutledge had studied in the Middle Temple before being called to the English Bar in 1772. He represented South Carolina in the Continental Congress, signed the Declaration of Independence, and in 1789 was representing Charleston in the South Carolina House of Representatives. *DAB.*

1. Thomas Pinckney (1750-1828), like his brother Charles Cotesworth Pinckney, matriculated at Oxford, studied law at the Middle Temple, and was called to the English bar in 1774. Late in that year, Thomas Pinckney returned to South Carolina and was admitted to its bar. He began his war service in 1775 and was wounded at the Battle of Camden in 1780 and taken prisoner. After the war, he resumed his legal practice in Charleston and served as president of the state convention which ratified the Constitution. Pinckney was governor of South Carolina in 1787 and 1788. In 1789 he declined appointment as United States judge for the district of South Carolina.

Pinckney later served as minister to England. As special commissioner and envoy extraordinary, he negotiated the treaty known as the Pinckney Treaty with Spain in 1795. The next year, Pinckney was an unsuccessful candidate for vice president. In 1797 he became a congressman from South Carolina and remained in the House of Representatives until 1801. *DAB; SEJ,* 1:31-32.

2. Other individuals also wrote from New York to report the appointment of one or more of the justices: John Brown to Harry Innes, September 28, 1789 (Harry Innes Papers, DLC); Alexander Hamilton to John B. Church, September 28, 1789 (*PAH,* 26:483-84); Daniel Hiester to James Hamilton, September 28, 1789 (PCarlH); Paine Wingate to Timothy Pickering, September 28, 1789 (Timothy Pickering Papers, MHi); Abraham Baldwin to Joel Barlow, September 29, 1789 (Abraham Baldwin Papers, CtY).

Individuals writing from places other than New York helped to spread word of appointments to the Supreme Court. Roger Sherman to Simeon Baldwin, September 28, 1789 (Roger Sherman Papers, CtY); Oliver Wolcott, Jr., to Jedediah Huntington, September 30, 1789 (Gratz Collection, PHi); George Mason to Zachariah Johnston, October 29, 1789 (*PGM,* 3:1179-80); John Rutledge, Jr., to William Short, November 4, 1789 (William Short Papers, DLC); Thomas Jefferson to William Short, December 14, 1789 (Thomas Jefferson Papers, ViW).

3. Charles Cotesworth Pinckney (1746-1825), brother of Thomas Pinckney and brother-in-law of Edward Rutledge, first studied law in the Middle Temple after matriculating from Oxford. Charles C. Pinckney was admitted to the English bar in January, 1769. After a few months of study in France, he returned home to South Carolina, where he gained admission to the bar in 1770. Pinckney's long career in public service in South Carolina began in 1769 when he sat in the provincial Commons House of Assembly. In 1773 he became acting attorney general for Camden, Georgetown, and the Cheraws. He served with distinction in the Revolutionary War and then resumed his career in law and public service. Pinckney represented South Carolina in the Constitutional Convention and supported ratification in his home state as well. He turned down President Washington's offer of an associate judgeship on the Supreme Court in 1791 and later declined Washington's offers of cabinet posts, first as secretary of war and then as secretary of state. Pinckney did, however, accept an appointment as minister to France in 1796 and the next year joined John Marshall and Elbridge Gerry in a special mission to that country. Pinckney was an unsuccessful candidate in the presidential election in 1800. *DAB.*

Erkuries Beatty to Josiah Harmar ————————————————
September 27, 1789   New York, New York

. . . The Officers in the judiciary department I hear is all appointed but have not been published_ M[r] Jay is Chief justice . . . M[r] Willson of Philad[a] is one of the five associate judges_ . . .

ARS (MiU-C, Josiah Harmar Papers). Addressed to the "Ohio River."

Erkuries Beatty (1759-1823) served in the Revolutionary War from 1775 to 1783 and then rejoined the army in 1784. From 1786 to 1788 he served as acting paymaster of the western army, and then for the next two years he commanded the outpost of Fort St. Vincent (present-day Vincennes, Indiana). Beatty resigned from the army in 1793. James Grant Wilson and John Fiske, eds., *Appletons' Cyclopædia of American Biography,* 7 vols. (New York: D. Appleton, 1894); *FFC,* 2:532.

Josiah Harmar (1753-1813), a Revolutionary War veteran, became commander of the army in 1784 and was stationed on the Ohio frontier. Harmar resigned from the army in 1792. From 1793 to 1799 he was adjutant-general of Pennsylvania. *DAB.*

Henry Chapman to Stephen Collins ———————————
September 27, 1789   New York, New York

... the Judiciary appointments are also made, Jay Supreme Judge, <u>Wilson</u> & Duane[1] two of the five Secondary Judges _ ...

ARS (DLC, Papers of Stephen Collins and Son).

Probably Henry Henley Chapman (1764-1821), a Maryland lawyer who had represented Charles County in the Maryland legislature in 1787 and 1788. Chapman was commissioned a justice of Charles County in 1789. He may have been in New York City in 1789 and was living next door to Stephen Collins in Philadelphia in 1790. He later returned to Charles County where he had a distinguished career in the state legislature, serving four terms as speaker of the House of Delegates. Reiman Steuart, *A History of the Maryland Line in the Revolutionary War, 1775-1783* (Towson, Maryland: Metropolitan Press, 1969), p. 66; Edward C. Papenfuse, et al., *A Biographical Dictionary of the Maryland Legislature, 1635-1789,* vol. 1 (Baltimore: Johns Hopkins University Press, 1979); Hodge, Allen, and Campbell, *The New-York Directory,* (1789), see additional listings, p. 100; U.S. Department of Commerce and Labor, Bureau of the Census, *Heads of Families at the First Census of the United States Taken in the Year 1790: Pennsylvania* (1908; reprint ed., Bountiful, Utah: Accelerated Indexing Systems, 1978), p. 220.

Stephen Collins (1733-1794) was a Philadelphia merchant. Daughters of the American Revolution, *DAR Patriot Index* (Washington, D.C., 1966); *1790 Census: Pennsylvania,* p. 220.

1. James Duane (1733-1797), a New York City lawyer, served as mayor of New York from February, 1784, until September, 1789. President Washington appointed him United States judge for the district of New York in 1789, and Duane served on the bench until his retirement in March, 1794. *DAB.*

Robert Morris to James Wilson ———————————
September 27, 1789   New York, New York

[*Morris notifies Wilson of Wilson's appointment as an associate justice of the Supreme Court. Morris mentions the other appointees and encourages Wilson to accept.*] ... the station is Honorable, and the Salary ... not contemptible altho neither comes up to my wishes for you. ...

Pr (Printed in *Carnegie Book Shop Catalog* 134 (1948), item 598).

Massachusetts Centinel ———————————
September 27, 1789   New York, New York

... I am happy in forwarding to you the following authentick list of
APPOINTMENTS,
which were not acceded to by the Hon. Senate until yesterday, although made on *Thursday* last.

* Hon. JOHN JAY, Chief-Justice.
Hon. † JOHN RUTLEDGE, of *S. Carolina,* ⎫
  ‡ JAMES WILSON, *Pennsylvania,*   ⎪
  § WILLIAM CUSHING, *Massa.*   ⎬ *Associate Jud*
  ‖ ROBERT H. HARRISON, *Maryl.*   ⎪
  ¶ JOHN BLAIR, *Virginia,*   ⎭

. . .

NOTES.

* Late Secretary of Foreign Affairs, and formerly President of Congress.
† Late Governour of South-Carolina, and Judge of Chancery.
‡ Of the Federal Convention, and a great Lawyer.
§ Chief Justice of Massachusetts, and late Vice-President of Massachusetts Convention.
‖ Late Governour of Maryland.[1]
¶ Judge of the Supreme Court of Virginia.
. . . I have added these notes for the information of strangers_ as it will add to their respect for our government, when they see that the men chosen to execute it, are eminent for their abilities and patriotism, and such as have been highly distinguished by their fellow-citizens. Indeed the whole chain of appointments are of men of equal eminence.

(Boston) October 3, 1789. This article is in the form of a letter; date and place are those of the letter.
    Reprinted in the *United States Chronicle* (Providence), October 8, 1789.
    Other newspapers also noted the appointments. One type of listing appeared in the *Daily Advertiser* (New York), September 28, 1789; the *Independent Gazetteer* (Philadelphia), October 1, 1789; the *Providence Gazette,* October 3, 1789; and the *Georgia Gazette* (Savannah), October 15, 1789. Another type appeared in the *Pennsylvania Packet* (Philadelphia), September 28, 1789, and the *State Gazette of North-Carolina* (Edenton), October 15, 1789. Some newspapers published notices of the appointments of one or two justices.
    1. Harrison never served as governor of Maryland.

George Washington to Edmund Pendleton ─────────
September 28, 1789 New York, New York

. . . Concurring in sentiment with some others of your friends that the functions of the Supreme Bench, which involve the fatigue of Circuit Courts, would be too much for the infirm State of your health, I beleived it necessary, to avail our Country of your abilities and the influence of your example, by nominating you to the office of Judge of the District-Court of Virginia, which will not require much greater personal exertion than the duties of your present Station_[1] . . .

Lb (DLC, George Washington Papers); DfS (DNA, RG 59, Miscellaneous Letters) with sections in hand of George Washington. Addressed "Virginia."
    1. Edmund Pendleton did not accept the appointment as federal district court judge for Virginia. J[ohn] Dawson to Tench Coxe, October 26, 1789. Tench Coxe Papers, PHi.

John Jay to Matthew Ridley
October 8, 1789   New York, New York

... Your favor of the 22 of last month did not come to my Hands untill the Day before Yesterday; and consequently the part of it w^h relates to Mr Chase, was not in Season for the Purpose intended by it. Whether if it had arrived sooner, it would have produced the desired Effect, I know not_ The Presidents personal Knowledge of destinguished Characters throughout the States, rendering it unnecessary for him to require or depend upon the Information[1] or Recommendation of others. ...

ARS (PHi, Dreer Collection); ADf (NNC, John Jay Papers). Addressed "To the Care of the Post master at Havre de Grace_   Maryland." Postmarked "New-York   Oct l[*number missing*]." Endorsed "Recd. the 15 Oct. 1789."

1. In the draft, John Jay wrote and then crossed out "of others_ in the present Case he certainly is perfectly well informed, and I have no Reason to believe that he commits himself."

John Adams to William Cushing
October 17, 1789   Middleton, Massachusetts

... Give me leave to congratulate you on your appointment to the national Bench, and to hope that you will soon give me an opportunity to see you and Mrs Cushing at New York. ...

ARS (MHi, Robert Treat Paine Papers). Addressed to Cushing "at M^r· Parsons's   Middleton."

John Hamilton to ?
October 17, 1789   Edenton, North Carolina

... Mr Iredell of this Place I understand has made application thro Doct^r Hugh Williamson for the Office of Judge[1] ...

C (DLC, George Washington Papers).

John Hamilton represented Edenton in the North Carolina legislature from 1789 to 1792. A native of Pennsylvania, Hamilton had read law at Edinburgh and Lincoln's Inn and may have been admitted to the Pennsylvania bar in 1784, but he later settled in North Carolina. In his newly adopted state, he was an outspoken supporter of ratification of the Constitution. In this letter, as well as in other letters, Hamilton sought an appointment under the new federal government, but he failed to achieve his goal. By June, 1790, he was "under indictment for extortionate fees" (*PTJ*, 16:477) further diminishing his chance for appointment. John L. Cheney, ed., *North Carolina Government, 1585-1979: A Narrative and Statistical History* (Raleigh: North Carolina Department of the Secretary of State, 1981), pp. 223, 225, 227-28; William Cumming to Doctor [Samuel?] Johnston, October 7, 1789, and February 10, 1790, George Washington Papers, DLC; *MBBP*, p. 275; Louise Irby Trenholme, *The Ratification of the Federal Constitution in North Carolina* (New York: Columbia University Press, 1932), pp. 215-16; Henry McGilbert Wagstaff, ed., *The Papers of John Steele*, 2 vols. (Raleigh: Edwards & Broughton Printing, 1924), 1:56-58.

1. See Hugh Williamson to James Iredell, August 12, 1789, and Hugh Williamson to George Washington, September 19, 1789.

David Humphreys to George Washington ——————
October 28, 1789 Petersburg, Virginia

[*Humphreys was passing through Petersburg, Virginia, on his way to New York and took this opportunity to convey to the president* "political intelligence" *from North Carolina.*] I have taken considerable pains to learn how the persons appointed to offices in the several States are considered by their fellow Citizens; I am happy to assure you that the appointments in general have met with almost universal approbation. The selection of Characters to fill the great Departments has afforded entire satisfaction: particularly in the Judiciary. I heard it repeatedly said in Halifax, that the Supreme Court would be the first Court in the world in point of respectability. These things cannot but augur well. . . .

ARS (DLC, George Washington Papers).
   David Humphreys (1752-1818), a Connecticut merchant, was a close friend of President Washington, having served him as an aide-de-camp during the Revolutionary War. Humphreys was appointed commissioner to the southern Indians on August 21, 1789, and later served as minister to Portugal (1790-1797) and minister to Spain (1797-1802). *FFC*, 2:485, 30.

Edward Rutledge to John Jay ——————————————
October 31, 1789 [Charleston, South Carolina]

For all the good Qualities which you possess my dear Friend, there was none which fixed you more firmly in my Esteem, than the inflexible Integrity which you discovered on all occasions. Judge then from hence, what Pleasure I felt at your appointment, to the Office of Cheif Justice of the United States— May you long live to discharge the Duties of it, much to your own Honor, and much to the Happiness, and approbation of your fellow Citizens. . . .

ARS (NNC, John Jay Papers). Place determined by reference to letter from Edward Rutledge to George Washington, October 31, 1789 (q.v.). Endorsed "and_ 16 Nov. 1789." Answering letter not found.

Edward Rutledge to George Washington ——————————
October 31, 1789 Charleston, South Carolina

. . . The Appointments you have made to the different Offices with the exercise of which we are acquainted, have given such perfect Satisfaction in this part of the Union, as to increase if possible, the public Confidence, asure a ready obedience to the Laws, & a faithful Administration of Justice. Of the two which were made from this Place to the Judiciary, my Brother[1] alone has accepted _ He has yielded to Considerations of a general Nature, & has added one more to a long list of private Sacrafices, for public good.[2] [*Rutledge discusses the reasons why Thomas Pinckney turned down the appointment as federal district court judge for South Carolina. Both Pinckney and Rutledge recommend William Drayton[3] for the position.*] If he is exceeded by any Man in this State, in legal Knowledge, it is only by General Pinckney, who cannot accept, & by my Brother who has already accepted an appointment. . . .

ARS (PHi, Gratz Collection); ADfS (ScHi, Miscellaneous Collection).

1. John Rutledge.

2. The draft of this letter reveals a slight change in focus as this sentence evolved: "He has
                              general   private
yeilded to Considerations of a ~~Public~~ Nature, & added one more to a long list of ^ Sacrafices for public good." Edward Rutledge to George Washington, October 31, 1789, Miscellaneous Manuscript Collection, ScHi.

3. William Drayton (1732-1790), a native of South Carolina, studied law at the Middle Temple, was called to the English bar in 1755, and began practicing in South Carolina in 1756. Drayton moved to East Florida after 1763 where he became chief justice of the province (1767), but personal and political differences ultimately led to his dismissal. He returned to South Carolina by 1780, where he became judge of the Admiralty Court and associate justice of the state Supreme Court. On November 18, 1789, President Washington forwarded to Drayton a commission as United States judge for the district of South Carolina (George Washington Papers, DLC). Drayton was confirmed by the Senate in February, 1790, and died three months later. *DAB; SEJ,* 1:38-40.

Catharine Ridley to John Jay
November 4, 1789   Bay Side, Maryland

. . . I should have wrote to Sister or you before had my health permited, a tedious fit of illness and a relapse since has deprived me of that pleasure _ & of Congratulating you on your late appointment, which from the General satisfaction it gives is very flattering to all your friends; to me it appears the most eligible in the united States. You will I hope excuse the application it leads me to make, Its with reluctance I assure you, knowing y⁻ delicacy on that subject that I do it, but my desire if I live to have it in my power to be nearer my friends encourages me to it, (circumstanced as they are I cannot even hope for a visit from them) & if this does not meet your approbation it need go no farther, being entirely between ourselves, M⁻ Ridley[1] left me before I knew there would be a Clerks place to be disposed of for the Supreme Court, & that your influence in that appointment would be considerable, the gentlemen who mentioned the subject to me considered it an object worth soliciting for, as delay in that case would not be prudent, otherwise I would have choose to have had M⁻ R sentiments; I know his attachment to my connections & his desire of bringing up our children among them, & that he would gratify me in residing among them at the expence of great labor to himself, & as little profit as we could live with so much is it my wish that I would prefer a few hundreds in that situation to as many thousands at this distance _ Should Mr Ridley be so fortunate as to get business in the Law (& not follow it without overtaking it as may be the case) the practise of it in this State obliges those of the profession to be almost entirely from their families; If it was not for my children I would rather live on <u>pone bread & homoniny</u> my life time then submit to such a sacrifise _ . . .

ARS (NNC, John Jay Papers). Catharine Ridley probably was writing from Havre de Grace, Maryland; see Matthew Ridley to John Jay, September 7, 1789.

Catharine Livingston (1751-1813), the sister of John Jay's wife, married Matthew Ridley of Baltimore in 1787. Edwin Brockholst Livingston, *The Livingstons of Livingston Manor* (New York: Knickerbocker Press, 1910), pp. 533-34.

1. Matthew Ridley, husband of Catharine Ridley.

George Walton to John Adams
November 7, 1789   Augusta, Georgia

Augusta, 7 November, 1789.

Sir,

You have my thanks for the letter which you did me the favor to write to me on the 25th of september last; and while I express some small disappointment on the subject of it, I beg leave to give you the assurance of a chearful acquiescence.[1] I know that disappointment has often been the cause of opposition and faction: but I trust that I have made a better estimate of men, and of the blessings of society and good Government, than to suffer myself to be governed by its influence. As a proof of this I take the liberty of repeating my application, in the same line, and to the same persons, for employment under the general Government._ Report says, at this place, that Mr Rutledge has declined accepting the appointment as one of the associate Judges; and the policy of diffusing the appointments will, no doubt, continue to operate. In this view I stand upon the same ground as Mr Rutledge did; and with respect to pretensions, if they do not evidence themselves, they ought not to be attended to. In any event your approbation will console me.

The sentiments you express upon the general principles of Government, and of the present condition of America, are perfectly satisfactory to my mind; and, as to Office, I have felt, perhaps, too confident on that foundation:[2] but I can truely assure you, that, since the 1st day of July 1776, my conduct, in every station in life, has corresponded with the result of that great question which you so ably and faithfully developed on that day _ a scene which has ever been present to my mind. It was then that I felt the strongest attachments; and they have never departed from me.

Should any principle, dangerous to the present views of future welfare, be generated in this quarter, or any thing otherwise eventful present itself, I will take an early occasion of communicating with you; and should you feel it justifiable to withdraw your attention from the engagements of your situation, and somtimes write to me, I shall be particularly obliged: for in truth, Sir,

I am, with the greatest respect and   esteem,   Your Most Obedient Servant,

GeoWalton

. . . I have just heard that Mʳ Drayton, of South-Carolina, is recommended. I am not acquainted with him: but the fact is, that, altho a native, he was a british subject, and a british judge, during the whole Revolution. What idea will be formed of Justice, if such men are preferred? _

His Excellency,
John Adams.

ARS (MHi, Adams Manuscript Trust).

George Walton (1741-1804) was born in Virginia. In 1769 Walton moved to Savannah, Georgia, where he studied law and was admitted to the bar in 1774. Walton represented Georgia in the Continental Congress. In 1783 the Georgia legislature elected him to be chief justice of the state. Six years later, Walton became Georgia's governor. After his service as governor, he was elected a judge of the Superior Court of Georgia in 1790. He was appointed in 1795 to fill out the unexpired Senate term of James Jackson. Walton served in the Senate until February 20, 1796. He again became a judge of the Superior Court of Georgia in 1799 and served until his death. *DAB; BDAC.*

1. On September 25, 1789, John Adams wrote to George Walton in response to a letter from Walton of August 30. In his August 30 letter, Walton had requested Adams to consider him as a candidate for the post of federal district court judge for Georgia. On September 25, Adams informed Walton that Walton's application had arrived after another person had been chosen for the position. Adams Manuscript Trust, MHi.

2. In John Adams's letter to George Walton of September 25, he briefly discussed principles of government conducing to "Union peace and liberty to North America . . . " He also discussed his attitude toward appointments: "I feel upon all occasions I own, a particular pleasure in the appointment to office of Gentlemen who are now well affected to the national Constitution who had some experience in life before the revolution and took an active part in the course and conduct of it." Adams Manuscript Trust, MHi.

Fisher Ames to John Jay
November 10, 1789 Boston, Massachusetts

Boston   November 10, 1789

Sir,

I presume the office of clerk of the Supreme Court of the United States will be sollicited by many candidates of merit and capacity for the trust. For, I think, pretenders of a different description will not delude themselves with any hopes of success. With this impression on my mind, I should not venture to recommend even common merit to your favour and patronage. John Tucker Esq, Clerk of the Supreme Court of Massachusetts, possesses so much worth, and is so eminently qualified for the office, that I feel myself authorised to recommend him to your notice. Being a gentleman in his manners as well as principles, and bred to the law, it was natural to expect from him fidelity assiduity and accuracy in the performance of his duty. And, accordingly, he has given uncommon satisfaction to the court, to the bar, and to the suitors. Mr Cushing, your honorable associate, is well acquainted with Mr Tucker's character and pretensions, and will furnish any further necessary information.

Please to accept my apology for the trouble of this application, and permit me to assure you that I am, with sentiments of the highest respect and esteem, Sir, your

most obedient and very humble   servant

Fisher Ames

Hon. Chief Justice Jay —

ARS (NNC, John Jay Papers). Addressed "New York." Postmarked "BOSTON NOV. 13." Endorsed "rec^d & an^d . . . 27 Nov 1789." Answering letter not found.

John Jay to Catharine Ridley ————————————————
November 11, 1789 New York, New York

Yesterday
. . . I rec^d ~~two Days ago~~ with great Pleasure your fav^r of the 4 Inst —[1] ~~Your~~
are
~~Illness had~~ We are all happy to find you so far recovered from an Illness which gave us great anxiety. The Interest you have uniformly taken in what concerned my welfare, renders your kind Congratulations very acceptable — I know them to be sincere —

Your wishes are natural, and correspond perfectly with mine — It would afford us great Satisfaction to have you nearer to us; & and I should gratify
as well as
my own Inclinations ~~as w~~ ~~not less than~~ yours by promoting it. It appears to me however that you overrate the object you mention — on such and indeed on all occasions it is best to be candid, and in my opinion it is ~~al~~ as improper to flatter delusive Expectations as to excite causeless apprehensions. In my Judgment the Place in Question will not be worth 200 a Year — that alone ~~therefore~~ will not afford a Living — how is the Deficiency to be supplied; or
w^h in Case it sh^d be attainable
w^d for it
how are the local advantages ∧ you ∧ ~~will~~ relinquish ∧ to be compensated by
or other
professional ∧ Pursuits here? These are matters of calculation, and should be well weighed and considered — talk the matter over with Mr Ridley — he ~~will~~ can estimate accurately these & a variety of other circumstances which are intimately connected with such a Plan — write to be[2] again without Reserve —

. . .

ADf (NNC, John Jay Papers).
1. Catharine Ridley had written to John Jay asking for his support in securing for her husband the position of clerk of the Supreme Court.
2. In this draft, John Jay wrote "be" instead of "me."

William Cushing to John Hancock ————————————————
November 17, 1789 Boston, Massachusetts

Boston   November 17ᵗʰ 1789.

Sir,

   Having received an appointment to a seat on the fœderal bench & thinking it my duty to accept;— it becomes necessary to resign the office which I have had the honor to hold in the Judicial department of this Commonwealth; which I do, not without regret at parting, in some degree, with many friends, with whom I have had the Satisfaction to live in a happy harmony.— My consolation is this— that I am still embarked in the Same good design of promoting Justice & of Supporting government, tending to Secure the union, the protection, the rights & liberties— & prosperity of all the good citizens of the United States. I have the honor to be, with the highest respect,

   Sir,   your Excellency's   most Obedient   humble Servant

WᵐCushing

His Excellency
   Govʳ Hancock—

ARS (MeHi, J. S. H. Fogg Collection). Endorsed "Rec'd Novʳ 20ᵗʰ 1789."

William Cushing to John Jay ————————————————
November 18, 1789 Boston, Massachusetts

Boston   November 18th[, 178]9

Sir,

   Having the honor of an appointment as one of your associates on the Supreme fœderal bench, I must beg the favor of a line from you respecting the time it will be necessary or convenient for me to attend at Newyork. If not inconvenient, I purpose to delay going till some time in January.— As to the stile of writs which seems to ₍be left to₎ the determination of the Judicial, I am informed your opinion is [tha]t it should be in the name of the President of the United States, to which [the] district Judges here will conform, & which I think is right. By the Act [re]gulating processes, the Supreme Court is to [pro]vide a Seal for the Circuit Courts.— The district Judges to provide t[he]ir own Seals. As it is said that persons here who wish to commence immediately in the Circuit Court, it [may?] be proper, assoon as a quorum of th[e Su]preme Court come together to [take an?] order in that matter. Would it [word missing] to direct that the ₍Seal of the₎ district Court may be used for the Circuit Court till further order?

I am informed that Mʳ Sedgewick wrote to you recommending Mʳ Tu[cker] a clerk of the Supreme fœderal Court[.] He studied law with M.ʳ Lowell [*word missing.*] which he was, about five years [ago?] [ap]pointed one of the Clerks of the [Supreme] Judicial Court of this State & has con[ducted to?] the general approbation; is a Gentleman [of good?] sense & agreeable temper [*phrase illegible*] a man of virtue & integrity.

I observe the law has prescribed the form of an oath for us, but has not said who shall administer it. I should be glad of your opinion relative to any of these matters, or any others respecting the business we about to be engaged in, that you may think proper to mention.

I have the honor to be with high regard & esteem,   Sir,   your most Obed.ᵗ hon.ᵇˡᵉ Servant

W.ᵐ Cushing

[The?] honorable
John Jay Esq.ʳ
[Chief?] Justice of the United States —

ADfS (Photocopy in MHi, Photostat Collection). This document is severely damaged along both margins; therefore, conjectural readings have been supplied in brackets.

Benjamin Hichborn to Henry Knox ——————
November 20, 1789   Boston, Massachusetts

. . . my principal view in this is to request your Influence with the Judges of ʸᵉ Supreme Jud.ˡ Court to have my worthy Friend Tucker who is Clerk of our Supreme Court promoted to the same office in theirs — his ability & Integrity in that line are too notorious to need proof — M.ʳ Jay & our late Chief Justice[1] are already engaged in his favour I presume you acquainted with all the rest & I know a word from you will go a great way I know I need not say more to induce you to do every thing that is proper I wish nothing else —

. . .

ARS (MHi, Henry Knox Papers). Addressed "New-York." Postmarked "BOSTON   NOV."
Marked "private."
    Benjamin Hichborn (1746-1817), a Boston attorney. Shipton, *Sibley's Harvard Graduates*, 17:36-44.
    1. William Cushing.

George Washington to Edward Rutledge ——————
November 23, 1789   New York, New York

. . . I have been favoured with your letter of the 31.ˢᵗ ultimo, and am very happy to learn that the appointments under the general Government have given so much satisfaction in your part of the Union. — Added to the consciousness of having brought forward such characters only to fill the several Offices in the United States, as, from my own knowledge, or the strictest inquiries, I conceived would do justice to the public & honor to themselves, I have the happiness to find, so far as my information extends, that they are highly acceptable to the good people of this Country.

Your brother's acceptance of his appointment has given me much pleasure . . .

C (DNA, RG 59, Miscellaneous Letters); Lb (DLC, George Washington Papers).

John Jay to Fisher Ames ————————————————————————
November 27, 1789 New York, New York

New-York, 27th November, 1789.

DEAR SIR,

I have this moment been favoured with your letter of the 10th of this month. Mr. Sedgwick has given me the same character of Mr. Tucker that you do.[1] There are at present several candidates for the place in question, and probably the number will be increased before the appointment takes place. As it should be the result of mutual information and joint consultation between the judges, it appears to me proper that I should in the mean time remain free from engagements, express or implied, to or for any gentleman, however well recommended. The reserve which this consideration imposes will not permit me to enlarge upon this subject; but I know of no consideration which should restrain me from assuring you very explicitly of the esteem with which I am, dear sir,

Your most obedient and humble servant,

JOHN JAY.

Pr (Printed in William Jay, *The Life of John Jay: With Selections from His Correspondence and Miscellaneous Papers,* 2 vols. (New York: J. & J. Harper, 1833), 2:201).
1. See Theodore Sedgwick to John Jay, September 23, 1789.

George Washington to Edmund Randolph ————————————————
November 30, 1789 New York, New York

. . . I shall now mention some matters to you in confidence.— . . . When I was about to make the nominations in the Judiciary, for the Union; the character & abilities of Mr Wythe did not escape me, and I accordingly consulted such Gentlemen from the State of Virginia (then in this City) as I thought most likely to have some knowledge of his Inclinations. There opinion was, that as he had lately been appointed sole Chancellor (an Office to which by inclination he was led) and engaged in other avocations which engrossed his attentions and appeared to afford him pleasure he would not exchange the former for a federal appointment.___ However, since these appointments have been announced, I have heared that it has been the wonder of some, in Virginia, that Mr Wythe should have been <u>overlooked</u>.___ The cause (if the epithet applies) I have assigned.___ ...

Lb (DLC, George Washington Papers); ADf[S?] (DNA, RG 59, Miscellaneous Letters). Addressed "Virginia." The last page of the draft is missing, and therefore it cannot be determined whether George Washington signed it.

Samuel Johnston to James Iredell —————————————————
December 1, 1789 Fayetteville, North Carolina

... Spencer[1] is here soliciting some further compensation to himself and brethren for their faithful service; but is not like to succeed; and so dissatisfied with the conduct of the Assembly, that he has expressed a wish to offer his services to the United States, and would condescend to accept an appointment in their courts, whether as a judge of the Supreme Court, or of the District Court, I have not heard. It is said that neither Cushing nor Rutledge will accept their appointments; and he has no doubt of his being equal to either of them in point of abilities and reputation. He has asked Col. Davie[2] to recommend him to Mr. Ellsworth, and Dr. Johnson:[3] he is to apply to me on the same subject, but has not yet done it, &c., &c. ...

Pr (Printed in *MJI*, 2:274-75). Published in *MJI* with "Fayette" given for the place. Samuel Johnston had written to James Iredell on November 23, 1789, from Fayetteville (*MJI*, p. 272). If Johnston did write "Fayette," he probably meant Fayetteville.

1. Samuel Spencer (1734-1793) graduated from the College of New Jersey (later Princeton) before moving to North Carolina to practice law. Spencer was appointed deputy clerk of the Court of Pleas of Anson County, North Carolina, in 1765. By 1777 he had become a district judge in that state and was soon elected to the North Carolina Superior Court. Spencer was a leading North Carolina anti-federalist. James McLachlan, *Princetonians: A Biographical Dictionary*, vol. 1, *1748-1768* (Princeton: Princeton University Press, 1976), pp. 289-92.

2. William Richardson Davie (1756-1820), a lawyer in Halifax, North Carolina, was serving in the state legislature at this time. Davie had been a member of the Constitutional Convention and played a prominent role in getting North Carolina to ratify the Constitution. In 1798 Davie was elected governor of North Carolina, but he resigned in 1799 when President Adams named him (along with Oliver Ellsworth and William Vans Murray) as envoy extraordinary and minister plenipotentiary to France. Richard A. Harrison, *Princetonians: A Biographical Dictionary*, vol. 3, *1776-1783* (Princeton: Princeton University Press, 1981), pp. 25-31.

3. Probably William Samuel Johnson.

John Jay to William Cushing

December 7, 1789   New York, New York

New York   7 Dec.ʳ 1789

Sir

I have been favored with yours of the 18ᵗʰ of last month, and I participate very sincerely in the general Satisfaction which your appointment has given. Your attendance at the Time mentioned in your Letter will in my opinion be sufficiently early. It gives me Pleasure to learn that writs from your District Courts will be in the name of "the President of the united States," and that you concur with me in thinking that Stile the most proper.

It is to be regretted that the Circuit Court cannot proceed for want of a Seal — but as the Statute enables the sup. Court, and not the Judges of it to provide one, I am inclined to think that no order on the Subject by the Judges out of Court, would be regular. if so, the Delay is unavoidable, and must continue untill the Sitting of the Court in February —

no particular Person being designated by Law, to administer to us the oaths prescribed by the Statute, I thought it best to take them before the Chief Justice of this State — and have since administered to different officers of Governm.ᵗ the oaths directed to be taken by them respectively.

Your character of M.ʳ Tucker corresponds with the accounts given of it by other Gentlemen. There will be other candidates for the Clerkship of the sup. Court. I have made it a Rule to keep myself free from Engagements, and at Liberty to vote as after mutual Consultation among the Judges shall appear most adviseable. — [1] It will I am persuaded occur to you that we shall want a Clerk immediately on opening the court, & that it would be convenient that he should reside at the seat of Governm.ᵗ — There are several matters which will demand early attention; and it would doubtless be useful to have some informal meetings before Court, in order to consider and mature such measures as will then become indispensable — Among these will be the Stile of writs — admission of Attorneys and Counsellors — some Rules of Practice &c — &c —

With great Respect & Esteem I have the Honor to be   Sir   Your most ob.ᵗ & h'ble Serv.ᵗ

John Jay

The Honble W.ᵐ Cushing Esq.ʳ
associate Judge — of the Sup Court of
the United States —

ARS (MHi, Robert Treat Paine Papers). Addressed "Boston." Postmarked "New-York   Dec. 9."

1. Twelve years earlier, John Jay had expressed some concern about the propriety of judges appointing clerks of their own courts. In 1777 he had opposed a section of the New York constitution which removed the power to appoint court clerks from the Council of Appointments and gave it to the judges of the respective courts. In a letter of April 29, 1777, to Robert R. Livingston and Gouverneur Morris, Jay wrote:

"That Clerks should be *dependent* is agreed on all Hands, on whom? is the only question. I think not on the Judges Because

The chancellor, and the Judges of the Sup. Court holding permanent Commissions, will be *tempted* not only to give these appointments to their Children Brothers Relatives and Favorites, but to continue them in Office against the public Good. You I dare say, know Men of too little Probity Abilities and Industry to fill an office well, and yet of sufficient art and attention to avoid such gross Misbehaveour, as might justify loud Clamors against them.

Besides, Men who appoint others to offices, generally have a Partiality for them, and are often disposed, on Principles of Pride as well as Interest, to support them. By the Clerks of Courts being dependent on the Judges Collusion becomes more easy to be practiced, and more difficult to be detected, and instead of publishing and punishing each others Transgressions, will combine in concealing palliating or excusing their mutual Defects or misdemeanours." *PJJ,* 1:389-402.

Edmund Randolph to George Washington —————————
December 15, 1789   Richmond, Virginia

. . . Your friendly favor of the 30ᵗʰ Ultimo is this moment delivered to me. . . .

You may be assured, that Mʳ Wythe neither wished nor expected to be the successor of Mʳ Pendleton.[1] I will candidly tell you the reason, upon which this assurance is founded. In the month of July it was intimated to me in a letter from Colᵒ Griffin,[2] that it was his desire to know, whether Mʳ Wythe would enter into fœderal employment. The intimation seemed to arise from a purpose to say something to you concerning him. I therefore took an indirect opportunity of communicating Colᵒ Griffin's request to Mʳ Wythe; whose answer was, that he could not make a reply in the then state of the application, and even if it were made in a stile, which permitted him to declare himself, he should say, that he was too old and too happy in his present situation to be induced to a change. It is true, that the office of the district-judge would not have compelled him to travel much beyond Richmond; but he sits in a

kind of legal monarchy, which ˄ to him is the highest possible gratification. We shall however enter into some general discourse, that will lead to a discovery of his true sensations; tho' I am confident, that he felt as much pleasure at the idea of being thought of, as an actual appointment would have afforded. . . .

ARS (DLC, George Washington Papers).

1. Edmund Pendleton had been appointed United States judge for the district of Virginia, but he declined the appointment. George Washington to Edmund Randolph, November 30, 1789, George Washington Papers, DLC.

2. Samuel Griffin. For more information about Griffin's letter, see Edmund Randolph to James Madison, July 19, 1789.

John Rutledge to Charles Pinckney ─────────────────────
December 17, 1789 Charleston, South Carolina

Charleston Dec̄: 17. 1789

Sir/

Having been appointed a Judge of the Supreme Court of the United States of America, I beg Leave to inclose, & resign, my Judicial Commission from this State ─ [1]

I have the Honour to be, with great Respect y.ʳ Exc̄ys most obed.ᵗ Serv.ᵗ

J: Rutledge

His Exc̄y the Governor
of S.º Carolina

ALS (ScCAH, Records of the General Assembly).

Charles Pinckney (1757-1824), second cousin of Charles Cotesworth Pinckney and Thomas Pinckney, was governor of South Carolina from 1789 to 1792. Like his cousins, he also was a lawyer, having been admitted to the bar in 1779; he also supported adoption of the Constitution. By 1795 his cousins were leaders of the federalist party, while Charles Pinckney had become a supporter of the republicans. In 1798 he was elected to the Senate. Three years later, he became minister to Spain. N. Louise Bailey and Elizabeth Ivey Cooper, eds., *Biographical Directory of the South Carolina House of Representatives, 1775-1790*, vol. 3 (Columbia: University of South Carolina Press, 1981), p. 556; *DAB*.

1. John Rutledge was resigning from his position as a judge of the High Court of Chancery for South Carolina. Walter B. Edgar and N. Louise Bailey, eds., *Biographical Directory of the South Carolina House of Representatives: The Commons House of Assembly, 1692-1775*, vol. 2 (Columbia: University of South Carolina Press, 1977), p. 580.

Edmund Randolph to George Washington ─────────────────
December 23, 1789 Richmond, Virginia

... I found a fortunate moment for a conversation with M.ʳ Wythe. He repeated what I wrote to you in answer to your favor of the 30.ᵗʰ Ult.º[1] Indeed he declared himself happy in believing, that he held a place in your esteem; and that he was confident, you had looked towards him with every partiality, which he could wish. Nay without going into the detail of your discourse, I am convinced from his own mouth, that the knowledge of his present situation is considered by him, as the only reason of a seat on the bench, not being tendered to him. ...

ARS (DLC, George Washington Papers). Addressed "New-York." Marked "Private." Postmarked "WILLIAMS[BG?] DEC [2]3."

1. See Edmund Randolph to George Washington, December 15, 1789.

Edmund Randolph to George Washington —————————
December 23, 1789 Williamsburg, Virginia

Williamsburg Dec.ᵗ 23. 1789.

Sir

I now do myself the honor of informing you <u>officially</u>, that I accept the commission, by which I have been appointed attorney general of the United States. I purpose to be present at the supreme court in february. But the peculiar situation of my family and of my private affairs will probably prevent me from fixing my residence in New-York immediately; if the nature of my duties will permit, (as I hope they will) my absence, until my final arrangements can be made.

I have the honor sir to be with due deference and respect yᵗ mo. ob. serv.

Edm: Randolph

ARS (DNA, RG 59, General Records of the Department of State).

John Jay to William Livingston —————————————
January 26, 1790 New York, New York

. . . our sup. Court opens next week — The Length of its Session is uncertain — none of the Associate Judges have as yet arrived. . . .

ARS (MHi, Livingston II Papers). Addressed to "Elizabeth Town" in New Jersey. Postmarked "New-York Jan 26."

William Livingston (1723-1790), John Jay's father-in-law, had been a New York lawyer and political leader before retiring to New Jersey in 1772. With the approach of the revolution, he quickly rose to political eminence, representing New Jersey in the Continental Congress. Livingston became New Jersey's first governor and served in that capacity for fourteen years. He later represented that state in the Constitutional Convention. *DAB.*

John Fenno to Joseph Ward ————————————————
January 31, 1790 New York, New York

. . . To morrow the Sup: Jud! Fed! Court is to be opened by the Chief Justice & Judges Wilson & Cushing . . .

ARS (ICHi, Joseph Ward Papers). Addressed "Boston." Marked "Honᵈ by Mʳ J Williams."

Boston-born John Fenno (1751-1798) was the editor of the *Gazette of the United States.* This newspaper was first published in New York City on April 15, 1789. Fenno moved the newspaper to Philadelphia when the capital moved there and began publication again on November 3, 1790. *DAB;* Brigham, *American Newspapers,* 1:645; 2:912.

Joseph Ward (1737-1812) had been a Boston schoolmaster before the Revolutionary War, at which time he had frequently contributed articles to newspapers and corresponded with political leaders. Both he and John Fenno were secretaries to General Artemas Ward, a distant cousin of Joseph Ward, during the Revolutionary War. After his war-time service, Joseph Ward became a broker but also continued his avocation of writing for newspapers and corresponding with political leaders. William Carver Bates, "Col. Joseph Ward, 1737-1812: Teacher-Soldier-Patriot," *Bostonian Society Publications,* 1st ser., 4 (1907): 57-76; *DAB* entry for John Fenno.

Massachusetts Centinel
January 31, 1790 New York, New York

Judge CUSHING arrived here on Thursday— and to-morrow the Supreme Judicial Court of the United States will be opened in this city, by the Chief Justice, Judge CUSHING, and Judge WILSON. . . .

(Boston) February 10, 1790. Date and place are those of news item.

Robert Morris to Gouverneur Morris
February 1, 1790 New York, New York

. . . M^{r}Chief Justice Jay, Judge Wilson & Judge Cushing opened the Supreme Court this day but M^{r}Rutledge & M^{r}Blair not being arrived and Mr Harrison of Maryland having Resigned they did not make a quorum— . . .

ARS (NNC, Gouverneur Morris Papers).

Gouverneur Morris (1752-1816) arrived in France in 1789 as the business agent for Robert Morris (no relation), whose assistant he had been when the latter was superintendent of finance in the early 1780s. He spent the next ten years abroad in both public and private capacities. In 1790 he undertook a special mission to England to settle controversies remaining from the Treaty of Paris, and in 1792 President Washington named him minister to France. *DAB.*

Gazette of the United States
February 3, 1790 New York, New York

On Thursday last arrived in this city, from Massachusetts the Hon. *William Cushing,* one of the Judges of the Supreme Court of the United States.

On Saturday the Hon. *James Wilson,* one of the Judges of the Supreme Court, arrived here from Philadelphia.[1]

Yesterday the Hon. *John Blair,* and the Hon. *Edmund Randolph,* arrived in this City from Virginia.[2] The former is a Judge of the Supreme Court— and the latter Attorney General for the United States.

THE SUPREME COURT,

Of the United States, convened on Monday in this City; but a sufficient number of the Judges not being present to form a quorum, the same was adjourned till yesterday.

The Hon. John Jay, Chief Justice of the United States.

The Hon. William Cushing, and

The Hon. James Wilson, Associate Judges, appeared on the bench.

John M'Kesson, Esq. acted as clerk.

The Court Room at the Exchange[3] was uncommonly crouded. _ [4] The Chief Justice and other Judges of the Supreme Court of this State; the Federal Judge for the district of New York; the Mayor and Recorder of New-York; the Marshal of the District of New-York; the Sheriff and many other officers, and a great number of the gentlemen of the bar attended on the occasion.

Yesterday the Supreme Court of the United States met at the Hall in the Exchange, a quorum of the Judges with the Attorney-General attending, their respective commissions were read _ [5] and the court then adjourned till this day at one o'clock.

(New York) February 3, 1790. Date and place from the item headline.

The part of this article which describes the events of Monday, February 1, 1790, had appeared—with some insignificant differences—in the *Daily Advertiser* (New York) of February 2, 1790, the day before the *Gazette of the United States* reprinted it. We publish the latter version because it was from the *Gazette of the United States* that newspapers outside of New York took their reports.

The *Boston Gazette* reprinted this report in full on February 15, 1790. Some newspapers reprinted it beginning with the proceedings on February 1: *Federal Gazette* (Philadelphia), February 6, 1790; *Independent Chronicle* (Boston), February 11, 1790.

A number of newspapers printed different reports about the proceedings of the Court on February 1 and 2. When these reports provide bits of information not available in the *Gazette of the United States,* they have been used as annotation. Other newspapers provided no additional information: *New-York Journal,* February 4, 1790; *Pennsylvania Packet* (Philadelphia), February 5, 1790; *Freeman's Journal* (Philadelphia), February 10, 1790; *Georgia Gazette* (Savannah), March 4, 1790.

1. The *Federal Gazette* (Philadelphia) on February 3, 1790, also noted the arrival of James Wilson in New York.

2. On February 2, 1790, James Madison wrote to Edward Carrington that John Blair and Edmund Randolph had arrived the day before and the Court had opened on February 2. *PMad,* 13:14-15.

3. The *Federal Gazette* (Philadelphia) of February 4, 1790, noted that the Court had "met at the Assembly Chamber, New-York."

4. The *United States Chronicle* (Providence), February 18, 1790, reprinted this article beginning with the proceedings of February 1 but left out the remainder of this paragraph.

5. John McKesson read the commissions. *Daily Advertiser* (New York), February 3, 1790; *Pennsylvania Mercury* (Philadelphia), February 9, 1790.

Independent Gazetteer ———————————————————————————

February 3, 1790 New York, New York

. . . Yesterday the Supreme Court of the United States, met agreeable to adjournment. Present,

John Jay, Esquire _ Chief Justice of the United States.

William Cushing, James Wilson, and John Blair, Esquires _ Associate Judges.

And Edmund Randolph, Esq. _ Attorney General of the United States.

The Marshall of New-York (Mr. Smith) attended, and Mr. M'Kesson officiated as Clerk.

The commissions of the Judges, and of the Attorney-General, were read.

The Jury from the District Court attended; some of the Members of Congress, and a number of respectable citizens, also.

As no business appeared to require immediate notice, the court was adjourned until 1 o'clock this day.

(Philadelphia) February 6, 1790. Date and place are those given in headline.
This article also appeared in the *Providence Gazette,* February 13, 1790.

Peter Allaire to George Yonge —————————————————
February 4, 1790 New York, New York

. . . Our Supreme Court was Opened the 2 Instant the [Inf]eriour Judges from the Other States having Arrived we [are] now in Every Respect _ A Nation[1]

We have now Sitting in this City: two Houses [o]f Congress, Supreme Court of the United States, Both houses [o]f the State of New York, Supreme Court of this State[,] [Co]urt of Chancery, Admiralty and Mayors Court, fine [ti]me for the Lawyers _ . . .

ARS (UkLPR, Foreign Office 4). Addressed "Stratford Place   London." Endorsed "R. 16th March." The margin of this text has been rendered illegible, because the letter has been bound into a volume. Text in brackets has been supplied from a transcript also in the Public Record Office.

Peter Allaire (1740-1820), a New York merchant of Huguenot descent, was acquainted with John Jay. At this time, Allaire was being paid by George Yonge £200 to report on American intelligence. During the Revolutionary War, Allaire had been a British spy. *PTJ,* 17:91n; Claude-Ann Lopez, "The Man Who Frightened Franklin," *Pennsylvania Magazine of History and Biography* 106 (1982): 515-26.

Sir George Yonge (1731-1812), a member of Parliament from 1754 to 1794, had held several cabinet positions and in 1790 was serving as secretary for war. Yonge was a friend of Peter Allaire. *DNB; PTJ,* 17:91n.

1. John Temple also reported the opening of the Court to the Duke of Leeds, February 4, 1790. Foreign Office 4, UkLPR.

Samuel Johnston to James Iredell —————————————————
February 4, 1790 New York, New York

. . . I am just returned from dining at the Presidents with a very respectable Company, the Vice President, the Judges of the Supreme Court & Attorney General of the United States, the Secretary at War[1] and a number of others[.] The President enquired particularly after you and spoke of you in a manner that gave me great pleasure . . .

ARS (NcD, James Iredell Sr. and Jr. Papers). Excerpt misdated as February 1, 1790, in *MJI*, 2:281-82.

1. Vice President John Adams, Attorney General Edmund Randolph, and Secretary of War Henry Knox. According to the diary of George Washington, Chief Justice John Jay and Associate Justices William Cushing, James Wilson, and John Blair attended. In addition Washington noted the presence of the judge, marshal, attorney, and clerk of the federal district court for New York. Senator Benjamin Hawkins of North Carolina and Secretary of the Treasury Alexander Hamilton were also there. *PGW, Diary*, 6:28.

Gazette of the United States ——————————————————————
February 6, 1790   New York, New York

Wednesday last the Supreme Court of the United States, met agreeable to adjournment. An order was read, appointing JOHN TUCKER, Esq. [late clerk to the Supreme Court of the Commonwealth of Massachusetts] their Clerk— who was accordingly qualified.[1] Two other orders were also read, to wit.

Ordered that the seal of *this* Court shall be, the arms of the United States engraven on a circular piece of steel of the size of a dollar, with these words in the margin— *the seal of the Supreme Court of the United States—* Ordered that the Seals of the *Circuit Courts*[2] shall be the arms of the United States engraven on circular pieces of silver of the size of half a dollar, with these words in the margin, viz. In the upper part— *The seal of the Circuit Court—* In the lower part— *the name of the District for which it is intended—* After which the court adjourned until one o'clock on Friday.[3]

Yesterday the Supreme Court of the United States met pursuant to adjournment. Among other business transacted, we hear, that

The Hon. ELIAS BOUDINOT, of New-Jersey,
The Hon. THOMAS HARTLEY,[4] of Pennsylvania,
The Hon. RICHARD HARRISON, of New-York,

were admitted Counsellors at the Supreme Court of the United States.

Ordered, That persons admitted as Counsellors shall not appear in the character of Attorneys, nor Attorneys in that of Counsellors, at the Supreme Court of the United States.

Ordered, That no person shall be admitted as an Attorney at the Supreme Court of the United States, who shall not have practised three years in the Supreme Court of a particular State, and who shall not sustain a just and fair character.

Ordered, That the Stile of all Writs and Processes from the Supreme Court of the United States, be in the name of THE PRESIDENT OF THE UNITED STATES.

The Court adjourned to Monday next.

———————————

(New York) February 6, 1790. Date and place are those given in the headline.

Some newspapers reprinted this article in full: *Herald of Freedom* (Boston), February 16, 1790; *Vermont Gazette* (Bennington), February 22, 1790; *State Gazette of North-Carolina* (Edenton), February 27, 1790. Other newspapers printed parts of it: *Federal Gazette* (Philadelphia), February 10, 1790; *Massachusetts Centinel* (Boston), February 13, 1790; *United States Chronicle* (Providence), February 18, 1790; *Georgia Gazette* (Savannah), March 18, 1790.

A number of newspapers printed different reports about the proceedings of the Court on February 3 and 5. When these reports provide bits of information not available in the *Gazette of the United States,* they have been used as annotation. Other newspapers provided no additional information: *Daily Advertiser* (New York), February 4, 1790; *New-York Journal,* February 4 and 11, 1790; *Federal Gazette* (Philadelphia), February 8, 1790; *Pennsylvania Mercury* (Philadelphia), February 9, 1790; *Freeman's Journal* (Philadelphia), February 10, 1790; *Maryland Journal* (Baltimore), February 12 and 16, 1790; *Pennsylvania Journal* (Philadelphia), February 17, 1790.

1. Brackets appear in the original. On February 6—the same day that this article appeared in the *Gazette of the United States*—Caleb Strong wrote to Nathan Dane that the Court was meeting and that John Tucker had been appointed clerk. Wetmore Family Papers, CtY.

2. The *Federal Gazette* (Philadelphia) reported on February 8, 1790, that the Court had adopted a design for the seals of the district courts. The *Maryland Journal* (Baltimore) of February 12 and the *Pennsylvania Journal* (Philadelphia) of February 17, both of which probably based their articles on that of the *Federal Gazette,* reported the same. These reports are inaccurate, which can be determined from the minutes of the Court, other newspaper accounts, and the letter from William Loughton Smith to Edward Rutledge on February 13, 1790 (q.v.).

3. Misinterpreting an article originally published in the *Federal Gazette* (Philadelphia) on February 8, 1790, the *Pennsylvania Packet* (Philadelphia) reported on February 9 that the Court had adjourned until Thursday.

4. Misspelled as "Thomas Harley" in the *Boston Gazette* reprint of this article on February 15, 1790, and in the *Providence Gazette* reprint on February 20, 1790.

Pennsylvania Packet
February 6, 1790   New York, New York

SUPREME COURT of the UNITED STATES.

AT a Supreme Court of the United States, held at the city of New-York, in the state of New-York (being the seat of government of the United States) on the first Monday in February, in the 14th year of the Independence of the said United States, and in the year of our Lord, 1790.

Present— John Jay, Esquire, Chief Justice; Wm. Cushing, Esquire, James Wilson, Esquire, Associate Justices.

Proclamation was made in the words following, viz.

This being the day assigned by law for the commencing the first session of the Supreme Court of the United States, and a sufficient number of justices to form a quorum not being convened, the Court is adjourned, by the Justices now present, until to-morrow, at one o'clock in the afternoon.

Tuesday, February 2.

Present— John Jay Esquire, Chief Justice; Wm. Cushing, Esq; James Wilson, Esq; and John Blair, Esq; Associate Justices.

Proclamation was made, and the Court opened.

Proclamation was made for silence, while the letters patent of the Justices present are openly read, upon pain of imprisonment; whereupon letters patent, under the Great Seal of the United States, bearing test the 26th day of September last, appointing the said John Jay, Esq; Chief Justice; letters patent bearing test the 27th day of September aforesaid, appointing the said William

Cushing, Esq; an associate Justice; letters patent bearing test the 29th September aforesaid, appointing the said James Wilson, Esq; an associate Justice; and letters patent bearing test the 30th day of September aforesaid, appointing the said John Blair, Esq; an associate Justice of this Court, were openly read.

Letters patent to Edmund Randolph, of Virginia, Esq. bearing test the 26th day of September aforesaid, appointing him Attorney-General for the United States, were openly read.

Ordered, That Richard Wenm[a]n be, and he is hereby appointed Crier of this Court.

Then the court adjourned until to morrow, at one o'clock in the afternoon

Wednesday, February 3, 1790.
Present as yesterday.

Ordered, That John Tucker, Esq; of Boston, be the Clerk of this court; that he reside and keep his office at the seat of the national government; and that he do not practice either as an attorney or a counsellor in this court, while he shall continue to be Clerk of the same.

The said John Tucker took the oaths prescribed by law.

Ordered, That the seal of this court shall be the arms of the United States engraven on a circular piece of steel, of the size of a dollar, with these words in the margin, "The Seal of the Supreme Court of the United States."

Ordered, That the seals of the Circuit Courts shall be the arms of the U. States engraven on a circular piece of silver, of the size of half a dollar, with these words in the margin, viz. In the upper part, "the seal of the Circuit Courts;" In the lower part, the name of the district for which it is intended.

Ordered, That the clerk of this court cause the beforementioned seals to be made accordingly, and when done, that he convey those for the Circuit Courts to the district clerks respectively.

Then the court adjourned until Friday, at one o'clock.

Friday, February 5.
Present the same as on Wednesday.

Ordered, That (until further orders) if it shall be requisite to the admission of attornies or counsellors to practice in this court, that they shall have been such for three years past in the supreme court of the state to which they respectively belong; and that their private and personal character shall appear to be fair.

Ordered, That counsellors shall not practice as attornies, nor attornies as counsellors, in this state.[1] That they respectively take the following oath, viz.

"I _____, do solemnly swear, that I will demean myself as an attorney (or counsellor) of the court, uprightly and according to law; and that I will support the constitution of the United States."

Ordered, That (unless and until it shall be otherwise provided by law) all process of this court shall be in the name of the President of the United States.

Elias Boudinot, of New-Jersey, Esquire, Thomas Hartley, of Pennsylvania,

Esq; Richard Harrison, of New-York, Esq.— respectively appeared in court, took the oath for that purpose, and were appointed counsellors of the said court accordingly

The court then adjourned till Monday next, at one o'clock in the afternoon.

(Philadelphia) February 11, 1790. Date and place from the headline. A reading has been supplied in brackets because of broken type.

The *Pennsylvania Herald* (York) on February 24, 1790, reprinted most of this version of the minutes of the Court for February.

This report may be based on rough minutes of the proceedings of the Court for February term, 1790. The rough minutes themselves no longer exist. For a fuller discussion of this matter, see the headnote to "Original Minutes."

1. Should be "in this Court."

DeWitt Clinton to Charles Clinton
February 8, 1790   New York, New York

... The City is at present filled with Legislatures and Law Courts— The Supreme Court of the U. States are in is now in session and ha[ve?] done no other business than admitting a few Counsellors and making a few rules— One of their orders "that all process shall run in the name of the President" tho' apparently unimportant smells strongly of monarchy— You know that in G. Britain some writs are prefaced with "George the 3ᵈ by the Grace of God &ᶜ" A federal process beginning with "George Washington by the grace of God &ᶜ will make the American President as important in Law forms as the British King. ...

ARS (NHi, Miscellaneous Manuscripts C). Addressed "Little Britain." Marked "Per Moses DeWitt Esqʳ."

DeWitt Clinton (1769-1828) had graduated from Columbia College in 1786. Clinton had opposed adoption of the Constitution. In 1790 he was completing his legal studies and acting as confidential secretary to his uncle George Clinton, then governor of New York. Admitted to the bar in April, 1790, DeWitt Clinton eventually served as state assemblyman and senator, United States senator, mayor of New York City, and governor of New York. *DAB;* Dorothie Bobbé, *De Witt Clinton,* new ed. (Port Washington, New York: Ira J. Friedman, 1962), pp. 52-55.

Charles Clinton (1767-1829) was an older brother of DeWitt Clinton. At this time, Charles Clinton was a surveyor. Charles B. Moore, "Sketch of the Clinton Family," *New York Genealogical and Biographical Record* 13 (1882): 173, 180; Bobbé, *De Witt Clinton,* p. 52.

Pierce Butler to James Iredell
February 10, 1790   New York, New York

... I should have been happy to have had you in Congress. The Union will no longer be deprived of your aid, and the benefit of your abilities. You have this day been nominated by the President,[1] and unanimously appointed by the Senate to a seat on the Supreme Federal Bench.[2] I congratulate the States on the appointment, and you on this mark of their well-merited opinion of you. I please myself with the expectation of seeing you soon here. I think you will save the lives of your children by bringing them here. Provisions, and every thing, but house rent, is cheaper here than with you. It is probable you will find it more convenient and eligible to settle your family somewhere to the North than keep them at Edenton. . . .

Pr (Printed in *MJI*, 2:280).
     1. James Iredell's nomination was sent to the Senate on February 9, not February 10.
     2. Notice of the Senate's action on the nomination of James Iredell appeared in the *Daily Advertiser* (New York), February 13, 1790, in the *Federal Gazette* (Philadelphia), February 19, 1790, in the *Massachusetts Centinel* (Boston), February 27, 1790, and in the *Georgia Gazette* (Savannah), March 11, 1790.

William Cushing to Charles Cushing
February 10, 1790 New York, New York

. . . We finished this term to day, after appointing a Clerk, Seals, admitting a Number of Gent, Consellors & Attorneys. Mʳ Harrison had resigned, Govʳ Rutledge could not Attend this term. I am told that a Mʳ Iredell of North Carolina is nominated[1] ^& appointed^ in yᵉ– room of MʳHarrison. . . .

ARS (MHi, William Cushing Papers). Addressed "Boston." Marked "favored by   MʳTucker." In this letter, William Cushing wrote that John Tucker would be leaving New York in the morning.
     1. The second "n" is written over a "t."

Roger Sherman to Simeon Baldwin
February 10, 1790 New York, New York

. . . P. S. The Supreme Court have Set here Some days. and have appointed a Clerk & admitted a number of attorneys & Counsellors. & Settled Some rules, the qualification for admission as attornies is 3 years practice in the Superiour Court of a State and a fair moral character. session closed this day. . . .

ARS (CtY, Roger Sherman Papers). Postmarked "New-York [*date missing*]." Part of the address cover is missing.
     Roger Sherman (1721-1793), a Connecticut congressman, was one of that state's leading figures of the revolutionary era. Sherman's public career began in 1755 with his election to the Connecticut General Assembly, a year after his admission to the bar. Sherman became a justice of the Superior Court in 1766 and served in the Continental and Confederation Congresses, 1774-1781 and 1783-1784. He attended the Constitutional Convention and supported ratification in his home state. In 1789 Sherman was elected to Congress and resigned his seat on the Superior Court. Two years later, he was elected to complete the term of William Samuel Johnson in the Senate and held that office until his death. *DAB*.

Simeon Baldwin (1761-1851), who had studied law with Charles Chauncey, was the city clerk of New Haven. In the spring of 1790, Baldwin was appointed clerk of the district and circuit courts of the United States for the district of Connecticut and served until 1803, when he was elected to Congress. Franklin Bowditch Dexter, *Biographical Sketches of the Graduates of Yale College,* 6 vols. (New York: Henry Holt, 1885-1912), 4:178-80.

Samuel Johnston to James Iredell ──────────────────────
February 11, 1790 New York, New York

. . . I have the pleasure to inform you that yesterday your Nomination to a Seat on the Bench of the Supreme Court of the United States was unanimously approved of by the Senate, (it was necessary, as you was not generally known to the Members, that some Member should inform them of your qualifications to execute that Office, that your friend Major Butler did in a manner which did honor to himself and to you, a Member from New Hampshire[1] said that tho he had the greatest Confidence in ~~wh~~ the Honor of the Gentleman from South Carolina he wished to hear the Sentiments of the Gentlemen from the State where you resided, upon this M.ʳ Hawkins[2] confirmed what Maj.ʳ Butler had said and added something of his own, the Senate were then perfectly satisfied.) . . .

ARS (Nc-Ar, Charles E. Johnson Collection). Addressed "Edenton." Endorsed "Ans.ᵈ"
    1. John Langdon and Paine Wingate were the senators from New Hampshire.
    2. Benjamin Hawkins (1754-1818) had represented North Carolina in the Confederation Congress (1781-1784, 1786-1787) and in 1789 was chosen to be a United States senator. Hawkins, who had negotiated Indian treaties in the 1780s, was appointed by President Washington in June, 1795, to be a commissioner to the Creek Indians. He was reappointed to that post in January, 1797. *DAB; SEJ,* 1:190, 192, 221, 224.

Federal Gazette ──────────────────────────
February 11, 1790 New York, New York

Yesterday the Supreme Court of the United States met, and adjourned until the first Monday in August next.

The following is a list of Attornies and Counsellors that were *sworn in* during the session:

ATTORNIES.

William Houston, Edward Livingston, Jacob Morton, Bartholomew De Haert, John Keese, Peter Masterton, and William Wilcocks ‒ of New-York.

COUNSELLORS.

Theodore Sedgwick, Fisher Ames, and George Thatcher ‒ of Massachusetts.

Richard Harrison, Egbert Benson, John Lawrence, Richard Varick, Robert Morris, Samuel Jones, Ezekiel Gilbert, and Cornelius J. Bogert ‒ of New-York.

El[i]as Boudinot, Abraham Ogden, Elisha Boudinot, and William Patter-
son_ of New-Jersey.
Thomas Hartley_ of Pennsylvania.
William Smith_ of South-Carolina.
James Jackson_ of Georgia.

(Philadelphia) February 15, 1790. Date and place are from item headline. Bracketed reading has
been supplied because type did not imprint.
The *Pennsylvania Herald* (York) also printed this on February 24, 1790.

New-York Journal —————————————————————————————————
February 11, 1790 New York, New York

...In the Supreme court of the United States, yesterday,_ Ordered, That
Arthur Lee, Esq. be admitted a Counsellor of this court.[1]
The court then adjourned to the next term, viz. the first day of August next.

(New York) February 11, 1790. Date and place from the headline.
Other newspapers merely noted that on February 10 the Court adjourned until August: *Federal
Gazette* (Philadelphia), February 15, 1790; *Georgia Gazette* (Savannah), March 18, 1790.
1. The minutes for February 10, 1790, do not mention the admission of Arthur Lee. Lee's
signature on the parchment counsellor roll (q.v., in "Admission to the Bar") is dated "Feb! 1790";
his is the last signature for the February 1790 term and follows that of Cornelius Bogert, dated
February 9. On March 6, 1790, the *Gazette of the United States* (New York) reported that "On the
15th ult. Arthur Lee, Esq. Barrister and Doctor of Laws, was, by a special order, of the Supreme
Court of the United States, admitted a Counsellor in the said Court." Lee could not have been
admitted on February 15, inasmuch as the Court adjourned on February 10. On January 5, 1791,
the *Virginia Gazette, and General Advertiser* (Richmond) reprinted the report from the *Gazette of the
United States,* noted that Lee was from Alexandria, and added the following paragraph: "We have
authority to say, that Mr. Lee intends to practise in the Supreme and District Federal Courts."

William Loughton Smith to Edward Rutledge ————————————
February 13, 1790 New York, New York

...I have to inform M⟨r⟩Drayton that the Supreme Court have not fixed any
thing as to the dress of the Courts, & that each District Court is to ~~fix~~ establish
its own Seal. They have fixed the Seals of the Supreme Court & Circuit Courts
according to the mode I suggested to M⟨r⟩ Jay, as he yesterday informed me.
You will see them in the papers_ The Ch. Justice & M⟨r⟩Cushing are to ride
the Eastern Circuit_ M⟨r⟩ Wilson & Blair the Middle_ Your Brother & M⟨r⟩
Iredell (appointed vice M⟨r⟩ Harrison, resigned) the Southern. I have been admitted a Counsellor, they have seperated the business of Counsellor & Attorney.— ...

ARS (ScHi, William Loughton Smith Papers). Addressed "Charleston   So. Car[ᵃ?]."
   William Loughton Smith (1758-1812), born in Charleston and educated abroad, was admitted
to the Middle Temple in 1774. Smith pursued higher education in Geneva from 1774 to 1778

and then returned to London in 1779 where he again studied law until his departure for America in 1782. He was admitted to the South Carolina bar in 1784. Smith's career in public office also began in that year when he was elected to the South Carolina House of Representatives, where he served until 1788. Smith was elected to the First Congress in 1789. He remained in Congress until July 10, 1797, when he resigned; on that same day, Smith was confirmed as minister to Portugal. Smith remained in a diplomatic capacity until September 9, 1801. *BDAC; DAB.*

Oliver Ellsworth to Ephraim Kirby
February 15, 1790 New York, New York

New York   Feby 15 _ 1790

Dear Sir,

I was seasonable & faithful in my application for you to the Judges of the Supreme Court, & probably should have been succesful had not Judge Cushing bro^t along with him Mr Tucker for the same birth. He had served with reputation as Clerk of the Supreme Court in Massachusetts, & being on the spot & well patronized he obtained the appointment. If any door should hereafter open that I can at once serve you & the publick I shall be happy to do it _
And am
    Sir.   Your hum^e Servt

Oliv̄ Ellsworth

Eph^m Kirbey Esq̄.

ARS (NcD, Ephraim Kirby Papers). Addressed "Litchfield   Connecticut." Postmarked "New-York   Feb 17."

John Jay to John DuMont
February 27, 1790 New York, New York

New York   27 Feb. 1790

Dr Sir

I was favored with yours of the 28th Ult.[1] ~~just~~ as I was preparing to go out of Town _ it was not untill last Evening that I returned, or I should have taken an earlier opportunity of answering your Letter _

Accept my thanks for your friendly Congratulations. I ~~am convinced of~~ believe them Sincere~~ty~~[2] and value them accordingly _ It would give me great Pleasure to ~~have opportunities of rendering your~~ see your Situation more comfortable _ on these occasions it is best to be very explicit _ it would neither be ~~candid nor~~ friend-ly nor candid ˄ to excite delusory Expectations, or to make Promises without a good Prospect of performing them _ There is not a single office in my Gift, nor do I recollect that there is more than one in the appointm^t of the Court, & I mean their clerk. as to Offices in the Gift of other Departments I think it my Duty

            nor to   it being improper for a Judge

not to interfere ~~with their affairs, or~~ ^ ask favors ~~from them~~ ^ _ ~~a Judge~~

                      on   official   he

~~ought not~~ to put himself under such obligations ~~to Men~~ ^ ~~whose~~ ^ ~~Conduct~~ ^

                         [*letters inked out*]

~~may~~ [*letters inked out*] ~~find himself called upon to pass Judgement. I shall always be ready to~~[3] ~~[on application?]~~ ~~to give them what Information~~ I am sincerely

                           can only

disposed to serve my Friends, and you among others, but ~~then~~ it ~~must~~ be in a way perfectly consistant with the Duties & Proprieties of my public Station_ These Considerations will I am persuaded have their due weight with you; ~~and~~ and rather ~~tend to~~ increase than Diminish the Esteem and attachment you have always expressed and manifested for me_ I regret that on this occasion I can-

                       but

not say things more consonant with your wishes [*phrase inked out*] ~~but~~ Sincerity

tho not always pleasing

^ is preferable to mer[e][4] Civility_ Be assured ~~nevertheless~~ of my constant regard & that I remain

     Your Friend

                                           J. J.

John Dumont Esqr

ADfS (NNC, John Jay Papers).

Probably John DuMont (1730-1811), a merchant and attorney in Kingston, New York. *DAR Patriot Index;* Gustave Anjou, *Ulster County, New York, Probate Records,* 2 vols. (New York, 1906), 2:126; H. Josephine DuMont, "Sheriff Egbert DuMont," *Olde Ulster* 5 (1909): 179.

1. Letter not found.

2. Originally John Jay wrote "I am convinced of their Sincerity." He then crossed out "am convinced of" and interlined "believe." He seems to have altered "their" to "them" and crossed out the "ty" in the word "Sincerity." Since Jay formed his "e" and his "i" similarly, the second "i" in "Sincerity" can also be read as an "e."

3. John Jay apparently crossed out this "to," finished drafting through the word "Information," and then crossed out the whole passage.

4. The edge of this page is damaged and, therefore, this reading has been supplied in brackets.

Pierce Butler to Archibald Maclaine ——————————
March 3, 1790   New York, New York

... You will have heard before this reaches you of the appointment of Mr Iredal to a seat on the bench of the Supreme Court. I was happy in the oppy of being instrumental in obtaining the appointment[.?] Indeed Mr Hawkins left nothing undone to serve Mr Iredel & he did materially serve him. ...

ALb (ScU, Pierce Butler Letterbook).

Archibald Maclaine (d. 1791) originally came to North Carolina to establish a mercantile business, but when that failed he studied law and became a prominent lawyer in Wilmington, North Carolina. Maclaine also represented that town in the state legislature. He was a close personal and political friend of James Iredell. *PJI*, 1:470-71n; *MJI*, 1:370-71.

James Iredell to John Jay ——————————————————
March 3, 1790 Edenton, North Carolina

Edenton   March 3ᵈ 1790.

Sir,

Having this day had the great honour to receive a Commission from the President appointing me one of the Associate Justices of the Supreme Court of the United States, I take the liberty to acquaint you that I have accepted of the important Trust, although with a becoming diffidence, as I can by no means equally rely on my abilities as on my application and fidelity in the discharge of the duties of it. I beg leave to request, Sir, that you will be so good as to acquaint me what Circuit I am to ~~prepare for~~ go, and I shall be happy to receive any other communications that you may think proper to send me.

I have the honour to be,   with great respect,   Sir,   Your most obedient and   most humble Servant

Ja. Iredell

ADfS (Nc-Ar, Charles E. Johnson Collection).

John Swann to James Iredell ——————————————————
March 5, 1790 [Pasquotank County, North Carolina]

... I beg leave to offer my warmest Congratulations on the Subject of your appointment. indeed, Sir, it must be highly pleasing to a delicate Mind to receive a distinction of that kind not solicited for, nor[1] perhaps thought of. however desirous I was that you shou'd have offered yourself as a Representative, I now very sincerely rejoice that you did not. I hope, Sir, you will now be relieved in a great degree from the many embarrassments[2] which surrounded you, at least that you will have leisure enough to make Pasquotank a Visit. ...

ARS (NcD, James Iredell Sr. and Jr. Papers). Place determined by evidence in letter. Addressed "Edenton." Sent by "Mr. Dawson."

Like James Iredell, John Swann (1760-1793) was related to Samuel Johnston through marriage, having married Johnston's daughter Penelope. Swann lived near Edenton in Pasquotank County, North Carolina. In 1788 he represented North Carolina in the last Confederation Congress. Swann supported the adoption of the federal Constitution. *BDAC* (where Swann's name is spelled with one "n"); *MJI*, 2:228.

1. Originally written as "not" and then altered to "nor."

2. John Swann probably is referring to financial difficulties. In a letter to Arthur Iredell (James Iredell's brother) on October 30, 1799, Samuel Johnston noted that James Iredell never seemed to have enough money: "unfortunately for his family he never realized any part of the money he received _ either for fees when at the Bar or for of his Salary after he [became a J?] was appointed

a Judge, ^tho^ he was guilty of no vicious excesses and his Wife is remarkable for her frugality and Economy, ^yet at the end of each Quarter, his purse was empty." Hayes Collection, NcU.

Daily Advertiser ———————————————————————————————
March 5, 1790   New York, New York

Yesterday ARTHUR LEE, Esq; took the oaths before the Hon. the Chief Justice of the United States, requisite to carry into execution the special order of the supreme court of the United States for admitting him a Counsellor in the said state.[1]

(New York) March 5, 1790. Date and place are those of headline.

1. For Lee's admission to the Court's bar, see *New-York Journal,* under date of February 11, 1790.

Samuel Johnston to James Iredell ———————————————
March 6, 1790   New York, New York

... I imagine you will before this have received your Commission. I suppose you ^will^ write to the President and beg you will at the same time write to your friend Maj.ʳ Butler who acted a very friendly part on that occasion. the people to the eastward opposed some person to you but I cannot discover who it was.
. . .

ARS (NcD, James Iredell Sr. and Jr. Papers). Addressed "Edenton."

Gazette of the United States ———————————————————
March 6, 1790   New York, New York

On Thursday last Mr. ARTHUR LEE took the necessary oaths for his admission to the bar of the Federal Court, as a Counseller at Law. _ [1] This gentleman, (whose talents and law knowledge so eminently distinguished him in the Courts of Westminster, prior to the commencement of the late glorious revolution, in the whole course of which his abilities and patriotism were so successfully exerted for the benefit of his country,)[2] will, we doubt not, be another shining ornament to the Federal Bar _ and will, we hope, meet with those returns from his fellow citizens, in the line of his profession, which his long-tried integrity, and high character justly entitle him to: Those considerations, we hear, have induced the Hon. Judges of the Supreme Court to dispense with a special rule of the Court in his favor, which precluded the admission of any person as a counsellor, who had not practiced as such in some of the Superior Courts of the States for three years antecedent to the adoption of the New Constitution.[3]

Every friend to America must be highly gratified, when he peruses the long list of eminent and worthy characters, who have come forward as Practitioners at the Federal Bar— where the most important rights of Man must, in time, be discussed, and determined upon, as well those of nations, as of individuals. Happy country! Whose Judges, (rendered independent— and selected for their wisdom and virtue,) constitute so firm a barrier against tyranny and usurpation on the one hand, and fraud and licentiousness on the other.

(New York) March 6, 1790. Date and place from headline.

This article reprinted in *Pennsylvania Mercury* (Philadelphia), March 11, 1790.

1. For Lee's admission to the Court's bar, see *New-York Journal,* under date of February 11, 1790.

2. For Arthur Lee's exertions during the Revolutionary War, see note to Arthur Lee to [Francis Lightfoot Lee], May 9, 1789.

3. The Court's rule on the admission of attorneys and counsellors did not specify practice "for three years antecedent to the adoption of the New Constitution," but rather required such service "for three years past"; see the Court's minutes, February 5, 1790.

James Iredell to Thomas Iredell ———————————————————
March 8, 1790   Edenton, North Carolina

Edenton North Carolina   March 8. 1790.

My dear & hon. Sir,

Though I have long forborne troubling you with any letter, fearing my correspondence was di[s]agreeable to you, yet I think it my duty to acquaint you of a very extraordinary & unexpected change which has lately taken place in my situation. Without the slightest application on m[y] part for any [o]ffice whatever, The President (Gen. Washington) has thought proper to confer upon me, with the unanimous approbation of the Senate, the high & important office of one of the associate Justices of the Supreme Court of the United States, an office held during good behaviour, & the Salary of which is 3500 Dollars a year, which & by the Constitution [*letters inked out*] this cannot be lessened during my continuance in office. The duty will be severe, but the station is so honorable & the income of so much value that I have accepted it with the utmost gratitude. There are [two?] to be 2 Sessions of the Supreme Court held at the seat of Gov. in each year, & a Circuit Court twice a year in each State. The United States are divided into three Circuits— one, called the Eastern, consisting of New Hampshire, Massachusets, Connecticut & New York; the middle, consisting of New Jersey, Pennsylvania, Delaware, Maryland & Virginia; and the Southern, consisting at present of South Carolina & Georgia, to which I imagine North Carolina will be added— ~~Two of the Justices of the Supreme Court are to attend~~ [*letters inked out*] The Circuit Courts are to consist of two Judges of the Supreme Court, and a Judge in each State appointed by the President who has in other respects a separate jurisdiction of a limited kind— Any two of these may constitute a Quorum— In consequence of this appointment, it is my intention as soon as possible to settle my Family in New York—[1] I have the happiness to have two lovely Children, the eldest a Daughter [*letters inked out*] a little more than 4 years old, ~~and~~ ^the youngest^ a Son (named James, at his Mother's earnest desire) who was born 2 Nov. 1788, and both are as fine Children as I could possibly wish them, but last Summer they suffered so much sickness & terrified us so much with the imminent danger of losing them, that I shall embrace with Joy this opportunity of fixing them in a more healthy climate. It is a circumstance also that gives me inexpressible Satisfaction that if it should please God to preserve my life I can, after a very short time, make my Mother's Circumstances perfectly easy. ~~which I~~ [*letters inked out*] My poor Brother Tom has had the Rheumatism with extreme severity almost the whole of this winter. He is now getting better but I greatly fear it is a chronic disease fixed upon him more or less for life— I expect next month to begin my Circuit, ~~tho'~~ [*phrase inked out*] ~~yet~~ tho' I[']m yet uncertain which it is to be. If you should honour me with a letter I beg the favour of you to direct it to me at New York, where I hope to be some time in July. Be ple[as]ed to direct it "To the care of The honorable Samuel Johnston Esq— Member of the Senate of the United States, New York—" I shall feel inexpressible anxiety to hear from you—

With the most sincer[e] wishes for your health & happiness, I am &—[2]

ADf (Nc-Ar, Charles E. Johnson Collection). This document is severely damaged and faded; conjectural readings have been supplied in brackets.

Thomas Iredell (d. 1796), James Iredell's uncle, was a wealthy and prominent Jamaican planter. As early as 1775, Thomas Iredell had warned his nephew not to involve himself with the American cause, lest he lose his inheritance. Thomas Iredell ultimately did disinherit James Iredell for taking an oath of allegiance to America and left the bulk of his estate to Arthur Iredell, a younger brother of James Iredell. *PJI,* 1:30n, 36n, 280; 2:423, 458-59.

1. In a letter to Robert Ferrier on September 18, 1790, Samuel Johnston noted the appointment of James Iredell to the Supreme Court and mentioned that Iredell had moved his family to New York. Hayes Collection, NcU.

2. On July 6, 1791, James Iredell, fearing that this letter had not reached his uncle, wrote from Philadelphia to inform Thomas Iredell of his appointment and position as an associate justice. Charles E. Johnson Collection, Nc-Ar.

John Jay to James Iredell ———————————————————
March 10, 1790   New York, New York

. . . Altho' I have not the Pleasure of being personally acquainted with you, yet your character renders your appointment to a Seat on the Bench, very satisfactory to me. I congratulate you on the occasion, and as your office will call you to this place at the ensuing Session of the SupCourt, my Endeavours shall not be wanting to make it agreable to You— ...

ARS (NcD, James Iredell Sr. and Jr. Papers). Endorsed "Rec^d & ans^d 8th April."

Archibald Maclaine to James Iredell —————————————————————
March 10, 1790   Wilmington, North Carolina

... I thank you, dear Sir, for your communications, and very cordially congratulate you on your appointment, and particularly on the honorable manner in which you have obtained it. I received your letter of 20^[h?] Feby[1] this day-week,[2] and the same day a New York paper appeared in town, mentioning your appointment in place of M^rHarrison of whose resignation M^rJohnston ˄had informed you. I had therefore no doubt but the paper published at the seat of Congress, and made probable by your own letters told the truth. I did I confess, and I think not unreasonably, suppose that you were appointed through the agency of M^rJohnston; but I am much better pleased to find that the President acted spontaneously, and that he had the unanimous approbation of the Senate ...

ARS (Nc-Ar, Charles E. Johnson Collection). Endorsed "Ans^d."
    1. Letter not found.
    2. The same day a week before. *OED*, under entry for "Day."

Silas Cooke to James Iredell —————————————————————————
March 15, 1790   New Bern, North Carolina

... We desire you to accept our very sincere congratulations, on your Accession to the appointment of Associate Justice, the Unanimous Voice of the Senate on an Occasion so interesting, not only reflects the most merited Honor on your self, but is to your friends a very sensible pleasure. [*Cooke concludes by asking for Iredell's aid in Cooke's efforts to be appointed clerk for the federal court in North Carolina.*]

ARS (NcD, James Iredell Sr. and Jr. Papers).
    Silas Cooke (born ca. 1754) was the clerk of the North Carolina Superior Court for the district of New Bern. Cooke took over the clerkship from his brother in 1782. *DAR Patriot Index;* Walter Clark, ed., *The State Records of North Carolina,* 16 vols. [numbered 11-26] (Winston, Goldsboro, and Charlotte, 1895-1906), 20:248; *PJI,* 2:3, 363-64.

Samuel Johnston to James Iredell ————————————————
March 18, 1790   New York, New York

...I am very much obliged to you for your Letter of the third[1] which has this moment come to hand, and am very glad to know that you have got your Commission and pray that you may live & keep your health long to enjoy it, I am told that the Southern Circuit is assigned to you and M[r] Rutledge for this time[.] it is expected that the Judges will take it in Rotation. it is not necessary that you should write to the Senate, it will be sufficient that you write to the President, Maj[r] Butler & Col[o]Hawkins ...

ARS (NcD, James Iredell Sr. and Jr. Papers). Addressed "Edenton."
   1. Letter not found.

Joseph Blount to James Iredell ————————————————
March 24, 1790   Edenton, North Carolina

Edenton   March 24th 1790

Sir

We received your very polite letter of the 22[d1] informing us of your late appointment as one of the Associate Justices of the supreme Court of the United States. We congratulate you on the event, and most sincerely applaud the choice of our President, who has very justly attested the preeminence of your merit;

We cannot help expressing how much we regret the loss of a Gentleman of the Bar of your abilities and integrity, and assuring you that the many important services you have rendered to this County will long remain impressed on our minds. if you have experienced at any time the politeness and regard of this Court, it is with pleasure we acknowledge that no person ever deserved it more

These are our sentiments and they are dictated by truth.

We can only add our sincere wishes for your health and happiness.

By order of the Worshipfull Court

Jos. Blount Clerk

Honorable James Iredell Esquire

ARS (Nc-Ar, Charles E. Johnson Collection). Endorsed "Ans[d]."
   Joseph Blount (1755-1794), clerk of the court for Chowan County, had served in the state legislature in 1782 and later held several civil appointments. *DAR Patriot Index;* J. R. B. Hathaway, ed., *The North Carolina Historical and Genealogical Register,* 3 vols. (1900-1903; reprint ed., Baltimore: Genealogical Publishing, 1970), 1:523-24; Cheney, *North Carolina Government,* p. 209; Clark, *State Records of North Carolina,* 24:455, 502, 736, 737. (Blount is identified as the clerk of the court for Chowan County in the endorsement on this letter to James Iredell.)
   1. Letter not found.

John Hay to James Iredell ————————————————————
March 24, 1790   Fayetteville, North Carolina

... A Letter from Mr Maclaine of the 19th informs me of Your appointment as one of the Judges of the Circuit Court. on this occasion I congratulate Yourself and the People to whom You are to dispense justice _ ...

ARS (Nc-Ar, Charles E. Johnson Collection). Addressed "Edenton." Endorsed "Ansd."

An Irish-born attorney from Fayetteville, North Carolina, John Hay represented Fayetteville in the North Carolina legislature in 1790. James Iredell stayed with Hay when Iredell was in Fayetteville. Samuel A. Ashe, ed., *Biographical History of North Carolina from Colonial Times to the Present,* 8 vols. (Greensboro: Charles L. Van Noppen, 1905-1917), 6:267-73.

John Tucker, Sr., to [Paine Wingate] ————————————————
March 27, 1790   Newbury, Massachusetts

... I intended, long before now, to have acknowledged your kind Favor of the 3d of Feby last,[1] which gave me the first Intelligence of my Son's Appointment to the Clerkship of the Supreme federal Court, but my health has been so poor, & my Spirits so low in the past winter, that I have Scarcely been capable of any Exertion, which must apologize for my neglect, and for the Barrenness of this.

I have not Seen my Son Since he returned from N. York, and am, as yet, uncertain whether he accepts of his Appointment. _ It depends, I believe, on his knowing what Support he may depend upon. If the Clerk is to have a fixt Salary, I Suppose the Quantum, will be determined by Congress, in which case I cannot doubt your using your Influence in his favor, So far as prudence & Equity will permit.

I cannot Say I like his going So far from us as N. York whatever may be his Emoluments, but Should be much better pleased would our genl Court make reasonable Provision for him in his present Office;[2] but I leave the Affair to a wise and overruling Providence. ...

ARS (MH-H, bMS Am 1198(97)). The card catalog at Houghton Library, Harvard University, notes in brackets that Paine Wingate was the recipient of this letter. The contents of the letter make Wingate a possible candidate because he was in New York at the right time and was a senator with the sort of influence John Tucker was seeking. A comparison of the endorsement on this letter with other examples of Wingate's handwriting makes the attribution probable.

John Tucker, Sr. (1719-1792), father of the first clerk appointed by the Supreme Court, was the minister of the First Congregational Church of Newbury, Massachusetts. Clifford K. Shipton, *Sibley's Harvard Graduates,* vol. 11, *1741-1745* (Boston: Massachusetts Historical Society, 1960), pp. 78-89.

1. Letter not found.

2. John Tucker, Jr., despite appointment as clerk of the Supreme Court, continued to be clerk of the Massachusetts Supreme Judicial Court.

James Iredell to Henry E. McCulloh ─────────────
March 31, 1790 [Edenton, North Carolina]

. . . I hope you will excuse my forbearing to write to you so long. The truth is I thought it probable that I should have offered to me (tho' I made not the least solicitation for that or any other Office) the place of District Judge, ~~under the United States~~ for this State, and under this [cert?] uncertainty I [*letters inked out*] felt an embarrassment about ~~answering your question~~ writing to you on

here
the subject of your Debts ~~in this State~~, which involved ~~you~~ questions of a most important & delicate nature on which I wished to keep my mind as unbiased

and
as possible ~~and~~ ^ At[1] the same time I was unwilling to mention that I had expectations which might be never realised. My expectations in that particular have not been exactly answered, but I have been promoted, beyond my most sanguine hopes, to the appointment of one of the Associate Justices of the S. C. of the U. S. which the President was pleased to confer upon me, with the unanimous consent of the Senate. This high honour is accompanied with severe duty, but it places me in a more desirable & independent situation, the office being held during good behaviour, & the salary 3500 Dollars a year, which ~~(by the Constitution)~~ cannot be lessened during my continuance in office. The first intimation I had of this great distinction being in contemplation for me was in a letter from Mr Johnston, wherein he mentioned that he had just received a message from the President by Major Jackson to know if he thought I would accept of that appointment, & signifying his intention to nominate me to it. In consequence of this change in my situation, I am resolved to remove my Family & settle altogether in New York which will be more convenient for me in other respects as well as extremely desirable on account of my Family's health. You will therefore be pleased to give me what direc-

your
tions you think proper in regard to ~~my~~ ^ affairs in my hands, as it will be utterly impossible for me to do any thing in them for the future. . . .

ADf (Nc-Ar, Charles E. Johnson Collection). Place determined by reference to contemporary James Iredell letters in the Charles E. Johnson Collection, Nc-Ar.

Henry Eustace McCulloh (ca. 1737-ca. 1810), James Iredell's cousin, had held several appointments in North Carolina during the colonial period, among them collector of the port of Roanoke (including Edenton), a post which he transferred to Iredell. After McCulloh returned to England, he served as the colony's agent. McCulloh inherited vast landholdings in North Carolina from his father, and Iredell handled legal affairs relating to the land. William S. Powell, ed., *The Correspondence of William Tryon and Other Selected Papers*, 2 vols. (Raleigh: Division of Archives and History, Department of Cultural Resources, 1980), 1:641; *PJI*, 1:xxxvii, xlviii-xlix.

1. The "A" is written over a lowercase "a."

Abraham Baldwin to Joel Barlow
April 7, 1790 New York, New York

. . . Iredil of North Carolina [*has been*] appointed in the place of old Mr. Harrison resigned. The supreme court sat here in Feb[y] four Judges and the attorney general quondam[1] Gov[r] Randolph attended, Rutledge & Iredil were not here.[2] There is little business but to organise themselves and let folks look on and see they are ready to work at them, the same new government has got some long roots down deep in the soil, I think it will stand a blow bye and bye. . . .

AR (CtY, Abraham Baldwin Papers). Endorsed "R[d] 28 May."

    1. Latin for "formerly."

    2. James Iredell was in North Carolina at the time he was commissioned on February 10, the last day that the Court met in February.

James Iredell to John Jay
April 8, 1790 Edenton, North Carolina

. . . I had not the pleasure of receiving your very obliging letter of the 10th March, till this day, owing to a mistake in the letter being forwarded to Newbern, which is near 100 miles to the southward of this Town, where I reside. The great honour of having so important an office conferred upon me is enhanced in a most agreeable manner by your kind expressions on the occasion, for which I beg leave to return my best thanks, and I shall think myself happy indeed if I can be so fortunate as to secure the continuance of your good opinion, and recommend myself to the approbation of the ^other^ very respectable Gentlemen with whom I have the honour to be joined.

   . . .

Highly sensible of the flattering distinction you shew me, by expressing a desire to make New York personally agreeable to me, & for which I feel sincere gratitude,

I have the honour to be with great respect, Sir, Your most obedient and most humble Servant

Ja. Iredell

ADfS (Nc-Ar, Charles E. Johnson Collection).

James Iredell to John Rutledge
April 9, 1790 Edenton, North Carolina

. . . This high appointment was as much beyond my expectations, as I fear it is above my merit. But I have every inducement which a Man can have to endeavour, by every means in my power, to render myself more and more worthy of it, not only in consideration of the weighty trust attending it, but from the very respectable characters of the Gentlemen with whom I have the honour to be joined. I assure you, Sir, it shall be my constant and anxious aim to recommend myself to your approbation and that of the other Judges of the Court. . . .

ADfS (NcD, James Iredell Sr. and Jr. Papers). Addressed "Charleston."

Samuel Spencer to James Iredell
April 9, 1790 Hillsborough, North Carolina

Hillsborough, 9ᵗʰ of April, 1790.

Dear Sir,

I had the Pleasure of reading your polite Note to the Judges,[1] by Mʳ Blair,[2] to whom we have given a Superior Court Licence. I have the Pleasure to think that his obtaining this Privilege so early in Life will be satisfactory to you, and I have no Doubt but upon further Application to the Study of the Law, he will do credit to the Bar.

I sincerely congratulate you on your Appointment to the very honorable and important Trust of one of the Associate Judges of the Supreme Court of the Nation. I have had the Pleasure of your Company on the Bench, and at the Bar for a Series of Years past, and have enjoyed many agreeable Hours in your Company. I cannot but regret the Loss of your Company for the future, and the real Loss the Bar must necessarily sustain in Consequence of your promotion. But I have the Consolation to think, that these Lossess will be amply compensated by the Benefit to the Public, and the Emolument to you, that will thereby accrue.

I am, Dear Sir, with very great   Respect, your very obedient,   humble Servant,

Samˡ Spencer

The Honᵇˡᵉ
James Iredell Esquire.

ARS (Nc-Ar, Charles E. Johnson Collection). Addressed "Edenton." Marked "Honᵈ by William Blair Esquire." Endorsed "Ansᵈ." James Iredell's answering letter not found.

1. James Iredell's letter to the judges of the Superior Court has not been found. Samuel Spencer was a judge on this court, the highest tribunal in North Carolina.

2. William Blair, James Iredell's nephew, had been appointed clerk of the North Carolina Superior Court for the Edenton district on November 17, 1787. Hathaway, *North Carolina Historical and Genealogical Register,* 2:458, 305.

Samuel Ashe to James Iredell ⸺⸺⸺⸺⸺⸺⸺⸺⸺⸺⸺⸺⸺⸺
April 10, 1790 Hillsborough, North Carolina

Hillsbor: Apʳ 10ᵗʰ 1790

Dear Sir,

Your polite favʳ of the 31ˢᵗ March,[1] informing us (the Judges) of your late appointment, was handed me by Mʳ Blair⸺[2] I am at once affected with different Sensations upon the occasion⸺ in the same instant, I rejoice & am Sad; in the moment that I regret your leaving us, & am Sensible of the loss we shall sustain; I am pleased that you are appointed to an office of such dignity & importance⸺ wᶜʰ I am sure you will fill, with reputation to yʳSelf, and the fullest Satisfaction to the public⸺ While you Sit, every Jealousy & fear will Subside, & every apprehension of encrochment from the newly erected Jurisdiction will cease⸺ from Mʳ Blair I understand, that yᵉ set off[3] immediately upon yʳ Southern Circuit, and that at your return, you mean to embark with Mʳˢ Iredel & family for New York; there to reside;⸺ in that case I despair of the pleasure of ever seeing you again, for my Glass is nearly run out, and before your 2ⁿᵈ Circuit this way, will take place, probably will be intirely exhausted⸺ but however that may be, be assured my dear Sir, that while I have the Power, I shall not cease to put up, my fervant & best Wishes for you⸺ Adieu my dear Sir, I had almost said forever⸺ May God have you in his favour & protection and every felicity attend you is the sincere Wish of

Yʳ ObᵗhˡServᵗ &c &c

Samˡ Ashe

James Iredell Esqʳ

ARS (Nc-Ar, Charles E. Johnson Collection). Addressed "Edenton." Marked as "Favᵈ by Mʳ Blair." Endorsed "Ansᵈ." James Iredell's answering letter not found.

Samuel Ashe (1725-1813) was the presiding judge of the Superior Court of North Carolina. One of the leading lawyers in the state, Ashe was appointed to the bench in December, 1777, along with James Iredell and Samuel Spencer. Ashe remained on the Superior Court until 1795 when he became governor. He served three one-year terms as governor. *DAB;* Clark, *State Records of North Carolina,* 11:825.

1. Letter not found.
2. William Blair.
3. Samuel Ashe wrote "set off" over a previously written phrase that is illegible. The earlier phrasing was preceded by "yᵉ," which Ashe did not alter to "you" when he changed the wording.

John Haywood to James Iredell ⸺⸺⸺⸺⸺⸺⸺⸺⸺⸺⸺⸺⸺⸺
April 10, 1790 Hillsborough, North Carolina

. . . To the congratulations of those of your friends who wish you best, you will permit me to ask, that mine may be added; and notwithstanding I am well aware of the multiplicity of business in which your late appointment and the necessary domestic arrangements preparatory to your leaving Edenton must have involved you, I will just trespass on your time to request, that you will be assured I am not only pleased, exceedingly pleased, that this unsolicitted distinction hath fallen to your lot, but that you will do me but justice in placing me in the number of those of your acquaintance who most sincerely rejoice and who experience the most heartfelt gladness on the occasion. _ that the fatiegues of the appointment may not injure your health, and that it may prove a source of profit and Happiness to you is my most sincere and cordial Wish.

. . .

ARS (NcD, James Iredell Sr. and Jr. Papers).
 John Haywood (1762-1826) of Halifax County, North Carolina. Haywood was a self-educated lawyer whose talents were well-respected. In 1785 the General Assembly elected Haywood to be judge of a court on the western frontier; he declined the offer. He was elected solicitor general of North Carolina in December, 1790. A year later, he became the state's attorney general, and in 1793 he was appointed a justice of the North Carolina Superior Court. Severely criticized for accepting a fee as a defense counsel in a major fraud case to be argued before the Superior Court, Haywood resigned in 1800 and returned to private practice. In 1807 he moved to Tennessee, and from 1816 until his death he served on the bench of the Supreme Court of Tennessee. *DAB*.

Alfred Moore to James Iredell
April 10, 1790 Hillsborough, North Carolina

Hillsboro 10ᵗʰ of April 1790
My Dʳ Sir
 I have to acknowledge the favour of two letters from you,[1] neither of which I had an opportunity to answer sooner_
 The event which has removed you from us is too honorable to be spoken of with regret[.] I hope you will believe me sincere when I assure you that every piece of good fortune that attends you will add to my happiness. What is in my power shall be done to make your situation easy with respect to your clients. I am very glad to learn that you are in health & that your family also is well_
 I am Dʳ very sincerely yours

A Moore

ARS (MeHi, J. S. H. Fogg Collection). Addressed "Edenton." Marked as "by favʳ of Mʳ Blair."
Endorsed "Ansᵈ." James Iredell's answering letter not found.
 1. Neither letter found.

John Brown Cutting to William Short ―――――――――――
April 23, 1790 London, England

... The President has appointed the officers in North Carolina ― also a Mr Iredell whose name I never before heard or saw ― an associate Judge in the place of Judge Harrison of Maryland ― I know not to what state he belongs. ―
...

ARS (DLC, William Short Papers).
    William Short (1759-1849), a Virginia-trained lawyer and intimate friend of Thomas Jefferson, accompanied Jefferson to France in 1784 as his secretary. Short remained in Paris after Jefferson's departure in 1789 and was named chargé d'affaires in June, 1789. Short later served in diplomatic posts in Spain and at The Hague. Wilson and Fiske, *Appletons' Cyclopædia of American Biography;* Dumas Malone, *Jefferson and His Time,* vol. 2, *Jefferson and the Rights of Man* (Boston: Little, Brown, 1951), pp. 8, 235, 258, 401, 405, 407, 411; *PTJ,* 7:148-49, 235-37; 15:202; 16:395-96.

Arthur Iredell to James Iredell ―――――――――――――
May 5, 1790 London, England

... You will do me the Justice, my dear Brother, to believe that I sympathized most cordially, upon reading your Letter of the 3^d of March,[1] in the Feelings you must have had when you wrote It. So flattering a Testimony to your merits, and so dignified & substantial a Reward of them, may well be supposed to have elated a mind that, like your's, is the least sensible to It's own Claims. It has made me, who can only shine with a reflected Light, extremely vain. I have always had Reason to be proud of my near Connection with you; but I have now, for the first time, occasion to triumph in your Success! That you will justify the Choice that has been made, arduous as your new Situation undoubtedly is, in an infant Government, more especially, I have not the slightest Doubt. My warm Wishes, and earnest Prayers are directed to another Object, to the Duration of a Life, highly valuable to your Family, but much, infinitely more so to a growing State, whose Laws you will assist in forming, whose Justice you will represent, and whose Happiness, in each Way, you will considerably promote. The Value of such a Life will soon be felt at the remotest Corners of that vast Continent over which you now judicially preside, and Millions will join with me in my Prayer! ― That It will be favorably heard by Him, under whose good Providence you may be instrumental to the greatest Ends, I am disposed to believe. And may I, at some future time, to which I shall not cease to look forward with the most lively Hope, see you, my dear James, in a Situation I deem the most enviable, administering equal Justice to all, but tempering Justice with Mercy. I would rather be a Judge, whose Ermine is not soiled by the Filth of Corruption or Partiality, or died in the Blood of unnecessary Victims, than the greatest Potentate upon Earth. You will be that Judge, my Brother, and you will perfect the Character with an Ability exceeded only by your Virtues. Can you pardon so just a Tribute to your Character?— You may as it comes from me. I did not mean to tell you what I have long felt; but the Tears of Joy which I now shed would witness, if you were present, to the Emotions of my Heart. My Mother has contributed to them by her Feeling when I communicated the Contents of your Letter to her— But I must have done with the Subject for the present; for it has taken a Turn which quite overpowers me.

I shall be impatient to learn what your last Plans have been. Do you settle your Family in New York? ...

ARS (Nc-Ar, Charles E. Johnson Collection). Addressed "Edenton   North Carolina   N° America." Marked "By the   New York Packet." Endorsed "Ans^d."
    Arthur Iredell (1758-1804), James Iredell's brother, was an Anglican minister in England. *PJI*, 1:36n.
    1. Letter not found.

Arthur Iredell to James Iredell
June 1, 1790 Guildford, England

... I had a few Days since the Pleasure [of] receiving your kind Letter of the 17th [April?]¹ confirming the good news a former one [*phrase missing*] me of your very honorable [Promotion to a?] Seat on the Bench of the Supreme C[ourt. I] wrote a few hasty Lines by the last [*word missing*] to congratulate you on this Event, and [*phrase missing*] fervently repeat my warmest Wishes [*word missing*] the Continuance of a Life that is become so [valua?]ble to that vast Continen! Your [r]emoval to New York is an Event particularly [pleas?]ing to my Mind, for It has always been prejudiced against Edenton on acc^t of It's Climate, Its unfavorable Communications between [It?] and this Country, and, in short, I had a thousand Objections against that Province which do [not?] at all affect New York, the Place of [*word missing*] [than?] I could most have wished you to remove[.] ...

ARS (Nc-Ar, Charles E. Johnson Collection). Addressed "to the Care of   The Honble Samuel Johnston   Member of the Senate of the United States   New York   America." Marked "By the   New York Packet." Endorsed "Ans^d." James Iredell's answering letter not found. One side of this letter is torn, accounting for several missing passages and conjectural readings that have been placed in brackets.
    1. Letter not found.

George Washington to the Marquis de Lafayette
June 3, 1790 New York, New York

... Many of your old acquaintances and Friends are concerned with me in the Administration of this Government.— By having Mr Jefferson at the Head of the Department of State, Mr Jay of the Judiciary, Hamilton of the Treasury and Knox of that of War, I feel myself supported by able Co-adjutors, who harmonise extremely well together. I believe that these and the other appointments generally have given perfect satisfaction to the Public. Poor Col? Harrison, who was appointed one of the Judges of the Supreme Court, and declined, is lately dead.[1] . . .

Lb (DLC, George Washington Papers); Df (DNA, RG 59, Miscellaneous Letters). Addressed "Paris."

In 1790 the Marquis de Lafayette (1757-1834) was a representative to the French National Assembly and commander of the Paris National Guard. *Encyclopedia Britannica*, 15th ed., entry for Lafayette.

1. The Marquis de Lafayette first met Alexander Hamilton and Henry Knox in August, 1777, when he came to George Washington's headquarters outside of Philadelphia; he probably met Robert Hanson Harrison on the same occasion. Hamilton, with whom Lafayette formed a strong friendship, was an aide-de-camp to Washington; Knox was an artillery general; and Harrison was Washington's secretary. Lafayette did not meet Thomas Jefferson until April, 1781, when Jefferson was governor of Virginia, and Lafayette was in Richmond in command of American forces. Lafayette admired Jefferson, and this first meeting began a fifty-year friendship, which deepened when Jefferson was stationed in Paris during the 1780s. Lafayette, who had corresponded with John Jay when Jay was president of the Continental Congress, became friendly with Jay when Jay was one of the peace commissioners in Paris in 1782. Louis Gottschalk, *Lafayette Joins the American Army* (Chicago: University of Chicago Press, 1937), pp. 26-33; James Thomas Flexner, *The Young Hamilton: A Biography* (Boston: Little, Brown, 1978), pp. 315-16; Gilbert Chinard, ed., *The Letters of Lafayette and Jefferson* (Baltimore: Johns Hopkins University Press, 1929), pp. xiii, 9; Malone, *Jefferson and the Rights of Man*, pp. 41-45; *PJJ*, 1:597-601; 2:12.

Pierce Butler to James Iredell —————————————————————
July 5, 1790   New York, New York

. . . If my little interest has been instrumental in placing you where you will do honor to the recommendation, and render so essential service to the country, my feelings are more highly gratified than I will venture to express. In paying a tribute to sincere friendship, I have at the same time not only discharged my public duty, but served the United States.

May you live long, my dear Sir, to enjoy the honorable station, where the unanimous voice of such of your fellow-citizens as had a right to a voice on the occasion has placed you, is my ardent wish. . . .

Pr (Printed in *MJI,* 2:291-92).

Henry E. McCulloh to James Iredell ————————————————————
August 1, 1790   London, England

. . . I am to acknowledge you fav. of the 9[:?] of March,[1] & congratulate you, on your Appointment. _ I shall certainly not enter into the mention of any matter that may be incompatible with your present Situation. _ . . .

ARS (NcD, James Iredell Sr. and Jr. Papers). Addressed "To the Care of Sam! Johnston Esq?
New York." Marked "φ Aug! Pac! 1790." Postmarked "AU 4 90."
    1. Letter not found.

Gazette of the United States ——————————————————————————
August 4, 1790   New York, New York

On Monday last the Supreme Court of the United States met at the Exchange, in this city_ Present, his honor Chief Justice *Jay*, associate Judges,
their honors *James Wilson, William Cushing, John Blair* and *James Iredell*, Esquires; Hon. *E. Randolph*, Esq. Attorney General. Adjourned till yesterday_
when the Court again met, and adjourned till January[1] next.[2]
    Hon. *Richard Bassett* and *John Vining* Esq. of the State of Delaware, and
Barnabas Bidwell, Esq. of the State of Connecticut, were admitted Counsellors
of the Supreme Court of the United States.

(New York) August 4, 1790. Date and place from the item headline.
    The *Federal Gazette* (Philadelphia) reprinted this in full on August 6, 1790, and the *Newport
Mercury* (Newport, Rhode Island) did so on August 16, 1790.
    The *Columbian Centinel* (Boston), August 11, 1790, printed a short report on the Court's August
term, but it did not include any new information.
    1. Should be February.
    2. The *New-Hampshire Gazette* (Portsmouth) of August 19, 1790, did not print the next para-
graph.

"Junius" to Thomas Adams ——————————————————————
Independent Chronicle
September 23, 1790   Boston, Massachusetts

MR. ADAMS
From the peculiar intricacy of the acts of Congress, it is evident, that a large
proportion of the Members are in a *"professional line,"* which makes it for their
interest to keep up as great a degree of law perplexity, as possible. The funding
bill is so complex, that but few can understand it.[1] A law, on which depends
the property of a great proportion of our citizens, is enveloped in mistery.
    The lenghty act relating to "sailors in the merchant's service," is calculated
to puzzle both owners, masters and mariners.[2]
    But not only laws, too intricate to be understood, are enacted, but it is
equally alarming to find so many Members of Congress, sworn into the Federal
Court, at its first sitting in New York.[3] The question then is, whether it is
proper that Congress should consist of so large a proportion of Members, who
are sworn Attornies in the Federal Courts; or whether it is prudent to trust
men to *enact laws*, who are *practising on them*, in another department;_ Le[t]
common sense answer.

If Congress does consist of practising Attornies, the laws enacted, may in a great measure, depend on the particular causes such individuals may have to manage in the judiciary; this being the case, the property of the people may in a few years, become the sport of Law-makers acting in the capacity of *interested Attornies.* _

JUNIUS.

(Boston) September 23, 1790. Date and place are those of the newspaper. Bracketed reading has been supplied because type did not imprint.

Thomas Adams was the publisher of the Boston *Independent Chronicle.* Brigham, *American Newspapers,* 1:307.

1. "An Act making provision for the [payment of the] Debt of the United States," August 4, 1790. *Stat.,* 1:138.

2. "An Act for the government and regulation of Seamen in the merchants service," July 20, 1790. *Stat.,* 1:131.

3. Of the twenty-seven lawyers admitted to the Supreme Court bar during the Court's first term in February, 1790, nine were congressmen (Fisher Ames, Elias Boudinot, Thomas Hartley, Egbert Benson, James Jackson, John Laurance, Theodore Sedgwick, William Smith, and George Thatcher) and one, William Paterson, was a senator. By the time of "Junius's" letter, two more congressmen had joined the bar: Senator Richard Bassett and Congressman John Vining. Both were admitted at the Court's August 1790 term. James R. Perry and James M. Buchanan, "Admission to the Supreme Court Bar, 1790-1800: A Case Study of Institutional Change," *Supreme Court Historical Society Yearbook* (1983), p. 11; *BDAC.*

John Brownrigg to James Iredell ————————————————
October 18, 1790   Dublin, Ireland

N° 23 Stephens Green Dublin   Oct^br 18th 1790
My Dear Sir

I have to return you many thanks for your favor of the 29 April[1] nothing could have given me more Pleasure then the hearing of you being appointed one of the Judges of the Supreme Court of the United States,[2] I am sure that our wrothy[3] and esteemed President could not have made a choice more to the Wish of every one who know your merit, Tho' you are Percluded from acting as my Attorney,[4] your advice as a Friend to the rest of my attornies will be acknowledged as a Favor By My Dear Sir your much Obliged
Sincere H^ble Ser^nt

Jno Brownrigg

ARS (Nc-Ar, Charles E. Johnson Collection). Addressed "Edenton   North Carolina." This address was crossed out and replaced with "Philadelphia." Endorsed "Ans^d." James Iredell's answering letter not found.

John Brownrigg's father, Richard Brownrigg, had owned a fishery near Edenton, North Carolina. John Brownrigg had inherited part of his father's estate. At this time John Brownrigg was living in Dublin, Ireland. Hathaway, *North Carolina Historical and Genealogical Register,* 1:530; 2:257-58; *PJI,* 1:33n.

1. Letter not found.

2. On October 12, 1790, John Brownrigg had written "I was made very happy when looking over Some American Papers by seeing your appointment as one of our Judges for North Carolina." Charles E. Johnson Collection, Nc-Ar.

3. I.e., worthy. In his letter of October 12, 1790, to James Iredell, John Brownrigg had written this correctly. Charles E. Johnson Collection, Nc-Ar.

4. John Brownrigg had earlier requested James Iredell to act as his attorney, a request which he repeated in his letter of October 12, 1790. Charles E. Johnson Collection, Nc-Ar.

Federal Gazette
February 5, 1791   Philadelphia, Pennsylvania

The Supreme Court of the United States will be opened in this city on Monday next.

(Philadelphia) February 5, 1791. Date and place are from item headline.

Joseph Anderson to George Washington
February [8-25], 1791   [Philadelphia, Pennsylvania?]

[*Anderson applies to be nominated as a judge of the Territory of the United States south of the Ohio River. In support of his application, he sends to George Washington*] a Certificate of my Admission as a Councellor at Law in the Supreme Court of the United States[1] . . .

ARS (DLC, George Washington Papers). This letter can be dated approximately by Joseph Anderson's reference to his admission to the Supreme Court bar (February 8, 1791) and by his application to be a judge in the Territory of the United States south of the Ohio, a nomination made by President George Washington on February 25, 1791. *SEJ*, 1:76-77. Place suggested by reference to contemporary Joseph Anderson letters in the George Washington Papers, DLC.

For identification of Joseph Anderson, see "Fine Minutes" under date of February 8, 1791.

1. This is the only reference discovered to such a certificate issued to a Supreme Court bar member. There is no evidence that the Court gave such certificates to all lawyers admitted. Most likely, Joseph Anderson had requested such certification for the purpose of enclosing it as part of his application to be appointed a territorial judge.

Clement Biddle to George Lewis
February 8, 1791   Philadelphia, Pennsylvania

. . . Altho' hurried beyond measure for two days past by my attendance on Court which is now over, I have not been inattentive to your business, tho' I had no time to write. . . .

ALbS (PHi, Clement Biddle Letterbook, 1789-1792).

Possibly George Lewis (1757-1821), a Virginia planter, merchant, and nephew of George

Washington. Richard A. Harrison, *Princetonians: A Biographical Dictionary*, vol. 2, *1769-1775* (Princeton: Princeton University Press, 1980), pp. 498-502.

Edward Burd to Jasper Yeates
February 8, 1791   Philadelphia, Pennsylvania

. . . The Supreme Court of the United States opened on Monday the 7th Inst. in which Chief Justice Jay and Judges Cushing, Wilson and Iredell sat. A number of ye Gentlemen of ye Bar of this City attended at their Lodgings and escorted them to the State House. The Court opened but there was no Business done.

The Gentlemen of the Bar applied for admission but a Rule of the Court stood in their way, which made it necessary previously to their Admission that they had practised in the Supreme Court of the State three years, and that they had good Moral Characters, and possessed good legal Abilities. I obviated the first Objection by my Certificate of their Admission in ye Supreme Court.

The Court took then as Evidence of ye latter Qualities, that Mr. Wilcocks was Recorder of the City: Mr. Bradford was Attorney General of ye State; Mr. Lewis was Attorney for ye District; Mr. Fisher was vouched for by Mr. Wilson, with apparent Reluctance as against his wishes to do it for any one. Mr. Sergeant proposed that as Mr. Fisher was admitted. He should vouch for ye rest of ye Bar, but ye Chief Justice said that they had determined that one lawyer should not vouch for another. However he remarked that Mr. Sergeant had been Attorney General which was an Evidence of his good Character and legal Ability, and therefore he was admitted. Mr. Ingersoll was then proposed, and Mr. Randolph stated to ye Court that he had been a Member of Congress, and of ye Federal Convention. Chief Justice Jay observed that he might be a very good Member of Congress, and yet no Lawyer. Mr. Ingersoll then formally withdrew his application for Admission till another period.

After a little while Mr. Wilson said that it was from no difficulty about either that Gentleman's Character or legal Ability, for every body knew that if he said any thing about him, he must have said that he was one of ye most eminent at ye Bar. He was admitted without any Renewal of his Application; and Mr. Jay also paid him some Compliments.

So many difficulties occurring the rest of the Bar declined bringing forward their Applications, having expected that from Mr. Wilson's knowledge of them, every thing might have been made easy.

The Court then adjourned till One o'clock, when the proper Certificates having been provided all who applied were admitted.

The Bar thought they might have been treated with a little more delicacy by a Gentleman who knew them all intimately. However I do not think that he meant any Offence to them, but merely adopted the Rule of discriminating between the deserving and undeserving of ye profession. It seems he might have acted with more fortitude if he had declared his good Opinion of some, and called for Certificates only as to such whom he did not know particularly;— or if he had positively refused to declare his opinion respecting any of ye profession without written Evidence.[1]

Pr (Printed in Lewis Burd Walker, ed., *The Burd Papers: Selections from Letters Written by Edward Burd, 1763-1828* (Pottsville, Pa.: Standard Publishing, 1899), pp. 168-70).

Jasper Yeates (1745-1817), a prominent Pennsylvania lawyer, was Edward Burd's brother-in-law. Both Yeates and Burd had studied law with Burd's uncle, Edward Shippen. In March, 1791, Yeates was appointed an associate justice of the Pennsylvania Supreme Court and served on the bench until his death. *DAB;* Randolph Shipley Klein, *Portrait of an Early American Family: The Shippens of Pennsylvania Across Five Generations* (Philadelphia: University of Pennsylvania Press, 1975), pp. 141-45.

1. For further discussion of this incident, see the headnote to "Admission to the Bar."

John Blair to Samuel Meredith
February 9, 1791 Williamsburg, Virginia

[*Blair instructs Samuel Meredith, treasurer of the United States, in the disbursement of funds from his salary.*] I expected to have settled with you in Philadelphia; but sickness has detained me til too late to go on— . . .

ARS (ViU, Walter R. Benjamin Collection). Addressed "Philadelphia—." Postmarked "WILLIAMS.B.G   FEBY 9."

Jacob Read to George Washington
February 10, 1791 Columbia, South Carolina

South Carolina
Columbia   10th February 1791—

Sir/

The Legislature of this state having at this Present Session Elected the Honorable John Rutledge (with his Consent) to the office of Chief Justice of the State and his Seat having thereby become vacant on the federal bench— I humbly presume to offer my self to your notice as a Candidate for that important Trust

I beg leave to assure your Excellency that 'tis with the utmost diffidence I come forth on this occasion— But if a regular Education in this Country and in Britain— a very Extensive practice in all the Courts of Law and Equity for many Years in this state— a Constant attention from the Year 1768 to the Courts of Law and Law readings— and the flattery of having been employed by my Country for a Series of Years past in several very important Offices & Trusts afford me any just Grounds of Confidence in my own Judgment and abilities I hope I shall not appear very presumptuous in thus presenting my self to public Notice

If I have the Honour to meet Your Excellency's nomination & the Senate's approbation I shall with pleasure devote my whole time to the Execution of the duties assigned me and make a faithful Exertion of my best abilities for the service of my Country

Possessed of some fortune and not having a large family to provide for I had determined very soon to relinquish the Lucrative but Laborious duties of my professional practice and if in my retirement I can be useful to my Country it will afford me more pleasure and Satisfaction than any other Consideration & I with truth add that the Emoluments of the office I now aspire to are no Inducement

I have one further request to make which is that your Excellency will be so good as not to mention this application from me to yourself, but shou'd I meet your approbation I pray that the nomination may Come as if from Yourself

I do not at present know of any Competitors— doubtless I shall have some— Coud I be informed who they were and shou'd they be persons whose Legal Knowledge, abilities and Standing in the Courts of Law I thought Superiour to my own— I shou'd with pleasure relinquish all pretensions to your favour or my Countrys notice in the present Instance

I have at several times been flattered with the Intreaties of my friends and many very reputable Citizens to take a seat on the bench of this State— but I declined that Honour as being an office little less Laborious than the practice of the Courts I am about to decline and which wou'd Confine me to a Constant residence in this State

I beg leave to tender my most respectful Compliments to Mrs Washington and intreat that your Excellency will accept my best Wishes for your health and happiness

I am with very great respect and regard   Your Excellencys most obedient and most faithful Servant.

Jacob Read

His Excellency
The President of the
   United States.

ARS (DNA, RG 59, Miscellaneous Letters).

Jacob Read (1752-1816), a Charleston attorney, began his political career in 1782 with election to the South Carolina House of Representatives. Read was in the General Assembly from 1782 to 1794 and served as speaker of the South Carolina House of Representatives from 1789 to 1794. In national politics, Read represented South Carolina at the Confederation Congress from 1783 to 1785 and was elected to the United States Senate in December, 1794. During his term in the Senate (1795-1801), Read voted for the Jay Treaty but also supported John Rutledge's nomination as chief justice of the Supreme Court. Bailey and Cooper, *Biographical Directory of the South Carolina House of Representatives*, 3:597-99.

Gazette of the United States ————————————————————————
February 23, 1791   Philadelphia, Pennsylvania

Names of the Counsellors and Attornies in the Supreme Court of the United States,
admitted and sworn at Philadelphia, Feb. 1791.

COUNSELLORS.

William Lewis, William Bradford, jun. Alexander Wilcocks, Miers Fisher,
Jonathan D. Sergeant, Jared Ingersoll, Edward Tilghman, James Monroe, Ed-
ward Burd, William Barton, Moses Levy, John F. Mifflin, Charles Heatley,
William Rawle, Jasper Moylan, A. I. Dallas, Thomas Leaming, jun. Peter S.
Du Ponceau, John Todd, jun. Joseph B. M'Kean, Joseph Henderson, and Ben-
jamin Chew, jun. Esquires, of *Pennsylvania.*
  Luther Martin, Esq. of *Maryland.*
  Hon. Alexander White, of *Virginia.*
  Hon. Samuel Johnston, of *North-Carolina.*

ATTORNIES.

John Caldwell, and Benj. R. Morgan, Esq'rs, of *Pennsylaania.*

(Philadelphia) February 23, 1791. Date and place are from item headline.
This item also appeared in the *Daily Advertiser* (New York), February 26, 1791.

Nathaniel Pendleton to James Iredell ————————————————
March 5, 1791   Savannah, Georgia

                                                              Savannah.   March 5th 1791.
Dear Sir
  You will have heard before this reaches you, that Mr Rutledge has resigned
or vacated his seat in the supreme Court, and accepted the appointment of
Cheif Justice of South Carolina, with a salary of £800 — ℔ annum.
  I have presumed to communicate to the president my wish to succeed him —
Suffer me to hope I shall have the aid of your good Offices on this occasion.
  When I solicited the appointment I now hold, I imagined Congress would
have made a more ample provision for the Judges of the District Court; and
when the salaries were fixed, and the Commission sent, I owed so much respect to the Character of the President, and felt so sensibly the honor he had
done me, I did not think I could with honor decline serving: and the more
so, as the President seemed to have a kind of right to call for the services of
those whom he had nominated for offices at their own request — this he did
by a very Obliging letter that accompanied the Commission. Thus circumstanced I accepted the appointment, and of course gave up a very lucrative

practice at the Bar, and it is impossible to return to it again. — I must therefore
now depend on the public for a provision for myself and family, and the Education of my Children. I am now the eldest District Judge in the Southern
Circuit, and if the President shall not find me deficient in Capacity and professional knowledge, I think I have just grounds to hope to be put in nomination — I presume the President will be governed as heretofore by the propriety
of Chusing the Judges nearly in an equal proportion from among the United
States; and if so, I know of none that would accept the appointment, who have
a preferable claim. M.ʳ Bee¹ is spoken of in Charleston; should he be appointed
it will, I confess, be a sensible mortification to me, because he is a younger
Judge, and South Carolina, hath already had her turn.

I beg you will please present my Compliments very respectfully to M.ʳˢ Iredell, in which M.ʳˢ Pendleton very sincerely joins.

With sentiments of the highest   Esteem and regard   I am, Dear Sir,   Your
most Obedient &   most humble serv.ᵗ

NathPendleton

ARS (NcD, James Iredell Sr. and Jr. Papers). Unlike most letters received by James Iredell, this
one has not been endorsed as answered.

Nathaniel Pendleton (1756-1821), nephew of Virginia judge Edmund Pendleton, moved to
Georgia following service in the Revolutionary War. Nathaniel Pendleton studied law and was
admitted to the Georgia bar on February 22, 1785. He later became attorney general of the state.
Pendleton was elected to, but did not attend, the Constitutional Convention in 1787; however,
he did serve in the Confederation Congress in 1789. Pendleton became chief justice of the Georgia Superior Court in January, 1789, and in September, 1789, was appointed United States judge
for the district of Georgia. Pendleton resigned in 1796 and moved to New York City, where he
practiced law. Allen D. Candler and Clement A. Evans, eds., *Cyclopedia of Georgia,* 4 vols. (1906;
reprint ed., Spartanburg, S.C.: Reprint Co., 1972); Allen D. Candler, comp., *The Colonial Records
of the State of Georgia,* vol. 19, part 2, *Statutes, Colonial and Revolutionary, 1774 to 1805* (Atlanta:
Charles P. Byrd, 1911), pp. 452-53; *FFC,* 2:493; *SEJ,* 1:29, 32; *BDAC.*

1. Thomas Bee (1739-1812), a Charleston lawyer and Colleton County planter, was admitted
to the bar on January 27, 1761. Bee began his fifty-year career in public service in 1762 when
he was elected to the South Carolina Commons House of Assembly. In addition to his service in
the legislature of South Carolina, he acted as assistant judge of the Court of General Sessions
(1776-1778), lieutenant governor of South Carolina (1779), member of the Continental and Confederation Congresses (1780-1782), and supporter of the Constitution in the state ratifying convention (1788). Nominated by George Washington to be United States judge for the district of
South Carolina on June 11, 1790, Bee was confirmed by the Senate three days later. He served
in that position until his death. Bailey and Cooper, *Biographical Directory of the South Carolina House
of Representatives,* 2:69-72; *SEJ,* 1:50-51.

Nathaniel Pendleton to [Henry Knox?] ————————
March 5, 1791   Savannah, Georgia

Savannah.   March 5ᵗʰ 1791 —

Dear Sir

M.ʳ Rutledge having accepted the office of Cheif Justice of the State of South-
Carolina, leaves a vacancy to be supplied in the Supreme Court. Being the

eldest District Judge in the Southern Circuit, I have made my request to the President[1] to be nominated to that vacancy.

My pretensions to hope for the honor of being appointed to that office, arise from the probability that the principle adopted in the first appointments, of chusing the Judges nearly in an equal proportion from the different parts of the Union, will still prevail; in which case, a citizen of Georgia not having yet been distinguished by an appointment in the[2] supreme Court, which a citizen in both the other States in the Southern Circuit have been; and being the eldest district Judge, South of Maryland, I have a double right to hope for that promotion, if I am not found deficient, in professional knowledge, and integrity. _ With respect to these qualifications, it becomes me to be silent; yet if I had not reason to hope they would bear the test of a minute enquiry, I should be very unwilling to subject them to the scrutiny of a Judge, who hath manifested on all occasions so nice a delicacy, as the President hath, in the appointments of public Officers_ If you shall think I possess these qualities in a sufficient degree, I flatter myself I may hope for the advantage of your friendship, in this affair. _

Altho the misfortune of a long Captivity from 1776 to 1780, and afterwards my duty in General Green's family in the Southern States, prevented me from an early opportunity of being personally acquainted with you, I was no Stranger to your public and private character; having received such an account of both, from that most excellent man, as to make me ambitious of succeeding to that friendship he always shewed for you. And altho accidents, hitherto, have disappointed me of an opportunity to cultivate a personal friendship, yet have they not lessened the high, and sincere respect, and esteem, with which I have the honor to be

Dear Sir   Your most obedient &   most humble Servant

Nath! Pendleton

ALS (MeHi, J. S. H. Fogg Collection).

Internal evidence suggests that Henry Knox may have been the recipient of this letter. First, the reference to a friendship between the recipient and General Nathanael Greene applies to Henry Knox, who was a close friend of Greene before the latter's death in 1786. Knox continued as a friend to Greene's widow. Richard K. Showman, ed., *The Papers of General Nathanael Greene,* vol. 1 (Chapel Hill: University of North Carolina Press, 1976), p. 221n.

Secondly, Nathaniel Pendleton refers to a friendship with the recipient, but he also states that events "prevented me from an early opportunity of being personally acquainted with you" and "accidents, hitherto, have disappointed me of an opportunity to cultivate a personal friendship." Both of these statements describe the relationship known to exist between Pendleton and Knox. In a letter to Catharine Greene, who was the widow of Nathanael Greene and a close friend of Nathaniel Pendleton, Henry Knox wrote in September, 1790, that "Judge Pendleton has lately arrived from Georgia. I have seen him only for a few minutes but he is to dine with us on Monday" (MiU-C, Nathanael Greene Papers). This is the first known meeting of Knox and Pendleton, just six months before Pendleton wrote a letter asking for a recommendation. (We gratefully acknowledge the aid of Richard Showman, editor of *The Papers of General Nathanael Greene,* who helped illuminate the relationship between Nathaniel Pendleton and Henry Knox.)

Thirdly, on April 17, 1791, Knox, who was in Philadelphia at the time, did write a letter to George Washington (q.v.) mentioning a letter from Pendleton requesting a recommendation. Pendleton's letter of March 5 would have had over six weeks to arrive in Philadelphia, more than enough time to make the trip from Savannah. In his letter to President Washington, Knox tactfully avoided endorsing Pendleton's application, a maneuver appropriate to the shortness of his personal acquaintance with Pendleton.

1. See Nathaniel Pendleton to George Washington, March 5, 1791.

2. Nathaniel Pendleton wrote "s"—the first letter of "supreme"—at the end of the line, but stopped and partially erased it and continued on the next line.

Nathaniel Pendleton to George Washington —————————
March 5, 1791   Savannah, Georgia

Savannah. Georgia   March 5th 1791.

Sir.

I am informed Mr Rutledge has lately accepted the appointment of Cheif Justice of the State of South Carolina, which will of course oblige him to resign his Office of Assistant Justice in the supreme Court of the United States.

When I solicited the appointment of Judge of this District, I imagined Congress would have made a more ample provision for their[1] Judges; but having, at my own solicitation had the honor to be nominated by you, I could not with propriety refuse serving: altho it will readily be admitted by those who knew the extant of my practice at the bar, that the salary allowed me, is[2] but a small compensation, nor is it indeed an adequate provision for a family in this Country.[3]

Permit me however, Sir, to assure you I feel with equal Sensibility, and gratitude the honorable proof you were pleased to give of your approbation of my Character and Conduct on that occasion. An honor I hope always to merit, as far as as fidelity and diligence can merit it, whenever I shall be so happy as to be distinguished by your nomination to a[4] public office.

Under the impression of these ideas, permit me to communicate my wish that it may be agreeable to you, to put me in nomination to succeed Mr Rutledge. I should not perhaps indulge so flattering a hope, on this subject, but from an idea that you will probably nominate some person residing in the Southern Circuit — in which I now have the honor to be the oldest district Judge.

If I were to make a particular profession, of the personal respect and admiration, I have always had for your Character and public services, it might[5] have the appearance perhaps, on this occasion, of flowing from other than the real motives — yet, having served under you as my General from a few weeks after your appointment to that important trust, to the end of the War, I hope to have the credit of sincerity, when I profess to be,

with Sentiments of the most respectful, and Unalterable Attachment, Sir, Your most Obedient, and most humble Servant

Nath¹Pendleton

George Washington, President of the United States.

ARS (DLC, George Washington Papers). There is also a duplicate ARS (DLC, George Washington Papers) marked by Nathaniel Pendleton as "Duplicate" and enclosed in his letter to George Washington of April 10, 1791 (q.v.).

1. In duplicate, "the."
2. In duplicate, "was."
3. On July 30, 1796, Nathaniel Pendleton wrote to George Washington resigning as United States judge for the district of Georgia. In this letter, Pendleton cited the inadequate salary which would not allow him to educate his children properly. Letters of Resignation and Declination from Federal Office, RG 59, DNA.
4. In duplicate, "any."
5. In duplicate, "would."

James Gunn to George Washington
March 7, 1791 Philadelphia, Pennsylvania

Sir

Should the appointing of Mr John Rutledge Cheaf Justice of the State of South Carolina, Occasion a vacancy in the Federal Judiciary, and The President Should think it proper to fill such vacancy with a professional character from the State of which I have the honor to be a deputy; I take the liberty to mention Mr John Houstoun[1] as a gentleman whose professional abilities are Inferior to but few in america, and Inferior to none in the State of Georgia; and I will add Should he be appointed the citizens of that State will feel themselves Obliged. —

It is necessary I Should Inform the President that this communication contemplates the Serving of the Republic and not the Individual for Mr Houstoun, and myself are not in the habits of Intimacy. —

I have the honor to be with the greatest respect Sir, your most Obt Hu[ble?] Sert —

James Gunn

Philadelphia March 7th [1]791

The President
of the united States

ARS (DLC, George Washington Papers).
James Gunn (1753-1801), a Georgia lawyer, served in the Senate from 1789 to 1801. *BDAC.*
1. John Houstoun (ca. 1750-1796), Revolutionary War governor of Georgia, read law in Charleston and began his legal practice in Savannah in 1771. In 1786 Houstoun was appointed chief justice of Georgia, but he never served in that position. Houstoun, who was a justice of the peace for Chatham County, had just completed his term as Savannah's first mayor when this letter was written. Edith Duncan Johnston, *The Houstouns of Georgia* (Athens: University of Georgia Press, 1950), pp. 52-53, 194, 214, 256-61, 275, 277, 286.

Charles Pinckney to George Washington ——————————
March 8, 1791 Charleston, South Carolina

... You will certainly before this have recieved M! Rutledge's resignation as
a federal Judge, on his having been appointed Chief Justice of this state. _ the
reasons which induced this step he has no doubt fully & satisfactorily stated,
and if the friendship which you have always honoured me with, may be considered as giving me a license to say, ₍so much,₎ permit me to wish that his vacancy may
be filled by some other Gentleman from this state. _ I do not say this from
any local or partial motives, but from an idea that the very great weight &
importance[1] of this country in a commercial view will probably engage more
of her citizens in concerns with foreigners than almost any other state in the
Union & that it would, I should suppose, always be pleasing to them to reflect
that when their suits were taken from one tribunal and carried to another
acting under a different authority, that still a citizen of their own was one of
the Judges_ but to your better Judgement this is very properly left & I trust
your goodness will excuse my even having said as much as I have_ I know
the people of this country wish it_ so do I_ but both they ₍& I₎
ought with pleasure to acquiesce As I am sure I shall in any appointment you
may concieve proper . . .

ARS (DLC, George Washington Papers); duplicate ARS (DLC, George Washington Papers).
  1. The "c" is written over a "t."

Nathaniel Pendleton to George Washington ——————————
April 10, 1791 Georgia

Georgia April the 10ᵗʰ 1791 _
Sir
  I was not apprized of the adjournment of Congress, nor your intention of
visiting the Southern States, til after I had sent to the northward, a Letter I
did myself the honor to address to you of the 5ᵗʰ of last month, of which I
take the liberty ₍now₎ to inclose a duplicate.[1] The recess of Congress makes a temporary appointment, to the office alluded to, necessary_ The information you
will obtain by being here, I trust will add weight to the motives I have ventured to suggest as the foundation of my application.
  I have the honor to be Sir with the highest respect and Esteem, Your
most Obedient and most Humble servant

                                                                Nath!Pendleton

George Washington
  President of the United States.

ARS (DLC, George Washington Papers).
  1. See Nathaniel Pendleton to George Washington, March 5, 1790.

Henry Knox to George Washington ———————
April 17, 1791   Philadelphia, Pennsylvania

... Being upon the subject of offices I beg leave further to state that Judge Pendleton district Judge of Georgia has requested me to mention his name to you as a candidate for the vacancy in the circuit Court occasioned by Mr Rutledges resignation.[1] In your tour you will be able to obtain all necessary information relative to him ...

ARS (DLC, George Washington Papers). Marked "Private."
   1. See note to Nathaniel Pendleton to [Henry Knox?], March 5, 1791.

Samuel Bayard to Caleb Strong ———————
May 23, 1791   Philadelphia, Pennsylvania

... You were so good, just previous to your leaving this city as to express a wish for my success in the business which I introduc'd to your attention. Presuming from what yourself & Mr Sedgwick intimated & from the circumstances of the case on M^r T__'s[1] resignation, I have ventured to write to the judges on the subject_ the answer to these letters has been wholly conditional as was proper_ But it would confer a benefit & obligation, if by any means you could reduce the matter more to a certainty, by ascertaining M^r T's plan & advi[si?]g me of it as early as possible_ ...

Whatever word you should receive from Mr T. I should be much oblig'd to you for a transcript_ I seem rather of opinion that Mr Wilson will have some favourite here whom he will be disirous of bringing forward but whatever should be the event_ I shall not repine_ ...

ARS (MNF, Stephen Strong Collection). Addressed "Northampton   State of Massachusetts." Postmarked "[N-YO?]RK may 28."
   1. John Tucker, clerk of the Court.

George Washington to Charles Cotesworth Pinckney and Edward Rutledge ———————
May 24, 1791   Columbia, South Carolina

Columbia   May 24th 1791.

Private

Gentlemen_

An address to you jointly on a subject of the following nature may have a singular appearance; but that singularity will not exceed the evidence which is thereby given of my opinion of, and confidence in you;_ and of the opinion I entertain of your confidence in, and friendship for each other._[1]

Charles Cotesworth Pinckney (1746-1825) by James Earl (1761-1796). Oil on canvas, ca. 1794-1796. Courtesy Worcester Art Museum.

The Office lately resigned by the Honble Mr J. Rutledge in the Supreme Judiciary of the Union remains to be filled.— Will either of you two Gentlemen accept it?— and in that case which of you?—[2] It will occur to you that appointments to Offices in the recess of the Senate are temporary, but of their confirmation in such a case there can be no doubt.—

It may be asked why a proposition similar to this has never been made to you before;— this is my answer— your friends whom I have often conversed with on like occasions, have always given it as their decided opinion that no place in the disposal of the gen^l Government could be a compensation for the relinquishment of your private pursuits; or, in their belief would withdraw you from them.— In making the attempt, however, in the present instance, I discharge my duty, and shall await your answer (which I wish to receive soon) for the issue.— Of my sincere esteem & regard for you both I wish you to be assured[3] and that

I am— Gentlemen   Your most Obed^t & Affect^e Humble Servant

G^oWashington

Chas Cotesworth Pi^nckney & Edwd Rutledge Esq^rs

ARS (ScC, George Washington Papers); Lb (DLC, George Washington Papers). Addressed "Charleston."

1. Charles C. Pinckney and Edward Rutledge were brothers-in-law. *DAB* entry for Charles C. Pinckney.

2. On October 1, 1800, the *Columbian Centinel* (Boston) sketched the life and character of Charles C. Pinckney, who was a candidate for vice president. This article mentioned briefly Pres-

ident Washington's offer of a seat on the Supreme Court. The newspaper erred, however, in noting that the offer was made to fill a vacancy caused by the resignation of either John Blair or Thomas Johnson; the offer was made to fill the vacancy caused by the resignation of John Rutledge. This article was reprinted in the *Federalist* (Trenton), December 2, 1800. President Washington's offer also was mentioned in the *Daily Advertiser* (New York), December 12, 1800.

3. In letterbook copy, "persuaded."

William Bradford, Jr., to Susan Bradford ——————————
May 30, 1791   West Chester, Pennsylvania

...I should wish to keep the federal Judiciary in view. But M^{r}Lewis[1] tells me that the President has declared his intention of supplying that bench in future with eminent Counsel directly from the bar._ This will hardly be the case if the state Judiciaries are annexed to the federal Gov^t._ [*Bradford speculates on a possible replacement for the recently deceased Francis Hopkinson, federal district court judge for Pennsylvania.*] Mr Randolph will certainly succeed Mr Rutledge_ ...

ARS (PHi, John W. Wallace Collection). Addressed "to the care of Hon. E. Boudinot Esq Elizabeth Town."

Susan Bradford (1764-1854), wife of Pennsylvania attorney general, William Bradford, Jr., was the daughter of New Jersey congressman Elias Boudinot. *DAB* entries for Elias Boudinot and William Bradford.

1. Probably William Lewis.

Charles Cotesworth Pinckney and Edward Rutledge to George Washington ———————————————————
June 12, 1791   Charleston, South Carolina

Charleston   June 12th 1791.

Dear Sir

We embrace the earliest opportunity which has presented itself to acknowledge the Receipt of your very friendly Letter of the 24th May, and return you our best Thanks for the Confidence with which you have treated us. Living as we do, and as we long have done, in the un-interrupted Habits of Friendship we feel a mutual Delight in every Measure which tends to the Happiness of either; and every Honor which may be confer'd on one, will unquestionably reflect Pleasure on the other.

Altho' our Minds had been long made up, with respect to the acceptance of Offices, yet the arrival of your Letter, very naturally called for a reconsideration of the Subject_ The Sincerity, with which the offer was marked_ the great Esteem which we entertain for you_ and an anxious desire to yield, to what appeared to be your wish, led us to review the Reasons which had formerly occasioned our Determination: and having done that we feel a deep Regret indeed, in being obliged to decline the acceptance of a Seat on the Federal Bench. Private Considerations have had their weight: but others of a general & more powerful nature have influenced our Resolution— We think we can be of more real Advantage to the General Government & to our own State Government by remaining in the Legislature than we could possibly be, by accepting of any Office under either, which fills the Public Eye with the appearance of being lucrative. Under this Opinion, you will be in Sentiment with us, that it is our indispensible Duty to continue in the Stations we are, so long as we possess the Confidence of the Public. But as we devoted a large portion of our early Years to the Service of our Country, so, whenever her Honor, or her Interest, shall seem to require our Aid, we shall chearfully lay aside all private or partial Considerations, & imitate as far as may be in our Power, the best, & brightest of Examples.

We beg to assure you of the sincere Esteem & Regard   with which we have the Honor to be Dear Sir   Your most obedient & affectionate   Humble Serv^{ts}

Charles Cotesworth Pinckney
Ed: Rutledge

The President of the United States—

ARS (DLC, George Washington Papers).

Edmund Pendleton to Thomas Jefferson ——————
July 13, 1791   Caroline County, Virginia

Caroline   July 13, 1791

Dear Sir

I have just received a Letter from my Nephew Nathaniel Pendleton jun^r of the State of Georgia,[1] informing me of the resignation of Mr Rutlidge as one of the Judges of the Supreme Fœdral Court, and requesting my Assistance to his wish of being appointed his successor

I can only hand you his pretensions founded on a chain of reasoning thus "He supposes the Vacancy will be filled from a Citizen of the Southern District— That as North and South Carolina have been already gratified in this respect, he supposes that Citizen will be sought for in Georgia— and that his being at present their District Judge will place him foremost there." How far this is well founded, the President will judge, and you, Sir, if, as is probable, you are consulted on such occasions; permit me to add that I have pleasure in hearing that his reputation is high in the State, and that if you can consistent with the Public good, serve him in it, it will particularly oblige

Dr Sir   Y^r mo. hble & Ob^t Servt

Edm^{d}Pendleton

ARS (DLC, Thomas Jefferson Papers). Endorsed "rec^d July 19."
1. Letter not found.

Edmund Pendleton to James Madison ————————————
July 13, 1791 [Caroline County], Virginia

Virg^a July 13th 1791.

Dr Sir

I take the liberty of troubling you once more in behalf of my Nephew Nathaniel Pendleton jun^r of Georgia, who wishes to succeed Mr Rutlidge in the Office he has resigned as $_\wedge$^a Judge of the Supreme Fœdral Court. He supposes a resident in the Southern district will be appointed, and that from Georgia, as the Carolinas have been already gratified; in which case he hopes his present rank of District Judge, will give him preference to any competitor there. I have pleasure in hearing he stands high in the Opinion of his fellow Citizens, and if you think his reasoning sound, and $_\wedge$^can give him aid in his pretensions, It will particularly oblige,

Dr Sir   Y^r very A[ff?]^e & Ob^t Servt

Edm^{d}Pendleton

ARS (DLC, George Washington Papers). Addressed "Philadelphia." Place suggested by the fact that Edmund Pendleton wrote from Caroline County to Thomas Jefferson on the same day (q.v.).

Federal Gazette ————————————————————————
August 5, 1791   Philadelphia, Pennsylvania

APPOINTMENTS.

Thomas Johnson, Esq. of Maryland, associate Judge, in the room of Mr. Rutledge, who has resigned. . . .

(Philadelphia) August 5, 1791. Date and place are those of headline.

This item also appeared in the *New-Hampshire Gazette* (Portsmouth), August 18, 1791, and in the *Georgia Gazette* (Savannah), September 1, 1791.

Charles Pinckney to George Washington ————————————
August 18, 1791   Charleston, South Carolina

. . . Mr Rutledge our Chief Justice was extremely sorry that from the necessary avocations of his Office he was absent.[1] I once took the liberty of mentioning to you our wish that his vacancy might be filled up by some Gentleman from this State but as there does not appear a disposition in those Gentlemen whom you have been the best acquainted with to accept—[2] & as my having mentioned it may perhaps in some measure be the means of your wish to confine it to this State it is proper in me to say that I am sure any Gentleman that

may be appointed from either of the southern States will be perfectly agreable
to us_ ...

ARS (DNA, RG 59, Miscellaneous Letters).

    1. John Rutledge had not been able to see George Washington during the president's visit to
South Carolina.

    2. President Washington had offered the position of associate justice to Edward Rutledge and
Charles Cotesworth Pinckney in a letter to both on May 24, 1791 (q.v.).

Federal Gazette ─────────────────────────────────────
November 7, 1791   Philadelphia, Pennsylvania

APPOINTMENTS.
NOVEMBER, 7th. 1791.

The President of the United States has appointed, by & with the advice and
    consent of the Senate, the following persons:

    Thomas Johnson, of Maryland, one of the associate [J]ustices of the Supreme
Court, vice John Rutledge, resigned. ...

(Philadelphia) November 7, 1791. Date and place are those of the headline. Reading supplied
in brackets because type did not imprint in original.

    This item also appeared in the *Columbian Centinel* (Boston), November 23, 1791, and in the
Georgia Gazette (Savannah), December 1, 1791.

John Jay to George Washington ──────────────────────
January 27, 1792   New York, New York

... As I shall be absent from the next sup: Court, obvious Considerations
urge[1] me to mention to You the Reasons of it: Early[2] in the next month I
expect an addition to my Family_[3] Mrs Jay's delicate Health (she having for
more than[4] three weeks past been confined to her Chamber) renders that
Event so interesting, that altho she is now much better, I cannot prevail on
myself to be <u>then</u> at a Distance from her;[5] especially as no Business of particular Importance either to the public, or to Individuals, makes it necessary_
...

ARS (DLC, George Washington Papers); ADfS (NNC, John Jay Papers).

    1. In draft, "induce" crossed out.

    2. In draft, "sometime" crossed out.

    3. In draft, "the number of my children" is crossed out and replaced with "my family."

    4. In draft, "near" crossed out and "for more than" substituted.

    5. On January 10, 1792, John Jay had mentioned in a letter to John Adams that Sarah Jay had
been confined to her chamber for over a week by "a severe Cold and Cough." In the draft of
this letter, John Jay wrote "the present State of her Health. added to the ~~extreme~~ Situation she
will soon be in, ~~render it doubtful whether I should~~ strongly oppose my leaving her." Thus Jay
seems to have been doubtful of his attendance at the February term as early as January 10. John
Jay Papers, NNC.

Pennsylvania Gazette ――――――――――――――――――――――――――――
February 1, 1792   Philadelphia, Pennsylvania

On Monday next the Supreme Court of the UNITED STATES will meet at
the new Court House[1] in this city, when it is expected, the important question
will be agitated and settled_ Whether a State can be compelled to appear and
answer to a Process issuing from that Court?[2]

(Philadelphia) February 1, 1792. Date and place are from item headline.

Reprinted in the *Virginia Gazette, and General Advertiser* (Richmond) on February 15, 1792, and
in the *Newport Mercury* (Newport, Rhode Island) on February 18, 1792. The beginning of this
article (through "city") appeared in *Dunlap's American Daily Advertiser* (Philadelphia), February 1,
1792.

1. In August, 1791, the Court took up new quarters in the Mayor's Court of the newly completed City Hall of Philadelphia. The Supreme Court held most of its February and August terms
there until the Supreme Court moved to Washington in 1801. Robert P. Reeder, "The First
Homes of the Supreme Court of the United States," *Proceedings of the American Philosophical Society*
76 (1936): 583-96.

2. The author probably is referring to *Oswald v. New York*. On February 11, 1792, plaintiff's
counsel made a motion for the issuing of a distringas to compel the appearance of the state of
New York. Two days later the motion was withdrawn by counsel, and the Supreme Court made
no ruling. See "Fine Minutes," February 11 and 13, 1792.

William Cushing to George Washington ――――――――――――――――
February 2, 1792   New York, New York

...I take the liberty to inform you that being on my journey to attend the
Supreme Court, which is to sit next monday, I have had the misfortune to be
stopt here, since Friday last, by a bad cold attended with somewhat of a fever,
so that the probability, at present, seems against my being able to reach Philadelphia by the time court is to sit. Assoon[1] as my health permits, however, I
design to proceed there. The travelling is difficult this Season:_ I left Boston,
the 13th Jany in a Phaeton, in which I made out to reach Middleton as the
Snow of the 18th began, which fell so deep there as to oblige me to take a
Slay, & now again wheels seem necessary. If Judge Blair & Judge Johnson
attend there will be a Quorum, I suppose, as two other Judges are upon the
Spot. The Chief Justice, I perceive, cannot be present this term._ ...

ARS (DLC, George Washington Papers).

1. From the fifteenth to the eighteenth century, "as soon" was commonly written as one word.
OED, s.v. "assoon."

James Wilson to William Cushing ――――――――――――――――――――
February 7, 1792   Philadelphia, Pennsylvania

                                        Philadelphia   7th February 1792.
Dear Sir,

With yours of the second instant[1] I have been favoured; and regret much
the Causes, which prevent my having the Pleasure of seeing the Chief Justice

and you at the Supreme Court. Mr Johnson wrote to me that he would be here; but has not, as yet, arrived; so that the Judges now in Town cannot make a Quorum. We adjourn from Day to Day.

So soon as the State of your Health will admit of it, you will oblige us by coming on to Philadelphia. Mr Blair and Mr Iredell beg to be remembered to you.

With much Regard and Esteem, I have the Honour to be,   dear Sir,   Your most obed^t h^{ble} Servt

James Wilson

Hon. William Cushing Esqr

ARS (MHi, Robert Treat Paine Papers).
   1. Letter not found.

William Loughton Smith to Edward Rutledge ————
February 13, 1792   Philadelphia, Pennsylvania

. . . A change of politics is about to take place at New York: Chief Justice Jay is a Candidate for the Government, & it is said he will succeed — his Successor is not talked of yet: do you think your Brother[1] would accept it? If I thought he would, I wo^d put the business in train: I am in hopes we shall in this Session abolish the system of making the Judges of the Supreme Court ride the Circuits throughout the Union; this has induced Mr Jay to quit the Bench; he was Seven months in the Year from his family, travelling about the Country. . . .

ARS (ScHi, William Loughton Smith Papers).
   1. John Rutledge.

James Iredell to John Jay ————
February 16, 1792   Philadelphia, Pennsylvania

. . . I hope you will forgive my regreting the danger we are in of losing you for our Chief Justice,[1] which however I should do the more if I did not believe the change under the present situation of the office would be personally agreeable to yourself — . Tho' it may be by means of your appointment to another more agreeable to you personally. . . .

ADf (NcD, James Iredell Sr. and Jr. Papers).
   1. On February 9, 1792, New York federalists meeting at Farmer's Hall in New York City voted that John Jay "be supported at the ensuing Election as a Candidate for the Office of Governor of the State." An account of this meeting appeared in the Philadelphia *Federal Gazette* on February 15—the day before James Iredell wrote this letter to John Jay.

Benjamin Bourne to [William Channing] ——————————
February 21, 1792 Philadelphia, Pennsylvania

... The Supreem Court which has been sitting here have done little or no business
... You have heard that M.ʳ Jay (who by the by was not at Court) is a Candidate for the Goverment of N York. Gentlemen of Information say he will undoubtedly succede, he did not consent to the use of his Name untill on enquiry he was told there was no likelihood of an alteration in the present arrangement of the Federal Judiciary. he had got quite tired of the Circuits.— His candidateship is too recent to admit any probable conjectures as to his successor— M.ʳ Cuishing however bids fairest to take his place.— ...

ARS (RHi, Benjamin Bourne: Rhode Island Historical Society Miscellaneous Collection). The identification of William Channing as the probable recipient of this letter results from a comparison of the contents of this letter with those of a letter from Benjamin Bourne to Channing, March 18, 1792. Channing-Ellery Collection, RHi.

Benjamin Bourne (1755-1808), a Providence lawyer, and advocate for the ratification of the Constitution, served in Congress from 1790 to 1796. In September, 1801, he became judge of the United States court for the district of Rhode Island. *DAB; BDAC.*

William Channing (1751-1793), a Newport lawyer and public official, was the United States attorney for the district of Rhode Island and Rhode Island's state attorney general. Harrison, *Princetonians,* 2:13-16.

"Aristogiton" to the Printers of the *Daily Advertiser* ——————————
Daily Advertiser
February 28, 1792 New York, New York

[*"Aristogiton" discusses the likelihood of different groups supporting John Jay's bid for the post of governor of New York.*] The lawyers certainly, are bound to him for the *decency* and *delicacy* with which they were treated when they applied to be admitted at the federal bar,[1] and for the pains he took to establish their reputation by *oaths* and *certificates,* and the rather as this favor was so distinguishingly bestowed on the lawyers of this state only. ...

(New York) March 1, 1792. Date and place are those of the letter.
1. In February 1790 term.

Thomas Johnson to James Wilson ——————————
March 1, 1792 Frederick, Maryland

Frederick March 1st 1792.

Dear sir:

I shall be much obliged to you to write me which Circuit I am expected to ride;[1] I wrote to M.ʳ Jay[2] but the State of his Family prevented his being in Phil.ᵃ and I have not heard from him— I have a discourging prospect as to

Health if it does not mend I shall not be able to discharge the Duties of the Office and must withdraw I some Times repent having engaged in it I am too old for Circuits.

If any Alterations have taken place in the Judiciary Act and some are very necessary I wish to be advised of them.

I am dear sir   Your most obed'Servant.

Th Johnson

ARS (PP, Hampton L. Carson Collection). Addressed "Philadelphia." Postmarked "BALT[*letters illegible*]6."

1. James Wilson wrote to Thomas Johnson on March 13, 1792, to notify him which circuit he would ride. Hampton L. Carson Collection, PP.

2. Letter not found.

"A Free Elector" to the Printers of the *Daily Advertiser* ——
Daily Advertiser
March 2, 1792   [New York, New York]

[*"A Free Elector" responds to the letter of "Aristogiton" of February 28, 1792 (q.v.).*] The conduct of the Chief Justice when he first presided in this state, stands not in need of any vindication. It was his duty not to admit any man whose character could be impeached, and the the court no doubt would have acted unjustifiably, had they not required satisfactory proof of the professional talents of each of the applicants. For this purpose it was requested that the gentlemen of the bar should produce certificates as to both these facts. The request was highly reasonabl[e], and it is strange that any man who was conscious that he could bear the scrutiny, should have taken the least offence at it[.] It may be, that Aristogiton himself had some difficulty in obtaining this certificate, at which he sneers with such supercilious disdain, or perhaps his self-importance and his high blown pride magnified the request into an insult. If this was the case, we can easily account for his spleen. *But because it operated as a hardship upon Aristogiton,* is the general principle to be condemned? *That Mr. Jay did not grant this distinguished favor to the gentlemen of the bar in the other states,* requires to be supported by some better testimony than the bare assertion of the *good and virtuous* Aristogiton[.] . . .

(New York) March 5, 1792. The date is that of the letter; the place is determined by evidence in article. Readings have been supplied in brackets because type did not imprint.

John Jay to Thomas Johnson ——
March 12, 1792   New York, New York

. . . I have been favored with your's of the 3ᵈ of last month,[1] & regret the Indisposition which detained you from Philadelphia— I hope your Health has been since re-established. The then daily Expectation of an addition to my Family, and which soon after took place, prevented my attending the Sup. Court. . . .

ARS (MdFre, Thomas Johnson Papers). Addressed "Frederick   Maryland." Postmarked "Mrh 13."
  1. Letter not found.

Thomas Johnson to James Iredell —————————————————
March 31, 1792   Frederick, Maryland

[*Johnson tells Iredell that he will not be able to join him on the southern circuit until it meets in Columbia, South Carolina. Poor health and family concerns will detain him.*[1]] if I see I cannot perform the Duties of the Office I shall not long fill it. . . .

ARS (Nc-Ar, Charles E. Johnson Collection). Addressed to James Iredell "now in Edenton ~~South Carolina~~   North Carolina." Endorsed "Ans^d."
  1. Writing from Georgetown on April 9, 1792, Daniel Carroll mentioned in a letter to James Madison that Thomas Johnson, "far from being well," was with him and probably unable to continue to South Carolina. James Madison Papers, DLC.

Tench Coxe to Richard Henry Lee ———————————————————
[April 11, 1792?]   [Philadelphia, Pennsylvania?]

. . . I feel a decided conviction that the offices of Chief Justice & the Secretaries of the three Departments should be put on such a footing that when vacant they should be unclog'd by the pretensions of any subordinate officer whatever. The man of the first abilities, that can be found should be induced into the Station. ~~wh~~[*letters inked out*] ₐ commander in chief in the army or navy, dull seniority and length of service should be considered as nothing. . . .

In appointing these officers, as in appointing a

ARS (ViU, Lee Family Papers). Place suggested by evidence in letter; contemporary letters from Tench Coxe also written in Philadelphia. Tench Coxe Papers, PHi.
  Internal evidence suggests that Tench Coxe wrote this letter, dated "Wednesday Evening," during the Senate debate of a bill subsequently enacted as "An Act making alterations in the Treasury and War Departments," May 8, 1792. *Stat.*, 1:279-81. The main debate on this bill occurred between April 10, when the bill was first read, and April 17, the date it was engrossed. *SLJ*, 1:422-28. An alternate but less likely date is April 4, the day after the Senate first appointed a committee to study a possible alteration of the 1789 statute establishing the Treasury Department. *SLJ*, 1:419; *Stat.*, 1:65-67. Richard Henry Lee, however, was not a member of that committee and was more likely to have solicited from Coxe the opinions expressed in this letter after the bill had been drafted and had its first reading and was being debated by the Senate.
  Richard Henry Lee (1732-1794), a brother of William Lee and Arthur Lee and a cousin of Charles Lee, was a senator from Virginia. Richard Henry Lee's public service began in 1757, when he became a justice of the peace for his native Westmoreland County. The next year he was elected to the House of Burgesses in which he served until 1775. Lee then served in the

Continental and Confederation Congresses. In 1788 he opposed adoption of the Constitution at the Virginia ratifying convention. Lee was elected to the Senate in 1789; he resigned from that office on October 8, 1792. *DAB; BDAC.*

Sarah Jay to John Jay
April 22, 1792 New York, New York

... Your friends at Philadelphia seem to relinquish the expectation of seeing you there again, at least in your official capacity,[1] as M⸢rs⸣ Morris has sent your Robe to you, which M⸢r⸣ Soderstrom was so obliging as to leave here this morning_ ...

ARS (NNC, John Jay Papers). Addressed to the chief justice "at   New Haven." Postmarked "[N-?]York   Apri[l 22?]."

    Sarah (Livingston) Jay (1756-1802) was a daughter of William Livingston, a New York lawyer and New Jersey patriot. A second cousin of John Jay's early law partner, Robert R. Livingston, Sarah Livingston married Jay on April 28, 1774. Livingston, *Livingstons of Livingston Manor,* pp. 553-59.

    1. John Jay's "friends at Philadelphia" probably expected Jay to win the New York race for governor and therefore resign as chief justice.

Gazette of the United States
August 8, 1792 Philadelphia, Pennsylvania

Monday last the Supreme Judicial Court of the United States met at the new City-Hall, in this city_ present, the Chief Justice and the whole bench of Associate Judges_ Business of great importance it is said is pending.

(Philadelphia) August 8, 1792. Date and place are from item headline.

    This item also appeared in the *Newport Mercury* (Newport, Rhode Island), August 20, 1792. A similar article appeared in the *National Gazette* (Philadelphia) on August 8, 1792, and this was reprinted in the *Argus* (Boston) on August 21, 1792. The *General Advertiser* (Philadelphia) on August 6, 1792, had announced the beginning of the Court's session.

House of Representatives
Gazette of the United States
January 18, 1793 Philadelphia, Pennsylvania

[*John Tucker, former clerk of the Supreme Court, petitioned Congress for payment for his services and expenses in that office.[1] Theodore Sedgwick moves for payment that would include compensation for Tucker's having traveled from Boston to New York to apply for the clerkship and attend the Court.*] The motion was opposed; it was said[2] that it would establish a dangerous precedent for the government to pay the voluntary expenses of an applicant for an appointment under the United

States; and that in the present case the actual services only ought to be compensated according to the provision made by a subsequent law.[3] In reply it was said[4] that it was taken for granted Mr. Tucker had applied for the appointment, but no evidence of this is adduced — several circumstances were mentioned to shew that the contrary was the fact, and that he was called to discharge the duties of the office. . . .

(Philadelphia) January 23, 1793. Date and place are those for the debate reported.

This item also appeared in the *State Gazette of South-Carolina* (Charleston), February 18, 1793.

1. The full account of the circumstances surrounding this petition will appear in the last volume of this series where the financial history of the Court will be presented.

2. Speaker unknown.

3. "An Act providing compensations for the officers of the Judicial Courts of the United States, and for Jurors and Witnesses, and for other purposes," March 3, 1791. *Stat.*, 1:216.

4. Speaker unknown.

John Jay to William Cushing
January 27, 1793 New York, New York

New York   27 Jany 1793 —

Dear Sir

I am prepared and purpose to set out for Ph^a Tomorrow if the weather should prove fair. for altho I have regained more Health than I had Reason to expect to have done so soon; yet I find it delicate, and not sufficiently confirmed to admit of my travelling in bad weather.[1] I mention this that in Case the ensuing week should be stormy, my absence from you may not appear singular — It is my wish as well as my Duty to attend the court, and every Exertion that prudence may permit, shall be made ^for that purpose — I hope the Benevolence of Congress will induce them to fix the Terms at more convenient Seasons, especially as the public good does not require that we should be subjected to the Cold of Feby or the Heat of August — [2] Mrs Jay joins me in requesting the favor of you to present our best Comp^{ts} to Mrs Cushing —

I am Dear Sir your affect^{te} & h'ble Servt

John Jay

The Hon'ble Judge Cushing —

ARS (MHi, Robert Treat Paine Papers). Addressed "Philadelphia." Postmarked "N-YORK jan 27."

1. John Jay had written about his illness in a letter to William Cushing on January 9, 1793 (Robert Treat Paine Papers, MHi). John Adams had also mentioned it in a letter to his wife Abigail on January 14, 1793. Adams Manuscript Trust, MHi.

2. As a postscript to his January 9, 1793, letter to William Cushing, John Jay had written: "The Terms of the Sup. Court should certainly be held at Seasons less severe to the Court & Parties than Feb^y & Aug^t —." Robert Treat Paine Papers, MHi.

James Gunn to George Washington

February 11, 1793 [Philadelphia, Pennsylvania?]

Sir.

At the time, that M.r John Rutledge was appointed Chief Justice of the State of South Carolina, I did myself the honor to address you on the Subject of filling his Vacancy, and I took the liberty of mentioning M.r John Houstoun, as a Gentleman whose professional abilities warranted my recommending him for an Appointment in the Federal Judiciary;[1] at that time, I did not know M.r Houstouns sentiments respecting a Federal Appointment. But I have since Conversed with him, and find him Solicitous to fill an Appointment in the Judiciary; and I will add, that his declining to come forward as a Senator from the State of Georgia, was owing to a wish of being Employed in the department suitable to his profession. — Being Informed of the resignation of Judge Johnson, it is my duty, to repeat the Application, and as the President have seen M.r Houstoun, since my first, he will Judge of the propriety of the present —

I have the honor to be with the highest respect Sir, Your Very Obed.t Serv.t

James Gunn

February 11th 1793

The President of the United States

ARS (DLC, George Washington Papers). Place suggested by the fact that James Gunn was a senator and Congress was still in session.

1. See James Gunn to George Washington, March 7, 1791.

Edmund Randolph to George Washington

February 18, 1793 Philadelphia, Pennsylvania

. . . I have made the enquiries, which you suggested this morning, from men, well-acquainted with the three characters.

M.r Cook[1] appears to possess integrity, industry, punctuality, and the qualities, suited to a collecting lawyer. Upon the scale of eminence, he has no just pretensions; altho' his vanity occasions him frequently to discover, that he conceives himself inferior to none of any bar.

M.r J. Chase[2] has the reputation of being upright, laborious, of a sound judgment, but of indifferent elocution. His acquired knowledge in law, or other walks of literature, scarcely places him on the roll of real fame.

M.r Houston[3] is not so absolutely within the scope of my researches. But if he exceeds the rank of a good county-court lawyer, I have been greatly misinformed.

Perhaps then, the competition is reduced to Governor Paterson and M.ʳ Potts.[4] To the former, not a point can be objected, but his position, and the uncertainty of his connection with the land-companies, which are now in motion against particular states. The latter is known, but little in detail, altho' he carries with himself universal esteem, as a valuable man, and a much approved practitioner.

But suffer me, sir, to submit to your view, what lies ~~very~~ near to my heart. When I consider, how many decisions must be very grating to the states; I am afraid, that the dissatisfaction will be increased by a distrust of the abilities of ˰ our judges; nay I do not hold it, impossible, that some of them may excite sentiments of a degrading kind. If such an idea gains ground, the state judiciaries will inevitably make a stand against the federal Bench. This temper has already broke forth; and can never be subdued but by preeminent talents. . . .

ARS (DLC, George Washington Papers).

1. Possibly William Cooke (d. 1817), an attorney in Annapolis, Maryland. Cooke was admitted to the Inner Temple in 1768. When he returned to Annapolis, he received an appointment as counsel for the crown. A loyalist during the revolution, Cooke was disbarred between 1777 and 1787; but with the renewal of his license, he quickly became one of the leading lawyers of the state. Edward Alfred Jones, *American Members of the Inns of Court* (London: Saint Catherine Press, 1924), pp. 51-52; Paul S. Clarkson and R. Samuel Jett, *Luther Martin of Maryland* (Baltimore: Johns Hopkins University Press, 1970), p. 157; Edward S. Delaplaine, *The Life of Thomas Johnson* (New York: Frederick H. Hitchcock, 1927), p. 467.

2. Jeremiah Townley Chase (1748-1828), a second cousin of Samuel Chase, had married a sister of Samuel Chase's first wife. Jeremiah Townley Chase probably had studied law with Samuel Chase and was admitted to the bar in Anne Arundel County, Maryland, in 1771. He spent most of his legal career in Annapolis, though he lived in Baltimore during the Revolutionary War. Chase served in several state and local offices as well as one term in the Confederation Congress. In 1789 he became an associate judge of the Maryland General Court and in 1799 chief judge of the same court. In 1806 he was named chief judge of the Maryland Court of Appeals and also of the Third Judicial District. Papenfuse, et al., *Biographical Dictionary of the Maryland Legislature, 1635-1789;* Carroll T. Bond, *The Court of Appeals of Maryland: A History* (Baltimore: Barton-Gillet, 1928), pp. 100-101.

3. Probably John Houstoun.

4. When Richard Potts (1753-1808) was elected to the Senate in 1792, he was chief judge of the Fifth Judicial District in Maryland. Before the Revolutionary War, Potts had read law with Samuel Chase and then moved to Frederick, where he became clerk of the county court in 1777. In 1784 he received an appointment as state's attorney for Frederick, Montgomery, and Washington Counties. Potts was commissioned in 1789 as United States attorney for the district of Maryland. *DAB.*

Independent Gazetteer ────────────────────────────────
March 6, 1793   Trenton, New Jersey

We hear that William Paterson, Esq. Governor of this state, is appointed by President Washington, a Judge of the Supreme Court of the United States, and that he has accepted the appointment. . . .

(Philadelphia) March 9, 1793. Date and place are those of headline.

A similar item appeared in the *Boston Gazette,* March 18, 1793. A variant appeared in the *General Advertiser* (Philadelphia) on March 8, 1793, and in the *Columbian Centinel* (Boston) on March 20, 1793. Other briefer notices appeared in the *Gazette of the United States* (Philadelphia), March 9, 1793; the *National Gazette* (Philadelphia), March 9, 1793; the *Boston Gazette,* March 18, 1793; the *Columbian Centinel* (Boston), March 20, 1793; and the *United States Chronicle* (Providence), March 21, 1793.

William Paterson to the Gentlemen of the New Jersey Legislative Council ———————————————
March 30, 1793   New Brunswick, New Jersey

. . . My acceptance of the Office of an Associate-Justice in the Supreme Court of the United States renders it improper, that I should continue in my present Station. I have accordingly this day delivered the great Seal to the honorable Elisha Lawrence, the Vice-President, and To-morrow I shall go out of the State, so that he may proceed to discharge his official Functions without any Obstacle or Difficulty. I now formally announce my Resignation of the Government; and in doing this my last Act, I feel inexpressible Sensibility, mingled with the liveliest Emotions of Gratitude and Respect for the Citizens of this peaceful and happy Land. Farewell, Gentlemen; and may the God of Heaven keep you in his holy Protection, smile upon your Endeavours to promote the Interests of this State, and the Prosperity of the Union at Large_ . . .

ARS (Nj, Vault Manuscripts). In the William Paterson Papers at Rutgers University, there is an autograph draft of this dated "March, 1793" and with a salutation "Gentlemen of the   General Assembly_." The text is the same as that reproduced here.

Dunlap's American Daily Advertiser —————————————————
April 3, 1793   New Brunswick, New Jersey

His Excellency Gov. Paterson being appointed one of the Associate Judges in the Supreme Court of the United States, and being about to take his departure from this place, on a circuit to the southern States; the Common Council and other inhabitants of New-Brunswick, having provided a dinner at the White-Hall on Saturday last, invited his Excellency to favour them with his company at the same, which he accepted.

At half an hour after two, a large and respectable company being met, the Common council and other citizens waited on the Governor and presented him with an address of which the following is a copy.

To his Excellency WM. PATTERSON, *Esq.*
The Address of the Common Council and other
inhabitants of the city of New-Brunswick

SIR,

It is not our design to introduce as the subject of our present address to you, the distinguished reputation you have so deservedly acquired in the discharge of the various duties belonging to the high and honourable offices to which you have from time to time been called by the voice of your country, or your exemplary private character; but as you are about to relinguish the office you hold by the unanimous and repeated suffrages of the representatives of this state as its chief magistrate, and to take upon yourself another very important trust under the general government: We the common council of the city of New-Brunswick, and other inhabitants, your friends and fellow citizens, cannot suppress declaring in this public manner our regret on the occasion,[1] as it deprives the State of New-Jersey of your superior aid and protection; while at the same time we felicitate our fellow citizens of the United States, that under your judicious management the department to which you are appointed, will be effectually secure.

Permit us to express our affectionate esteem and respect for you as a citizen and a public officer, and as the period is at hand for you to commence your journey on a circuit to the southern States, in the execution of your office; We beg leave to assure you of our best wishes during your absence, for your safe return to your domestic connections and friends, and that the divine blessing may constantly attend your person, your family, and public administration.

Signed by order of Common Council and   other inhabitants

JOHN SCHUREMAN, President.

To which his Excellency replied,
To the Common Council and other Inhabitants
of the city of New-Brunswick

Gentlemen,

With liveliest sensibility I receive your affectionate address. It calls forth the tenderest emotions of my soul. In return, be pleased to accept the warmest acknowledgements of a heart, overflowing with gratitude and respect for the citizens of this happy land.— With wishes the most pure and fervent for your individual felicity, I bid you, my friends and fellow-citizens, an affectionate farewell. May peace be your lot on earth, and never-ending peace your portion in heaven.

Wm. Paterson.

At three o'clock the company sat down to dinner.

On Monday morning at 11 o'clock, Judge Paterson set out from his house in Burnet Street, escorted by the B[r]unswick company of Light Infantry, and a large number of respectable citizens, to Capt. Hillyer's sloop, on board which he embarked with some other gentlemen for New-York on his way to Georgia, amidst repeated testimonials of deserved respect and esteem for the man who has served his country in many high and important offices with distinguished reputation._ *Virtue will have its reward.*[2]

On the departure of Judge Paterson.

SEE the once father, ruler of our State,
Throng'd by the rich, the poor, the great._
Why all this bustle? was it to revere
A crested monarch, not with *love_* but *fear:*
The *patriot's merits* with his *deeds* combin'd,
Their hearts united, and their voices join'd:
While gratitude sincere inspires their praise,
With sorrow on the parting ship they gaze.
Ye gales propitious!_[2] to the destin'd shore
Waft him_ kind heav'n protect him evermore.

(Philadelphia) April 5, 1793. Date and place are those of the headline. A reading has been supplied in brackets because type did not imprint.

1. In newspaper, "occasiou."

2. The last paragraph of this article appeared in the *Gazette of the United States* (Philadelphia) on April 6, 1793, and in the *New-York Journal* on April 13, 1793.

3. In newspaper, "propitions."

Egbert Benson to Rufus King

December 18, 1793 New York, New York

... It having been supposed necessary that something ought to be done at Albany, during the ensuing Session of the Legislature, respecting the next Election for Governor, some <u>Freinds</u> waited on M⁅ Jay, a few evenings since, to know his Wishes and Determination_ He answered, that when, on the Request of his <u>Freinds</u>, he consented to become a Candidate at the last Election, the Office of a Judge of the Supreme Court of the U. S. was in a Degree intolerable, and therefore almost any other Office of suitable Rank and Emolument was preferable, but that, in consequence of the Releif which Congress have since given to the Judges,[1] he would rather continue in his present Office than be Governor of the State, at the same time however <u>as his Freinds had not deserted him</u> he certainly would not desert them, and if therefore upon the whole <u>they</u> still judged it most advisable that he should again be a Candidate, that he would as certainly acquiesce and if elected would accept_ ...

ARS (NHi, Rufus King Papers). Addressed "Philadelphia." Postmarked "N, YORK 'Dec. 18.'"
    Egbert Benson (1746-1833), a New York lawyer, served in Congress from 1789 to 1793.
DAB.
    1. On August 9, 1792, John Jay and the associate justices of the Supreme Court sent a rep-
resentation to Congress requesting relief "from their present painful and improper situation" that
required them to hold twenty-seven circuit courts a year "in the two most severe seasons of the
year" (RG 46, DNA). Congress responded to this plea with the passage, on March 2, 1793, of
"An Act in addition to the Act, entitled 'An Act to establish the Judicial Courts of the United
States.'" Among other things, the act provided a measure of relief from the rigorous circuit riding
schedule by reducing the required attendance at a circuit court from two Supreme Court justices
to one. *Stat.,* 1:333.

James Iredell to John Jay ————————————————————
January 21, 1794   Williamston, North Carolina

... It is with the most sensible mortification that I have[1] to inform you of the
disappointment of my expectation of attending at the Supreme Court in February, at which time[2] I was extremely anxious to attend on account of the
variety[3] of important business which probably will then come on,[4] and of the
novel and peculiar nature of a part of it. I accordingly set off so early as the
14th, but was unfortunately taken sick when I had rode about 40 miles, and
obliged to return.[5] My health has since got better, but not so much so as to
enable me to proceed. [*Iredell discusses the allotment among the justices of spring
circuits and the possibility of altering through legislation the month in which the Supreme Court holds its winter term.*]
    You will be so good as to inform the other Judges of the circumstance which
has unfortunately prevented my having the pleasure to meet them,[6] and I beg
the favour of you at the same time to assure them of the high respect I constantly feel for them ...

ARS (NNC, John Jay Papers); ADf (Nc-Ar, Charles E. Johnson Collection). Addressed "Philadelphia." Marked "Recommended to the care of the   Honorable Judge Wilson."
    1. In draft, "have" written over crossed-out "am obliged."
    2. In draft, "a Court which" crossed out and "at a time when" interlined.
    3. In draft, the word "great" crossed out preceding "variety."
    4. In draft, "which probably will ~~come on at that time~~ then come on" interlined above "~~de-
pending on it.~~"
    5. On February 13, 1794, James Iredell wrote to Edmund Randolph a similar account of his
efforts to reach Philadelphia to sit with the Supreme Court. Charles E. Johnson Collection, Nc-
Ar.
    6. James Iredell had originally drafted the following passage and then crossed it out: "I beg
the favour of you to lay this letter before the other Judges, whom I heartily regret that I lose the
pleasure of meeting."

Edmund Pendleton to Nathaniel Pendleton —————————————
February 3, 1794   Edmundsbury, Caroline County, Virginia

... I have hitherto declined writing on the Subject of your wish to rise in the Fedral Judiciary Corpse,[1] on account of the late situation of Phil[a]_ [2] I mean however to write to the President & present Secretary[3] on the Subject, whose appointment may prove a favourable circumstance to you. I will write more freely to Madison & Col[o] Taylor[4] on the Subject, wishing to assist you in what I consider as a laudable Ambition to serve your Family & the Public in Offices, justly esteemed useful to Society. ...

ARS (CtY, Nathaniel Pendleton Papers). Addressed to Nathaniel Pendleton "at Savañah   Georgia." Edmundsbury was the estate of Edmund Pendleton.

1. I.e., corps.
2. Between August and November, 1793, a yellow fever epidemic caused many inhabitants of Philadelphia to flee the city. The death toll exceeded five thousand individuals. *PAH,* 15:325n.
3. Secretary of State Edmund Randolph was appointed on January 2, 1794. *SEJ,* 1:144.
4. John Taylor of Caroline (1753-1824), a Virginia lawyer and planter, served in the Senate from 1792 to 1794 and on two later occasions. Taylor, who later gained fame for his political and agricultural writings, was raised by his uncle, Edmund Pendleton, who was also a first cousin of John Taylor's father. Nathaniel Pendleton was Taylor's second cousin. *DAB;* Mays, *Edmund Pendleton,* 1:139; 2:44, 170-71.

William Paterson to Euphemia Paterson —————————————
February 20, 1794   Philadelphia, Pennsylvania

... I expected to have reached home about this time, but the business of the court has been greater than I supposed it would have been. I have no prospect of the court's rising for several days to come, as there is yet much business to be dispatched. ...

ARS (NjR, William Paterson Papers).

Euphemia (White) Paterson (1746-1832), wife of William Paterson. Elizabeth Morris Lefferts, comp., *Descendants of Lewis Morris of Morrisania* (New York: Tobias A. Wright, 1907), Chart L.

Although Paterson dated this letter 1794, internal evidence suggests he meant 1795.

Edmund Pendleton to George Washington —————————————
March 5, 1794   Virginia

                                                            Virg[a]   March 5th 1794.
Dear Sir

Unwilling as I am to trouble you with Applications respecting the Appointments to Public Offices, I feel it a duty I am inclined to fulfill, to mention my Nephew M[r] Nathaniel Pendleton, the present Fedral District Judge of Georgia; who, having heard that you intended to supply the next Vacancy in the Supreme Court, by appointment of a resident of that state, wishes to be con-

d
sidered as a Candi̭ate for that Office, and as such to be recommended to your
notice. He supposes that his only Competitor will be a M.ʳ Houston, the State
Chief Justice,[1] before whom he thinks he stands in Grade, and modestly wishes
to be refer'd to the Professional Gentlemen acquainted with both, for information as to their comparative legal Abilities, & mentions amongst others M.ʳ
Baldwin,[2] a Member of Congress from the State, as a good Judge & has an
intimate knowledge of both. Having thus mentioned him, I have only to Add
that I am far from wishing him success, unless the public good will be at least
as well answered by him as another, but in that case shall esteem the preference to him as a Singular Favor to
    D.ʳ Sir,   Y.ʳ mo. Aff.ᵉ & Ob.ᵗ Serv.ᵗ

                                                    Edm.ᵈ Pendleton

ARS (NjMoNP). Addressed "Philad.ᵃ."
    1. John Houstoun never served as chief justice of Georgia. In 1786 Houstoun was appointed
chief justice of Georgia; but upon receiving his commission on March 4, 1786, he wrote a letter
declining the post. Shortly thereafter, he was suspended from the post, although he never officially
had accepted the appointment. The suspension was related to a political dispute between the governor and officials of Chatham County. The state of Georgia then reorganized its judicial system
and created a Superior Court composed of three justices. Houstoun was commissioned on January
17, 1792, as one of these justices and served until his resignation in December, 1792. Johnston,
Houstouns of Georgia, pp. 256-61, 278-81; Stephen F. Miller, *The Bench and Bar of Georgia*, 2 vols.
(Philadelphia: J. B. Lippincott, 1858), 2:96-100.
    2. Abraham Baldwin, a Georgia congressman.

Thomas Hall to Samuel Bayard ───────────────────
March 17, 1794   Charleston, South Carolina

                        Charleston S.ºCarolina   17ᵗʰ March 94
Dear Sir
                        so
I take the Liberty to request you will be ̭ o[b?]ging as to furnish me with a
Writ of Error Certif.ᵈ formally, the one which arrived here was by an accident
lost by one of our Attorneys— You may rest assured that you will not be
again called on by me again on the same account
    Remaining with much respect   Yr V.ʸ Obed.ᵗ Serv.ᵗ

                                                    Thomas Hall
                                                    District Clerk

ARS (DNA, RG 267, Records of the Office of the Clerk). Addressed to "The Clerk of the
Supreme Court of the United States of America at Philadelphia." Postmarked
"CHAs.TON*MAR, 24."

George Washington to Edmund Pendleton ——————
March 17, 1794 Philadelphia, Pennsylvania

... Your letter of the 5th instᵗ came duly to hand.— I know not from what
source, a report that, the next associate Judge was to be taken from the state
of Georgia, could have been derived.— Nothing from me, I can venture to
say, gave rise to it;— first, because there is no vacancy on that bench at present.— 2ᵈ because, whenever one does happen, it is highly probable that a
geographical arrangement will have some attention paid to it;— and (although
I do— at all times— make the best enquiries my opportunities afford, to
come at
obtain the fittest characters for offices, where my own knowledge does not
give a decided preference) because, 3ᵈˡʸ, no one knows my ultimate determination until the moment arrives when the nomination is to be laid before the
                                                                              might
Senate.— My resolution, not to create an expectation, which thereafter ᴧ em-
barrass my own conduct (by such a commitment to any one as might subject
me to the charge of deception) is co-eval with my inauguration; and in no
instance have I departed from it.— The truth is, I never reply to any applications for offices by letter; nor verbally, unless to express the foregoing sentiments; lest something might be drawn from a civil answer, that was not intended.— ...

ARS (MHi, Washburn Papers); Lb (DLC, George Washington Papers).

George A. Baker to Samuel Bayard ——————————
March 28, 1794 Philadelphia, Pennsylvania

Please examine whether there are any Judgments on Record in the Supreme
Court of the United States against Robert Morris Esquire.— Philadelphia
28th March 1794.

George A. Baker

Samuel Bayard Esqʳˡ
Clk of Supreme Court of United States.—

ARS (PWacD, Sol Feinstone Collection).
    George A. Baker (1736-1816) was a Philadelphia accountant, surveyor, and scrivener. *DAR
Patriot Index;* Clement Biddle, *The Philadelphia Directory* (Philadelphia: James & Johnson, 1791);
James Hardie, *The Philadelphia Directory and Register* (Philadelphia: T. Dobson, 1793).
    1. Samuel Bayard wrote back to George A. Baker on the bottom of the sheet of paper used
by Baker to write to Bayard; see Samuel Bayard to George A. Baker, March 28, 1794.

Samuel Bayard to George A. Baker ————————————
March 28, 1794   Philadelphia, Pennsylvania

I do hereby certify that there are no judgment, or judgments against Robert Morris Esq.ʳ of Pennsylvania, at the suit of any one or more persons, on the records of the Supreme Court of the United States —

SamˡBayard
Clk. Sup. Cur. UStates

Philadᵃ 28 Maͬ 1794

6s 1¹/₂ᵈˡ

ARS (PWacD, Sol Feinstone Collection). This letter was drafted at the bottom of the piece of paper that George A. Baker had used to write to Samuel Bayard; see above under date of March 28, 1794.

1. This is Samuel Bayard's notation of the clerk's fee due for his services.

John Jay to George Washington ————————————
April 30, 1794   New York, New York

. . . I was this day honored with your's of yesterday.[1] There is nothing I more ardently wish for than Retirement, and Liesure to attend to my Books and papers: but parental Duties not permitting it, I must acquiesce, & thank God for the many Blessings I enjoy. If the Judiciary was on its proper footing, there is no public Station that I should prefer to the one in which you have placed me— it accords with my Turn of mind, my Education & my Habits— . . .

ARS (DLC, George Washington Papers); ADf (NNC, John Jay Papers).

1. John Jay had been appointed envoy extraordinary to England on April 19, 1794. Ten days later, President Washington had written to Jay confidentially to offer him the post of resident minister plenipotentiary at London. In declining the offer, Jay wrote the passage printed here. *SEJ*, 1:152; George Washington Papers, DLC.

William Cushing to William Paterson ————————————
July 20, 1794   Scituate, Massachusetts

. . . I hope I may be absent from August Court without inconvenience; as I expressed my wish to be, in February, notwithstanding the absence of the Chief Justice, you are not remote, Judge Wilson on the Spot; Judge Blair promised me to attend, if not prevented by some unforeseen necessity, & Judge Iredell will doubtless be present, as he was absent in February. The Extremity of the heat disagrees much with my Constitution, & I could wish if it were practicable, to have that term in a better Season of the year. . . .

ADf (MHi, Robert Treat Paine Papers).

William Paterson to William Cushing ———————
August 9, 1794   New Brunswick, New Jersey

. . . I have just returned from Philadelphia. No business was done in the supreme court, except the assignment of judges for the fall circuits. . . .

ARS (MHi, Robert Treat Paine Papers). Addressed "Scituate   Massachusetts." Postmarked in writing "NBruns^k Augt 11."

Henry Lee to George Washington ———————
August 17, 1794   Richmond, Virginia

. . . When I saw you in Philad^a I had many conversations with you respecting Mr Henry[1] & since my return I have talked very freely & confidentially with that gentleman— [I?] plainly perceive that he has credited some information which he has received (from whom I know not) which induces him to beleive that you consider him a factious seditious character & that you expressed yourself to this effect on your return from S^o Carolina [i?]n your journey thro this state[2] as well as elsewhere— Assured in my own mind that his opinions are groundless I have uniformly combated them, & lament that my endeavours have been unavailing— He seems to be deeply & sorely effected. It is very much to be regretted, for He is a man of positive virtue as well as of transcendent talents, & was it not for his feelings above expressed, I verily beleive he would be found among the most active supporters of your administration— Excuse me for mentioning this matter to you, I have long wished to do it in the hope that it will lead to a refutation of the sentiments entertained by Mr H. . . .

ARS (DLC, George Washington Papers).

    1. Patrick Henry (1736-1799) was licensed to practice law in Virginia in 1760. Henry's brilliant oratory soon made him one of Virginia's leading lawyers and a spokesman for the revolutionary movement. His career in public service began in 1765 with his election to the House of Burgesses. Henry served in the Continental Congress (1774-1776) and as governor of Virginia (1776-1779, 1784-1786). He played a prominent role in drafting Virginia's new constitution in 1776. Henry later became the foremost opponent of ratification of the federal Constitution in the Virginia convention of 1788. After 1788 Henry resumed his law practice and, during the 1790s, eventually became a supporter of George Washington's administration and the federalist party. Henry declined offers to be in the Senate, on the Supreme Court, in the cabinet, and in the diplomatic service. In 1799 he stood for election to the Virginia House of Representatives as a federalist. He won the election but died before taking office. *DAB; BDAC.*

Patrick Henry by Lawrence Sully (1769-1803). Watercolor on ivory, 1795. Courtesy Mead Art Museum, Amherst College.

According to George Washington's response to Henry Lee on August 26, 1794 (q.v.), these conversations had taken place "in the winter preceeding the last." This would mean during the winter of 1792 to 1793. Henry Lee, then governor of Virginia, had traveled to Philadelphia in the winter of 1793 on state business. He left Virginia on January 28, 1793, and returned at the beginning of March. Inasmuch as Washington's letter implies that Patrick Henry's name came up in reference to a possible appointment to the Supreme Court, the conversation may have centered on seeking a replacement for Thomas Johnson, who resigned on January 16, 1793. William Paterson was commissioned on March 3, 1793. Sherwin McRae, ed., *Calendar of Virginia State Papers* vol. 6 (1886; reprint ed., New York: Kraus Reprint Corporation, 1968), pp. 266-67, 301.

2. On March 21, 1791, Washington left Philadelphia for his tour of the southern states. His route took him through Virginia, North and South Carolina, and as far south as Savannah, Georgia. He returned to Mount Vernon on June 12, 1791. *PGW, Diary,* 6:96-97, 163.

George Washington to Henry Lee ————————————
August 26, 1794   Germantown, Pennsylvania

[*Responding to Lee's letter of August 17, 1794 (q.v.), Washington writes that he considers the Pennsylvania Whiskey Rebellion* "as the first formidable fruit of the Democratic Societies."] A part of the plan for creating discord, is, I perceive, to make me say things of others, and others of me, wch have no foundation in truth.— The first, in many instances I know to be the case— and the second I believe to be so.— but truth or falsehood is immaterial to them, provided their objects are promoted.

Under this head may be classed, I conceive, what it is reported I have said
                                        I
of M.ʳ Henry＿ ...With solemn truth then ˄ can declare, that I never expressed such sentiments of that Gentlemen, as from your letter, he has been
led to believe.＿ I had heard, it is true, that he retained his enmity to the
Constitution; but with very peculiar pleasure I learnt from Col.º Coles[1] (who I
am sure will recollect it) that M.ʳ Henry was acquiescent in his conduct, & that
though he could not give up his opinions[2] respecting the Constitution, yet,
unless he should be called upon by official duty he w.ᵈ express no sentiment
                                              a
unfriendly to the exercise of the powers of ˄ government which had been chosen by a majority of the people; or words to this effect:＿ Except intimating
in this conversation (which to the best of my recollection was introduced by
Col.º Coles) that report had made M.ʳ Henry speak a different language;＿ and
afterwards at Prince Edward Court house, where I saw M.ʳ Venables[3] & finding
I was within eight or ten miles of M.ʳ Henry's seat & expressing my regret at
not seeing him the conversation might be similar to that held with Col.º
Coles;＿ I say, except in these two instances, I do not recollect, nor do I believe, that in the course of the journey to & from the Southward I ever mentioned M.ʳ Henry's name in conjunction with the Constitution, or the government.＿ It is evident therefore, that these reports are propagated with evil
intentions＿ to create personal differences.＿ On the question of the Consti-
                                            known,
tution M.ʳ Henry & myself, it is well ˄ have been of different opinions; but
personally, I have always respected and esteemed him;＿ nay more,＿ I have
conceived myself under obligations to him for the friendly manner in which
he transmitted to me some insiduous[4] anonymous writings that were sent to
him in the close of the year 1777, with a view to embark him in the opposition
that was forming against me at that time.

I well recollect the conversations you allude to in the winter preceeding the
last;＿ and I recollect also, that difficulties occurred which you, any more than
                             not
myself, were ˄ able to remove.＿ 1.ˢᵗ though you believed, yet you would not
undertake to assert, that M.ʳ Henry would be induced to accept any appointment under the General Government; in which case, & supposing him to be
inemical to it, the wound[5] the government would receive by his refusal, and
the charge of attempting to silence his opposition by a place, would be great;＿
2.ᵈ because you were of opinion that no office which would make a residence
at the Seat of the government essential would comport with his disposition, or
views;＿ and 3.ᵈˡʸ because if there was a vacancy in the supreme Judiciary at
that time (of which I am not at this time certain) it could not be filled from
Virginia without giving two Judges to that State, which would have excited
unpleasant sensations in other states.＿ Any thing short of one of the great
Offices, it could not be presumed he would have accepted; nor would there
(under any opinion he might entertain) have been propriety in offering it.＿

What is it then, you have in contemplation, that you conceive would be rel-
ished? _ and ought there not to be a moral certainty of its acceptance? _ This
being the case, there w^d not be wanting a disposition on my part _ but strong
inducements on public & private grounds, to invite Mr Henry into $_\wedge$ employment under the General Government to which his inclination might lead, &
not opposed by those maxims which has been the invariable rule of my conduct. . . .

AR[S?] (ViHi, Lee Family Papers); Lb (DLC, George Washington Papers). The recipient's copy
is incomplete. Marked "(Private)."

    1. Isaac Coles (1747-1813) of Halifax, Virginia, was an anti-federalist congressman (1789-1791,
1793-1797). In the First Congress, Coles represented the district that included Prince Edward
County, then the home of his cousin, Patrick Henry. George Washington, on his southern tour
of 1791, dined at Coles's house. *BDAC;* Herbert Clarence Bradshaw, *History of Prince Edward
County, Virginia* (Richmond: Dietz Press, 1955), p. 317; Richard R. Beeman, *Patrick Henry: A
Biography* (New York: McGraw-Hill, 1974), p. 170; Robert Douthat Meade, *Patrick Henry: Prac-
tical Revolutionary,* vol. 2 (Philadelphia: J. P. Lippincott, 1969), p. 269.

    2. In letterbook, "opinion" follows "~~conduct~~."

    3. The Venable family was very prominent in Prince Edward County, and President Washing-
ton may have seen several of them at the courthouse. The conversation reported by Washington
may have been with Abraham Bedford Venable (1758-1811), congressman from the district which
included Prince Edward County in the Second Congress; or it may have been with his younger
brother, Richard N. Venable (1763-1838), an attorney who was at the Prince Edward courthouse
on June 7, 1791, and recorded in his diary that the road along Washington's route was crowded
with people "anxious to see the Saviour of their Country & object of their love." Elizabeth Marshall Venable, *Venables of Virginia* (New York: J. J. Little and Ives, 1925), pp. 15-41; Harrison,
Princetonians, 3:306-10, 388-92; *PGW, Diary,* 6:161.

    4. In letterbook, "insidious."

    5. In letterbook, followed by "~~it would give~~."

Samuel Bayard to Edmund Randolph ——————————
October 25, 1794   [Philadelphia, Pennsylvania?]

. . . By this days mail _ I have written to ~~th~~ 2 of the Judges of the Sup. Court
explaining the reason of my leaving the U. S. _ [1] requesting their concurrence
and approbation & apprizing them of my having ~~provided~~ a suitable $_\wedge$ person to de-
pute in my place as Clk of the Court _ approv'd by yourself[2] & by the Att^y
General _ I shall write to the others to morrow.[3] I should be happy to learn
whether any arrangements have been made between M^{r}Hallowell and yourself
respecting the house which I occupy at present, _ On this subject, & others
of more importance I shall do myself the honor of waiting on you at any hour,
most agreeable to you, & when you will be least liable to interruptions, from
other quarters _ . . .

ARS (DNA, RG 59, Despatches from Special Agents). Place suggested by evidence in letter. Addressed "Market Street," Philadelphia. Endorsed "recd."

1. President Washington recently had appointed Samuel Bayard unofficial agent of claims and appeals to manage cases pending in British admiralty courts involving American ships captured or condemned by the British. *Columbian Centinel* (Boston), November 19, 1794; Instrument of Indemnification, Samuel Bayard before James Graff of Bird, Savage, & Bird, January 10, 1795, and Samuel Bayard to Edmund Randolph, April 17, 1795, Letters Received from Samuel Bayard, RG 76, DNA; Samuel Bayard to Timothy Pickering, July 27, 1796, Instructions to Diplomatic Officers, RG 59, DNA.

2. Deputy clerk Jacob Wagner, Samuel Bayard's temporary replacement, was working at that time in the offices of the Department of State, where Edmund Randolph was secretary of state. See headnote to "The Clerks and Their Record."

3. None of Samuel Bayard's letters to the justices of the Supreme Court has been found.

Jeremiah Smith to William Plumer
February 7, 1795   Philadelphia, Pennsylvania

... The Supreme Court commenced their session on monday._ Much of the dignity of the Court is lost by the absence of the Chief Justice_ Judge Cushing has not attended every day_ He is under the Care of a Physician for a Cancer on his Lip_ He attends part of the Time & in those Causes where they cannot make a quorum without him._ ...

ARS (Nh, Plumer Papers).

Jeremiah Smith (1759-1842), New Hampshire's leading jurist, had attended Harvard but completed his studies at Queen's College (later Rutgers), graduating in 1780. Smith was admitted to the bar in 1786. He served in the House of Representatives from 1791 to 1797. Following his resignation from Congress in 1797, he became the United States attorney for the district of New Hampshire. In 1801 he received an appointment as circuit judge under the judiciary act passed that year, but he lost the position when the act was repealed. A year later he became chief justice of New Hampshire. *DAB.*

William Plumer (1759-1850), a New Hampshire lawyer, was a leader of the federalists in that state. Plumer served in the state legislature (1785-1786, 1788, 1790, 1791, 1797-1800); in 1791 and 1797, he was speaker of New Hampshire's House of Representatives. *DAB.*

John Adams to Abigail Adams
February 9, 1795   Philadelphia, Pennsylvania

... The Judges are now here   Judge Cushing is under the Hands of Dr Tate who is said to have wrought many Cures of Cancers and particularly one for the President. The Judge appears to be under serious apprehensions for something in his Lip which he thinks is a Cancer but his hopes from Tates Prescriptions seem to be lively. ...

AR (MHi, Adams Manuscript Trust).

Abigail (Smith) Adams (1744-1818), wife of John Adams. They had married in 1764. *DAB.*

James Iredell to Hannah Iredell —————————————
February 13, 1795 Philadelphia, Pennsylvania

... Our Court is yet sitting, and probably will till some time next week. ... I am so much engaged with Court Business that I cannot possibly write now to any body else_ ...

ARS (Nc-Ar, Charles E. Johnson Collection). Addressed "Edenton North Carolina." Postmarked "13 FE."

   Hannah (Johnston) Iredell (1747-1826), wife of Associate Justice James Iredell, was the sister of Samuel Johnston. *PJI,* 1:88n.

James Iredell to Hannah Iredell —————————————
February 20, 1795 Philadelphia, Pennsylvania

... Our Court is yet sitting, and probably will for three or four days longer and the business before us is of such great importance as to require almost our constant attention. This will prevent me, I fear writing to any body else, though I much wish it. ... I am now busily engaged in particular in preparing to deliver my opinion on a very important and difficult case the argument of which lasted eight days.[1] ...

ARS (Nc-Ar, Charles E. Johnson Collection). Address partly obliterated; "Carolina" still visible. Postmarked "20 FE."

   1. *Penhallow v. Doane's Administrators.*

Jeremiah Smith to William Plumer —————————————
February 24, 1795 Philadelphia, Pennsylvania

... I shall attend the Supreme Court to day_ I am told that the Judges will this day deliver their opinions seriatim in the McClary Cause_[1] This indicates that a difference in opinion exists on the Bench_ They miss the chief-Justice_ He was the ornament of the Bench_ between ourselves Cushing is superannuated & contemptible_ Patterson is unquestionably the ablest Judge_ Well I shall tell you more about it in the afternoon_ [*Smith continues the letter in the afternoon with a long report of the Court's decision in* Penhallow v. Doane's Administrators. *He particularly praises Justice Paterson's opinion.*]

   You would have been delighted_ The rest of the Court were like amolehills beside the Alps_ I speak the general sentiment_ How rideculous to appoint old men to such offices; Patterson appears to be a young man, perhaps 45_[2] It is astonishing how so good a man should ever have been appointed a Governor?

                                    a
If we only had ⌃ few such men the Lord would save this Country as he
promised to do Sodom⎯ But you know I am extravagant in my praises as well
as Censures⎯ What ever I do I do with all my might⎯ . . .

ARS (Nh, Plumer Papers).
   1. *Penhallow v. Doane's Administrators.*
   2. At this time, William Paterson was forty-nine years old.

James Iredell to Hannah Iredell ⎯⎯⎯⎯⎯⎯⎯⎯⎯⎯⎯⎯⎯⎯
February 26, 1795 Philadelphia, Pennsylvania

[*Iredell explains that because he will ride the Eastern Circuit*] I have no expectation
that I can get home until after the Supreme Court in August, which will probably have a very long session, as perhaps the great Virginia cause[1] and some
others will then come on. . . .

Pr (Printed in *MJI,* 2:440-41).
   1. *Ware v. Hylton.*

Jeremiah Smith to William Plumer ⎯⎯⎯⎯⎯⎯⎯⎯⎯⎯⎯⎯
February 28, 1795 Philadelphia, Pennsylvania

. . . The supreme Court remain in session & it is probable we shall leave them
sitting
   Walker ThBartlett & Calfe[1] would have settled all the Business that has been
before them in a less number of hours than they have spent days.⎯ Justice
seems to sleep here, with us she rides post.⎯ . . .

ARS (Nh, Plumer Papers). Addressed "Epping   New Hampshire" via "Exeter   Post Office."
Postmarked "28   FE."
   1. Timothy Walker (1737-1822), Thomas Bartlett (1745-1805), and John Calfe (1741-1808)
were justices of the Court of Common Pleas in Rockingham County, New Hampshire. Shipton,
Sibley's Harvard Graduates, 14:107-11; Ezra Scollay Stearns, *Genealogical and Family History of the
State of New Hampshire,* 4 vols. (New York: Lewis Publishing, 1908), 1:159-60; Ann Calef Board-
man, *Robert Calef of Boston and Some of His Descendants* (Salem, Mass., 1940), pp. 52-53; D. Hamilton Hurd, comp., *History of Rockingham and Strafford Counties, New Hampshire* (Philadelphia: J. W.
Lewis, 1882), p. 2.

James Iredell to Hannah Iredell ⎯⎯⎯⎯⎯⎯⎯⎯⎯⎯⎯⎯⎯⎯
March 6, 1795 Philadelphia, Pennsylvania

. . . Our Court did not break up till Tuesday, and tho' we were all very much
fatigued we should probably have sat several days longer but for Judge [*letter*
                Cushing's
inked out] ⌃ indisposition who suffers severely by a cancer on his lip. Unfortunately now so much important business has been deferred till August that I
have no doubt we shall sit thro' the whole of the month, if not later.[1] . . .

ARS (Nc-Ar, Charles E. Johnson Collection). Addressed "Edenton   North Carolina."
    1. In a letter written from Springfield, Massachusetts, on May 7, 1795, James Iredell again
mentioned to his wife that "I believe we shall have a long Court in August." Charles E. Johnson
Collection, Nc-Ar.

James Iredell to Helen Tredwell ————————————————————
March 7, 1795   Philadelphia, Pennsylvania

. . . I did intend to have written to you much sooner, but our Court lasted an
unexpected long time, and during its continuance it required almost unre-
mitted attention. . . .

ARS (Nc-Ar, Charles E. Johnson Collection). Addressed "Edenton."
    Helen (Blair) Tredwell (1763-1802), known as Nelly, was a niece of the Iredells. Wilma Cart-
wright Spence, comp., *Tombstones and Epitaphs of Northeastern North Carolina* (Baltimore: Gateway
Press, 1973), p. 65; *PJI*, 2:169n.

James Iredell to Hannah Iredell ————————————————————
March 13, 1795   Philadelphia, Pennsylvania

[*My health*] is very good. It was a little affected, but not much, by the incessant
and important business of our Court blended with many kind entertainments.
. . .

ARS (Nc-Ar, Charles E. Johnson Collection). Addressed "Edenton   North Carolina." Postmarked "13   MR."

William Bradford, Jr., to Samuel Bayard ————————————
June 4, 1795   Rosehill, Philadelphia County, Pennsylvania

                    the New York
. . . The event of M͟r͟ ͟J͟a͟y͟s͟ election is yet unknown: but it may probably be
ascertained before the William Penn sails.— Should Mr Jay be chosen the
choice of his successor will be an embarrassing business. In a constitution like
ours which carefully seperates the great departments of gov^t & strives to prevent the least dependence of the Judiciary on the Executive, the principle of
Rotation would be the least exceptionable in that point of view:— but as cases
may often occur in which the succession of the eldest puisne judge would be
wholly improper, it will be impossible to establish such a system. The public
voice seems already to have excluded Mr C.[1] who stands next to M^r. Jay— &
it is even supposed by some that neither h[e?] nor his friends for him would
desire it— But these are premature reflections as I hope we shall yet keep
Mr Jay: but it is confidently said that he w͟i͟l͟l͟ has a considerable majority. . . .

ARS (PHi, Gratz Collection). Endorsed "recd 10ᵗʰ July & ans'd 11." Written at "Rosehill," the country estate of Elias Boudinot, the father-in-law of William Bradford, Jr. J. J. Boudinot, ed., *The Life, Public Services, Addresses and Letters of Elias Boudinot, LL.D.,* 2 vols. (1896; reprint ed., New York: Da Capo Press, 1971), 2:37.

1. William Cushing.

Peter Augustus Jay to Essex Ridley ————————————
June 10, 1795 Philadelphia, Pennsylvania

. . . My Father is now here perhaps for the last time— He has been chosen during his absence to an Office which will not oblige him to be at a distance from Home, and you know his disposition to well to suppose that he will again wish to quit his family & friends— . . .

ARS (MHi, Ridley Papers). Addressed "Baltimore." Postmarked "11   IV."
Peter Augustus Jay (1776-1843), eldest child of Chief Justice John Jay, accompanied his father to England to serve as his secretary during the negotiations for the Jay Treaty. Peter Jay returned to New York at the conclusion of the mission, studied law, and was admitted to the bar in 1797. *DAB.*
Essex Ridley (1776-1796), son of the late Matthew Ridley (John Jay's friend and brother-in-law). *PJJ,* 2:12, 122, 591; Livingston, *Livingstons of Livingston Manor,* p. 533.

John Blair to William Cushing ————————————————
June 12, 1795 Williamsburg, Virginia

Wᵐsburg— June 12ᵗʰ 1795.

Dear Sir,

Your letter on my last leaving Philadelphia, inclosing me a hundred dollars on account of my taking the Southern circuit, expressed a wish that you might be excused from attending the Supreme Court in August next, as in that hot season little is to be done, & as the middle circuit would probably be assigned to you, at that siting, which would make it necessary for you to leave home in Septʳ after— As far as this was to depend upon me, I was determined to do every thing in my power, for gratifying your desire, & had fully ~~determined~~ resolved to attend the August-Term my self— ~~And~~ This is still my design, if a calamity which has befallen me do not prevent it— I think, however, I ought to inform you, that a malady which I have had for some years, in a smaller degree, has since I had the pleasure of seeing you increased so greatly as to disqualify me totally for business— It is a rattling, distracting noise in my head— I had much of it at Savannah; besides almost continual cholic. I would fain have declined the decision of several Admiralty cases there, if I had not been told that delay would be greatly injurious, on account of the prize-goods being stored at a very great daily expense— This circumstance prompted me to go thro that

business, altho in a condition not fit for any; & I have some reason to fear
that in doing so I have effected nothing but work for the Supreme court,
                                                                                   to
by undoing what I have done. It is, however, a consolation to me, that there
is yet a court where my errors may be corrected ___ When I came to Columbia,
I found much business of the same sort; but as in those cases bond & security
had been given, & the goods not stored, altho I heard an argument on two
of them, I thought it adviseable (my disorder still increasing) to decline making
any decree & adjourn the court ___ The same cause induced me to decline hold-
          but make the best of my way home,
ing the court at Raleigh, ^ having first done every thing I could to prevent
the fruitless attendance of others; & from every thing I have experienced since
my being at home, I have little encouragement to think that I shall be able to
attend court in August; I fear I never shall; & if I find no speedy amendment,
so as to justify an expectation that I may be again qualified to execute the
duties of my office, I shall certainly resign it ___ [1] In case the writ of error for
reversing the judgment of the circuit-court at Richmond, which was continued
in Feby ___ on account of the absence of the Chief Justice, should be brought
on in August, I ought to remind you, that I have all along declined siting in
that cause ___ [2] I flatter my self that Dr Tate has long before now removed all
your apprehension on account of the disorder of your lip, & that Mrs Cushing,
as much as ever, may have all reason to consider it as the seat of bliss.

Pray present to her my most respectful compliments ___

With great regard, I am, dear sir,   Your humble servant

John Blair

ARS (MHi, Robert Treat Paine Papers). Addressed "Massachusetts." Postmarked "W^{ms}.burg
June 12 1795."

1. John Blair sent his letter of resignation to George Washington on October 25, 1795 (q.v.
in "Appointments to the Bench," under "John Blair: Appointment as Associate Justice in 1789").

2. *Ware v. Hylton.*

James McHenry to George Washington ———————
June 14, 1795   Baltimore, Maryland

. . . In the event of a new arrangement in the judiciary department I beg leave
to suggest to your consideration the present chief justice of this state, at the
same time I would remark (having had no conversation with Mr Chase) that
I do not know whether he would incline to relinquish the office he now holds
for one that would be attended with greater fatigue.

Among the inducements I feel for presenting his name on this occasion is
his general conduct since the adoption of our government, and the sense I
entertain of the part he bore in the revolutionary efforts of a long and trying
crisis. You know that his services and abilities were of much use to the cause
during that period, sometimes by the measures he proposed or had influence

to get adopted, and sometimes by the steady opposition he gave to the intrigues raised against yourself; and that if some of his conduct procured him enemies, whatever might have been exceptionable in it was greatly exaggerated at that moment,[1] by the zeal of patriotism, which makes no allowance for human situations, and afterwards by persons, who seem to me, to have been always more intent upon removing obstructions to their own advancement than in promoting the public good, or doing justice to the merits of competitors. Your experience has long since enabled you to form a just estimate in such cases, and to distinguish between a mans real character and the representation made of it during the fermentation of a party, or by those, who approaching your councils may have a special interest in the continuance of its obscuration. In this respect the public has done Mr Chase justice with the exception of a few men who seem determined to pursue him to old age with a rancour, which in my eyes no political quarrel can excuse or honourable ambition justify. In making this allusion I do not mean I assure you Mr Carroll whose sentiments of Mr Chase I have reason to think correspond pretty much with my own, as mine does, I am persuaded with most persons in the State of influence and discernment.

It is, Sir, after having weighed all these circumstances since our conversation respecting him; after having reflected upon the good that he has done, and the good that he may still do; after having debated within myself whether his political or other errors (which exist no longer) have been of such a cast and magnitude as to be a perpetual bar to his holding any office under the United States; after having considered the impressions which an appearance of neglect[2] is apt to produce in minds constructed like his, that I have thought it a dúty to mention him as a subject of consideration for present or future attention.

I ought to add perhaps that Mr Chase and I are neither upon good nor bad terms, neither friends nor enemies; that we speak to each other when we meet and do business ~~together~~ without quarrelling when matters of a public nature bring us together. He is always decent in his behaviour to me and I do not know that I am otherwise to him. It is on such occasions that I have thought I discovered reason to[3] infer that he would have no objection to a change of position,[4] and from all these considerations united, that I have ventured to speak of him as not wholly to be neglected unless such a step should be opposed by some striking and imperious circumstances.[5]

I need not tell you that to his professional knowledge he subjoins a very valuable stock of political science and information; but it may be proper to observe that he has discharged the office which he fills without the shadow of imputation upon the integrity of his decisions. . . .

ARS (DLC, George Washington Papers); ADfS (DLC, James McHenry Papers). The draft is dated "13 June 1795."

1. In draft, "time" crossed out and "moment" interlined.
2. In draft, "~~determined~~ neglect."
3. In draft, "discovered reason to" interlined over an inked-out word.
4. In draft, "a change of position" interlined over "~~national appointment~~."
5. In draft, this paragraph has been written after the closing and keyed as belonging here by a reference mark.

John Adams to Abigail Adams
June 18, 1795 Philadelphia, Pennsylvania

. . . His Excellency Governor Jay returned Yesterday to N: York_ He has been very sociable and in fine Spirit[s?]_ His Health is improving. We have no C. J. as yet nominated. . . .

ARS (MHi, Adams Manuscript Trust).

William Cushing to John Jay
June 18, 1795 Scituate, Massachusetts

. . . I cannot so heartily relish the gubernatorial office, which is presented to you and with so much advantage in the choice. It will doubtless be for the good of N. Y., as well of the public in general, & what is of some consequence, more for your ease & comfort, than rambling in the Carolina woods in June. If you accept, as the Newspapers seem to announce, I must, though reluctantly, acquiesce.

I was in hope to get clear of going to Phila this hot season, but suppose it will not to do, to risque the want of a quorum, unless you give me permission to Stay at home. A Virginia cause was continued to August term, for your presence,[1] whether that will be consistent with your situation, I know not. The middle circuit will of course fall to me next; In the Summer or fall I expect the pleasure of calling to pay my respects to you_ . . .

ARS (NNC, John Jay Papers). Addressed "Newyork." Postmarked "BOSTON 1 IV." Endorsed "and 11 July." John Jay's answering letter not found.

1. *Ware v. Hylton.*

William Bradford, Jr., to Samuel Bayard
June 20, 1795 Rosehill, Philadelphia County, Pennsylvania

. . . I had the pleasure of a good deal of conversation with Mr Jay, who returned to New York a few days ago. I regret his absence from the bench & I know not how the loss will be supplied: but he will no doubt give a tone to the state of New York, of great importance in a government constructed like ours._ . . .

ARS (CtY, Miscellaneous Manuscripts Collection).

Federal Orrery
June 27, 1795 New York, New York

A gentleman, not a little fortunate in his dreams, dreamt, last night, that the following promotions will take place on or about wednesday next, viz.

Jay, governor of the state of New-York, vice Clinton.[1]

Cushing, chief Justice of the United States, vice Jay. . . .

(Boston) July 9, 1795. Date and place are those of the headline.

1. John Jay's resignation of the chief justiceship was reported in the *Columbian Centinel* (Boston), July 11, 1795.

William Bradford, Jr., to Alexander Hamilton ————————
July 2, 1795 Philadelphia, Pennsylvania

. . . Your squabbles in New York have taken our Chief Justice from us— ought you not to find us another?— I am afraid that department "as it relates neither to War, finance nor Negociation," has no charms for you: & yet when
one considers how immensely important it is one a government where they
                                               is,
have the power of paralizing the measures of the goverment by declaring a law unconstitutional, it is not to be trusted to men who are to be scared by
                                    -minded
popular clamor or warped by feeble ^ prejudices.— I wish to heaven you would permit me to name you:— If not, what think you of Mr Randolph? . . .

ARS (DLC, Alexander Hamilton Papers).

James Iredell to Hannah Iredell ————————————
July 2, 1795 New York, New York

. . . I am perfectly well, but extremely mortified to find that the Senate have broke up without a Chief Justice being appointed, as I have too much reason to fear that owing to that circumstance it will be unavoidable for me to have some Circuit duty to perform this fall [*Iredell discusses the continuing burden of circuit riding with particular emphasis on the amount of time that he must be away from his family,* "so that I must either resign or we must have in view some residence near Philadelphia."] Mr Jay was sworn in as Governor yesterday. He was in danger of dying on his passage, and does not look well now. I am told, which has greatly astonished me, that he did not send his resignation of Chief Justice till two or three days ago, since the Senate broke up. Whatever were his reasons, I am persuaded it was utterly unjustifiable. The President may himself make a temporary appointment, but it is not much to be expected, I fear, as few Gentlemen would chuse to accept under such circumstances I expect to go in a few days to Philadelphia. . . .

ARS (Nc-Ar, Charles E. Johnson Collection).

Dunlap's American Daily Advertiser ————————————
July 3, 1795 Philadelphia, Pennsylvania

We understand from authority, that Mr. Jay has resigned the office of Chief Justice of the United States: In consequence of this vacancy, the writs issued

from the Supreme and Circuit Courts of the United States must be tested as
is directed by the following extract from the act of the 8th May, 1792.[1]

"Be it enacted by the Senate and House of Representatives of the United
States of America in Congress assembled, that all writs and processes issuing
from the Supreme or a Circuit Court, shall bear test of the Chief Justice of the
Supreme Court (or if that office be vacant) of the associate Justice next[2] in
precedence."

(Philadelphia) July 3, 1795. Date and place from item headline.

This article was reprinted in the *Boston Gazette* on July 13, 1795. It was summarized in the
Aurora (Philadelphia) on July 4, 1795, and the summary version also appeared in the *Richmond
Chronicle,* July 14, 1795.

1. "An Act for regulating Processes in the Courts of the United States, and providing Compensations for the Officers of the said Courts, and for Jurors and Witnesses," May 8, 1792. The
passage as printed in *Dunlap's American Daily Advertiser* differs insignificantly in capitalization from
the version printed in the statutes at large. *Stat.,* 1:275.

2. In newspaper, "uext."

Edmund Randolph to George Washington ———————
July 7, 1795 Philadelphia, Pennsylvania

Private

Philadelphia, July 7. 1795

Dear Sir

I this morning received the inclosed letter.[1] It relates to a subject, which,
notwithstanding the suggestions of M.ʳ King, M.ʳ Burr,[2] M.ʳ Bradford and some
other gentlemen, I positively forbid to be mentioned to you.[3] Why I forbid
it, the reasons are very, very many; for altho' the wish of the most respectable
of the bar in this city might have seemed to countenance it; yet One reason
overpowered in my mind every other; that I did not think it right in itself,
and that the world would not think ʌ it so. It shall never be said, that I would
ask for myself, what would be improper for your character to grant.

But this letter has really led me into a train of reflection, which I have
endeavoured to suppress, but ʌ which pours too rapidly into my mind to be resisted.

I foresee, as I believe with certainty, that the present chief-magistrate[4] will
not be prevailed upon to continue in office after the expiration of this term;
and I cannot well reconcile to myself the idea of serving, where I now am,
under any other— This is not all— With an abstinence from company, which
does not comport with my station, I run in debt, and hazard again those difficulties, from which the sales of my estate are likely to relieve me. The incessant anxiety of my wife, founded upon the experience of the last eighteen
months, [~~persuades?~~] ʌ urges me even now, to adopt an alternative, either to put down
my carriage, and live in a very circumscribed style; or to go again into the
practice of the law— That the latter is the most lucrative course is to me obvious. But it would inevitably throw me into the lower parts of Virginia, and
I do not wish to go farther south than Alexandria at any rate— The former

does not correspond with public expectation; and public expectation must in a degree be consulted.

Time ~~Years~~ has[5] rolled so fast and unperceived over my head, that I have not, until a year or two past calculated, how few remain for very active exertion. Nor have I, until a year or two ago, been persuaded, that, if an accident should befal you, the union is split in twain, unless it should be placed above the machinations of its enemies during your administration. In the event of a dissolution, Virginia will not be, for me or my family, a proper country to dwell in.

Thus circumstanced, and looking to all events, I think I ought to capacitate myself to take my position, in whatsoever part of the U. S. I may find most comfortable. Philadelphia is at present the most so; and no place appears likely to come into competition with my wishes, until the federal city shall receive congress. There, if the Union should remain intire, I mean to fix the fortunes of my son.

I am now brought to that stage of my reflections, at which my sensibility is most alive. A transposition into M[r] Blair's office would seem to seperate me rather more from you. As to yourself, my continuance on my present ground can be no farther important, than to close the weighty matters, now depending. These I would not quit, for my own honor, if I could not [*word inked out*] go through them notwithstanding. ~~The only~~ It is among the most pleasant of my sensations, that in spite of the ferment, raised by a few wicked men, I shall have some future credit in being in your confidence until you have established peace and order in the United States

I shall intrust none Sir,[6] but yourself, with these thoughts; never meaning to say to you thro' a second hand any thing of this nature. It is probable, that until after the supreme court, the subject will lie dormant; and that there may be no necessity to think of it until ~~the spring,~~ february. My only object is now, to relieve myself from a course of reflection, which might otherwise lie heavy upon my mind.

I have the honor to be my dear sir, with the most cordial and grateful attachment,   y[r] affectionate and sincere   hble serv.

                                                                Edm: Randolph

The President
    of the U. S.

ARS (DLC, George Washington Papers).

1. Letter not found.

2. Following service in the Revolutionary War, Aaron Burr (1756-1836) studied law and was admitted to the New York bar in 1782. Burr became one of the leading lawyers in New York City. In September, 1789, he became attorney general of New York. Two years later, Burr was elected to the Senate, where he remained through 1797. He then served for two years in the New York legislature. After being defeated for reelection in 1799, Burr returned to the legislature in 1800. In 1801 he became vice president of the United States. *DAB*.

3. The subject referred to was speculation that Edmund Randolph might replace John Jay.

4. George Washington.

5. Originally Edmund Randolph wrote "Two Years have"; he altered "Two" to "Time," crossed out "Years," and changed "have" to "has."

6. Edmund Randolph seems to have written "no man" and then altered the "no" to read "none" and wrote "Sir" over "man."

Aurora
July 7, 1795 Baltimore, Maryland

The senate having recommended to the President further friendly negocia-tions;[1] probably Mr. Jay has resigned his office as chief justice, to be ready for another voyage to the court of London. The late display of his political and commercial talents, must highly recommend him _ besides we are persuaded that royal George[2] will sqeeze him by the hand, the cunning Charlotte[3] vouch-safe her gracious smiles, and even the maids of honour be strangely delighted at his return, for they always received great pleasure from the Quxiote[4] visage of the American plenipo.

(Philadelphia) July 10, 1795. Date and place are from headline.

1. On June 24, 1795, the Senate ratified the Jay Treaty on condition that those sections of Article XII that regulated trade between the United States and the British West Indies be sus-pended and that further negotiations be undertaken on that subject. *SEJ*, 1:186.

2. King George III.

3. Charlotte Sophia (1744-1818) had married George III in 1761. William H. Harris and Judith S. Levey, eds., *The New Columbia Encyclopedia* (New York: Columbia University Press, 1975).

4. In newspaper, "Qnxiote."

Samuel Bayard to Elias Boudinot
July [10-31], 1795 London, England

... By some of the late papers from N. Y. which come as far down as the 15. June we find that M[r] J. had been elected Governor of N. York. by a majority of 1580 _ The President I apprehend will be under some difficulty in finding a proper person to fill his place _ By a letter from M[r] Bradford,[1] I find that it is the general opinion _ that M[r] C. _[2] who holds the next seat on the bench cannot be the man. Who will he be _ from what state be taken _ Will there be no resignation that will give the President an opp[y] of taking a distinguish'd from one of the large states? In short I see there must be con-siderable difficulty in the final choice _ The change of situation must however be agreeable to M[r3] J. _ Independently of his income being increas'd (in these dear times) _ Of his being more at ho[me] with his family _ & of his gen[l] preference of an executive to a judicial situation _ it would been embarrassing for him to have decided points arising out of the very treaty he had negociated.
...

ARS (NHi, Bayard-Boudinot-Pintard Papers). This letter is dated "July. 1795." It had to have been written after July 10, because of Samuel Bayard's reference to his receipt of William Bradford's letter to him of June 4, 1795 (q.v.); the endorsement on the Bradford letter indicates that Bayard received it on July 10. The margin of Bayard's letter has been reinforced with tape which renders some text illegible; as a consequence, readings have been supplied in brackets.

1. William Bradford, Jr., to Samuel Bayard, June 4, 1795 (q.v.).
2. William Cushing.
3. The "M" is written over a "J."

Edmund T. Ellery to David L. Barnes
July 15, 1795 Newport, Rhode Island

Newport July 15ᵗʰ 1795 —

Dear Sir,

I received a letter from you yesterday in which you write for two exons, one against Carpenter, the other against Mulbone — There is a difficulty arises in my opinion respecting the Test of the Exons — I find by the papers that Mʳ Jay has resigned his office as a Judge [a]nd taken the oath of Office as Governor [o]f New York — I think the law provides that in case of vacancy &c — the next Judge Writs of exons are to bear the Test of the next Judge, who I presume is Mʳ Cushing — You will be pleased to inform yourself whether I can put Judge Cushings name to the Writs &c not knowing <u>officially</u> that Judge Jay has resigned — be pleased to write me immediately, & in the mean time I will make out the Exons leaving a blank for the Judge's name — to be filled up as you may think [*letters inked out*] proper — You will undoubtedly be at newport the first of August, and then you may confer with the other gentlemen of the Law respecting this business — Judge Marchant[1] chooses to be silent about the matter, only mentioning, that I had better write you, previous to the Exons [issuing — ?]

With esteem, I am your humble servant

Edmund T: Ellery

ARS (RHi, Rhode Island Manuscripts). Addressed "Providence." Text is missing because it adhered to the wax seal when the letter was opened; therefore readings are supplied in brackets.

Edmund Trowbridge Ellery (1763-1847), son of the chief justice of Rhode Island, was the clerk of the federal district and circuit courts for Rhode Island. Harrison Ellery, "Ancestors of Hon. William Ellery, Signer of the Declaration of Independence," *Newport Historical Magazine* 4 (1883): 181-82; *PAH,* 16:452.

David Leonard Barnes (1760-1812), a Providence attorney. Judicial Conference of the United States, Bicentennial Committee, *Judges of the United States* (Washington, D.C.: Government Printing Office, 1978).

1. Henry Marchant (1741-1796) had studied law with Edmund Trowbridge of Cambridge, Massachusetts. Marchant settled in his native Newport, Rhode Island, where he rose to prominence in law and politics. He served as attorney general of Rhode Island from 1771 to 1776 and later supported adoption of the federal Constitution in his home state. Marchant was appointed United States judge for the district of Rhode Island on July 3, 1790, and remained on the bench until his death. *DAB; SEJ,* 1:53.

William Bradford, Jr., to Samuel Bayard —————————————
July 16, 1795   Philadelphia, Pennsylvania

... No appointment of Chief Justice is yet made_ but Mr Rutledge, (Ch Jus. of S. Carolina) will be the man if he inclines to accept it._ Mr Blair, talks of resigning his seat_ and I suspect Mr Wilson will not continue long on the bench._ ...

ARS (PHi, Gratz Collection). Endorsed "Recd. 24. Aug. & ansd 25. ___ 95."

South-Carolina State-Gazette —————————————————
July 17, 1795   Charleston, South Carolina

Yesterday,[1] agreeably to[2] notifications in the several gazettes, the citizens convened in the Exchange.

On this momentous occasion, we were happy in the appearance of veterans, whose services and patriotism, so often exerted, and whose great age were thought to have withdrawn them from public service. G[e]n. Gadsden,[3] was selected from them for speaker, which office he accepted so far, as to adjourn the meeting to St. Michael's church, which prom[i]sed better accomodation; but urged his age as a competent reason for declining the other duties of that capacity. His acceptance and resignation were both received with plaudits of veneration.

Judge Mathews[4] was called unanimously to the chair. After the speaker had informed the meeting that they had been assembled to consider whether the impending treaty of amity, commerce and navigation, between the United States and Great Britain, is not[5] degrading to the national honour, dangerous to the political existence, and destructive of the agricultural, manufacturing, commercial and shipping interests of the people of the United States, and requested of those who had come prepared, to offer their sentiments on the occasion.

Mr. Goodwin,[6] introduced the business, by declaring his opinion of the treaty, in the plainest terms of disapprobation. He called upon the friends, if such there were, to come forward, to shew its merits, and those opposed, were requested to discuss its de-merits. He then requested to submit a motion, that a committee be appointed to draw up a remonstrance assigning their reasons, &c. and that the same be forwarded to the president.

Chief Justice Rutledge[7] rose. He contended in the first instance, that the title was a perversion of terms_ that it was stiled a treaty of amity, commerce and navigation, but in fact, it was an humble acknowledgement of our dependence upon his majesty; a surrender of our rights and privileges, for so much of his gracious favour as he should be pleased to grant.

That the first article securing friendship and peace to people of every degree, was extending favour to all those who were under banishment or amercement, which was improper.

He adverted to the frequent inattention to the proper use of words throughout this puerile production. Diplomatic characters were generally particular in this respect, and it was inconceivable how such perversion of terms should take place. "His majesty *will* withdraw his troops, &c. within the boundaries *assigned* by the treaty of peace, &c."[8]

WILL, he contended, implied it[9] as a favour. It should have been SHALL withdraw his troops. It is not possible[10] to conceive it a matter of will, even in his most gracious majesty. But the whole of this clause he contended was improperly introduced.

Mr. Jay should have demanded an unconditional relinquishment of those posts[11] as a right; 'till which was granted and until Lord Grenville[12] had given orders to Lord Dorchester[13] to that effect, open,[14] to be sent to our President to be by him forwarded, he should not have opened his lips upon the treaty. It was prostituting the dearest rights of freemen and laying them prostrate at the feet of royalty. Assigned by the treaty of peace "[15]was an expression that ought not to have been admitted by one who knew the territory to have been fought for, to have been attained with our freedom and who should have insisted upon the possession of it.

He adverted to the tricks, easy to be discovered in every article and clause of the treaty that were put upon our envoy. But his admitting, that "it is uncertain whether the river Missisippi extends so far northward as the lake of the woods as to be intersected by a line drawn due west from the lake of the woods in the manner mentioned in the treaty of peace,"[16] and whereas "doubts have arisen what river was truly intended under the name of the river St. Croix,"[17] are the grossest absurdities; particularly when assented to by a man who absolutely signed[18] that treaty,[19] and had before him maps that excluded both uncertainty and doubt. To be diplomatically chaste, it should have been, "as we are uncertain" and whereas doubts have arisen with us" &c.

The appointment of the commissioners[20] was a measure that could operate to the advantage of but one party, the British, in case it should be properly conducted, but he asserted that the chance was greatly against fairness and he doubted not that it would be little better than a direct relinquishment of all it was intended they should decide upon.

After observing that he hoped a full discussion would not take place this day, he insisted that there was but one article or clause in the whole that had the appearance of reciprocity, an idea requisite in the conception of a treaty,[21] or conferring advantage to the United States, and that was the one, allowing us the West India trade _ [22] a deception, a trick that adding[23] insult to injury.

In pointing out the improprieties of negociations of any kind with England, the chief justice was led to the state of the French successes. He lavished[24] the highest encomiums on that brave and heroic nation. The Alexanders, the Cæsars, and the Charles of antiquity,[25] gave place to a whole nation of heroes. Their deeds of heroism were great _ but nobler ones were daily acted[26] in all parts of France. As a nation they had conquered all her opposers. Holland owned her conquest, Prussia felt her energy, Germany retired from her arms, Spain was suing for peace and the perfidious, the boasting the assuming nation Great Britain, that had arrogated for ages, power never possessed, that assumed the sovereignty of the sea and monopolized the commerce of the whole world, was hoping for peace upon whatever terms France might grant it. To negotiate, she could not hope— She was reduced to the last gasp and were America to seize her by the throat she would expire in agonies at her feet.

One[27] thing appeared to him right, it was justice, and he hoped his country would always maintain it— he alluded to the intent of the article[28] that secured to the British creditors their debts in the United States.[29] Although he was well convinced that their interest in the funds bought at two or three shillings in the pound is now worth twenty; tho' the indent had been obtained by the soldier as the reward of his laborious services at the expense perhaps of life or limb, and that he parted with it thus depreciated, observing it to be the *price* he paid for his country's freedom, yet he was for allowing them their just demand, but we ought not to bind ourselves to it by treaty.

To take the power of deciding upon those claims from our state courts; to deny to trust the supreme court of the United States, and submit the causes to a few commissioners[30] was ridiculous and inadmissible.

To attempt to do justice to the energy, the eloquence, the decided and manly firmness of this sage republican, is a rashness that we disclaim, we only seek to sketch the outlines, not without some hopes however, of extending the rays of his patriotism, by even our humble efforts.

To hear his abhorrence of the whole instrument, unmoved, would argue a want of that spirit which the union now finds necessary to her existence. When he declares he had rather, the President should die, dearly as he loves him, than he should sign that treaty— when he pronounces for *war* rather than his country should approve the measures that will effect her annihilation, we are roused into a sense of our danger. When the same energy is exerted to advise a calm, firm and decisive line of conduct, and the most deliberate and cool discussion, we cannot deny it weight,[31] nor fail to disavow all outrageous expressions of disapprobation, either of men or measures. The effect was thus with the auditory; the most implicit confidence followed his spirited remarks, and the most determinate assent was obtained by his moderation. [*Goodwyn's motion, made before John Rutledge spoke, was adopted. An election would be held in Charleston to choose fifteen men to draft a statement to be sent to President George Washington opposing the Jay Treaty.*][32]

(Charleston) July 17, 1795. Date and place are those of the headline. Readings in brackets have been supplied because of broken type.

Because of the importance of John Rutledge's speech in subsequent efforts to negative his nomination, all copies found thus far are listed here: *Dunlap's American Daily Advertiser* (Philadelphia), July 28, 1795; *Philadelphia Gazette,* July 28, 1795; *Aurora* (Philadelphia), July 29, 1795; *Pennsylvania Gazette* (Philadelphia), July 29, 1795; *Argus* (New York), July 30, 1795; *Federal Intelligencer* (Baltimore), August 1, 1795; *Independent Gazetteer* (Philadelphia), August 1, 1795; *Rich-*

mond Chronicle, August 1, 1795; *Independent Chronicle* (Boston), August 6, 1795; *Providence Gazette,* August 8, 1795; *Lamson's Weekly Visitor* (Exeter, New Hampshire), August 11, 1795; *State Gazette of North-Carolina* (Edenton), August 13, 1795.

Newspapers were notoriously careless about the placement of quotation marks. We have not noted variations in placement from newspaper to newspaper.

1. *Dunlap's American Daily Advertiser* (Philadelphia), July 28, 1795, preceded this item with the following: *"By the Sloop Dispatch, Capt. Bird, arrived last Sunday morning, we have the following."* The news reported arrived on July 26—"last Sunday morning." The same introduction appeared in the *Philadelphia Gazette,* July 28, 1795; *Pennsylvania Gazette* (Philadelphia), July 29, 1795; *Argus* (New York), July 30, 1795; *Independent Chronicle* (Boston), August 6, 1795; *Lamson's Weekly Visitor* (Exeter, New Hampshire), August 11, 1795.

2. The newspaper printed "agreeabl yto."

3. Christopher Gadsden (1724-1805), a Charleston merchant, had been a leader of radical forces in South Carolina at the outbreak of the Revolutionary War. Gadsden served in the South Carolina legislature almost continuously from 1757 to 1784 but thereafter withdrew almost entirely from politics. His career included service in the Stamp Act Congress (1765), the Continental Congress (1774-1776), and South Carolina's ratifying convention (1788). He was lieutenant governor of South Carolina from 1780 to 1782. When elected governor in 1782, he declined the office because of his age and health. Edgar and Bailey, *Biographical Directory of the South Carolina House of Representatives,* 2:259-63.

4. John Mathewes (1744-1802) previously had been a member of the South Carolina legislature, a representative to the Continental Congress, and a governor of South Carolina. In 1784 he became chancellor of the Court of Equity; in 1791 he became a judge of the Court of Equity and served on the bench until 1797. Edgar and Bailey, *Biographical Directory of the South Carolina House of Representatives,* 2:438-40.

5. In the *Independent Gazetteer* (Philadelphia), August 1, 1795, this word appears as "now."

6. Charles Goodwyn (ca. 1756-1827) was a native of England who gained admission to the bar in Charleston in 1784. Goodwyn represented the Winton district in the South Carolina House of Representatives, 1800-1801. Teresa E. Wilson and Janice L. Grimes, comps., *Marriage and Death Notices from the Southern Patriot, 1815-1830,* vol. 1 (Easley, S.C.: Southern Historical Press, 1982), p. 165; John A. Chapman, *History of Edgefield County from the Earliest Settlements to 1897* (1897; reprint ed., Spartanburg, S.C.: Reprint Co., 1980), pp. 176-77, 182-83; John Bolten O'Neall, *Biographical Sketches of the Bench and Bar of South Carolina,* vol. 2 (1859; reprint ed., Spartanburg, S.C.: Reprint Co., 1975), pp. 146-47; Walter B. Edgar, ed., *Biographical Directory of the South Carolina House of Representatives,* vol. 1, *Session Lists, 1692-1973* (Columbia: University of South Carolina Press, 1974), pp. 254-58.

7. "Chief Justice" Rutledge probably refers to John Rutledge's position as chief justice of South Carolina, a post he held from February 18, 1791, to July 29, 1795. President Washington had appointed Rutledge chief justice of the Supreme Court on July 1, 1795, but news of his appointment did not appear in Charleston newspapers until July 20, 1795. Edgar and Bailey, *Biographical Directory of the South Carolina House of Representatives,* 2:580; for Rutledge's resignation, see below, John Rutledge to Arnoldus Vanderhorst, July 29, 1795; for notice of Rutledge's appointment, see below, *Philadelphia Gazette* under date of July 20, 1795.

8. This quotation is from Article II of the Jay Treaty. *ASP, Foreign Relations,* 1:520.

9. The word "it" was left out in the *Providence Gazette,* August 8, 1795.

10. This appears as "impossible" in *Dunlap's American Daily Advertiser* (Philadelphia), July 28, 1795; the *Philadelphia Gazette,* July 28, 1795; the *Aurora* (Philadelphia), July 29, 1795; the *Pennsylvania Gazette* (Philadelphia), July 29, 1795; the *Argus* (New York), July 30, 1795; the *Federal Intelligencer* (Baltimore), August 1, 1795; the *Independent Gazetteer* (Philadelphia), August 1, 1795; the *Independent Chronicle* (Boston), August 6, 1795; the *Providence Gazette,* August 8, 1795; and *Lamson's Weekly Visitor* (Exeter, New Hampshire), August 11, 1795.

11. Under Article VII of the Definitive Treaty of Peace (1783), British forces were to withdraw with "all convenient speed" from American soil. While British troops under Sir Guy Car-

leton withdrew from New York, those occupying a string of frontier posts running from Fort Michilimackinac on the Straits of Mackinac to Dutchman's Point on Lake Champlain did not. For over twelve years, the British held these forts, ostensibly to protect their fur trade. The Jay Treaty established June 1, 1796, as the evacuation date of the posts, and by the summer of that year the withdrawal was complete. Samuel Flagg Bemis, *Jay's Treaty: A Study in Commerce and Diplomacy* (New York: Macmillan, 1923), pp. 1-14; Lester J. Cappon, ed., *Atlas of Early American History: The Revolutionary Era, 1760-1790* (Princeton: Princeton University Press, 1976), pp. 61, 129.

12. William Wyndham Grenville (1759-1834), the British secretary of state for foreign affairs, had been the principal British negotiator for the Jay Treaty. *DNB; ASP, Foreign Relations,* 1:520.

13. Guy Carleton, Lord Dorchester (1724-1808), had been governor of Quebec at the outbreak of the Revolutionary War. Following military service and a return to Britain, Carleton returned to North America in 1782 as commander-in-chief of British forces in America. In 1786 he was reappointed governor of Quebec and later became governor of Canada, a post he held until July 9, 1796. As governor, Carleton had repeated contacts with the Washington administration (particularly with Alexander Hamilton) about the possibilities of an Anglo-American alliance. *DNB;* Jerald A. Combs, *The Jay Treaty* (Berkeley: University of California Press, 1970), pp. 47-53.

14. The word "open" was left out in the *Independent Chronicle* (Boston), August 6, 1795, and *Lamson's Weekly Visitor* (Exeter, New Hampshire), August 11, 1795.

15. The phrase "assigned by the treaty of peace" appears in Article II of the Jay Treaty. It refers to the boundary lines drawn between the United States and Canada as a result of the Definitive Treaty of Peace (1783). *ASP, Foreign Relations,* 1:520; also, see note 11 above.

16. This phrase appears in Article IV of the Jay Treaty. *ASP, Foreign Relations,* 1:521.

17. This phrase appears in Article V of the Jay Treaty. *ASP, Foreign Relations,* 1:521.

18. This word appears as "figured" in the *Richmond Chronicle,* August 1, 1795.

19. John Jay, along with American commissioners Benjamin Franklin and John Adams, signed the Definitive Treaty of Peace in Paris on September 3, 1783. *PJJ,* 2:579.

20. John Rutledge was referring to Article V of the Jay Treaty. Article V provided for the appointment of three commissioners—one named by Great Britain, one by the United States, and one chosen by the other two—who would determine which river was intended to be the St. Croix River mentioned in Article II of the Definitive Treaty of Peace (1783). The St. Croix River was designated as the northeastern boundary of the United States. *ASP, Foreign Relations,* 1:521; Bemis, *Jay's Treaty,* p. 325n.

21. The phrase "an idea requisite in the conception of a treaty" was left out of the *Argus* (New York), July 30, 1795; *Independent Chronicle* (Boston), August 6, 1795; and *Lamson's Weekly Visitor* (Exeter, New Hampshire), August 11, 1795.

22. The reference is to Article XII of the Jay Treaty. *ASP, Foreign Relations,* 1:522.

23. This was rendered as "added" in the *Aurora* (Philadelphia), July 29, 1795; the *Pennsylvania Gazette* (Philadelphia), July 29, 1795; the *Federal Intelligencer* (Baltimore), August 1, 1795; the *Independent Gazetteer* (Philadelphia), August 1, 1795; the *Providence Gazette,* August 8, 1795; and the *State Gazette of North-Carolina* (Edenton), August 13, 1795. It appeared as "was adding" in the *Argus* (New York), July 30, 1795; the *Independent Chronicle* (Boston), August 6, 1795; and *Lamson's Weekly Visitor* (Exeter, New Hampshire), August 11, 1795.

24. Appears as "wished" in *Dunlap's American Daily Advertiser* (Philadelphia), July 28, 1795; the *Philadelphia Gazette,* July 28, 1795; and the *Federal Intelligencer* (Baltimore), August 1, 1795.

25. Probably a reference to Charlemagne (742?-814), Carolingian king of the Franks (768-814) and emperor of the West (800-814). *New Columbia Encyclopedia.*

26. Appears in the newspaper as "dailyacted."

27. "One" appears as "The" in the *Philadelphia Gazette,* July 28, 1795, and in the *Federal Intelligencer* (Baltimore), August 1, 1795.

28. Appears as "articles" in *Dunlap's American Daily Advertiser* (Philadelphia), July 28, 1795; the *Aurora* (Philadelphia), July 29, 1795; the *Pennsylvania Gazette* (Philadelphia), July 29, 1795; the *Argus* (New York), July 30, 1795; the *Independent Gazetteer* (Philadelphia), August 1, 1795; and the *Providence Gazette,* August 8, 1795.

29. The reference is to Article VI of the Jay Treaty. *ASP, Foreign Relations,* 1:521.

30. Article VI provided for five commissioners—two appointed by Great Britain, two by the United States, and one chosen by the other four—to examine and decide all claims. The awards were to be considered final and conclusive both as to justice and amount, and the United States would pay all judgments. Because the article did not stipulate that a creditor exhaust all judicial remedies first, critics argued that it would be possible for a creditor to bypass the federal courts in favor of proceeding before the commissioners. *ASP, Foreign Relations,* 1:521; Combs, *Jay Treaty,* p. 152.

31. The phrase "it weight" was printed as "it right" in the *Independent Gazetteer* (Philadelphia), August 1, 1795, and as "its weight" in the *State Gazette of North-Carolina* (Edenton), August 13, 1795.

32. The following newspapers mentioned the meeting in Charleston and noted John Rutledge's participation: the *Columbian Centinel* (Boston), August 5, 1795, and the *Rutland Herald* (Rutland, Vermont), August 17 and 24, 1795. In addition, the *Independent Chronicle* (Boston), which had printed the Rutledge speech on August 6, 1795, mentioned again, on August 10, the Charleston meeting and Rutledge's part in it.

Philadelphia Gazette ——————————————————————
July 20, 1795 Charleston, South Carolina

From the most undoubted authority, we announce to our fellow-citizens the offer of Chief Justiceship of the United States, made to that true patriot and friend of man — JOHN RUTLEDGE, Esq. Chief Justice of this state.

His acceptance or rejection of the office, we are not yet informed of.

The uncertainty agitates the feelings of his cauntrymen. On the one hand they must lament his separation from them, and the want of his more immediate services to themselves — on the other, reap consolation from the idea of advantage to the Union, in the acceptance of so important a trust, by a man of tried Republican principles.

Honor and ambition, ye touch him not — He has reached the goal, in the universal love of Carolinians.

(Philadelphia) August 17, 1795. Date and place from headline.

Printing under an obviously incorrect title of August 20, the *Independent Chronicle* (Boston) republished this article on August 10. Under a Charleston headline of July 31, the *Boston Gazette* on August 17 also noted the appointment of John Rutledge.

Edmund T. Ellery to David L. Barnes ——————————————
July 23, 1795 Newport, Rhode Island

Newport July 23ᵈ 1795

Sir —

I had no doubt in my mind when I wrote you respecting the Test of Executions,[1] that Mʳ Jay had resigned his office as Chief Justice, and that Mʳ Cushing was the next in Office; — but I then thought, and do now think that some other information, different from that of a Newspaper should be given; — not that I had the vanity to suppose that the President would give me an Official letter on the subject, but might leave me, <u>leave me</u>, as you are pleased to express yourself, to find out this <u>important</u> circumstance in the best way I could __ I think I have found a guide to direct me, and therefore do not hesitate to test the enclosed executions with the name of Judge Cushing. __

As you undoubtedly glory in being esteemed a Yankee, __ I wish you had shewed me a little more of the candor of a Yankee, and instead of attempting to ridicule my ignorance, had imparted to me a portion of your superior knowledge __

I am   Sir   Your most   Humble servant

Edmund T: Ellery

David L: Barnes esq^r

NB. Your letter, from mistake, had not your name affixed to it,[2] but from a knowledge of your handwriting __ I have addressed this letter to you[*letters inked out*] __

ALS (RHi, Rhode Island Manuscripts).
  1. Edmund T. Ellery had written to David L. Barnes on July 15, 1795 (q.v.).
  2. Letter not found.

James Iredell to Hannah Iredell
July 24, 1795 Philadelphia, Pennsylvania

. . . No Chief Justice yet appointed, that I know of. I suppose Brother Cushing does not augur well from the delay.

ARS (Nc-Ar, Charles E. Johnson Collection). Addressed "Edenton   North Carolina." Postmarked "24   IV."

James Iredell to Hannah Iredell
July 24, 1795 Philadelphia, Pennsylvania

. . . We have yet no Chief Justice appointed, that I know of __ I presume it arises from the difficulty of fixing on a proper Person, but it may prove very distressing to the other Judges. If there is not one appointed by the Supreme Court I see no possibility of my avoiding some Circuit in the fall, which I can't bear to think of. . . .

ARS (Nc-Ar, Charles E. Johnson Collection). Addressed "Edenton."

Edmund Randolph to George Washington ——————————
July 25, 1795   Philadelphia, Pennsylvania

... The proposed nomination of Mr Rutledge, tho' mentioned without reserve, is not known to have excited much, if any sensation, among his colleagues. But it is very seriously whispered, that within these two months he is believed in Charleston to be deranged in his mind. The report comes from a letter, which M[r] Desaussure[1] has received from a practising lawyer, of some eminence there.[2] ...

ARS (DLC, George Washington Papers). Marked "Private."

1. Henry William De Saussure (1763-1839), was a Charleston lawyer. De Saussure represented Charleston in the South Carolina General Assembly (1790-1794, 1796-1798, and 1800-1802). He served briefly as director of the United States Mint, receiving a temporary commission on July 9, 1795, and remaining in office until October 28, 1795. *DAB; PAH,* 19:298n.

2. Letter not found.

Argus ————————————————————————————
July 27, 1795   Charleston, South Carolina

We are informed that on Friday last John Rutledge, Esq. received, by post, a commission[1] appointing him CHIEF JUSTICE of the UNITED STATES, in the room of *John Jay,* Esq. resigned.[2]

(New York) August 7, 1795. Date and place are from headline.

This item also appeared in the *Aurora* (Philadelphia), August 10, 1795; *Richmond Chronicle,* August 18, 1795; *Rutland Herald* (Rutland, Vermont), August 24, 1795. A variant appeared in the *Federal Intelligencer* (Baltimore) on August 11, 1795, and in the *United States Chronicle* (Providence) on August 13, 1795.

1. John Rutledge did not receive his commission until August 12, two days after his arrival in Philadelphia (see "Appointments to the Bench," under "John Rutledge: Appointment as Chief Justice in 1795," Edmund Randolph to John Rutledge, August 12, 1795). Rutledge may have received official notice of his nomination on July 24, 1795 ("Friday last"), but news of the nomination first appeared in Charleston on July 20, 1795; see the article reprinted from the *Philadelphia Gazette* under date of July 20, 1795.

2. Other newspapers noting Rutledge's appointment included the *Philadelphia Gazette,* August 8, 1795; *Newport Mercury* (Newport, Rhode Island), August 11, 1795; *Providence Gazette* (Providence), August 15, 1795; *Virginia Gazette, and General Advertiser* (Richmond), August 26, 1795; *State Gazette of North-Carolina* (Edenton), August 27, 1795.

Oliver Wolcott, Jr., to Alexander Hamilton ————————
July 28, 1795   Philadelphia, Pennsylvania

... to my astonishment, I am recently told that M[r] Rutledge has had a tender of the office of Chief Justice—[1] By the favour of heaven the Com[n] is not issued, and now I presume it will not be.— but how near ruin & disgrace has the Country been? ...

ARS (DLC, Alexander Hamilton Papers).

Oliver Wolcott, Jr. (1760-1833), of Connecticut served in the Treasury Department throughout the 1790s: auditor, 1789-1791; comptroller, 1791-1795; secretary of the treasury, 1795-1800 (resigned in December). *DAB.*

1. Oliver Wolcott's "astonishment" may have been prompted by a report published in two Philadelphia newspapers (*Dunlap's American Daily Advertiser* and the *Philadelphia Gazette*) on the day he wrote this letter. The articles printed in great detail the inflammatory speech delivered by John Rutledge in Charleston on July 16 in opposition to the treaty negotiated by John Jay with Great Britain.

Edmund Randolph to George Washington ─────────
July 29, 1795 Philadelphia, Pennsylvania

. . . The newspapers present all the intelligence, which has reached me, relative to the treaty. Dunlap's of yesterday morning conveys the proceedings of Charleston.[1] The conduct of the intended Chief Justice is so extraordinary, that Mʳ Wolcott and Colº Pickering[2] conceive it to be a proof of the imputation of insanity. By calculating dates, it would seem to have taken place, after my letter, tendering the office to him was received; tho' he has not acknowledged it.[3] . . .

ARS (DLC, George Washington Papers). Marked "Private."

1. *Dunlap's American Daily Advertiser* (Philadelphia) on July 28, 1795, published the text of John Rutledge's speech.

2. Timothy Pickering had become secretary of war on January 2, 1795, and succeeded Edmund Randolph as secretary of state in August, 1795. *DAB.*

3. According to an article appearing in the *Argus* (New York) under a Charleston headline of July 27 (q.v.), John Rutledge had received notice of his appointment on July 24, a week after his speech of July 16.

John Rutledge to Arnoldus Vanderhorst ─────────
July 29, 1795 [South Carolina]

Sir

Having accepted the Office of Chief Justice of the United States, I resign to your Excellency, the Commission of Chief Justice which I held, under this State. ─

I have the Honor to be, with great respect and Esteem,   Sir   Your most Obedient Servant

                                                            J: Rutledge

July 29ᵗʰ 1795
His Excellency
    The Governor.

RS (ScHi, Vanderhorst Papers). Place determined by fact that John Rutledge did not leave South Carolina until July 31, 1795; see note to article from *Philadelphia Gazette* under date of August 12, 1795.

Arnoldus Vanderhorst (1748-1815), governor of South Carolina (1794-1796). Edgar and Bailey, *Biographical Directory of the South Carolina House of Representatives,* 2:686-88.

Chauncey Goodrich to Oliver Wolcott, Jr. ────────
July 30, 1795 Hartford, Connecticut

. . . many of the warmest advocates for the present measures are hurt by Mr Rutledges appointment, and are difficulted to account for it, but impute it to want of information of his hostility to the Goverment, or some hidden cause, which justifies the measure; We shall be loth to find faction is to be courted at so great a sacrifice of consistency. . . .

ARS (CtHi, Oliver Wolcott Jr. Papers).
Chauncey Goodrich (1759-1815), the brother-in-law of Oliver Wolcott, Jr., was a Hartford, Connecticut, lawyer and served as a congressman from 1795 to 1801. *DAB.*

Oliver Wolcott, Jr., to Alexander Hamilton ────────
July 30, 1795 Philadelphia, Pennsylvania

[*Wolcott, concerned about the British perception of the United States, remarks on the halting progress of ratification of the Jay Treaty, comments on the hostile reception of the treaty by some Americans, and ends with the final outrage:*] A driveller & fool appointed Chief Justice— . . .

ARS (DLC, Alexander Hamilton Papers). Marked "Private."

Timothy Pickering to George Washington ────────
July 31, 1795 Philadelphia, Pennsylvania

. . . The supreme court is to sit here next week, and perhaps the gentleman named for Chief Justice may arrive. Private information as well as publications of his recent conduct relative to the treaty, have fixed my[1] opinion that the [*word inked out*] commission intended for him ought to be withheld. . . .

ARS (DLC, George Washington Papers); ADfS (MHi, Timothy Pickering Papers). ARS marked by Timothy Pickering "(This letter is for your own eye alone)."
1. In draft, Timothy Pickering interlined "my" above "~~our~~."

Edmund Randolph to George Washington ——————————
July 31, 1795   Philadelphia, Pennsylvania

. . . I have heard nothing of M[r] Rutledge, or from him, except what I have already had the honor of writing to you. . . .

ARS (DLC, George Washington Papers). Marked "Private."

William Bradford, Jr., to Alexander Hamilton ——————————
August 4, 1795   Philadelphia, Pennsylvania

. . . The crazy speech of M[r] Rutledge joined to certain information that he is daily sinking into debility of mind & body, will probably prevent him to receiving the appointment I mentioned to you. But should he come to Philad[a] for that purpose, as he has been invited to do— & especially if he should resign his present Office— the embarrassment of the President will be extreme— but if he is disordered in ^mind^ the manner that I am informed he is,— there can be but one course of procedure.— . . .

ARS (DLC, Alexander Hamilton Papers). Addressed "New York." Postmarked "5   AV."

Lewis Morris, Sr., to Lewis Morris, Jr. ——————————
August 4, 1795   Morrisania, Westchester County, New York

. . . Hamilton has taken upon himself to defend the treaty his papers are under the Signature of Camillus and in my opinion very convincingly are his arguments that it was the best Treaty M[r] Jay could get tho it is with much diffidence that I differ from Chief Justice Ruledge who I observe under the Charlestonhead is very warm against the the treaty but many people Since Camillus came out have altered their opinions and confess their error I should be pleased to hear that the Chief Justice had done the Same tho perhaps he has too much pride tho if he comes forward to write I hope it may come this way . . .

ARS (N, Signers of the Declaration of Independence). Addressed "Charleston   South Carolina." Marked "[p̄r?] Cp[t]- Bliss." Morrisania was the estate of Lewis Morris, Sr. *DAB*.

   Lewis Morris, Sr. (1726-1798), brother of New York's Chief Justice Richard Morris and half-brother of Gouverneur Morris, was a major landowner in New York. Lewis Morris served in the Continental Congress, signed the Declaration of Independence, and fought in the battles around New York in 1776. He later became a Westchester County judge and from 1777 to 1790 served intermittently in the New York Senate. *DAB*.

   Lewis Morris, Jr. (1752-1824), son of Lewis Morris, Sr., was a country gentleman with estates in New York and South Carolina. Harrison, *Princetonians*, 2:415-20.

Edmund Randolph to George Washington ——————————
August 5, 1795   Philadelphia, Pennsylvania

... No answer has been received from M.ʳ Rutledge; but the reports of his attachment to his bottle, his puerility, and extravagances, together with a variety of indecorums and imprudencies multiply daily. ...

ARS (DLC, George Washington Papers). Marked "Private."

The Defence No. V by "Camillus" ——————————
Argus
August 5, 1795   New York, New York

[*Alexander Hamilton, writing under the pseudonym of "Camillus," discusses the importance of calm reflection about the Jay Treaty and stresses the desirability of maintaining peace.*] The ravagings of anger and pride are mistaken for the suggestions of honor. Thus are we told in a delirium of rage, by a gentleman of South Carolina,[1] that our envoy should have demanded an *unconditional* relinquishment of the Western Posts as a right; 'till which was granted, and until Lord Grenville had given orders to Lord Dorchester to that effect, *open to be sent to our president, to be by him forwarded,* he should not have *opened his lips about the treaty. It was prostituting the dearest rights of free men, and laying them prostrate at the feet of royalty.*

In a case of incontestable, *mutual* infractions of a treaty,[2] one of the parties is to demand, peremptorily of the other, an *unconditional* performance on his part, by way of preliminary and without negociation. An envoy sent to avert war, carrying with him the clearest indications of a general solicitude of his country, that peace might be preserved, was at the very first stept of his progress to render hostility inevitable, by exacting, not only what could not have been complied with, but what must have been rejected with indignation. The government of Great Britain must have been the most abject on earth, in a case so situated, to have listened for a moment to such a demand. And because our envoy did not pursue this frantic course; did not hold the language of an IMPERIOUS BASHAW[3] to his TREMBLING SLAVE, he is absurdly stigmatized as having *prostrated the rights of freemen, at the f[e]et of royalty.* What are we to think of the state of the mind which could produce so extravagant a sally? Would a prudent people have been willing to have entrusted a negociation which involved their peace to the author of it? Will they be willing to take him as their guide in a critical emergency of their affairs?*[4] ...

No man in the habit of thinking well either of Mr. Rutleges head or heart, but must have felt at reading the passages of his speech, which have been published, pain, surprise, and mortification. I regret the occasion, and the necessity of animadversion.

(New York) August 5, 1795. Date and place are those of the newspaper. A reading has been supplied in brackets because type did not imprint.

1. John Rutledge.

2. While Americans objected to British occupation of the western posts, the British felt that Americans had reneged on their treaty commitments. During the revolution, several states had passed property confiscation and debt sequestration laws. Article IV of the Treaty of Peace of 1783 specified that there should be no lawful impediments to the recovery of debts. Article V called on Congress to recommend to the states the restitution of confiscated property and the dismantling of any legal impediments to recovery suits. The United States had not successfully enforced these two articles of the treaty, thus arousing British complaints of noncompliance. John Bassett Moore, ed., *International Adjudications, Ancient and Modern: History and Documents,* modern series, vol. 3, *Arbitration of Claims for Compensation for Losses and Damages Resulting from Lawful Impediments to the Recovery of Pre-War Debts* (New York: Oxford University Press, 1931), p. 3; Bemis, *Jay's Treaty,* p. 14.

3. I.e., pasha. *OED.*

4. The following passage appears as a footnote at the bottom of the column.

Federal Orrery ————————————————————————————————————

August 6, 1795   Boston, Massachusetts

The citizens of Charleston (S. C.) have had a meeting on the subject of the treaty. Judge Rutledge appears to have been the principal *spouter* on the occasion. In the course of his declamation, the imagination of the learned chief justice seems to have broken its *franum.*[1] At times, however, he descends from the *empyreum* of rhetoric to the *analysis* of syntax. Dismounting, in full gallop, from the great horse of Dr. Johnson, he commences a more leizurely rout on the *slow pacing nag* of a grammarian.

After having learnedly descanted on the specific qualities of "WILL" and "SHALL," he resumes his majesty of gait; and as the heroism of the French is so admirably calculated to explain the merits of a treaty with Great Britain, he proceeds to the following *splendid puff.*

He wished the highest encomiums on that brave and heroic nation. The Alexanders, the Cæsars, and the Charleses of antiquity, gave place to a whole nation of heroes. Their deeds of heroism were great; but nobler ones were daily acted in all parts of France. As a nation, they had conquered all her opposers. Holland owned her conquest. Prussia felt her energy. Germany retired from her arms. Spain was suing for peace; and the perfidous, the boasting, the assuming nation, Great-Britain, that had arrogated, for ages, power never possessed, — that assumed the sovereignty of the sea, and monopolized the commerce of the whole world, was hoping for peace upon whatever terms France might grant it. To negociate she could not hope. She was reduced to the last gasp; and were America to *seize her by the throat, she would expire in agonies at her feet!!!*

(Boston) August 6, 1795. Date and place are those of the newspaper.

1. The frænum linguæ is a folded tissue running vertically from the underside of the tongue to the floor of the mouth. The writer wanted to imply that Rutledge's tongue was loose or wagging. Henry Gray, *Anatomy, Descriptive and Surgical: A Revised American, from the Fifteenth English, Edition* (New York: Bounty Books, 1977), p. 811.

Thomas Shippen Diary Entry ——————————————
August 9, 1795   Philadelphia, Pennsylvania

. . . I am delighted to hear of Chief Justice Rutledge's appointment to the office of Chief Justice of the U. S. and hope that he will not fail to accept it, as he may be able to stem the Torrent of the N. York faction which has for so many years brought mischief & corruption into our Councils. . . .

AD (DLC, Shippen Family Papers).

   Thomas Lee Shippen (1765-1798), son of a prominent Philadelphia physician and nephew of Richard Henry Lee, was a member of the Philadelphia bar. Klein, *Shippens of Pennsylvania,* pp. 332, 214-19.

Oliver Wolcott, Jr., to Oliver Wolcott, Sr. ——————————
August 10, 1795   Philadelphia, Pennsylvania

. . . N: B— I <u>find</u> that it is true that Jn.º Rutledge has been invited to be C. Justice but he is not <u>Commissioned</u>[1] & I must presume he will not be, after his late Conduct— . . .

ARS (CtHi, Oliver Wolcott Jr. Papers). Marked "Private."

   Oliver Wolcott, Sr. (1726-1797), a leading public official of Litchfield County, Connecticut, represented Connecticut in the Continental and Confederation Congresses. Wolcott supported the adoption of the Constitution. He was serving as lieutenant governor of Connecticut in 1795 and became governor in 1796. *DAB.*

   1. John Rutledge's temporary commission passed the seal of the United States on August 12, 1795, and Edmund Randolph forwarded it to him the same day; see "Appointments to the Bench," under "John Rutledge: Appointment as Chief Justice in 1795," note to temporary commission under date of July 1, 1795, and Edmund Randolph to John Rutledge, August 12, 1795.

Independent Chronicle ———————————————————
August 10, 1795   Boston, Massachusetts

We congratulate the public on the late appointment of Citizen JOHN RUT-LEDGE, late Chief-Justice of the State of *South-Carolina,* to the Chief-Justiceship of the United States. We hope that illustrious patriot, who has ONCE refused that office,[1] will NOW accept this important trust; for our Rights and Liberties will be safe in such hands.

(Boston) August 10, 1795. Date and place are those of the newspaper.

   Reprinted in *Dunlap's American Daily Advertiser* (Philadelphia), August 17, 1795.

   1. John Rutledge had not been offered the office of chief justice of the United States before 1795.

John Rutledge to James Iredell
August 11, 1795 Philadelphia, Pennsylvania

August 11. 1795.

Dear Sir/

I thank you for your very kind Letter,[1] & shall be happy to see you, as soon as convenient— I cannot take my Seat at the Bench, to day— when the Court rises, I will be obliged to you, for a Sight of your Gown, or, if Mʳ Jay's, or Mʳ Blairs, is here, be pleased to order the Officer of the Court, or the person who has Charge of 'em, to send one of them, to my Lodgings.—

I am   dʳ Sir   Sincerely yours

J. Rutledge

ARS (NN, Emmet Collection).
   1. Letter not found.

Columbian Centinel
August 12, 1795 Boston, Massachusetts

Mr RUTLEDGE, who is appointed Chief Justice of the United States, has been one of the foremost in advocating federal measures. His consistency cannot be doubted; and therefore we can cordially congratulate the public in his appointment. Mr. RUTLEDGE'S appointment is another evidence of that watchful patriotism which has ever marked the conduct of our beloved PRESIDENT, as notwithstanding the known abilities and integrity of the Judges of the Supreme Court, the appointment of them, he foresees may be drawn into a precedent, which might at some future period, be highly disadvantageous.[1]

(Boston) August 12, 1795. Date and place are those of the newspaper.
   1. In newspaper, "disadvautageous."

Philadelphia Gazette
August 12, 1795 Philadelphia, Pennsylvania

On Monday evening arrived in town from Charleston,[1] via Baltimore,[2] John Rutledge, Esq. late Chief Justice of the state of South Carolina, now Chief Justice of the United States.

(Philadelphia) August 12, 1795. Date and place are from the headline.
   1. Monday evening was August 10. *Dunlap's American Daily Advertiser* (Philadelphia) on August 12, 1795, reported, however, that John Rutledge had arrived in Philadelphia on August 11. It also noted that William Cushing and William Paterson were in town. The *Boston Gazette* reprinted this article on August 24. This report of Rutledge's arrival on the 11th seems to be inaccurate. Corroboration for his arrival on the 10th comes from the *Georgia Gazette* (Savannah) of September

10, 1795. On that date, the *Georgia Gazette* printed under a "Charleston, September 2" heading an extract of a letter from Philadelphia dated August 18. The letter noted Rutledge's arrival in Philadelphia on the 10th. The *Virginia Gazette, and General Advertiser* (Richmond) on August 19, 1795, carried an article indicating that Rutledge had arrived on August 10. The *Lamson's Weekly Visitor* (Exeter, New Hampshire) on August 25, 1795, merely noted Rutledge's arrival in Philadelphia without specifying the date.

2. The Argus (New York) on August 8, 1795, reported under a Charleston headline of July 31 that Rutledge had left Charleston on July 31 aboard the *Swift Packet* bound for Baltimore. This article appeared in several other newspapers as far north as Rutland, Vermont (in the *Rutland Herald* of August 24, 1795) and as far south as Philadelphia (in the *Philadelphia Gazette* on August 10, 1795). The *Georgia Gazette* (Savannah) of August 6, 1795, paraphrased this news from Charleston and mistakenly reported that Rutledge had left on July 30.

The *Federal Intelligencer* (Baltimore) noted in its August 11, 1795, edition that Rutledge had passed through Baltimore on August 8, 1795.

James Iredell to Hannah Iredell
August 13, 1795   Philadelphia, Pennsylvania

... I greatly flattered myself I could have fixed tomorrow a day for my departure, but it is impossible, we have so much business to do, & the Lawyers so scandalously long in arguing the causes. We have one cause[1] now depending that began on Thursday of last week & probably will not end till Saturday. M.r Rutledge (my old Friend) is arrived; and yesterday took his seat as Chief Justice of the United States. Tho' I very much lament his intemperate expressions in regard to the Treaty, yet altogether no Man likely for the appointment would have been personally more agreeable to me. I have now great hopes of resting entirely this fall.[2] ...

ARS (Nc-Ar, Charles E. Johnson Collection). Addressed "Edenton   North Carolina." Sent via "M.r Devereux."
   1. The case was *Talbot v. Jansen.*
   2. James Iredell hoped to be relieved of riding a fall circuit.

Independent Chronicle
August 13, 1795   Boston, Massachusetts

Judge *Rutledge* of Carolina, has said in a late speech on the Treaty, that he had rather the President should die than sign that puerile instrument— and that he preferred *war* to an adoption of it. The Centinel of yesterday[1] congratulates the public on the appointment of this gentleman to the Chief Justiceship of the United States, as a firm and decided *Federalist,* and a warm supporter of all federal measures.

(Boston) August 13, 1795. Date and place are those of the newspaper.
   1. See the *Columbian Centinel* under date of August 12, 1795.

Christopher Gore to Rufus King ————————————
August 14, 1795   Waltham, Massachusetts

[*Gore writes that opposition to the treaty negotiated by John Jay with Great Britain
will continue to grow unless President Washington indicates his support by ratifying
the treaty[1] and delivering an address to the American people explaining his action.*] Of
all the critical situations in which the government has been placed; this is the
most extreme— prejudices against the English, love for the french, a false idea of
our own strength, & of that of Britain— the character of the opponents in
Charlestown, especially if Rutledge is appointed Chief Justice, together with
the conclusions that will be drawn from the President's conduct, will require
more strength & influence to oppose than can be expected from the few firm
friends to order which may be found in Massachusetts— ...

ARS (NHi, Rufus King Papers).

1. The Senate ratified the Jay Treaty on June 24, 1795, but recommended that further negotiations be undertaken to modify Article XII regulating trade with the British West Indies. President Washington wanted to follow the Senate's advice, but the Senate had provided no guidance
on how the revised Article XII was to be approved. He decided to seek the advice of his cabinet
and former Secretary of Treasury Alexander Hamilton. Before Washington reached a final decision, he received word on July 7 that the British had begun to seize the cargoes of American
ships bound for France. With the exception of Secretary of State Edmund Randolph, all of Washington's cabinet counseled the president to ratify the treaty but to include a memorandum ob-
jecting to the British seizures. The president, however, decided to follow Randolph's advice to
withhold ratification until the British promised to halt the practice. During the next several weeks,
Washington grew increasingly concerned at the public outcry over the treaty, but he was determined to wait for a change in British policy. The president was finally forced to make a decision
on August 11 when Secretary of War Timothy Pickering and Secretary of Treasury Oliver Wolcott, Jr., relying on French documents captured by the British, accused Edmund Randolph of
conspiring with and seeking a bribe from the French. Rather than risk accusations of being under
French influence, Washington decided to sign the treaty except for Article XII. The decision was
announced at a cabinet meeting on August 12, and the treaty was signed on August 14. Five days
later, Randolph was confronted with the bribery charges and he resigned that same day. The
instruments of ratification, including an additional article suspending Article XII, were exchanged
in London on October 28, 1795. Hunter Miller, ed., *Treaties and Other International Acts of the
United States of America*, vol. 2 (Washington, D.C.: Government Printing Office, 1931), pp. 267-
74; John Alexander Carroll and Mary Wells Ashworth, *George Washington*, vol. 7, *First in Peace*,
completing the biography by Douglas Southall Freeman (New York: Charles Scribner's Sons,
1957), pp. 242-98; James Thomas Flexner, *George Washington*, vol. 4, *Anguish and Farewell, 1793-
1799* (Boston: Little, Brown, 1972), pp. 209-30.

Independent Gazetteer ————————————————————
August 14, 1795   Philadelphia, Pennsylvania

[*The headline indicates that this article was taken from the* "STATE GAZETTE,"
probably the South-Carolina State-Gazette, *published in Charleston. Therefore, the
meeting described takes place in Charleston.*]

SOCIETY OF THE SANS-CULOTTES

Sitting of the 22d of July, 1795.

It was unanimously agreed, that on account of the distinguished manner in which the citizens, chief justice Rutledge & Charles Pinckney former governors of this State have spoken of the French nation, an address of thanks should be presented to them from this society, by means of the public papers.

To Citizens Rutledge and Pinckney.

. . .

This address of gratitude, that we are so happy in offering you this day, is infinitely more pleasing to us, as you have merited it in the most particular manner.

All your observations made to your fellow citizens, on The Treaty, which disgraces and afflicts them; your distinguished attachment to our nation; the high idea you have conceived of us, has been generally known for years past; but at the last assembly of your fellow-citizens, shone forth with more than common splendor, in concert with that respectable OLD MAN*[1] whom we infinitely love and esteem.

You have called forth to the recollection of your countrymen, that to the blood of the French, mixed in your combats, partaking your misfortunes, your dangers, your victories, America was greatly indebted for the enjoyment of her liberty: Citizens it is true. The French People flew to your assistance, and the remembrance is sweet, that in you they protected humanity oppressed — but it shall never again be repeated, unless to strengthen the bonds, by which all Freemen should be united in their common cause. . . .

(Philadelphia) August 14, 1795. Date and place are those of the newspaper.
   1. At the bottom of this column, the "OLD MAN" was identified as Christopher Gadsden.

Oliver Wolcott, Jr., to Oliver Wolcott, Sr. ——————
August 17, 1795   Philadelphia, Pennsylvania

. . . M.͏ʳ Rutledge is Chief Justice — the Pres.͏ᵗ was [*letters inked out*] pledged in such a degree, that the Com.͏ⁿ could not be denied — the Senate will have the off[ices?] to determine, when a permanent appointment is made, whether M.͏ʳ R. shall be the man. — I mention this to correct an intimation in a late Letter[1] . . .

ALS (CtHi, Oliver Wolcott Jr. Papers).
   1. See Oliver Wolcott, Jr., to Oliver Wolcott, Sr., August 10, 1795.

Independent Chronicle —————————————————————————————
   August 17, 1795   Boston, Massachusetts

A humorous occurrence is reported a few days since on the appointment of
the illustrious RUTLEDGE, by our "beloved President," to the Chief Justiceship
of the Union:— One of the *aristocratic enragers,* in favor of the Treaty, was
inveighing bitterly against the character of the present Chief Justice on account
of his late patriotic oration in Charleston against it; and among other assertions
which discovered his profound Ignorance, as well as malignancy, he roundly
declared that Mr. RUTLEDGE was actually *Insane:*— Have you reason for this
assertion? (says a cool observer who was present)— Oh, undoubtedly, (says
the other), there is no doubt of it at all: I had it from Mr. H—G————N,
the *man midwife to the Chamber of Commerce:*—[1] I am sorry for it, (says the
gentleman) indeed, for the President has lately made him Chief Justice to the
United States, and you must be guilty of a vile calumny, or the President is
more crazy than the Judge. The *tory* hung his under jaw, and retired amidst
the ridicule and hootings of the company.

(Boston) August 17, 1795. Date and place are those of the newspaper.
   1. Stephen Higginson, the Boston merchant, was a founding member of the Boston Chamber
of Commerce, established in 1794. Higginson favored the adoption of the Jay Treaty; and the
Boston Chamber of Commerce apparently did as well, for they passed resolutions of support for
President Washington's foreign policy. *Rules and Regulations of the Boston Chamber of Commerce Established March 17, 1794* (Boston: Ezra W. Weld and William Greenough, 1794), p. 13; Gerald
H. Clarfield, *Timothy Pickering and the American Republic* (Pittsburgh: University of Pittsburgh Press,
1980), p. 157; Justin Winsor, ed., *The Memorial History of Boston,* 4 vols. (Boston: James R. Os-
good, 1881), 3:204.

James Iredell to Simeon Baldwin ———————————————————————
   August 18, 1795   Philadelphia, Pennsylvania

. . . I should much sooner have acknowledged your obliging letter,[1] but that
we have been so incessantly employed in business in the Supreme Court that
it has been scarcely possible for us to attend to any thing else— One Cause
began on the 6th instant and is not yet ended, and one Lawyer spoke three
days in it.[2] . . .

ARS (CtY, Baldwin Family Papers). Addressed "New Haven   Connecticut." Postmarked "18
AV."
   1. On July 15, 1795, James Iredell had forwarded to Simeon Baldwin, clerk of the circuit court
for the district of Connecticut, a copy of the grand jury charge that Iredell had delivered in New
Haven. The grand jury had requested that it be published. Baldwin acknowledged the receipt of
the charge in a letter to Iredell dated July 27, 1795. Baldwin Family Papers, CtY.
   2. The case was *Talbot v. Jansen.*

Oliver Ellsworth to Oliver Wolcott, Jr. ——————————
August 20, 1795   Windsor, Connecticut

... With regard to Mʳ Rutledge, it certainly was difficult after he had come, not to commission him. If the evil is without remedy, we must as in other cases, make the best of it._ Beleive not my dear Sir, that I have ~~any~~ feelings on this occasion,[1] which are not common to all the well informed friends of the Government. ...

ARS (CtHi, Oliver Wolcott Jr. Papers). Endorsed "ansᵈ Aug 24. 95."
  1. The comma is crossed out.

Independent Chronicle ——————————————————————
August 20, 1795   Boston, Massachusetts

The heads of the departments are met at Philadelphia_ We have *now* a RUTLEDGE instead of JAY._ The spirit of this illustrious patriot it is hoped will purify the dregs of the HAMILTONIAN faction, who are left behind.

(Boston) August 20, 1795. Date and place are those of the newspaper.

Aurora ————————————————————————————————
August 21, 1795   Philadelphia, Pennsylvania

A report is very industriously circulated, that Mr. Rutledge has changed his sentiments, & has become a friend to the treaty since he has received the commission of Chief of the U.S. This is so infamous a libel upon the character of that gentleman, that no man who believes him to have any principles will give it credit. His pointed, his unequivocal disapprobation at the meeting in Charleston cannot leave a doubt of his repugnance to the treaty & a report to the contrary must be designed to exhibit him in a light very derogatory to his real character.

(Philadelphia) August 21, 1795. The date and place are those of the newspaper. This item was headlined "FROM A CORRESPONDENT."

"A Real Republican" to John Rutledge ——————————
Columbian Centinel
August 26, 1795   Boston, Massachusetts

TO HIS HONOR
JOHN RUTLEDGE, ESQUIRE,
Late Chief Justice in the State of *South-Carolina*

SIR,
The newspapers have announced to the public your appointment, by the

President of the United States, to the elevated and important station of Chief Justice of the Federal Court, an office too important and dignified for a character not very far above mediocrity.

To fill that station with advantage to the public, and with reputation to himself, a man must be eminent for his talents and his integrity— for a dignified reserve, and a deliberate investigation before he forms, much less avows an opinion. He should be conspicuous for his love of justice in his private dealings, and in his official conduct; for if any thing can be discovered in either, that suggests even a doubt on this point, he must lose the confidence and respect of the people, his usefulness and his reputation are gone for ever.

A close and fair inquiry, whether you possess those qualities for the office, in the estimation of the public, or even in the opinion of your friends, should be made by yourself, before you accept the present appointment, *which is but temporary,* and must be renewed at the next session of Congress.

Now suppose a number of suits to be brought forward against you, to recover, in equity, for your own bonds, taken up at one third, or one half the sums which they promised, and which you received from the persons to whom they were given. Suppose a claimant to come into the Court, where you intend officially to preside, and to say, that "he called upon you to pay your bond for £.1000; that you laughingly, told him you could not pay, that it was not the fashion of the day to pay bonds— that, being much distressed for the money, he offered you a discount of 20 per cent. if you would make some exertion to pay him, to which you replied, his offer was no inducement to you to pay, as you could go every day to the Coffeehouse, and buy up your own bonds, at 50 per cent discount"[1] Suppose another to come forward and declare, that, finding he could get no payment from you, he had sold your bond at 50 per cent. discount, to pay his own debts, and relieve his own wants; and that he afterwards found you were the purchaser; that you had found money to buy up your own bond to him for £.1000, with £.500 cash, though you had just before declared, you had not and could not get money to pay him £.200, on account of the same bond. Suppose, sir, these things to appear and be substantiated against you, can the people possibly have any confidence in your integrity, or be willing you should preside in their highest Court of Justice? It is impossible to believe that a man, who would do such things, would not sell, at a good price, his official opinion.[2]

Suppose, again, a steady, judicious man, to read, in the *Charleston* newspapers, the account there published of your conduct and opinion, delivered at a meeting convened to damn the treaty with *Britain;* when he reads your *silly rant* upon that subject, and fancies you, QUIXOTTE-like holding *Great-Britain* by the throat, in your clenched fist, until should[3] expire in agonies at your feet. When he examines your assertions, that Mr. JAY ought not to have opened any negotiation, until *Britain* had previously conceded every thing in dispute, he must believe, that you have no correct ideas of treaties, or the way to effect them, no habit of deliberate investigation, nor any just notions of consistency or propriety. And when he sees you mounted upon the head of a hogshead, harranguing a mob, assembled purposely to reprobate the treaty, and insult the Executive of the Union— when he finds you insinuating, that Mr. JAY and the Senate, were fools or knaves duped by British sophistry, or bribed by British gold, he must not only think you destitute of the dignity and prudence necessary to the station in question, but must conceive you also to be deficient in common sense, and without regard to character, which all decent men possess and exhibit upon common occasions.

It is to be lamented, upon public principles, that the President had not known better your real character before the appointment. His motives in making it, cannot however, be questioned, every one knows and confesses his integrity and zeal to do right; but he cannot know every man in the *United States;* and the information he gets from others, cannot always be relied upon.

To save yourself from disgrace, it is the earnest wish of your friends that you may decline the appointment; since with these charges, exhibited by common fame, and believed by the people, it will be impossible for the President to nominate, or for the Senate at their next session, to approve your being appointed Chief Justice of the United States: You will then have to retire from that exalted station, with the marked disgrace of being dropped, or indirectly displaced for your follies, if not your vices.

If, Sir, the suggestions of common report be true, as to your morals— if the accounts published in the public newspapers, relative to your speeches and conduct upon the subject of the treaty, are near the truth, your are wholly destitute of every qualification for that important station. You had better not expose still more conspicuously your vices and follies; but you had better retire into some interior[4] situation in your own country, where vice and folly have their votaries, and where you will find no contrasts, to blast your reputation, and keep you in the shade. Be assured, that, with present impressions, you will find no admirers in the middle and nothern states; but, instead of a cordial respect, due to the office, you will, from your own demerits, be put into Coventry[5] where ever you go[.] No man, who regards his own reputation, will admit you into his house; but whilst he respects and notices your brethren on the Bench, every man must, in his own defence treat you with neglect.

These Sir, are the honest sentiments of

A REAL REPUBLICAN.

(Boston) August 26, 1795. Date and place are those of the newspaper. Headlined "FOR THE COLUMBIAN CENTINEL." A reading has been supplied in brackets because type did not imprint.

Also reprinted with some variations in the *Newport Mercury* (Newport, Rhode Island) on September 1, 1795; the *Connecticut Journal* (New Haven) on September 2, 1795; the *Connecticut Courant* (Hartford) on September 7, 1795; and the *North-Carolina Gazette* (New Bern) on November 7, 1795. Variations have been noted in the copy published here.

1. Three newspapers either omitted a part or changed the wording of the sentence beginning "Suppose another . . . "; but they left the meaning intact. *Connecticut Journal* (New Haven), September 2, 1795; *Connecticut Courant* (Hartford), September 7, 1795; *North-Carolina Gazette* (New Bern), November 7, 1795.

2. According to one of his biographers, John Rutledge had been "collecting debts and paying

little or nothing" on them for years. Richard Hayes Barry, *Mr. Rutledge of South Carolina* (New York: Duell, Sloan and Pearce, 1942), p. 359. Although Barry's biography of John Rutledge is unreliable in many instances, Rutledge's financial problems are documented elsewhere; see note to John Rutledge, Vindicated: "A South Carolinean" to Benjamin Russell, under date of August 28, 1795.

3. All reprintings read "until she should."

4. The *Newport Mercury* (Newport, Rhode Island) of September 1, 1795, has "inferiour."

5. "*To send (a person) to Coventry:* to exclude him from the society of which he is a member on account of objectionable conduct." *OED.*

"My Country's Friend" to the Editors ————

Independent Chronicle

August 27, 1795   Boston, Massachusetts

CITIZENS,

I send you a copy of a letter from an old gentleman in the country, who after having served his country in public life, in the cabinet and in the field, throughout the whole of her struggle for liberty, has retired to private life, beloved and esteemed.

———————

"*My Dear Sir,*

We are much amused in the country with your political controversies in the town. We observe that in the CENTINEL, and some other papers devoted to the British interest. every man who has rendered himself conspicuous for republican sentiments and principles is abused.

The appointment of JOHN RUTLEDGE, Esq. who was the great leader of *South Carolina* in the late revolution, who signed that instrument which emancipated us (*for a time at least*) from the domination of Great-Britain; who aided in forming the Federal government; who was the first Governor of *South-Carolina* after the revolution; was one of the first Judges appointed by the President under the General Government for the Supreme Judicial Court; but who returned to the office of Chief-Justice of his own State, at the earnest solicitation of his fellow-citizens there, who allowed him one thousand pounds lawful money of this state annually, for his salary.

He is now appointed by the President, to whom his virtues and abilities are well known, to the head of the Judicial Department in Government. For this he is abused by those Britons who reside in our[1] country, and by their slaves and coadjutors. There was a time when these men would not dare to treat our distinguished patriots in this way.

Since the establishment of the Federal Government, the President has been much in the vortex of these men's politics, and they have been too successful with the people in getting into place and office the men who originally opposed the revolution, and are friends to Monarchy and enemies to Republicanism_ ["*My Country's Friend" continues with a discussion of the rise of the* "enemies to Republicanism."]

. . . Did they not treat HANCOCK then as they do RUTLEDGE now? Did they not frequently advertize him as a bankrupt, when in fact he has since died worth seventy thousand pounds.

. . .

The great object with the British party is, to have the government in their own hands, to promote their own friends, who are the enemies of civil freedom, and our independence. The fact is, that they want to establish what they call a mixed government, a King, Nobility and Commons, or to restore the States to the condition of British Colonies; or at least to place us under the complete controul of that nation's politics. The appointment or election of an old whig, has therefore become obnoxious to them; unless it be of such, who having altered their political opinions, can now unite in their measures. . . ."

(Boston) August 27, 1795. Date and place are those of the newspaper.

Reprinted in *Lamson's Weekly Visitor* (Exeter, New Hampshire), September 1, 1795.

1. In newspaper, "onr."

Independent Chronicle ———————————————————————————

August 27, 1795   Boston, Massachusetts

Upon the nomination of Mr. Rutledge to the office of Chief Justice, it was observed in the Centinel, that this gentleman was *a staunch Federalist,* and an *honest man*[.] S[i]nce which, a writer has come forward in that paper, with an attack upon this gentleman's character, that would disgrace an Hottentot.

The writer has held up Judge Rutledge, as the most abandoned character, both in a political and moral view[.][1] Such writers only serve to enlighten the people; as we cannot suppose that the President would nominate a man, so despicable in his reputation. The reflections on Judge Rutledge, apply as forcibly to the conduct of the *President,* as to him. If he is a man thus abandoned, why did the President nominate him? Where is the INFALLIBILITY of the President in this instance? It comes with an ill grace from those who openly declare the President "can do no wrong:' But the apology is, that the President did *not know his real character*_ Poor wretches are ye, who presume to justify the President on this ground; did he not know the character of Judge Rutledge; a man, with whom he had set in Congress, in the earliest period of the Revolution? Who was a member of Congress before the establishment of the Constitution; and who was a member to frame it? Is it possible that the President should not know Mr. Rutledge, after being with him in various trying situations! The President DID KNOW HIM, and on the strength of *his knowledge,* considered him as the most proper person, at this alarming crisis, to fill the important office of Chief Judge of the United States.

The President knew Judge Rutledge, long before he heard of the WALTHAM *Gentleman Farmer.*[2] If the President had been acquainted with all the characters appointed to important offices; it is probable, many who are now enjoying the blessings of that independence, to which they and *their Fathers* were opposed, would have been confined to their Lawyers office, and would be obliged to *their friends* for the assistance of a few guineas to purchase a decent apparel.

Washington not to know Rutledge, "would argue *himself* unknown.' His appointment of this firm patriot at this period, must evince, that the President *has not Ratified the Treaty* in the manner expected by the British Faction —[3] but has *anticipated* the period, when it will be necessary to have the sentiments of a Rutledge upon it.

The YEOMANRY by expressing their opposition to the treaty, will enable both Washington and Rutledge to save the United States from British rapacity.

(Boston) August 27, 1795. Date and place are those of the newspaper. Readings have been supplied in brackets because type did not imprint.

1. See "A Real Republican" to John Rutledge, August 26, 1795.

2. The reference is to Christopher Gore, United States attorney for the district of Massachusetts and a leading federalist, who owned a country farm and estate in Waltham, outside Boston. Under the pseudonym of "A Federalist," Gore had been writing articles in favor of the Jay Treaty. Pinkney, *Christopher Gore,* pp. 49, 62-63; the *Independent Chronicle* (Boston) on August 6, 1795, carried an article attacking the gentleman farmer of Waltham.

3. In fact, George Washington had signed the Jay Treaty on August 14, 1795; and by August 18 the British minister, George Hammond, was already on his way to London with the instrument of ratification. Flexner, *Anguish and Farewell,* p. 233; see also note to Christopher Gore to Rufus King, August 14, 1795.

John Rutledge, Vindicated: "A South Carolinean" to Benjamin Russell

Columbian Centinel
August 28, 1795   "Rhode-Island State"

MR. RUSSELL,

If there were the remotest probability, that the Chief Justice of the United States would reply to the audacious[1] indecencies and untruths of the writer in your paper of the 26th inst. under the signature of *"A Real Republican,"* I should not have desired you to obtrude upon the public, these observations upon that publication. It were unreasonable to expect, that our public officers, should themselves descend to defence against the many shafts of malice and insiduousness which have been levelled of late against them, by a party of disappointed and wicked characters, even though they occasionally croud so thick into the political atmosphere of this country as to throw a temporary gloom around the brilliant virtues of the Patriot, like the clouds which drive under the sun, and for a moment hide its lustre from the sight of those below it. They know that the force of them, however well directed, will spend itself, even though unresisted, before they reach the eminence of political integrity. Their consciousness of rectitude precludes any solicitude in them, to dispel the gloom below them, and the good citizen also, who has reaped advantages from their exertions, knowing the source of it, and it[s?] necessary inefficacy, may think it is as useless to interpose a shield to the reputation of his country's benefactor, against suggestions made by such characters, though extrinsic[2] from truth, and positions calculated to delude the unwary.

But when a writer who professes to be an enemy to those disappointed characters, comes forward to attack an old veteran of '75, who assisted in the counci[l]s of confederated *America* with abilities that were then looked up to, and greatly relied upon, who has since lived uniformly under the shade of those laurels which his patriotic exertions during our revolution acquired to him, and now presides over the administration of the laws in our highest Courts of Judicature, every good citizen who knows the injustice done to such a character, feels the force of reasons of another nature, prompting him to step forward— he feels for the name, for the national character which his country may incur— lest, what some late occurrences may have suggested to the minds of many, that ingratitude towards our public officers, should become a distinguishing feature in the character of *America,* whether occasioned by the combination of natural causes, or necessarily resulting from the spirit and influence of a republican form of government. In the present instance, the author of the piece I answer, makes an appearance, as one of those who would submit to have the administration of our constitution and laws, conducted by those whom we have appointed for the purpose— and yet betrays at the same time, a spirit of revolt against an act done by the first political character in our Commonwealth.[3] He points with derision at, and strives to disgust his fellow-citizens, with a man, who has been tried in the hour of calamity and adverse fortune, and was found faithful to the end, and whom therefore, and on account of great and distinguished abilities still to serve his country in the capacity he now is, the President of the United States has preferred to fill the seat of Chief Justice of the United States. If the choice of the President in this instance, is to be reproved, his system of nomination uniformly ought to be so— That of selecting men to preside and watch over, to preserve and administer those rights, the difficulty of gaining which they have experienced.

"A Real Republican" has no where shewn so much art, as in excusing the President for promoting Mr. RUTLEDGE to the office of Chief Justice, whilst he rails against the man who is promoted, as unworthy of it. His excuse is, that the President was either ignorant, as he cannot be supposed to know *every man* in the United States, or misinformed of the man he appointed by those on whose information he cannot always rely. I would ask, is it necessary to know every man in the United States, to nominate a Chief Justice, or could the President be supposed by a rational man, or would it be consistent with the rest of his conduct, that he should have elevated a citizen to the high and important office of Chief Justice of the United States, whom he did not know? But the President is not the only object of crimination by this writer, and I am therefore surprized, that he should be the only object of excuse; this is not the first time Mr. RUTLEDGE has been upon the Bench of the Supreme Federal

Court of the Union— And how came he there; by the nomination of the President, and the approbation of the Senate. How came the Senate so ignorant— Oh, perhaps says this writer, he was well qualified for being next to the Chief Justice, but no more. A paltry subterfuge, unworthy of *"A Real Republican."* Chief Justice is but a nominal discrimination from the rest of his brethren. I cannot suppose, from the production of this writer, that he presumed to aim at the office, or the little reason with which he opposes the appointment, would have led me to suspect some disappointment, which had made it expedient for him to get into the opposition, and try what that might afford him.

That Mr. RUTLEDGE was known, well known [t]o the President, cannot be doubted— And if *"A Real Republican"* was himself ignorant of him, and his high legal reputation, he ought out of tenderness to himself, not to have exposed his ignorance, of a man who was eminently distinguished by the part he took in the late Revolution. If there is one man in the United States, fit for the office of Chief Justice, Mr. RUTLEDGE is that man. His legal abilities, are generally admitted by the learned of the Bar, to be without superiority in the Union.— His domestic embarrassments,[4] occasioned by abstracting his attention from his own affairs, and devoting it entirely to the public good, during the war, is not a solid objection against his eligibility to become Chief Justice. Pecuniary independence is not prescribed by the Constitution, as a qualification necessary to such as fill that office— No specific fortune or amount of property, either in possession, or without incumbrance. If it were so, it were to confine honor to wealth,[5] and to make poverty a disgrace to virtue and talents.

If *"A Real Republican,"* by his suppositions, would insinuate that Mr. R. ever told a creditor in Court, laughingly, who demanded payment of a bond from him there, that it was not the fashion of the day to pay bonds, &c.— he is mistaken. Mr. R. I believe said, as a man of observation and of useful experience, that in *South-Carolina,* at that day, to pay debts, was unfashionable, and the truth of the remark gave it a currency, by which *"A Real Republican"* probably came to hear of it. But mark the ungenerous perversion which this writer has made of his expression, and of the application of it— For shame— for shame— if Mr. RUTLEDGE was unable to answer on demand, every debt he owed, it was his misfortune. If *"A Real Republican"* on the contrary, is able to satisfy his debts, he ought to have been content to be thankful for his own good fortune, and not to have insulted another, who may not have been as fortunate as himself. Mr. RUTLEDGE was thought in his own State, where his integrity was well known, to preside as Chief Justice, in their Courts of Justice. His private moral character has nothing to do with his official uprightness; but even that defies the tongue of calumny, although *"A Real Republican"* would hint at, he says not what, to excite a suspicion against it.

The Speech of the Chief Justice, relative to the treaty, was never fairly represented in the newspapers. I believe it would puzzle him more to have spoken as he is represented to have done on that occasion, than to speak in a manner worthy of a Chief Justice of the United States. The sketch of his speech, originated in a paper printed in *South-Carolina,* by two young men,[6] meritorious for their inclination and endeavours to please and gratify their readers; but illy qualified to deal out to the world, the substance of a speech made by Mr. RUTLEDGE, upon a subject the most difficult to comprehend.

If Mr. RUTLEDGE differed in opinion, from the President and the Senate, as to the merits of the treaty, no doubt it was from a conviction in his own mind, that the treaty ought not to be ratified, and that he supposed they would be pleased to learn the observations and opinion upon a subject of so great magnitude and importance, of a man whose observations and opinions were not used formerly to be despised or treated lightly by them.

It was not from party spirit, or an opposition to government, I would hazard to assert, and submit to the continuity of his public conduct to come, as well as past, to evince the fallacy or truth of the assertion. That his sentiments of the treaty are wrong, I wish, and am rather inclined to think; but no man can yet be positive that they are. Though they be wrong, he may differ on a point of policy, without affecting his legal character or judgment. If *"A Real Republican"* is alarmed, lest Mr. RUTLEDGE should be a professed railer at the measures of government, he will no doubt be mistaken. The conduct of the Chief Justice, in this particular instance, is not sufficient evidence of it, and no other can be adduced against him.__ The independent manner in which he spoke publicly his sentiments on this subject, though they militated with the projections and measures of those who are in office, and to whom he has generally adhered, ought to be considered as a pleasing presage, that upon the Bench of Justice he will not be influenced or prevailed upon to deviate from what his own judgment dictates him to be right; but will rather observe faithfully, that rule of strict rectitude on all occasions, of *"fiat Justitia, ruat cœlum."*[7]

A SOUTH CAROLINEAN.

Rhode-Island State, 28th Aug.

(Boston) September 2, 1795. Date and place are those of the letter. Readings have been supplied in brackets because type did not imprint. Benjamin Russell was the publisher of the *Columbian Centinel.* Brigham, *American Newspapers,* 1:277.

Reprinted in the *Connecticut Courant* (Hartford), September 14, 1795.

1. In newspaper, "andacious."

2. The *Connecticut Courant* (Hartford), September 14, 1795, reprints this as "intrinsic."

3. President George Washington.

4. A reference to John Rutledge's financial problems. Unlike James Wilson, Rutledge never went to jail for his debts. In two memoranda dated October 30, 1795, and November 12, 1796, John Rutledge, Jr., the son of Chief Justice Rutledge, listed his father's debts and noted that in order to pay his father's creditors he was forced to borrow "from the Banks__ And altho' it appears there that I am their debtor to [a?] considerable amount, yet, most of this money, was borrowed for the purpose of taking up notes which I had endorsed for the Chief Justice." John Rutledge eventually repaid his son, at least in part, by conveying to him his Union Plantation valued at £500. Barry, *Mr. Rutledge of South Carolina,* p. 359; Memoranda, October 30, 1795, and November 12, 1796, John Rutledge Papers, NcU.

5. In *Connecticut Courant* (Hartford), September 14, 1795, this appears as "honour with wealth."

6. John Rutledge's speech appeared in the *South-Carolina State-Gazette* (Charleston) on July 17, 1795. The newspaper was published by Benjamin Franklin Timothy (1771-1807) and his brother-in-law, William Mason. Douglas C. McMurtrie, "The Correspondence of Peter Timothy, Printer of Charlestown, with Benjamin Franklin," *South Carolina Historical and Genealogical Magazine* 35 (1934): 123-29; Brent H. Holcomb, comp., *Marriage and Death Notices from the (Charleston) Times, 1800-1821* (Baltimore: Genealogical Publishing, 1979), p. 182; Leona M. Hudak, *Early American Women Printers and Publishers, 1639-1820* (Metuchen, N.J.: Scarecrow Press, 1978), p. 480; Brigham, *American Newspapers,* 2:1040.

7. "Let right be done, though the heavens should fall."

Stephen Higginson to Timothy Pickering ————————————
August 29, 1795   Boston, Massachusetts

. . . the account of M[r] Randolphs resignation[1] we have by various channels, all of them attended with conjectures as to the cause, but none that give full satisfaction. I rather conjecture, upon comparing circumstances that it has resulted from some points relative to the appointment of JRutlege to the office of chief Justice; & from the whole derive hopes he is not yet commissioned, in which ^case I presume he never will receive a Commission. it would be an unfortunate thing for the public, if hes been commissioned, as well ^as for himself; since, with the present public opinion as to his conduct & character, he never can have the confidence of the people, nor be confirmed by the President & Senate at the next Session of Congress.— . . .

ARS (MHi, Timothy Pickering Papers). Addressed "Philadelphia." Postmarked "31   AV."

1. Edmund Randolph resigned as secretary of state on August 19, 1795. His position in President Washington's cabinet had been compromised by the British capture of French dispatches which seemingly incriminated Randolph in a plot to influence United States policy toward France in return for money. One particular document—labeled Dispatch No. 10, dated October 31, 1794, and written by Jean Antoine Joseph Fauchet, French minister to the United States—was shown by George Hammond, British minister to the United States, to Secretary of Treasury Oliver Wolcott on July 28, 1795. Wolcott shared it with other members of the cabinet the next day. President Washington was called back to Philadelphia from Virginia; and on August 19, Washington, with Wolcott and Secretary of War Timothy Pickering present, confronted Randolph with the document and asked for an explanation. Thinking that the interview was unfair and humiliating, Randolph resigned. *PAH,* 18:527ff.

Arthur Iredell to James Iredell ————————————
September 1, 1795   "near Lewes," Sussex County, England

. . . I have hope . . . from One Part of your Letter[1] ^i.e. that no Chief was put upon Your Bench— : for I hardly think Washington will not appoint the very Successor to M[r] Jay, whom I sh[d] name, were I President of the United States— If it should prove so!— Well! there w[d] be little to wonder at, tho much to delight me— You know how long I have dreamt of seeing you distribute Justice in America— the Seeing you at the Head of the Law on that Continent w^d indeed be an enviable Sensation!— If I could want an Inducement for crossing the Atlantic, that w^d be a powerfull one— ...

ARS (Nc-Ar, Charles E. Johnson Collection). Addressed "Philadelphia   N America" and sent "By the New   York Packet." When this letter arrived in the United States, "Philadelphia" was crossed out and "Edenton" was substituted. The letter was then postmarked "7   NO."
  1. Letter not found.

Aurora ————————————————————————

September 1, 1795   Salem, Massachusetts

A Correspondent observes,

———————

That while the friends of the treaty have discovered moderation, they have gained the public favour, but that the late attack upon Judge Rutledge, in the Columbian Centinel,[1] is more licentious than any thing which the pen of faction has yet produced. It not only displays a want of candour in the present controversy about the treaty, but a violent faction in favour of the present measures. Nothing has yet appeared more alarming. While our pleas for the President are from his long public services, a contemporary patriot, who has held the highest offices of state, is damned for an error in judgement, as base and wicked, as unknown, and the object of public detestation and punishment. Alas, the ingratitude of faction!

(Philadelphia) September 8, 1795. Date and place from headline.
  Also printed in the *Rutland Herald* (Rutland, Vermont), September 14, 1795.
  1. See "A Real Republican" to John Rutledge, *Columbian Centinel* under date of August 26, 1795.

The Lamentation ————————————————————

Independent Chronicle
September 3, 1795   Boston, Massachusetts

O the Jacobins! Messrs. Printers, the Jacobins! the Jacobins! What shall we do? The whole continent are turning Jacobins. For all the continent are condemning the *Treaty,* and all who do condemn this treaty are Jacobins. What[1] is to be done? From Georgia to Maine, they act as if the D——l was in them; yet I hope, and trust and pray, that there is still a chosen few, who have preserved themselves from the contagion of this universal mania. *Only* Messrs. Printers, *only* let the people know, who those are, that take the lead in these impious transactions, and I am sure they will not be longer influenced by them. As I am sure *they* do *not know*. I will tell them, I will enlighten their dark understandings, I will shew the *"swinish multitude"* that the ring leaders of this cursed business, are blinded by partiality and hatred; and that they are, and ever since 1775, have been prejudiced against our new, I mean our *old friends* the British. To begin then at the south__ there is that arch rebel, John Rutledge, many years a member of the old continental Congress, in time of the war; what better could be expected from him; is it ye[t] forgotten, that when he was Governor of South Carolina, and the British had possession of Charleston, his capital, that he hung[2] all the British he could catch; as well as all such as would not assist him in fighting them; and dont you think he knows, that if the treaty takes place, and the British again bear rule, that they will hang him in turn; what better then could you expect from such a man as he?__ Self preservation our parson says, is natures first law; and if he knows that the British will hang him if they come, is it not natural for him to try to prevent their coming? Tis true, our President did make him Judge of the Supreme Court of the United States; but he afterwards suffered his own State to buy him off, by creating him their Chief Justice, with a higher salary. I hope therefore the people will not be influenced by the doings of such a man. . . .

(Boston) September 3, 1795. Date and place are those of the newspaper. Readings have been supplied in brackets because type did not imprint.

    1. Appears in the newspaper as "Whrt."

    2. Appears in the newspaper as "hnag."

"A Real Republican" to "The South-Carolinean" ─────────
Columbian Centinel
September 5, 1795   Boston, Massachusetts

TO THE "SOUTH-CAROLINEAN,"

─────────

Vindicator of Judge RUTLEDGE, *dating in* Rhode-
Island, *but residing in* Boston: __ [1]

SIR,

We naturally feel for, and share by sympathy, the honor or the disgrace, which our townsmen, our acquaintance, and much more our particular friends and relations may incur; but we ought to be cautious, that our feelings do not impel us to attempt a defence, when, from the facts and circumstances in the case, we can only, at best, make bad *worse;* and increase the disgrace of our friends, whom we mean to defend. But you, sir, have not yet lived long enough, it seems, to be master of your own feelings; and have been urged so, by family pride, perhaps, to vindicate a cause not capable of defense. In your first paragraph, there appears a singular medley and confusion of ideas, which plainly indicates, that your pen was much more under the direction of your feelings__ than of your judgment. You express great surprize and apprehension, that so eminent a man as Judge RUTLEDGE, should be attacked in his character, whilst you think very lightly of his insinuating, that Mr. JAY, and the *Senate,* are *"fools or knaves,"* by what rule or principle can it be right for him, to insult them by insinuations, which the world believes to be most *infamously false*, that will not at least justify our saying that of him, which every one believes, and you cannot even attempt to disprove, because the fact bears hard upon his reputation. If it be improper, or criminal to speak truths of the Judge, because they tend to injure his reputation, it must be *infamous indeed*, to attempt to slander Mr. JAY, and the *Senate* by palpable falsehoods.

You admit in that paragraph, that the shafts of the real Republican were *"well directed";* but you console yourself in the fond belief, that they will spend their force before they reach to the height of the Judge's eminence. This may be taken as a specimen of your own and the Judge's ideas of democratic equality; or we may account for this singular sentiment, by the partiality which we all know to be natural for our friends and relations.

In your second and third paragraphs you express great anxiety lest our national character should suffer, and its government be brought into contempt, because the Judge, who is not yet, we hope, a component part of it has been attacked; but you seem to have no such fears or feelings, when Mr. JAY and the *Senate,* whose weight in the public estimation, is as a MOUNTAIN to a *mole-hill* compared with his, were by him most vilely abuse. The *"Real Republican"* did not, sir, reprove the appointment of the Judge; but he recommended it to the Judge not to accept the office, should it be offered him, upon the personal ground of saving himself from disgrace, and assigned his reasons.— But where, *Mr Vindicator,* did you learn, that the Judge had received the approbation of the Senate, or that he is now Chief Justice of the United States, by their consent. Had you read the *"Real Republican"* with attention and candour, you would not have committed this blunder. The Senate were not in session, and could not therefore have approved of the Judges' appointment, if it has really been made; and one of the strongest reasons urged to induce him to decline it, was, that it would be impossible for the Senate, whom he had so *scandalously traduced,* to confirm his appointment at their next session. Or where, sir, do you find in the *"Real Republican"* an admission that your Towns man is well qualified for an inferior or *puisne* Judge, though not well fitted for Chief Justice? The *"Real Republican"* has admitted no such thing, on the contrary his objections will operate an utter disqualification for the lowest seat in that bench.

Your attempts in your fourth and fifth paragraphs, to puff off the Judge as the first law character in the Union, as the highest and the best for the office of Chief Justice, would pass better in another quarter, perhaps, than here. Those are comparitive or relative terms; the same man, may appear first in one circle, and last in another. But the most unfortunate point in your feeble vindication, is, that to exculpate the Judge from hav[i]ng refused to pay his debts, you transfer the impu[t]ation from him to the State, or the people of *South-Carolina,* at large, a compliment for which they will no doubt confess themselves much indebted to you. The only mark of prudence you discover, is in not denying the fact as to the Judge, personally and particularly, it being too notorious; and in attempting to shield him under a general imputation of the same kind of injustice upon the whole state. This friendly act of yours toward them, we leave you to make the most of with your fellow-citizens at your return home. They ought at least, we think, to honor you with a *Civic Feast,* and place you at the *top* of the table with the Bonnet rouge, *alias, a "fools Cap"* upon your head. But where, good Sir, did you learn, that a *"moral character has nothing to do with official uprightness?"* Is there no affinity between morality and integrity? Can a man who wrongs his neighbour, be as fully relied on to dispense Justice, as one conspicuously moral and just in all his dealings? This may be true in *South-Carolina,* from your own description of the people; but such is not the *New-England* creed.

It is not possible to admit your apology for the Judge's ranting speech about the treaty; nor can it be true, that the sketch of it we have seen published in the newspapers, is essentially different from what he delivered. If the wild declamation which has been ascribed to him be not true; if he did not on that occasion insinuate that Mr. JAY and the *Senate,* were *"fools or knaves,"* for having made and recommended the treaty; if he did not then say, that it were better THE PRESIDENT should die than ratify the treaty, and that he would declare for war, at the hazard of loosing our country, rather than not have his choice of *"will* or *shall,"* words of similar import, and equally apt for the purpose in view; is it to be believed, that the judge would not have corrected the mistake, when we recollect, that the first publication was made at his own door, and under his own eye? Is it credible, that he would have permitted so many wild, illiberal, and silly sentiments, to have been palmed upon him?

In your last paragraph, you exhibit the Judge upon the *stool* of repentance, as acknowledging his folly and crying *peccavi,*[2] by you his proxy; and having asked forgiveness of his past weakness and imprudence on that occasion, he is made to promise, by you, who are his surety, that he will not again attempt to excite opposition, nor to *rail* at the measures of government. How far you may have been authorized by the Judge, thus to make his public recantation, and to promise that for the future he shall behave better, we will not controvert. But anxious indeed must a man be for promotion, and great must be his prouess[3] to intemperate sallies, who can one day set all decency at defiance, to indulge the mean passion of railing at his *betters,* and on the next descend to such humiliating concessions, as you have made for him[,] to court their favour, and gratify his own ambition.

You seem to rely much on Mr. RUTLEDGE'S being one of your '75 men, and having had a great share in pulling down the existing government of that day. We also have here our men of the same stamp, who still possess, like the Judge, the spirit of '75; and who, like him, not perceiving the difference between our then and our present situation, conceive it to be the duty of a good patriot, to defame and oppose the existing government, be it what it may; such men are good *fellows* to effect a revolution; but they are wholly unfit to be entrusted with the administration of an infant republic.

You rely also on the plea of poverty, to excuse the Judge for refusing to pay his debts; but such inability will neither excuse nor account for getting rid of a debt on payment only of one half of it; an honest man would acknowledge the other moiety still to be due, with a promise to pay it when he shall have the means. But this plea cannot be admitted, even by the Judge and his family, who value themselves much upon his wealth; and all others from that State, beside yourself, speak of him as one of the most wealthy men in that country.

Upon the whole, Mr. Vindicator, I think you had much better been quiet, for you have by medling, most clearly traduced the State you came from, and you have implicated yourself, without relieving the judge. These are truly, the honest sentiments of

A REAL REPUBLICAN.

(Boston) September 5, 1795. Date and place are those of the newspaper. The headline indicates that this article was "FOR THE COLUMBIAN CENTINEL." Readings have been supplied in brackets because of type that did not imprint.

1. See John Rutledge, Vindicated: "A South Carolinean" to Benjamin Russell, *Columbian Centinel* under date of August 28, 1795.

2. I have sinned.

3. The writer may mean "prowess," and the printer substituted a "u" for the "w" by mistake; but alternatively the writer may have meant "proneness," in which case the printer has omitted an "ne" and inverted the other "n."

Thomas Jefferson to James Monroe ─────────────────────────
September 6, 1795   Monticello, Albemarle County, Virginia

... P. S. ... I omitted in my letter to mention that J. Rutledge was appointed Chief Justice in the room of m̅r Jay, and that he, Govr Pinckney[1] & others of that Southern constellation had pronounced themselves more desperately than any others against the treaty.─ ...

AR (DLC, James Monroe Papers); APc (DLC, Thomas Jefferson Papers).

James Monroe (1758-1831), fifth president of the United States, studied law in Virginia under Thomas Jefferson, with whom he maintained a lifelong friendship. Monroe entered public service in 1782 with his election to the Virginia legislature. He served in the Confederation Congress and later opposed ratification of the Constitution in the Virginia convention in 1788. In 1790 Monroe was elected to the Senate to fill a vacancy. He left the Senate in June, 1794, when he was appointed minister to France. Monroe was recalled in 1796 and in 1799 was elected governor of Virginia, a position he held until 1802. *DAB.*

1. Charles Pinckney.

Boston Gazette ─────────────────────────
September 7, 1795   Boston, Massachusetts

Our beloved PRESIDENT, it appears, is not without his enemies.─ The *"Real Republican,"* in that *pure, chaste,* paper, the CENTINEL,[1] of *shifting* principles, holds this great character up to view, as extremely ignorant of the abilities and integrity of the citizens of the United States in general, particularly of those of Mr. RUTLEDGE, Chief Justice of the Union. _ This assassin of the PRESIDET, says, "*it is to be lamented, upon public principles, that the President had not known better his real character before the appointment; but he cannot know every man in the United States; and the informations he gets from others, cannot be always relied upon.* _ A truly *insurgent* charge this against the first Magistrate of America! _ What, the PRESIDENT to be *betrayed* by the Senate and other official characters! _ Were not WASHINGTON'S character too firmly rivetted in the good opinion of the LITERATI of the world, universally, it is barely possible, this scribbling ATOM might gain a proselyte to his infamous assertion. _ But, CO-LUMBIANS! whilst this illustrious Patriot and venerable Statesman[2] is at the head of affairs in this country, such contemptable wretches as this *"Real Republican"* has proved himself to be, will only receive the pity of the real Federalists of America for his folly, rather than any other severity for an *attempt* to injure the character of a man, whose prudence, virtue, and abilities, eclipse all monarchs of the world.

(Boston) September 7, 1795. Date and place given are those of newspaper. The following phrase precedes this article: *"Unavoidably omitted last Week."*

1. See "A Real Republican" to John Rutledge, *Columbian Centinel* under date of August 26, 1795.

2. In the newspaper, the words "venerable Statesman" appear without a space between them.

Federal Intelligencer ———————————————————
September 7, 1795 Charleston, South Carolina

... Judge Rutledge in the short time of his absence, sat upon the bench consequential of his late appointment to the chief justiceship of the United States,[1] and came on board the packet a few hours after the adjournment of the court. ...

(Baltimore) September 29, 1795. Date and place are those of the article.

This article also appeared in the *Independent Chronicle* (Boston), October 12, 1795.

1. A brief article noting that John Rutledge had taken his seat as chief justice appeared in the *Independent Chronicle* (Boston), September 17, 1795; the *Argus* (New York), September 21, 1795; and the *New-Hampshire Gazette* (Portsmouth), September 22, 1795.

Letter from an Anonymous Correspondent ———————————
Aurora
September 8, 1795 Carlisle, Pennsylvania

"I find the opposition to the treaty still continues notwithstanding the President has ratified it. There is one thing I would be glad to know; whether the President sent the commission of chief justice to citizen Rutledge before or after he knew of his opposition to the treaty; if after, it would seem it was given him as a quietus. I have too good an opinion of the patriotism of the chief justice to suppose he would change from his former principles on account of his filling the above office, therefore conclude he is still inimical[1] to the treaty and will always oppose it in his private and official capacity, as the treaty is a violation of the constitution which he has covenanted to support. Although the conduct[2] of some men in the United States would lead many[3] to believe the sentiment of *Walpole* "Show me the man and I will shew his *price*," I cannot as yet subscribe to it. ... "

(Philadelphia) September 8, 1795. The date is that of the newspaper; the place is that given for the letter.
1. Appears in the newspaper as "icimical."
2. Appears in the newspaper as "couduct."
3. Appears in the newspaper as "mauy."

Essay by "Cathmor"
Virginia Gazette, and General Advertiser
September 8, 1795   Blue Ridge, [Virginia?]

[*The* "gigantic powers" *of* "*Camillus*"] have given birth to those haughty sentiments of superiority, that strongly mark his invectives against Mr. Rutledge.[1] To arraign a man's understanding and confute his arguments, is widely different— from asserting that his reasoning, exhibits a weak head and contravenes the supposition of a good heart— For the human mind is not infallible— her errors are not considered as crimes, while those of the heart are justly supposed corrupt or selfish, neither can apply to Mr. Rutledge— but he has reprobated the treaty— and that unpardonable sin, absorbs judgment— contracts discernment— erases recollection of intrepid patriotism.— The active federalist, the able advocate for the new Constitution, is scarcely justly distinguished and rewarded by an appointment to the head of the judiciary, when administration have to lament his strictures on the treaty, and repine least official and natural dignity uniting together, may extend the progress of opposition.— Camillus had he freely unfolded his real sensations, in place of declaiming on heads and hearts, would exhibit a poignant sorrow at the appointment of Mr. Rutledge, his nervous eloquence would seemingly anticipate the danger of a friend or friends— in the line of impeachment, from a virtuous man— an incorrupt republican— an able lawyer, the friend, the supporter of the Constitution, presiding in the seat of ju[st]ice.

I do not presume a cap[a]city to advise C[a]millus, I avow the reverse, but a common s[e]nse truly humble, may possess refl[e]ction adequate to investigate political interest— perhaps justly differ in opinion, with, and refuse assent to the most r[e]fined intuitive perceptions, supported by logical arrang[e]m[e]nt— enforced by the most powerful elocution— ...

(Richmond) September 30, 1795. Date and place are those given by author. Readings have been supplied in brackets where type did not imprint. Headlined "FOR THE VIRGINIA GAZETTE, &c."
1. See The Defence No. V by "Camillus," *Argus* under date of August 5, 1795.

John Blair to James Iredell
September 14, 1795 Richmond, Virginia

... my trip up the country has not brought me any relief from the strange disorder, which for a considerable time past has afflicted my head, and renders me incapable of business, which I have been obliged to neglect, in a degree very painful to me. Sensible of the advantages of my official character, I have not been in haste to resign. I have been willing to take every chance for a removal of the complaint, consistent with a resolution I have taken, in case an unexpected recovery should not prevent it, to resign so long before the court in February next, as to give the President sufficient time to supply the vacancy against that court. The time I had limited for that purpose will shortly expire, and then I shall not think of any further experiment. ... My infirmity will, I fear, deprive me of the pleasure of ever seeing you again. ...

Pr (Printed in *MJI*, 2:454-55).

Columbian Centinel
September 19, 1795 Boston, Massachusetts

We learn, that Judge RUTLEDGE dined with THE PRESIDENT, during his stay at *Philadelphia*. We mention this circumstance, as evincive of cordiality between those two distinguished characters, notwithstanding any difference of political sentiment between them.

(Boston) September 19, 1795. Date and place are those of the newspaper.

Henry Lee to Patrick Henry
September 30, 1795 [Virginia]

Sepr 30th, 1795.

DEAR SIR:

I set out in a few days for Phila. where I wish to do whatever I can for you. If you have any business write to me by post. The political fever has much abated, the people everywhere begin to understand the views of faction and obey their government. What a happy crisis for you to come forward. Certain I am that you would have been long ago called to high office, if men pretending to know your sentiments and wishing to withhold your weight from administration, had not constantly declared your unwillingness to accept.

Pray tell me as your friend, whether I may contradict, if I find a proper occasion, this opinion where the contradiction may lead to serve you.

I think Mr. Rutledge's late appointment will probably be dissented to on the part of the Senate.

That office exactly suits you, and I always wished to see you fill it. Be unreserved and decided in your reply— I will instantly commit the let[r] to flames, & use its purport only for your favor and the public good. God bless you.

Yours ever,

H. LEE.

TO PATRICK HENRY, ESQ.

Pr (Printed in William Wirt Henry, *Patrick Henry: Life, Correspondence, and Speeches*, 3 vols. (New York: Charles Scribner's Sons, 1891), 2:561). Place determined from evidence in letter.

Anecdote of Chief Justice Rutledge
Rutland Herald
October 5, 1795   Rutland, Vermont

He was president of South Carolina in March 1778, when the general assembly and legislative council of that state presented to him the new constitution, by them adopted, for his assent; when, by virtue of the negative power delegated to him by the temporary constitution, he refused to pass it, and on that occasion delivered to them a speech, recited at large in Ramsay's history of the revolution in that state, vol. I, p. 132,[1] of which the following is an extract:

"The people also preferred a compound or mixed government to a simple democracy, or one verging towards it. However unexceptionable democratic power may appear at first view, its effects[2] have always been found arbitrary, severe, and destructive."

(Rutland, Vermont) October 5, 1795. Date and place are those of the newspaper. Marked *"From the Providence Gazette."*

1. The text of John Rutledge's speech is given in David Ramsay, *The History of the Revolution of South-Carolina, from a British Province to an Independent State*, 2 vols. (Trenton: Isaac Collins, 1785), 1:132-39. The quotation given here—slightly misquoted—is found on pages 137-38. The correct quotation is: "The people also preferred a compounded or mixed government to a simple democracy, or one verging towards it, perhaps because, however unexceptionable democratic power may appear at the first view, its effects have been found arbitrary, severe and destructive."

2. The words "its effects" appear without a space between them in the newspaper.

John Blair to James Iredell
October 10, 1795   Williamsburg, Virginia

WILLIAMSBURG, Oct. 10th.

Your favor of the 24th ult. reached me yesterday.[1] I feel much gratitude for the concern which you and Mrs. Iredell take at my loss of health, for your anxiety that I should not resign, and for your obliging readiness to assume for my accommodation still further fatigue of duty than is properly your own.[2] You may, probably, be right also in the confidence you express, that in this the rest of the Judges would willingly concur with you; but this appears to me so unreasonable an imposition that I cannot think of it. . . .

My complaint is nothing but an overbearing noise in my head, which distracts my attention; but which, from experience, seems to be consistent with good health in other respects, &c., &c.

Your faithfully affectionate friend,

JOHN BLAIR.

Pr (Printed in *MJI*, 2:455).

1. Letter not found.

2. Because of illness, John Blair sent his resignation to President Washington on October 25, 1795; see "Appointments to the Bench," under "John Blair: Appointment as Associate Justice in 1789." James Iredell took Blair's place at the circuit court meeting in Richmond in November, 1795. John Blair to James Iredell, September 14, 1795, and James Iredell to Hannah Iredell, November 12, 1795, in *MJI*, 2:454-57.

Letter from an Anonymous Correspondent ————————————
Gazette of the United States
October 10, 1795   Philadelphia, Pennsylvania

. . . You have doubtless seen or heard of the scandalous publications in a Boston Paper against the chief justice and an intended vindication said to be written by Mr. K———n, and a reply to the defence.[1] I fear a cabal is forming to reject the appointment in Senate. . . .

(Philadelphia) November 12, 1795. Date and place are those given for the letter. "A Friend to the People" had sent this extract of a letter from Philadelphia to the *South-Carolina State-Gazette* (Charleston) which had printed it. "Crito" forwarded it to the editor of the *Gazette of the United States.* For the comments of "Crito," see the *Gazette of the United States* under date of November 12, 1795.

The item published here also appeared in the *Richmond and Manchester Advertiser* (Richmond, Virginia), November 11, 1795.

1. See "A Real Republican" to John Rutledge, *Columbian Centinel* under date of August 26, 1795; John Rutledge, Vindicated: "A South Carolinean" to Benjamin Russell, *Columbian Centinel* under date of August 28, 1795; and "A Real Republican" to "The South-Carolinean," *Columbian Centinel* under date of September 5, 1795.

The identity of "Mr. K———n," who wrote under the name of "The South-Carolinean," is unknown.

Elias Boudinot to Samuel Bayard ————————————————
   October 17, 1795   Rosehill, Philadelphia County, Pennsylvania

[*Writing to Bayard in England, Boudinot describes the town gatherings in opposition
to the Jay Treaty.*] Of all these Meetings that of Charles Town in South Carolina
was the most extraordinary, on account of the puerile, declamatory & violent
Speech from the present Chief Magistrate of the United States— Nothing can
excuse this instance of democratic fury, but the reported state of Mind, of this
once worthy Man— I am told, but cannot answer for the truth of it, that he
is now much ashamed of his Conduct— In short I believe many good, but
weak men, have been imposed upon, to give their assent to some very reprehensible Acts on this Occasion . . .

ARS (NjP, Bradford Papers).

Aurora ————————————————————————————
   October 20, 1795   Philadelphia, Pennsylvania

[The abuse so liberally bestowed on Judge Rutledge by a certain class of prints
   in the United States will be recollected. The following extract from a London Print of the same stamp will shew, that the conductors of such papers,
   on either side of the Atlantic, are as uniform in their abuse of the real
   friends of the people, as if they had given one another the word.][1]

   ————————————————

In a morning paper of last Friday, devoted to French principles, there appeared a long letter from Charleston, South-Carolina, giving an account of the
debate that took place in that city, on the late Treaty between this country and
America.
   The most prominent orator on that occasion was Judge Rutledge, who ut-
tered the most gross invectives both against the President Washington, as well
as Mr. Jay, for having sacrificed the interests of the American States to the
king of Great Britain; and concluded with a severe philippic against royalty.
   It will not, however, be improper to acquaint the public of the character of
this flaming orator, who is now employed to administer justice in America, as
Chief Justice of South Carolina. This man fled the country for debt. He was
educated near the metropolis, and when he married, he ordered wedding
cloaths, a chariot, and other necessaries, which the person who superintended
his education paid for. To the present moment these debts are owed for by
Judge Rutledge, the same as another debt to a poor English clergyman at Amsterdam who educated his son.[2]
   It is thus that the out-casts of their country carry revolutionary principles
into every place where they find shelter; and scatter about the seeds of dis-
content and disorganization. Every where they are the irreconcileable enemies

of regular governments, and the active instruments of the overthrow of states. In France, the Genevese were the busiest destroyers of all order; in England, French jacobins are preaching up the most unconstitutional doctrines; and in in America we see a Rutledge, who was obliged to leave this country for fraudulent practices, with the utmost impudence insult the most respectable personages, and declaim against the most beneficial treaties.

(Philadelphia) October 20, 1795. Date and place are those of headline.

1. The *Federal Orrery* (Boston) did not include any such explanatory paragraph when it published the article which follows on October 12, 1795.

2. No evidence has been found either to prove or disprove these charges. For the precarious state of John Rutledge's finances, see notes to "A Real Republican" to John Rutledge, *Columbian Centinel* under date of August 26, 1795, and John Rutledge Vindicated: "A South Carolinean" to Benjamin Russell, *Columbian Centinel* under date of August 28, 1795.

George Washington to Alexander Hamilton ————————
October 29, 1795 Philadelphia, Pennsylvania

... M.̅ Chase of Maryland[1] is, unquestionably, a man of abilities; and it is supposed by some, that he w.̅d̅ accept the appointment of Attorney General.＿ Though opposed to the adoption of the Constitution, it is said he has been a steady friend to the general government since it has been in operation.＿[2] But he is violently opposed in his own State by a party, and is besides, or to speak more correctly has been, accused of some impurity in his conduct.＿[3] ...

ARS (DLC, Alexander Hamilton Papers). Marked "(Private & confidential)."

1. Samuel Chase.

2. For this information, George Washington may have been relying on James McHenry's letter to him of June 14, 1795 (q.v.).

3. Probably a reference to Samuel Chase's involvement in flour speculation during the Revolutionary War; see "Appointments to the Bench," headnote to "Samuel Chase: Appointment as Associate Justice in 1796." It should be noted that, less than three months after writing these comments, George Washington nominated Chase to fill a vacancy on the Supreme Court.

Letter from an Anonymous Correspondent to a Gentleman in Philadelphia ————————————————————————
American Mercury
November 5, 1795 London, England

... The language of Mr. ————,[1] was such at Charleston respecting the treaty, as has shocked here every man that has read it, and yet that same person has been called upon to take his seat at the head of the Supreme Court of Justice; I suppose when the President named him for that high and honourable station, he could not possibly have been informed of his gross conduct and behaviour upon a subject sanctioned by the law of his country, and to which law every man ought to bow obedience; and if Americans know their own interest, they will steadily and faithfully adhere to and support a constitution, framed and fitted for their future welfare and happiness. . . .

(Hartford) January 25, 1796. Date and place are those given for the letter. Published under a New York headline dated January 18.

1. John Rutledge.

"Crito" to an Anonymous Correspondent in Philadelphia ———
Gazette of the United States
November 12, 1795 Philadelphia, Pennsylvania

[*"Crito" responds to the author of a letter written October 10, 1795, and printed in the* Gazette of the United States *on November 12, 1795 (q.v. under date of October 10, 1795).*] If the writer was disposed to recollect the publications which appeared in the Charleston papers some years since, on the subject of Mr. Rutledge's conduct towards Capt. Thompson, for a supposed insult to his mulatto wench, and which publications were well received by the republican party at that time in Charleston, he would be compelled to acknowledge, that the Judge has been very tenderly handled at Boston.[1] . . .

(Philadelphia) November 12, 1795. Date and place are those of newspaper.

1. In 1784, when John Rutledge was a member of the South Carolina House of Representatives, he had Captain William Thompson, a Charleston tavern keeper, jailed for contempt. Thompson had had a dispute with one of Rutledge's slaves and then insulted Rutledge when Rutledge chose to believe his slave's account of the incident. Thompson's version of the incident was reported in the *Gazette of the State of South-Carolina* (Charleston) under the title "The 10th Chapter of the Book of Chronicles" on April 8 and 15, 1784. Thompson's affadavit was printed on April 29, 1784.

Edward Carrington to George Washington ———
November 13, 1795 Richmond, Virginia

                  as to
. . . Will you be so good ˄ pardon my presumption in offering to your consideration for a vacancy which I learn has taken place, a character lately under your contemplation for another?[1] I allude to the resignation of Judge Blair, & to Col? Innes[2] as his successor. Gen¹ Marshall & myself have had a private consultation on the subject of mentioning the latter Gentleman to you— we agree in this, that in point of talents & legal acquirements his pretensions are
                                       on
surpassed by none— & for steadiness & zeal founded ˄ sincere attachment to the constitution and Government of the UStates, he yields to none. the in-

dolence of which are[3] apprised is all that can operate against him, and this we
  believe he will sufficiently counteract from a sense of pride, a stimulus that
^
may be added to, by a communication which we might make at the time of
sounding him as to an acceptance. We believe he would accept, because he
reluctantly declined the former proposition; and certainly would not have done
so, from any other consideration but the inadequacy of Salary. You may be
assured Sir that the present suggestion rests intirely with Gen[l] M— & myself,
and will there expire should you from any considerations forbear to adopt it.
I am sure that the Gentleman who is the subject of it, has not a suspicion of
our having thought of it. . . .

ARS (DLC, George Washington Papers).
  Edward Carrington (1749-1810) was the supervisor of the revenue for the district of Virginia.
Carrington was married to John Marshall's sister-in-law, Eliza Ambler Brent. *PJM*, 1:117; 2:309.
  1. On September 28 and October 9, George Washington ha·l written to Edward Carrington
asking Carrington and John Marshall their opinions on whether james Innes would be qualified
for and accept appointment as attorney general of the United States. Fitzpatrick, *Writings of George
Washington*, 34:317-18, 331-33; Leonard Baker, *John Marshall: A Life in Law* (New York: Macmillan, 1974), pp. 168-69.
  2. James Innes (1754-1798) had attended the College of William and Mary before the Revolutionary War. A lawyer by occupation, Innes declined an appointment as judge advocate general
of the Continental Army in 1782. He was later elected attorney general of Virginia in 1786 and
supported ratification of the Constitution in 1788. Innes worked with Patrick Henry and John
Marshall for the defendants in the· British debt cause (1791-1793). At the request of President
Washington, Innes temporarily left his job as attorney general for six months (1794-1795) to go
to Kentucky to explain the progress of negotiations with Spain regarding navigation of the Mis-
sissippi River. He resigned his post in 1796 when he was appointed one of the American commissioners under Article VI of the Jay Treaty. *DAB; PJM*, 2:290; Moore, *International Adjudications*,
3:19-21.
  3. Edward Carrington probably meant to write the word "we" before "are."

Ralph Izard to Jacob Read ————————————————
November 17, 1795   Charleston, South Carolina

                                            Charleston   Nov[r] 17th 1795.—
Dear Sir
  By the accounts from the Northward I find that the enemies of the Government are making every possible exertion to do mischief. They are in hopes
that the Senate will not confirm the appointment of M[r] Rutledge as Chief Justice; & if so, will immediately raise a clamor, & endeavor to ascribe the rejection to party. I most sincerely hope that the Senate will agree to the nomination, & that the Anarchists may be disappointed. No man could be more
afflicted than I was at the part M[r] Rutledge took in opposition to the Treaty.
I am sure he is now very sorry for it himself. After the death of his Wife, his
mind was frequently so much deranged, as to be in a great measure deprived
of his senses; & I am persuaded he was in that situation when the Treaty was

under consideration[.] I have frequently been in company with him since his return, & find him totally altered. I am of opinion that no Man in the United State would execute the Office of Chief Justice with more ability, & integrity than he would. I hope therefore you will make every possible exertion on the subject with our Friends in the Senate. The minds of people in this State begin to be calmed, & I wish that everything may be avoided which will be likely to rekindle the flame, which has already given us too much trouble. My regard for M.ʳ Rutledge, & my love of tranquillity would not have induced me to write to you on this subject if I were not perfectly convinced of the propriety of confirming the appointment. Be pleased to communicate my opinion on this business, with assurances of regard, & affection, to my Friends M.ʳ Cabot;[1] M.ʳ Strong, M.ʳ Ellsworth, & M.ʳ Frelinghuysen.[2]

I am Dear Sir   Your most ob.ᵗ Servant

Ra. Izard

. . .

ARS (NN, Emmet Collection). Originally addressed "New York." When the letter arrived in New York, that city's name was crossed out and the letter was forwarded to "Philadelphia." Postmarked "N-York-DEC 4."

1. George Cabot (1752-1823), a Massachusetts merchant, served in the Senate from 1791 to 1796. A federalist, Cabot was a supporter of the Jay Treaty. *DAB*.

2. Frederick Frelinghuysen (1753-1804), a New Jersey lawyer, had served in the Continental and Confederation Congresses. He entered the United States Senate on December 5, 1793, and resigned in May, 1796. *DAB*.

Oliver Wolcott, Sr., to Oliver Wolcott, Jr. ─────────
November 23, 1795   Litchfield, Connecticut

. . . I am apprehensive that no more than a strong Minority in the house of Representatives will appear to support the constituted authorities[1] and the na-
                    but
tional characters ─ ˄ I hope We may rely upon the firmness of the Senate ─
                                                              treating
The Virtuous Motives which have induced the [treated?] with regard, Men who avow and act upon principles inconsistent with the preservation of order,
                      them
to influence ˄ to a more just conduct, has and will be ineffectual ─ I hope therefore no such appointments will be made nor sanctioned ─ any yielding to those people does but increase their Violence ─ however disagreable it may be as it will imply an Error in Judgment in the President to appoint M.ʳ Rutledge, that He will not be confirmed in his office ─ I wish that another Person of a more confidential character than M.ʳ M[u]roe[2] may supply his place ─ and
            be
that We are ˄ an independent nation not in name only ─ . . .

ARS (CtHi, Oliver Wolcott Jr. Papers).

1. Originally Oliver Wolcott, Sr., seems to have written "authority" and then altered the ending to "ies."

2. James Monroe, appointed on May 28, 1794, as minister plenipotentiary to the French Republic. His strong pro-French leanings and opposition to the Jay Treaty made him very unpopular with the federalists, and George Washington finally decided to recall him in July, 1796. Oliver Wolcott, Sr., may have been expressing only his own feelings or responding to sentiments already current within Washington's cabinet. *SEJ,* 1:157; Fitzpatrick, *Writings of George Washington,* 35:124-27; *DAB.*

Columbian Centinel ——————————————————————————
November 27, 1795   Philadelphia, Pennsylvania

. . . "It is said Judge R.[1] if nominated to the Senate, will not be chosen Chief Justice — notwithstanding all the reports of his conversion."

(Boston) December 9, 1795. Date and place are those of the article. The quotation marks in this excerpt have been reproduced as they appear in the *Columbian Centinel;* they indicate that the paragraphs probably were taken from a letter.

1. John Rutledge.

Abigail Adams to John Quincy Adams ——————————————
November 29, 1795   Quincy, Massachusetts

. . . It is thought the Senate will have some difficult discussions before them, there Judas may not pass uncensured, and the Chief Justice may possibly receive a Negative, the Appointment was extrodonary; some person asked General Knox how the p. t came to make such an appointment. left of God, replied Knox. for the first Time, the circumstances which took place after ward, were not foreseen by the p.   and I must suppose that he was ignorant of the present Character of the man, I am sure the p.   never adopted the Sentiment, of a Southern writer, who in aiming to defend his Character, asserted that a mans moral Character, had no connextion with his political Character; a Judge like the wife of Ceasar, ought not to be suspected. . . .

ARS (MHi, Adams Manuscript Trust). Addressed "Holland or England." Endorsed "1. Feb[y] 1796. rec[d] London.   ans[d]."

Arthur Iredell to James Iredell ——————————————————
December 1, 1795   "near Lewes," Sussex County, England

. . . I was sensibly mortified the other Day by reading in the Papers the Appointment of another Person to the Chiefship in your Court, — for I had

worked myself up to the Persuasion that Washington could not in Justice withhold it from you_ By the bye, is it to be the Fashion in America, as here, to
select a Chief from the Bar?_ It is, I think, a very improper & injudicious
Custom anywhere_ I wish very much to know the Characters of your learned
Brethren; but I dare not ask you to sketch their Likeness for me_ Send me,
however, printed Cases &ᶜᵃ, as you have lately done, that I may puzzle out an
Opinion of my own_ . . .

ARS (Nc-Ar, Charles E. Johnson Collection). Addressed "Philadelphia   N America." Sent "By
the New   York Packet."

Aurora ————————————————————————————————————
December 1, 1795   Charleston, South Carolina

By a gentleman who left Camden[1] on Wednesday last,[2] we are informed
that the Chief Justice of the United States left that place on the Saturday preceding,[3] on his way to hold the Circuit Court in North Carolina; that on the
evening of that day he reached Evan's tavern, on Linch's Creek, which he left
the next morning, a few hours after, he was taken so unwell that he was
obliged to return to Mr. Evans's. When the account came away, he was so
much indisposed as to make it doubtful whether he would be able to proceed
in time to hold the court in North-Carolina.[4]

(Philadelphia) December 23, 1795. Date and place are from the headline.
   This item also appeared in the *Columbian Centinel* (Boston), January 2, 1796.
   1. Camden, South Carolina.
   2. November 25, 1795.
   3. November 21, 1795.
   4. The Circuit Court for the district of North Carolina was not held that term.

Jacob Read to Ralph Izard ————————————————————————
December 8, 1795   Philadelphia, Pennsylvania

. . . I am obliged to you my dear sir for your Letter of the 17ᵗʰ of Novʳ I have
long thought and anxiously too of the Subject on which it is written. I see that
the Senate will be exceedingly embarrassed on that business_ Altho' the
Gentleman spoken of has treated me exceedingly Cruelly_ wantonly Charged
me & mis-represented my Views and in his speech held a very different Language than that he used to me & which for aught he knew might have greatly
influenced my mind_ yet when my Country's peace & welfare are at stake I
hope I am Incapable of revenge_ I have forgiven & shall Study to forget all
that passed when I was absent & no one to take my part. I believe with you
that a weakness of the moment not to be accounted for was the Cause of that
unwise Speech & Violent Conduct which has Indeed done great mischief_ I
have long been a Witness to the abilities of that Gentleman & 'twill give me

pleasure if his appointment is Confirmed— Mr Smith & my self have had some Conversations on the Subject— We shall Consult again & you may be assured I will shew your Letter to the Friends you desire— I this day shewed it to Mr Cabot he said it wou'd be he feared Utterly impossible to raise that Gentleman in the Esteem of the people of the Eastern States. He spoke of the opinion expressed in those States of his Conduct & gave me no hopes of any Co operation We are to have another Conversation and I shall See what can be done— If the nomination shou'd not be confirmed I beg you'l do me the Justice to Say that my Efforts in M^r R_____'s[1] favour have not been wanting[—] . . .

ARS (ScU, Ralph Izard Papers). Addressed "Charleston."
    1. John Rutledge.

Henry Lee to George Washington
December 9, 1795 Richmond, Virginia

. . . I hope soon to hear from M^r H;[1] in case a certain office may be vacated[2] I wish you to know his mind— If Virg^a furnishes not the C. J. I hope she will supply the present judiciary vacancy.[3] Should this be thought proper Mr Innes is considered among us here the fit character— you will Judge for yourself—
. . .

ARS (DLC, George Washington Papers).
    1. Patrick Henry.
    2. If the Senate did not confirm John Rutledge's nomination as chief justice, that position would be available.
    3. John Blair had sent his resignation to President Washington on October 25, 1795; q.v. in "Appointments to the Bench," under "John Blair: Appointment as an Associate Justice in 1789."

John Adams to John Quincy Adams
December 12, 1795 Philadelphia, Pennsylvania

. . . The Conduct however of some of our old Men, such as Rutledge . . . has been not only illegal and unconstitutional but indiscreet in a high degree. . . .

ARS (MHi, Adams Manuscript Trust).

Alexander Hamilton to Rufus King
December 14, 1795 New York, New York

. . . An extraordinary press of occupation has delayed an answer to your letter[1] on [a~~certain~~?] the subject of M^r R[2] Though it may come too ^late, I comply with your request as soon as I can—

The subject is truly a perplexing one; my mind has several times fluctuated—
If there was nothing in the case but his imprudent sally upon a certain occasion
I should think the reasons for letting him pass would outweigh those for opposing his passage— But if it be really true— that he is sottish or that his mind
                                      or that he
is otherwise deranged, and if he has exposed himself by improper conduct in
pecuniary transactions, the byass of my judgment would be to negative— And
as to the fact I would satisfy myself by careful inquiry of persons of character
who may have had an opportunity of knowing—

It is now, and in certain probable events will still more be, of infinite consequence that our Judiciary should be well composed. Reflection[3] upon this in
its various aspects weighs heavily on my mind against M[r] R, upon the accounts
I have received of him, and ballances very weighty considerations the other
way . . .

ARS (NHi, Rufus King Papers). Addressed "Philadelphia." Postmarked "N-York. DEC 15."
  1. Letter not found.
  2. John Rutledge. Alexander Hamilton appears to have written "M[r]___" and then wrote the
"R" over the dash.
  3. The "R" is written over "The."

John Adams to Abigail Adams ───────────────────────────
December 16, 1795   Philadelphia, Pennsylvania

. . . The Senate have refused their Consent to the Nomination of M[r] Rutledge.
I hope that Chief Justices at least will learn from this to be cautious how they
go to popular Meetings [at?] especially unlawful:[1] assemblies to Spout Reflections and excite opposition to the legal Acts of Constitutional Authority.[2] . . .

ARS (MHi, Adams Manuscript Trust).
  1. John Adams probably wrote this colon when he intended to conclude the sentence at this
point. He then continued the sentence but neglected to cross out the colon.
  2. At the time John Rutledge delivered his speech, he probably did not know that President
Washington had appointed him chief justice, ad interim.

Jeremiah Smith to William Plumer ─────────────────────
December 16, 1795   Philadelphia, Pennsylvania

. . . The Senate have this day refused to concur in the appointment of John
Rutledge as Chief Justice of the United States—[1] you will be pleased to recollect his speech at Charleston on the Treaty a speech which would have disgraced the lips of an Idiot.— There must have been some thing wrong in the
Heart of the man who could utter it

I am sure you will be pleased with this act of the Senate.— I doubted of
their firmness & am agreeably disappointed.— . . .

ARS (Nh, Plumer Papers). Addressed "Epping   New Hampshire." Sent to "Exeter Postoffice." Postmarked "16   DE."

1. Jeremiah Smith mistakenly reports the rejection as taking place on December 16. In fact, it happened on December 15. William B. Giles wrote a brief mention of it to Thomas Jefferson on Tuesday, December 15. Thomas Jefferson Papers, DLC; see also Jacob Read to Ralph Izard, December 19, 1795.

Columbian Centinel
December 16, 1795   Philadelphia, Pennsylvania

"You will learn by the papers, that the Senate have negatived the nomination of Judge RUTLEDGE.[1] This is as it should be; and what he ought to have expected, after his imprudent and virulent attack he made on their characters in *Charleston.* THE PRESIDENT having appointed him *ad interim,* before he knew of his late proceeding, was of necessity, obliged to put him in nomination: But since it has been known, how *passionately* he arraigned a measure, before he had time to consider; or perhaps before he read it; he has been judged (all politicks apart) to be a very unfit person for a Chief Justice of the United States.

. . .

"The opening of the doors of the *Senate,* though very inconvenient on account of the building, will *open* the eyes of many people; who will therein see many of the first rate talents, patriotism and firmness.[2] The negative they have put on the nomination of R. is an instance of the latter.

(Boston) December 26, 1795. Date and place are those of the article. The quotation marks in these excerpts have been reproduced as they appear in the *Columbian Centinel;* they indicate that the paragraphs probably were taken from a letter.

1. The *Aurora* (Philadelphia) on December 16, 1795, briefly noted the Senate's rejection of John Rutledge. Other newspapers reported the Senate's vote and, therefore, are included in annotation to the Senate rejection on December 15, 1795, in "Appointments to the Bench," under "John Rutledge: Appointment as Chief Justice in 1795."

2. On December 9, 1795, the Senate for the first time opened its doors to the public. Previously the Senate had met in closed session. *SLJ,* 2:197.

John Adams to Abigail Adams
December 17, 1795   Philadelphia, Pennsylvania

. . . The Negative put by the Senate on the Nomination of Mr Rutledge gave me pain for an old Friend, though I could not but think he deserved it. C. Justices must not go to illegal Meetings and become popular orators in favour of Sedition, nor inflame the popular discontents which are ill founded, nor propogate Disunion, Division, Contention and delusion among the People.[1] I never thought him the greatest Man in the World, nor had any fixed Confidence in his Penetration or his Constancy or Consistency. I have also had Reason to suspect that the French had too much Influence with him to leave him perfectly neutral or impartial. The Disarrangement of his affairs the Reports of his Eccentricities &c had not made so much Impression upon me. But all Things considered, the Senate were very decided that such an Example ought to be made. . . .

ARS (MHi, Adams Manuscript Trust).

   1. As in his letter of the day before (q.v.), John Adams mistakenly implies that John Rutledge knew he had been appointed chief justice, ad interim.

Henry Lee to Patrick Henry —————————————————
December 17, 1795 Richmond, Virginia

. . . You never have told me what you would do if a vacancy in the Chief Justice's place should happen, and I really hoped you would have expressed to me unequivocally your mind, as I should have only used it for your own and the public good.[1] . . .

Pr (Printed in Henry, *Patrick Henry,* 2:562).

   1. See Henry Lee to Patrick Henry, September 30, 1795.

Jacob Read to Ralph Izard —————————————————
December 19, 1795 Philadelphia, Pennsylvania

. . . on Tuesday last the vote was taken in the Nomination by the President of Jn° Rutledge Esqʳ to be Chief Justice of the United States when the appointment was negatived the Numbers being 14 to 10,— as I assured you I wou'd, so in fact I did use every exertion in my power with our friends   but in vain   they declared to me that it woud be utterly impossible to raise Mʳ Rutledge in the Esteem of the thinking & respectable part of the Community in the Eastern & middle States— that it was one thing to punish a man and another to reward, that altho they had no Idea of Suppressing the Sentiments of Gentlemen   yet it woud be very unwise in Gouverment to put that man in the first Seat of Justice in the Union who had headed a Town meeting & urged & excited the Citizens to do what woud in a very little time if pursued totally destroy all gouvernment & defeat our respresentative System intirely— for if after knowing Mʳ Rutledge's conduct the Senate shoud confirmed the appointment how cou'd they hereafter venture to condemn the Conduct of any other popular Demagogue or disorganizer, very full reports of his pecuniary embarrassments were also circulated but these formed a very inferiour objection: the ill effect of rewarding a man with the first Honours & offices who had advised a system & headed a tumultuous assembly which if repeated cou'd not fail to unhinge all order & destroy our Gouverment was the true & real objection & in this the friends of order were immovable.

I represented in private the weight of that Gentleman in our State, his connexions, & the Effect I feared it might have in them, his great law knowledge, his having resigned a situation equally Lucrative & nearly as Honorable to accept this[,] my hopes that his opinion on Maturer reflexion was changed & above all that I dreaded it wou'd split the federal Interest & Serve as a new rallying point for the Mischievous & Enemies to order, but all was in vain_ When the question was about to be put I again by as conciliating and as moderate, tho' as highly recommendatory a Speech as I coud make, endeavoured to remove objections & to procure a vote of confirmation_ I was the only person who spoke on the occasion. nothing was said in opposition but the majority was ⌃as I have said immoveable_ had the vote been delayed till next day it wou'd have been 16 to 10 as Govr Bradford[1] & Mr Vining[2] came into Senate, Mr Vining declaring that he might almost say he was Instructed on the point so general was the sentiment in Delaware against Mr Rutledge & were it taken now I believe the votes wou'd be 18 to 10 if not a greater majority_ I am sorry for this, as it will hurt the Old Gentleman's feelings and perhaps disgust his Connexions, but had he been my Father I cou'd not have done more for him_ I perhaps exerted my self the more because as Mr Rutledge had differed from me in a vote & opinion, I had given, I felt a pleasure in shewing him I did not therefore respect him the less nor feel any resentment tho' I have Suffered severely in consequence of that ferment, which it is believed he contributed so much to raise & tried by his Speech to Countenance_ You will but do me Justice in saying to Mr Rutledge's friends that my endeavours were Zealously & Sincerely offered in his behalf_ ...

ARS (ScU, Ralph Izard Papers).
    1. William Bradford (1729-1808), an attorney from Bristol, Rhode Island, served in the Senate from March 4, 1793, until October, 1797. *BDAC.*
    2. John Vining (1758-1802) was a Delaware lawyer, who had served in the House of Representatives from 1789 to 1793. In 1793 Vining was elected to the Senate, where he was a strong supporter of the Jay Treaty. He resigned from the Senate on January 19, 1798. W. Emerson Wilson, *Forgotten Heroes of Delaware* (Cambridge, Mass.: Deltos Publishing, 1969), p. 98; *BDAC.*

Robert R. Livingston to Edward Livingston ———————
December 20, 1795   New York, New York

... I am sorry for the mortification Rutledge will feel in being made the sport of a party[.?] If his appointment is now so improper how has it happened that many of the Senators who now vote against him were formerly his advocates for the second place on the bench?_ Who is to succeed him? I suppose Paterson or Wilson the place is too important for a native American.[1] ...

ARS (NHi, Robert R. Livingston Papers). Addressed "Philadelphia   Market Street." Postmarked "N-York DEC 21."
    Robert R. Livingston (1746-1813), brother of Congressman Edward Livingston, was the chancellor of New York. Robert R. Livingston, a lawyer, briefly had shared a law practice with John

Jay and later served with distinction in the Continental and Confederation Congresses. In 1788 Livingston supported the adoption of the Constitution at the New York convention, but he later joined the republicans and led opposition to the Jay Treaty. He was defeated by John Jay in 1795 in New York's gubernatorial election. Livingston held the chancellorship from 1777 to 1801. In the latter year, he became minister to France. *DAB*.

Edward Livingston (1764-1836) was a lawyer and a republican congressman from New York. Elected in 1794, Livingston served in Congress until 1801 when he was appointed United States attorney for the district of New York. Shortly thereafter, he became mayor of New York City. *DAB;* William B. Hatcher, *Edward Livingston: Jeffersonian Republican and Jacksonian Democrat* (Baton Rouge: Louisiana State University Press, 1940), p. 76.

1. William Paterson was born in Ireland and James Wilson in Scotland.

John Adams to Abigail Adams
December 21, 1795 Philadelphia, Pennsylvania

... My old Acquaintance Mr Walton, who served in Congress, with me in 1776 and 1777 is returned a Senator from Georgia in the room of General Jackson[1] who has resigned. He is or has lately been Chief Justice. As old acquaintances are easily sociable We soon fell into Conversation about affairs old and new. I asked him whether The Negative of Mr Rutledge would have any ill Effect at the southward. He says No by no means— on the Contrary he is sure it will have a very good Effect. He adds he was rejoiced when he heard upon his arrival that it was done, because it saved him & his Colleague from the Necessity of giving a disagreable Vote: but that they both came to Town with a determination to vote against the appointment. He says that a Disarrangement of Intellect certainly exists and has been more decissive lately than formerly. That he has not been able to attend the Circuit Court in Georgia nor in North Carolina. That he attempted to attend in N. Carolina but was so bad that he could not. That he even attempted to make way with himself. He was himself at the House and made himself fully acquainted with the Facts.

He adds that M^r R's Conduct, as Chief Justice of the state of S. Carolina has been lately so unsatisfactory that several Grand Juries have presented him for what they thought Misconduct or at least Negligence of his Duty. The Embarrassment of his private affairs has lately pressed harder upon him than ever and produced or at least accellerated and increased the Disorder of his Mind. These Things being so we shall hear of no very sharp Rebukes Upon the Senate, for the Vote they have passed and the President will have avoided giving any offence to particular Friends. This is all in Confidence between you and me as I know you will have some anxiety upon this subject, as I have had a great deal. I have felt for an old Friend and his Friends. He is a Brother of your Friend Mrs Smith[2] whom you knew in London and has been a worthy Man. But the Man who plunges into Debt will soon get out of his Depth. You must mention these Things with great discretion and only in Confidence.
...

ARS (MHi, Adams Manuscript Trust).

1. James Jackson (1757-1806), a Georgia lawyer, served in Congress from 1789 to 1791. Elected to the Senate in 1793, he resigned in 1795 to return to Georgia to contest the state legislature's sale of land to the Yazoo Company. Jackson was elected governor in 1798 and served through 1801 when he returned to the Senate. *DAB*.

2. Mary Rutledge (1747-1832), John Rutledge's sister, married Roger Smith, a prominent South Carolinian, in 1768. Mabel L. Webber, comp., "Dr. John Rutledge and His Descendants," *South Carolina Historical and Genealogical Magazine* 31 (1929-1930): 13.

George Washington to Edward Carrington ———————
December 23, 1795 Philadelphia, Pennsylvania

... It had been expected that the Senate wou'd not confirm the appointment of M.r R— and so it has happened.— This induced me to delay the nomination of a successor to M.rBlair; and as the Department of War is yet unfilled; I am waiting (expecting[1]) information to make a general arangement— or rather distribution of these offices before I decide upon either separately.— ...

Lb (DLC, George Washington Papers); ADfS (DLC, George Washington Papers).
1. In draft, "expected."

William Vans Murray to James McHenry ———————
December 24, 1795 Philadelphia, Pennsylvania

... I <u>have</u> several times brought up M.r Chace to view while the official wheel was in motion— I have taken pains to place his & Martins politics in the true point of view— as yet no consequence has follow'd— except perhaps a <u>prep-aration</u>. Yes— Rutledge was rejected—[1] It is said openly that he is in an un-happy <u>state of mind</u>— & often deranged— by gentlemen immediately from his own country. ...

ARS (DLC, James McHenry Papers). Addressed to "near Baltimore."
1. On the same day that he wrote this letter to James McHenry, William Vans Murray also sent one to Samuel Chase with a report of the rejection of the Rutledge nomination (abstract in James McHenry Papers, MdHi). Letter not found.

American Minerva ———————
December 24, 1795 New York, New York

Authentic accounts from Charleston South-Carolina, inform us that John Rutledge, late Chief Justice, is so much deranged in his mind, as to require constant watching to prevent his committing violence on himself.

(New York) December 24, 1795. Date and place are from the headline.
A similar item appeared in the *Aurora* (Philadelphia), December 28, 1795, and in the *Connecticut Courant* (Hartford), January 4, 1796.

Charles Simms to George Washington ——————————————
December 25, 1795 Alexandria, Virginia

Alexandria   Decr 25.th 1795

Sir

I Trust it cannot be deem'd improper in a Citizen who is willing to serve his country in any office, to make known his desire to that department of Government which has the appointment to the office he wishes to hold.

Under that impression and being inform'd that Mr Blair has lately resigned the office of an Associate Justice of the Supreme Court of the United States, I beg leave to inform you that I am willing to fill the vacancy occasion'd by his resignation, if you think proper to nominate me for that office. With due respect

I am your Obed.^t Servt

Ch: Simms

ARS (DLC, George Washington Papers). Addressed "Philadelphia."

Charles Simms (1755-1819) was a lawyer in Alexandria, Virginia. Simms had gained admission to the bar in Augusta County, Virginia, in 1773 and practiced law in that region, near Pittsburgh. In 1776 he represented Augusta County for one term in the Virginia House of Delegates. Simms was a lieutenant colonel during the Revolutionary War. Before the end of the war, Simms moved to Alexandria where he resumed his law practice. He represented Fairfax County in the House of Delegates, 1785-1786, 1792, and 1796. He also represented Fairfax County in the Virginia convention of 1788, where he supported ratification of the Constitution. *PGW, Diary,* 4:123n; 5:286n; Lyman Chalkley, *Chronicles of the Scotch-Irish Settlement in Virginia,* 3 vols. (1912-1913; reprint ed., Baltimore: Genealogical Publishing, 1965), 1:175.

Henry Lee to Patrick Henry ——————————————————
December 26, 1795 Richmond, Virginia

. . . I wrote to you the other day[1] by Mr Call — to this le.^r no reply —

[*It is*] necessary for me to know your mind on a confidential subject.

The Senate have disagreed to the P. nomination of Mr Rutledge & a vacancy in that important office has taken place — For your countrys sake for your friends sake for your familys sake tell me you will obey a call to it —

You know my friendship for you, you know my circumspection & I trust you know too that I should not address you on such a subject without good grounds —

Surely no situation better suits an individual than[2] that will you — you continue at home only when on duty —[3] Change of air & exercise will add to your days

The salray excellent & the honor very great. Be explicit in your reply . . .

ARS (MB, Mss. Acc. 594). Addressed to "Long Island." Long Island was in Campbell County, Virginia; Patrick Henry to George Washington, October 16, 1795, Gratz Collection, PHi.

1. The letter referred to is probably that of December 17, 1795, from Henry Lee to Patrick Henry.

2. The "n" was written over a "t."

3. Henry Lee may have meant to write "when not on duty."

Henry Lee to George Washington

December 26, 1795 Richmond, Virginia

... Till very lately Have I felt myself well enough to discharge my daily dutys & now hardly fit for writing_ But your le'[?] (without date)[1] rec[d] last ev[g] as well as my constant desire to administer to your information so far as I can, induces me to sieze the first opportunity of replying_

M[r] H was written to by me in a way to obtain his answer by a direct opportunity which was presented in the course of the last ten days.[2]

It is now about the proper time to receive his reply, but least any accident may interrupt my receipt of it, I have this day repeated the contents of my le[r] & shall send it off in the morning by express_[3] The mail succeeding my hearing from him will bear my communication of his mind to you.

In my correspondence I have never mentioned you or any authority from you_ this I purposely avoided.

...

In my le[r] to M[r] H I make private business its plain object & I send it under cover from a friend_[4]

ARS (DLC, George Washington Papers).

1. Letter not found.

2. See Henry Lee to Patrick Henry, December 17, 1795.

3. See Henry Lee to Patrick Henry, December 26, 1795.

4. This sentence appears as a postscript after Henry Lee's signature.

Henry Tazewell to James Monroe

December 26, 1795 Philadelphia, Pennsylvania

... When M[r]Jay was appointed Gov[r] of New York_ Jn[o] Rutledge of S. C. succeeded by the Presidents appointm[t] in y[e] recess of the Senate to the office of Chief Justice_ After his appointm[t] his Sentiments which were given in a public meeting at Ch[s] Town ag[t] the Treaty were~made public_ [became known] When the Senate met the other day, the confirmation of his appointment was refused, & now the office is vacant. This incident cannot fail to add to the embarrassments experienced by the Executive in filling the high offices of y[e] Government. ...

ARS (NN, James Monroe Papers).

Henry Tazewell (1753-1799) was a prominent Virginia jurist. He became chief justice of the Virginia General Court in 1789 and was appointed to the Court of Appeals in 1793. Tazewell, an anti-federalist, succeeded John Taylor of Caroline in the Senate in 1794 and in February, 1795, was elected the Senate's president pro tem. In the Senate, Tazewell opposed the adoption of the Jay Treaty and voted for John Rutledge's appointment as chief justice of the Supreme Court. *DAB; SEJ,* 1:196.

Columbian Centinel ————————————————————————————

December 26, 1795   Philadelphia, Pennsylvania

"Judge RUTLEDGE you will hear is insane. The fact is daily corroborated. I have it from authority which mingles in the information the tears of pity and commiseration.

(Boston) January 6, 1796. Date and place are those of news item. The quotation mark in this excerpt has been reproduced as it appears in the *Columbian Centinel;* it indicates that the paragraph probably was taken from a letter.

This article also appeared in the *New-Hampshire Gazette* (Portsmouth), January 9, 1796.

William Read to Jacob Read ————————————————————————

December 29, 1795   Charleston, South Carolina

. . . I verily believe Mr Rutledge has lost ground more by his behaviour lately than his life time of services will regain, & I have reason to think that many see that the rock his Mark has split on is his jealousy of you, for on that alone, I have thought, his hatred is built

. . . The unfortunate Judge Rutledge has been much Housed, said to be indisposed, ever since his return from a half finish'd circuit — on sunday morn^g1 that miserable old man attempted to put an end to his Life by drowning himself — They say he is mad — Tho' on this occasion there appear'd much consistent arrangement — He left his House by stealth early in the morning, & went down to Gibbes's Bridge — there, with his clothes on he went deliberately into the water — It was just day light — a negro child was near, & struck with the uncommonness of the sight she call'd to some negroes on the Deck of a Vessell[—] he had now gone beyond his depth & had sunk, but struggleing sometimes rose — The Fellows had the presence of mind to run with a Boat hook & catch hold of his arm — he made violent opposition to them but they draged him out & detaind him by force, they calling out for assistance, while he cursed & abused them, & would drive them away. The noise brought out Jack Blakes[2] House-keeper who he also scold'd, & drove her away, she gave Mr Blake the alarm, he ran out & secured the miserable old man, brought him to his House where he attempted to reason him out of such design — He is related to have had a Razor in his Pocket — He was prodigiously agitated, & shook with cold & perhaps shame — He persisted in his intention said he had a right to dispose of his own life as he pleased — "he had long been a Judge & he knew no Law that forbid a man to take away his own Life" "that if he had not been prevented he would by this time have been happy" M^r B reasond with him on a regard for reputation, on the disgrace such an end would bring on his children— He reply'd that his Life was his own that he care'd not a Button for his children Thus spoke this unfortunate wise old man— his conduct to most people is unaccountable as ˄'tis extraordinary— some suppose it arrising from his reflections on his late Political conduct— I hear that he was reasonable & calm today— It has been said that he made an attempt to drown himself at Camden— Every Body appears to pity & lament Mr Rutledges situation— Young Ned[3] has been severely shook with Fever— this will almost kill him— ...

AR[S?] (ScU, Jacob Read Papers). Whether this letter was signed cannot be determined because the end of the letter is missing.

William Read (1754-1845), brother of South Carolina's Senator Jacob Read, was a planter and physician in South Carolina. Bailey and Cooper, *Biographical Directory of the South Carolina House of Representatives,* 3:599-600.

1. Sunday morning would have been December 27. The same day that William Read wrote this letter to Jacob Read, Benjamin Moodie also wrote one to Jacob Read in which Moodie reported that John Rutledge had "made an attempt to drown himself at Old Cap̄ Blake's Wharf South Bay" (Jacob Read Miscellaneous Papers, NN). Moodie mentioned that the incident had occurred on Saturday, December 26, and this date was confirmed by an anonymous Charleston correspondent who wrote on December 31, 1795 (q.v., below). On December 28, 1795, Rutledge sent to President Washington his resignation from the office of chief justice; q.v. in "Appointments to the Bench," under "John Rutledge: Appointment as Chief Justice in 1795."

2. Probably John Blake (1752-1810), a Charleston merchant and member of the South Carolina House of Representatives. Blake inherited the property near Gibbes's Bridge from his father. Bailey and Cooper, *Biographical Directory of the South Carolina House of Representatives,* 3:72-73; Caroline T. Moore, comp. and ed., *Abstracts of Wills of Charleston District, South Carolina, 1783-1800* (Columbia, S.C.: R. L. Bryan, 1974), p. 339.

3. Ned could be short for Edward—if so, then Ned probably refers to John Rutledge's fourth child, Edward Rutledge (1767-1811). The use of the word "Young" may have been meant to distinguish Edward Rutledge (son of John Rutledge) from Edward Rutledge (brother of John Rutledge). Webber, "Dr. John Rutledge and His Descendants," pp. 14-17.

Thomas Jefferson to William B. Giles —————————————
December 31, 1795   Monticello, Albemarle County, Virginia

... the rejection of m̄r Rutledge by the Senate is a bold thing, because they cannot pretend any objection to him but his disapprobation of the treaty. it is of course a declaration that they will recieve none but tories hereafter into any department of the government. ...

ARS (NNPM, #9184.3); ACS (DLC, Thomas Jefferson Papers).

William Branch Giles (1762-1830), a Virginia lawyer, entered Congress in 1790. An outspoken supporter of Thomas Jefferson's policies, Giles strenuously opposed the Jay Treaty. He resigned in 1798 but later returned to Congress for one term in 1801. *DAB.*

Letter from an Anonymous Correspondent ————————
Federal Gazette
December 31, 1795   Charleston, South Carolina

A letter from a gentleman in Charleston, of the 31st ult. mentions, "That chief justice Rutledge, on Saturday last,[1] attempted to drown himself, but was taken out of the water by some negroes. It is said, he had discovered symptoms of derangement for some weeks past."

(Baltimore) January 8, 1796. Date and place are those of the letter.

This item also appeared in the *Aurora* (Philadelphia) of January 15, 1796, and in the *Columbian Centinel* (Boston) of January 23, 1796.

1. "Saturday last" was December 26. William Read reported to his brother Jacob Read that this incident had occurred on Sunday, December 27; see letter under date of December 29, 1795.

Independent Chronicle ————————————————
December 31, 1795   Boston, Massachusetts

The negative of the Senate on the nomination of the President of Judge Rutledge, appears an unparalleld instance of party spirit; whether the affront is more aimed at the President, than the Judge is difficult to determine. The nominationn by the President, we are to suppose, was from a full knowledge of the abilities and integrity of Mr. Rutedge. He was personally acquainted with the President; his character was high in his estimation— otherways it is not probable he would have been appointed to so important an office. If we doubt this, it is an impeachment of the President's judgment. Nothing has since taken place, to convince the public, that he is not the same virtuous, honest, and qualified person, as when he was first nominated. The Senate have not given any reasons to shew that he is altered in any respect, and that he is not still entitled to that confidence which the President placed in him. What then can be the cause of the negative? is it because he was in opposition to the late British Treaty? Because he spoke his sentiments like an honest man on this subject? Because he gave his voice in public, against an instrument, which consigns this country into the hands of the British nation? Because he felt for the honor of his country, in sacrificing every principle of gratitude to the French, and wantonly courting a connection, with Britain, in opposition to the constitutions and the feelings of every friend to republicanism? Are not these the apparent causes, which the Senate have in this instance showed their resentment to the President, and exercised their power to wound the reputation of an honest man? If these are not the reasons it is difficult to say, what are.— Why is Mr. Rutledge held up as unfriendly to the Government— because he is against the Treaty, when the President himself was opposed to it, according to the statement of Mr. Randolph.

Is it become necessary, to support our Government, that we should attempt to controul the opinions of the citizens? That no man must expect an appointment, but such, as pay implicit submission to every transaction, done by a particular body of men?_ The Treaty, at the time Judge Rutledge expressed his mind, was a subject of public investigation; and every freeman was in duty bound to declare his sentiments with respect to it. The Judge exercised this right, and for doing it he is abused in the public papers, and even marked by an official act, as an enemy to the Government. But however, the honorable Judge, must feel a satisfaction, from a consciousness of having acted becoming a free citizen, and can retire from that eminence to which the President *at-tempted to ellevate him,* with a serenity of mind, which his enemies can "neither give, nor take away."

(Boston) December 31, 1795. Date and place are those of the newspaper.

This item appeared without a dated headline in the *Aurora* (Philadelphia), January 9, 1796, and in the *City Gazette* (Charleston), January 22, 1796.

Aurora
January 2, 1796 Philadelphia, Pennsylvania

There is a remarkable occurrence in our affairs, the refusal of the Senate to confirm the President's nomination of Mr. RUTLEDGE as Chief Justice of the United States._ It is the first instance in which they have differed with him in any nomination of importance, and what is remarkable in this case, is that the minority of the members on the Treaty were the minority on this nomination. The face of the thing exhibited a well digested plan, and as common decency made a nomination necessary, management with the Senate must have rendered the appointment abortive._ Senators who had been in an uniform habit of acting with the President would hardly have abandoned him of a sudden, had not the thing been well understood.

(Philadelphia) January 2, 1796. Date and place are those of newspaper. Headlined "FROM A CORRESPONDENT."

Reprinted in the *City Gazette* (Charleston) on January 23, 1796.

Henry Sherburne to Benjamin Bourne
January 5, 1796 Newport, Rhode Island

... The presidents Nomination of Mr Rutledge is truly strange,_ we have ever been taught to beleive that he always looked well before he leaped, if so, it is probable he must have been acquainted with his situation,_ this is difficult to reconcile. ...

ARS (RHi, Peck Collection). Addressed "Philadelphia." Postmarked by hand "Newport 5. Jan^y."

Henry Sherburne (1748-1824) was a justice of the peace in Newport, Rhode Island. In 1791 Sherburne had been appointed Rhode Island commissioner to settle accounts with the United States. He was appointed treasurer of Rhode Island in 1792. James N. Arnold, *Vital Record of*

Rhode Island, 1636-1850, 1st ser., 20 vols. (Providence: Narragansett Historical Publishing, 1891-1911), 4:113; *Biographical Cyclopedia of Rhode Island* (Providence: National Biographical Publishing, 1881), pp. 150-51; Joseph Jencks Smith, comp., *Civil and Military List of Rhode Island, 1647-1800* (Providence: Preston and Rounds, 1900), pp. 555, 488.

Columbian Centinel ————————————————————————
January 6, 1796   Boston, Massachusetts

The *Salem* paper of yesterday contains the following paragraph; "By a southern paper, we learn, that Judge RUTLEDGE is so disordered in his intellects, as to render it necessary to have him constantly guarded, he having threatened and even attempted his own destruction."[1] ☞ *Accounts from the southward confirm this; and the paragraph in the last* CENTINEL *extracted from a South-Carolina paper makes the event highly probable.*[2]

(Boston) January 6, 1796. Date and place are those of newspaper.
   This item was reprinted in the *New-Hampshire Gazette* (Portsmouth), January 9, 1796.
   1. The preceding quote was taken from the *Salem Gazette,* January 5, 1796.
   2. On January 2, 1796, the *Columbian Centinel* had republished the article that had appeared in the *Aurora* on December 23, 1795 (q.v. under date of December 1, 1795).

Aurora ————————————————————————————————
January 7, 1796   Philadelphia, Pennsylvania

[*In a highly sarcastic tone, this article points out that President George Washington had serious misgivings about the Jay Treaty.*] but it would have been highly derogatory to the dignity and convenience of the Senate and President that they should split upon the subject. If the President had differed from them in *deed* as well as *opinion* he would have lost their support and then in return[1] the President could not have depended on theirs. The effects of such a division would already have been felt in the case of Chief Justice RUTLEDGE, whose appointment might have been confirmed contrary to the President's *second thoughts.*

(Philadelphia) January 7, 1796. The date and place are those of the newspaper.
   1. Appears as "retrun" in the newspaper.

Independent Chronicle ————————————————————————
January 7, 1796   Boston, Massachusetts

It is difficult to account for the publications in certain papers, that Mr. Rutledge is insane. This was said of him, immediately on his expressing his disapprobation of the Treaty; but since that time, he has officiated as Chief Justice, and so far from shewing any evidence of what was *formerly* called insanity, he gave the strongest marks of professional abilities. It seems however that *insanity* by the political quacks of the present day is, an independent mind, uninfluenced by the funds, banks, or land jobbing. If a man has not a due proportion of these stimulus's in his political constitution, he will soon get deranged in his intellects, his circulation will deaden, and the vital *stamina* will quickly decay.

The blood of the body politic, receives vigor, and nourishment by feeding on a new patent composition of 6 per cents, 3 per cents, bank shares and land scrip. These well mixed in a small proportion of *deferred stock* and new emission, and run through a *negociating strainer,* will preserve the health to an astonishing degree. It has been known to raise men from the *lowest stage of life,* to an uncommon healthy corpulency. It has a peculiar property to make real small men, nominal big men; and what is most extraordinary, it is said to carry off the peccant humours contracted by an old fashioned malady called *patriotism.* It is of a soothing nature, as it will absorb every passion, but that which is within the immediate focus of its physical operation,

Mr. Rutledge not being in the habit of taking this balsamic, we are afraid that the account of his insanity is too true.

This cordial composition may be obtained, provided you can produce a certificate that you are in favor of Mr. *Grenville's* Treaty, *witnessed* by our *extraordinary* envoy.

(Boston) January 7, 1796. Date and place are those of the newspaper.
Reprinted in the *Aurora* (Philadelphia), January 15, 1796.

Samuel Johnston to James Iredell ———————————
January 9, 1796   Hermitage, New Hanover County, North Carolina

... I neither regret nor wonder that the Senate have refused their Assent to Mᵣ Rutledge's appointment, it would have unfortunate, after what has appeared, if they had concurred, the only disagreeble circumstance attending is that the Enemies of good order will endeavor to impress it on the minds of the people that the Majority were influenced by improper motives, at the same time I most sincerely lament, with you, the melancholy cause of Mᵣ R's. disgrace. ...

ARS (Nc-Ar, Charles E. Johnson Collection). Addressed "Edenton." Endorsed "Ansᵈ." Hermitage was the home of John Burgwin, a wealthy merchant. It was located a few miles north of Wilmington, North Carolina, on Burgwin's Castle Hayne plantation in New Hanover County. Donald R. Lennon and Ida Brooks Kellam, eds., *The Wilmington Town Book, 1743-1778* (Raleigh: Division of Archives and History, North Carolina Department of Cultural Resources, 1973), p. 157.

George Read to Henry Latimer ————————————————
January 9, 1796   New Castle, Delaware

... I do not apprehend that much Notice will be taken of the Senate's rejection of Mᵣ Rutledge's nomination, the natural heat of this Man's political mind with his known unsteadiness or occasional timidity in that line will prevent his becoming a sainted Martyr in the Cause of Democracy. The friends of Order and good Governm! will always be well pleased to see a firmness of Conduct in the Senate, and such it hath heretofore pretty generally Exhibited. It is a principle when duly exercised greatly tendsﬓg[1] to publick Safety and quiet, and deservedly applied by the Senate to the President in their late address not merely from the Act, which some seemed to confine it to, but from the general tenor of his Conduct in publick life. The Members of that branch of the Legislature while it exercises this principle must expect occasional abuse from the demagogues in the Union and their numerous followers in the respective districts, pretty generally the San-culotes. this is a price they must expect to pay for the Station they hold: few Men in active political life ever escape it. . . .

ARS (DeU, Latimer Family Papers).

George Read (1733-1798) was chief justice of Delaware. Read had served in the Senate from 1789 to 1793. Prior to that, he had been a judge of the Court of Appeals in Cases of Capture and a member of the Continental Congress. *DAB*.

Henry Latimer (1752-1819), a physician and surgeon, served in Delaware's House of Representatives in 1787, 1788, and 1790 (when he was speaker). Latimer entered the Third Congress in February, 1794, after successfully contesting the election of another candidate. He was then elected to fill the Senate seat left vacant by George Read's resignation in 1793 and entered the Senate on February 28, 1795. Latimer resigned from the Senate six years later. *BDAC*, pp. 53n, 1196-97.

1. The "s" is written over an "i."

Letter from an Anonymous Correspondent ————————
Aurora
January 9, 1796   Charleston, South Carolina

"About ten days since Judge RUTLEDGE attempted to drown himself. I was at the spot when he was taken from the water. Two negroes saw him jump in and ran to his assistance ― He damned them for rescuing him. I believe he was a *little insane.* About a week afterwards we heard of his appointment being negatived by the Senate. . . . "

(Philadelphia) February 3, 1796. Date and place are those given for letter.

This item also appeared in the *Federal Orrery* (Boston), February 15, 1796.

Letter from an Anonymous Correspondent in Philadelphia ———
City Gazette
January 9, 1796   Charleston, South Carolina

"I can easily figure to myself your astonishment, at hearing the senate have negatived the appointment of the chief justice. Although he is revered in Carolina by the glories of his actions, particularly those which illumined your po-

George Read by Robert Edge Pine (1730-1788). Oil on canvas, ca. 1784. Courtesy National Portrait Gallery, Smithsonian Institution.

litical hemisphere during the difficult times in which he held the reins of government; yet, such is the violence of party spirit, the force of stock-jobbing influence, and the prejudice of our prejudiced Anglomen here, that 'tis regarded as wise in the senate to keep out of office every one who has spoken disrespectfully of the treaty lately made, or Mr. Jay. In the majority of the senate are gentlemen who are personally acquainted with the chief justice, intimately acquainted with his splendid talents and sound judgement, and who, in their conversations, *out of senate,* do homage to his pure patriotism and republican firmness; but the fact is, that Mr. Hamilton, who manages the senate, has become a perfect terrorist, and his satellites and votaries disseminate with uncommon industry the following principle: "That it is ruinous to admit into administration any man who may refuse to go all lengths with it; that our citizens, who expressed their disapprobation of the commercial treaty, are enemies to the general government; that most of them are in the pay of France, and the object of their service is the overthrow of the constitution." If your citizens preserve the political honesty they were so rich in when I knew them, this sort of doctrine will shock them; they will exclaim, What political blasphemy! What effrontery! But here, where stockjobbers, speculators and American Anglomen have duped many of our honest, unsuspecting, and many of our timid citizens, it passes as orthodox.

. . .

"The Georgia senators[1] are arrived, and chagrined that the appointment of the chief justice had been submitted to the senate when their state was unrepresented: the thing looks disrespectful, but might have been accidental. . . . "

(Charleston) January 9, 1796. Date and place are those of newspaper. The letter had to have been written after the Senate's rejection of John Rutledge on December 15, 1795.

This article also appeared in the *Federal Gazette* (Baltimore) on February 4, 1796, and in the *Boston Gazette* on February 22, 1796.

1. James Gunn and George Walton.

Letter from an Anonymous Correspondent ———————
Columbian Centinel
January 9, 1796   Philadelphia, Pennsylvania

"GENTLEMEN,

"I observe a paragraph in the *Boston Chronicle*,[1] reflecting upon the majority of the Senate, for negativing the PRESIDENT'S nomination of Mr. RUTLEDGE for Chief Justice—the writer imputes it to a vindictive and party spirit; this is a wrong representation; the majority of the Senate of the United States, have certainly more magninimity than to seek vengeance upon any one, and more especially upon an individual, merely because he had, when in a fit of lunacy, manifested a high degree of indiscretion—the fact is, however painful it may be to relate, Mr. RUTLEDGE frequently incapacitates himself, and plunges into *voluntary lunacy,* and not only so, but we are credibly informed, that he lately made an ATTEMPT UPON HIS OWN LIFE!

"The former of these circumstances the Senate were acquainted with, before they negatived his nomination; the latter, it is true, came to their knowledge within two or three days after. Certainly the Senate are justifiable in not placing a *lunatic* at the head of the Judiciary—but it may be asked, why the President nominated such a man? the reason is, he did not know his infirmities at the time he made the nomination. The President knew Mr. RUTLEDGE was a man of great legal knowledge, and of splendid abilities, and that he *had been* a Patriot, and deserved well of his country, he therefore nominated him? in this respect, as in all others, the PRESIDENT has acted a prudent and magnanimous part."

(Boston) January 23, 1796. Date and place are those of the letter. Published under the following headline: "MASSACHUSETTS.   SPRINGFIELD, JAN. 19, 1796."

Reprinted on January 25, 1796, in the *American Mercury* (Hartford) as a letter that had been sent to the editors of a Springfield newspaper; also reprinted in the *New-Hampshire Gazette* (Portsmouth), February 6, 1796.

1. The reference is to an article in the Boston *Independent Chronicle* (q.v. under date of December 31, 1795).

Abigail Adams to John Adams ————————————
January 10, 1796   Quincy, Massachusetts

. . . one general rule will hold good with respect to appointments to office, that a man destitute of private virtue must want principle,[1] and the man who wants principle[2] cannot be actuated by pure motives, nor can he possess so exalted an affection as a Rational and disinterested Love of his Country. this has been so recently exemplified in the late Chief Justice, that no other instance need be quoted. the publick papers have mentiond almost every circumstance you related,[3] and his insanity will Sheild the Senate from, even Jacobinical censure, ~~I should suppose~~ for his Friends I am Sorry, it is a pitty that he was made so conspicuous in his Fall . . .

ARS (MHi, Adams Manuscript Trust).
    1. The "le" is written over "al."
    2. Abigail Adams appears to have written "principal" and then altered it to read "principle."
    3. See John Adams to Abigail Adams, December 21, 1795.

George Washington to Henry Lee ————————————
January 11, 1796   Philadelphia, Pennsylvania

Philadelphia 11th Jany 1796.[1]

My dear Sir,
    Your letter of the 28th[2] Ult.º has been received, but nothing from you since; which is embarrassing[3] in the extreme;[4] for not only the nomination of Ch__f. J_____ but of As_____te J_____ and Se_____ of W__ have been suspended on the answer you were to receive from _____ ;[5] and what renders the want of it more to be regretted;[6] is, that the first monday in next month, (which happens on the first day of it) is the time appointed by law for the meeting of the Supreme Court of the U. States. in this city; at which, for particular reasons the bench ought to[7] be full. __[8] I will add no more at present than that I am,
    Your Affect.^e

(signed) G.ºWashington

Gen.! Lee

a true copy   Geo:[ᵍ]:Brown

L (ViHi, Lee Family Papers); ADfS (DLC, George Washington Papers).
    1. In draft, George Washington mistakenly wrote the year as "1795."
    2. In draft, the date given is the "26th," which is the correct date.
    3. In draft, "embarrassing to me."
    4. In draft, "extreme."
    5. In draft, "have been . . . _____ " appears as "are depending upon the answer I ex-

pected." George Washington was waiting to hear whether Patrick Henry would accept an appointment as chief justice.

6. In draft, "more to be regretted" appears as "more unfortunate, if any thing can add to my present perplexity on the occasion."

7. In draft, this has been written above "should."

8. In draft, the following sentence has been crossed out: "I am really at a loss to know what measures now to adopt; could I have supposed that it would have taken 'till this time to have ascertained the opinion of a certain character I should have relinquished the idea altogether. _ "

Oliver Wolcott, Sr., to Oliver Wolcott, Jr. ————————
January 11, 1796   Litchfield, Connecticut

... The negative of the appointment of Mꞏ Rutledge is as farr as I know highly agreable, it certainly is to to me, as I think that it would have been disgraceful to America that after what he had done, he should be confirmed in his Office _ ...

ARS (CtHi, Oliver Wolcott Jr. Papers).

Gabriel H. Ford to Timothy Ford ————————————
January 13, 1796   Morristown, New Jersey

... I expressed some Joy to Mꞏ D.[1] that the Senate had rejected the nomination of Mꞏ Rutledge whose wild, intemperate speeches had sunk him as an able Statesman quite below mediocrity, for I could not ⌃the Reports of his
(credit)
infirmity. It is since then established by a paragraph in one of your papers that disarms me of my former opinion and I am ready to believe freely that when in health he was the able, profound, good man which so many of you represented him to be _ ...

ARS (ScHi, Ford Family Papers). Addressed "Charleston   South Carolina." Endorsed "Ansꝺ 20. Febꞃy. 96."

Gabriel H. Ford (1765-1849) was a lawyer in Morristown, New Jersey. Francis Bazley Lee, ed., *Genealogical and Memorial History of the State of New Jersey,* 4 vols. (New York: Lewis Historical Publishing, 1910), 4:1564-65.

Timothy Ford (1762-1830), brother of Gabriel H. Ford, was a New Jersey native who moved to South Carolina. In 1786 Timothy Ford entered into a law practice with his brother-in-law, Henry William De Saussure. Ford represented Charleston in the South Carolina House of Representatives from 1792 to 1797. Harrison, *Princetonians,* 3:401-4.

1. Probably Henry William De Saussure, who had been the director of the United States Mint from July 9, 1795, to October 28, 1795. De Saussure was married to Elizabeth Ford, the sister of Gabriel H. Ford and Timothy Ford. *PAH,* 19:298n; Harrison, *Princetonians,* 3:401-4.

Robert Lindsay to Samuel Johnston ─────────────────
January 13, 1796 Charleston, South Carolina

late
. . . Your Friends here are all well exept the ^ Chieff J. Jnọ R. . . .e, who attempted, about ten days ago, to drown himself in Ashley River, but was taken out, by some negroes, before he finished the end of his career in this world ─
. . .

ARS (NcU, Hayes Collection).
 Robert Lindsay (d. 1803) was a Scottish merchant living in Charleston. William M. MacBean, *Biographical Register of Saint Andrew's Society of the State of New York,* 2 vols. (New York: Saint Andrew's Society, 1922-1925), 1:322-23; Moore, *Wills of Charleston,* pp. 117-18, 219.

James Iredell to Hannah Iredell ─────────────────
January 20, 1796 Suffolk, Virginia

. . . There is n[o ac]count of any appointment of Judges, nor any news but such as I imagine the [post carried?] on Tuesday. . . .

ARS (Nc-Ar, Charles E. Johnson Collection). Addressed "Edenton." Readings have been supplied in brackets because the document is damaged.

David Daggett to Roger Griswold ─────────────────
January 23, 1796 New Haven, Connecticut

. . . Where is the Chief justice Rutledge and who is moral enough to suc[c?]ede him? ─ . . .

ARS (CtY, David Daggett Papers). Addressed "Philadelphia." Postmarked "N. HAVEN JAN. 25."
 David Daggett (1764-1851), a New Haven attorney, was the speaker of the lower house of the Connecticut General Assembly. Daggett, a federalist, later served in the United States Senate and on the bench of the Connecticut Superior Court and Supreme Court of Errors. *DAB.*
 A Connecticut lawyer and an outspoken federalist, Roger Griswold (1762-1812) sat in Congress from 1795 to 1805. Griswold later served as a Superior Court judge, lieutenant governor, and governor of Connecticut. *DAB.*

Henry Tazewell to [John Ambler?] ─────────────────
January 24, 1796 Philadelphia, Pennsylvania

. . . Mr Cushing the federal Judge has been created Chief Justice of the US. in the place of MRutledge who was voted out ─ some say because he was

insane__ otherwise because he was unfriendly to the Treaty with England.
Mᵣ S. Chase of Maryland has been appointed a Judge in the place of MᶜBlair
who has resigned__[1] ...

ARS (DLC, Miscellaneous Manuscripts Collection). The recipient of this letter has been tentatively
identified as John Ambler from a later letter Henry Tazewell wrote to him on April 4, 1796
(Miscellaneous Manuscripts Collection, DLC). In the April 4 letter, Tazewell discusses a debt to
a Mr. Andrews that Tazewell also had mentioned in his letter of January 24. Some question as
to the correctness of this identification arises, however, from the fact that the endorsements on
these two letters appear to be written in different hands, and Tazewell is spelled "Tazwell" in the
endorsement on the January 24 letter.

John Ambler (1762-1836) was a Virginia planter who had represented James City County in
the Virginia House of Delegates in 1793 and 1794. *PJM,* 1:122n.

1. George Washington sent the nominations of William Cushing and Samuel Chase to the
Senate on January 26, 1796; see Joshua Coit to Elias Perkins, January 26, 1796. The Senate
consented to the appointments on January 27. Henry Tazewell wrote about Cushing and Chase
toward the end of his letter of January 24 which may, in fact, have been written over a period
of several days because of the serious illness mentioned by Tazewell early in the letter.

Joshua Coit to Elias Perkins ———————————————
January 26, 1796 Philadelphia, Pennsylvania

... the President has this day nominated to the Senate Judge Cushing for
Cheif Judge__ a MᵣChace of Maryland Judge vice Blair resigned[1] ... it is of
course with the Senate to let them lay over till tomorrow before they act on
them__ ...

ARS (CtNlHi, Perkins Collection). Addressed "New London   Connecticut." Postmarked "27
IA."

Joshua Coit (1758-1798), a lawyer in New London, Connecticut, and a congressman from 1793
to 1798. *BDAC.*

Elias Perkins (1767-1845), a lawyer in New London, Connecticut, was a representative in the
Connecticut General Assembly. A federalist, Perkins became an assistant judge of New London
County in 1799. Dexter, *Graduates of Yale College,* 4:502-3.

1. Jonathan Trumbull, senator from Connecticut, reported this same news in a letter of January
27, 1796, to William Williams of Lebanon, Connecticut. Peter Force Papers, DLC.

The *Federal Gazette* (Baltimore), January 30, 1796, also noted the nominations of William Cushing and Samuel Chase.

James Iredell to Hannah Iredell ———————————————
January 29, 1796 Baltimore, Maryland

... I just hear that Mᵣ Cushing has been nominated Chief Justice of the United
States; and Mᵣ Chase (I believe the Chief Justice of this State[1]) an Associate
Judge. ...

ARS (Nc-Ar, Charles E. Johnson Collection). Addressed "Edenton,   North Carolina." Postmarked "BALT-JAN 31."

1. Samuel Chase was chief judge of Maryland's General Court at the time of his nomination to the Supreme Court of the United States. James Haw, et al., *Stormy Patriot: The Life of Samuel Chase* (Baltimore: Maryland Historical Society, 1980), p. 167.

Jeremiah Smith to William Plumer ─────────────────
January 29, 1796 Philadelphia, Pennsylvania

... You will Observe that Cushing is appointed Ch. Jus.— Chace of Maryland now Ch Jus of the state Assoc. Judge vice Blair resigned—[1] who will supply Cushings place it doth not yet appear— The two last appointm[ts] are no improvement of the Bench C. is too old for Ch Justice & Chace I am told by some of the Maryland Gentry takes Beer aboard— Possibly this may be scandal— at all events I find they are very glad to get rid of him which is a very bad Symptom.— ...

ARS (Nh, Plumer Papers).
1. An announcement of William Cushing's appointment as chief justice and Samuel Chase's appointment as associate justice appeared in *Claypoole's American Daily Advertiser* (Philadelphia) on January 28, 1796. This item also appeared in the *Rutland Herald* (Rutland, Vermont) on February 17 and the *Georgia Gazette* (Savannah) on February 18. A variant was printed in the *Philadelphia Gazette,* January 28, 1796, which also appeared in the *Federal Gazette* (Baltimore), February 1, 1796.

Henry Tazewell to Richard Cocke ─────────────────
January 30, 1796 Philadelphia, Pennsylvania

... Mr. Rutledge of So. Carolina who was in the recess of the Senate appointed Chief Justice of the U. S. by the President, commissioned, and acted in the Court, was lately nominated to the Senate for confirmation. Without a single word being publicly said agnst him, the nomination was rejected by the Senate. Some say it was because he is insane. Others say it was because he made a speech agnst the Treaty. Let it be as it may, he is rejected and Cushing appointed in his place. Saml. Chase of Maryland is appointed in Mr. Blair's place[1] ...

Tr (Typescript at ViW, Henry Tazewell Papers). Addressed "Grayland Surry County, Virginia To be left at the Cross Roads."
Richard Cocke (1748-1816), a planter in Surry County, Virginia, had been a sheriff and justice of the peace in that county during the 1780s. Cocke served in the House of Delegates in 1782 and 1783, at the same time that Henry Tazewell was there representing Williamsburg. *DAR Patriot Index* under Cox; James C. Southall, "Genealogy of the Cocke Family in Virginia," *Virginia Magazine of History and Biography* 5 (1897-1898): 73-76; U.S., Department of Commerce and Labor, Bureau of the Census, *Heads of Families at the First Census of the United States Taken in the Year 1790: Virginia* (1908; reprint ed., Bountiful, Utah, Accelerated Indexing Systems, 1978), pp. 43, 78; Wilmer L. Hall, ed., *Journal of the Council of the State of Virginia,* vol. 3 (Richmond: Virginia State Library, 1952), pp. 38, 390; Earl G. Swem and John H. Williams, *A Register of the General*

Assembly of Virginia, 1776-1918, and of the Constitutional Conventions (Richmond, 1918), pp. 361, 436.

1. In a letter written to Harry Innes on January 28, 1796, John Brown mentioned the rejection of John Rutledge and the appointments of William Cushing and Samuel Chase. Harry Innes Papers, DLC.

John Adams to Abigail Adams ————————————————————————————
February 2, 1796 Philadelphia, Pennsylvania

. . . Judge Cushing declines the Place of Chief-Justice on Account of his Age and declining Health. . . .

ARS (MHi, Adams Manuscript Trust).

John Adams to Thomas Welsh ————————————————————————————
February 2, 1796 Philadelphia, Pennsylvania

. . . I pray that my Country may take from me all temptation to remain in office ~~after the app~~ before the Approach of Dotage shall take from me the Capacity of doing any thing but Mischief to the Public and dishonour to my Character.

Whatever Tenderness of Friendship I may feel for a Gadsden a Rutledge a Dickinson,[1] a Warren[2] or an Adams,[3] with all of whom I have acted on the Public stage in earlier Life, I am Stunned and astonished at their Vanity Presumption and Ignorance— I cannot but ascribe it to the Imbecility ^and^ of decrepitude of Age.

In their Solitudes, unable to read, to converse or to think, destitute of all the Information which Government possesses do they think to dictate and to domineer, like Pædagogues over school boys? . . .

ARS (MHi, Adams-Welsh Papers).

Thomas Welsh (ca. 1752-1831), a Boston physician and close friend of the Adams family, had married a first cousin of Abigail Adams in 1777. *PJA, Diary,* 3:234n.

1. John Adams first met John Dickinson (1732-1808) in August, 1774, in Philadelphia where Adams was attending the First Continental Congress. Dickinson's last public office was as a delegate to the Constitutional Convention, where he strongly supported adoption of the Constitution. In the 1790s he became deeply interested in international affairs; and in August, 1795, at a public meeting in Wilmington, Delaware, Dickinson spoke at length about his objections to the Jay Treaty. *PJA, Diary,* 2:117; *DAB;* Milton E. Flower, *John Dickinson: Conservative Revolutionary* (Charlottesville: University Press of Virginia, 1983), pp. 274-76.

2. James Warren (1726-1808), a gentleman farmer and merchant of Plymouth, Massachusetts, had been a close friend and ally of John Adams prior to the outbreak of the Revolutionary War. In 1775 Warren became the president of the Provincial Congress of Massachusetts, and when the legislature was reorganized, he became speaker of the lower house. In the 1780s, however, he and John Adams increasingly differed politically. Warren opposed the adoption of the Constitution because it lacked a bill of rights. In his later years, he supported the Jeffersonian democrats. *DAB.*

3. While serving as governor of Massachusetts, Samuel Adams opposed adoption of the Jay Treaty and characterized it as "pregnant with Evil" because it favored Great Britain. Paul Goodman, *The Democratic-Republicans of Massachusetts: Politics in a Young Republic* (Cambridge: Harvard University Press, 1964), p. 71.

Aurora
February 2, 1796   Philadelphia, Pennsylvania

The carpers at Executive administration, who have so often intimated that none but Federal men were the objects of Presidential favor, must effectually be silenced on that head, by the late appointment of Mr. SAMUEL CHASE to the Federal bench, as his pointed and unwearied opposition to the Constitution may still be remembered by all— But then he circulated and obtained a dozen signers to an address in favor of the Treaty, and this like the mantle of charity will cover a multitude[1] of sins— this will wash an antifederalist whiter than snow— It was objected to Judge RUTLEDGE, that he was in debt— But Mr. S. C. is disencumbered of such shackles, as the records of Maryland (recourse being thereunto had) will fully shew— or it is presumed he would not have been appointed to diffuse the streams of justice among the people, whose hallowed fountain ought never to be contaminated by a hand that is impure.

(Philadelphia) February 2, 1796. Date and place are those of newspaper.
   This item also appeared in the *Federal Orrery* (Boston), February 15, 1796.
   1. Appears as "multitnde" in the newspaper.

John Adams to Abigail Adams
February 6, 1796   Philadelphia, Pennsylvania

...Judge Cushing has been wavering, sometimes he would and sometimes he would not be C. J.— This will give the P. some trouble. Mr Chase is a new Judge, but although a good 1774 Man his Character has a Mist about it of suspicion and Impurity which gives occasion to the Enemy to censure. He has been a warm Party Man, and has made many Ennemies. His Corpulency, which has increased very much since I saw him last in England, is ~~much~~ against his riding Circuit very long. ...

ARS (MHi, Adams Manuscript Trust).

James Madison to Thomas Jefferson
February 7, 1796   Philadelphia, Pennsylvania

... There is some reason to think that Jno Rutledge is not right in his mind. Cushing has been put at the head of the Bench, but it is said will decline the

pre-eminence. Chase in the place of Blair!!!! _ a vacancy remains to be filled. M⸢Henry Secretary at War _ Through what official interstice can a ray of re-
now
publican truths ⌄ penetrate to the P____ . . .

AR (DLC, James Madison Papers). Addressed "Charlottesville   via   Richmond." Postmarked "8   FE." Endorsed "recᵈ Feb. 20."

James Iredell to Hannah Iredell ————————————————————————
February 10, 1796 Philadelphia, Pennsylvania

. . . M⸢ Cushing, with an extraordinary degree of moderation and modesty, has declined the office of Chief Justice, on account of his age and infirm state of health, but retains his seat on the Bench _ no new appointment has yet been made _ . . .

ARS (Nc-Ar, Charles E. Johnson Collection). Addressed "Edenton, North Carolina." Marked "Recommended to the care of Watson Stott Esq⸢ Suffolk _ ,   Virginia." Postmarked "10   FE." This letter is published in *MJI,* 2:460, under the incorrect date of February 20.

Uriah Tracy to Oliver Wolcott, Sr. ————————————————————
February 10, 1796 Philadelphia, Pennsylvania

. . . M⸢ Cushing, who was appointed Chief Justice (in room of M⸢ Rutledge resigned) has declined the preferment _ of course, a chief Justice will, prob-ably, soon be nominated; who will be the man, is not known, M⸢ Patterson of N. Jersey is thought of, but our President keeps his own counsel tolerably well, till he acts Officially. _ . . .

ARS (CtHi, Oliver Wolcott Jr. Papers). Addressed "Litchfield   Connecticut."
    Uriah Tracy (1755-1807), a Connecticut lawyer and state's attorney for Litchfield County, served in the House of Representatives from March 4, 1793, to October 13, 1796. In 1796 he succeeded Jonathan Trumbull in the Senate and remained in the Senate until his death. *BDAC.*

Chauncey Goodrich to Oliver Wolcott, Sr. ——————————————
[February 12?], 1796 Philadelphia, Pennsylvania

. . . The Supreme Court is in session _ a good deal of important business be-fore them. Mr. Cushing refuses his appointment as Chief-Justice. No successor has been appointed. . . .

Pr (Printed in George Gibbs, *Memoirs of the Administrations of Washington and John Adams, Edited from the Papers of Oliver Wolcott, Secretary of the Treasury,* 2 vols. (New York: W. Van Norden,

1846), 1:297-98). This letter was printed with a date of January 12, 1796. The letter's reference to the Court as "in session" dates it after February 1, 1796, when the Court opened. It is not known whether the inaccuracy was that of Chauncey Goodrich or those who prepared the printed edition of these letters.

Oliver Wolcott, Sr., to Oliver Wolcott, Jr. ———————————
February 15, 1796 Litchfield, Connecticut

... Mʳ Cushing I understand has declined his preferment— he is a good and respectable Character— I know Sam Chase and to you I will say, that I have but an unworthy Opinion of him— The Character of the Government will depend upon that of their officers, to respect a man because he is of a party, ^and^ to gratify them, will always be found false policy, a publick officer is neither to attach himself to, nor fear ^any^ no one— ...

ARS (CtHi, Oliver Wolcott Jr. Papers).

Jonathan Arnold to Welcome Arnold ———————————
February 16, 1796 Philadelphia, Pennsylvania

... The [court?] has passed over two weks and tryed but one [c]aus[e] and to day the judges all met but Cushing who is Sick on Account of his indisposition the court adjourned till to Morrow ...

ARS (RPJCB, Welcome Arnold-Greene Papers). This document is damaged along the margin; as a result, readings have been supplied in brackets.

Jonathan Arnold (d. 1806), brother of Welcome Arnold, was in the lime burning and shipping business with his brother. Jonathan Arnold evidently represented the business in Charleston. Arnold, *Vital Record of Rhode Island,* 7:265; Franklin S. Coyne, "Welcome Arnold (1745-1798), Providence Merchant: The Founding of an Enterprise" (Ph.D. diss., Brown University, 1979), pp. 54n, 56.

Welcome Arnold (1745-1798) was a Providence merchant with extensive shipping interests. Arnold had played a prominent role in supporting Rhode Island's ratification of the Constitution. Phillip Dismukes, ed., *The Arnold Family* (Arlington, Va.: American Genealogical Research Institute, 1972), p. 89.

Jeremiah Smith to William Plumer ———————————
February 17, 1796 Philadelphia, Pennsylvania

... The supreme Court have been in session two weeks & have in imitation of us done but little Business— tho' they have a great deal before them.—

30, or 40 Causes it is said & they are generally important.— ...

Cushing refuses to accept the appointment of chief Justice— Some say Wilson will have the offer & some say the President will leap over his head to Patterson which G of his infinite mercy grant— If <u>Marshall</u> would accept he should have <u>my Vote.</u>— ...

ARS (Nh, Plumer Papers).

Elias Boudinot to Samuel Bayard ————————————————
February 18, 1796   Rosehill, Philadelphia County, Pennsylvania

... M.ʳ Cushing has been appointed Chief Justice, but discovered great wisdom in refusing it— The President seems in the State of old Judge [Vangiesen?],[1] who <u>was</u> [*word illegible*]. It is not known [who?] he contemplates for that important Office— M.ʳ Sam.ˡ Chace is appointed in the room of M.ʳ Blair, who resigned. ...

ARS (NjP, Bradford Papers).
    1. Possibly Rinear Vangieson (1704-1784), who had been a judge, justice of the peace, and member of the New Jersey General Assembly from Bergen County. Larry R. Gerlach, *Prologue to Independence: New Jersey in the Coming of the American Revolution* (New Brunswick: Rutgers University Press, 1976), p. 364.

William Plumer to Jeremiah Smith ————————————————
February 19, 1796   Dover, New Hampshire

... Why did judge Blair resign? From the little acquaintance I have had with him, I consider him as a man of good abilities— not indeed a <u>Jay</u>— but far superior to Cushing— A man of firmness, strict integrity, & of great candour— qualities essentially necessary to constitute a good judge.

I am disappointed in the appointment of Cushing as Chief Justice. He is a man I love & esteem. He once possessed abilities, firmness, & other qualities requisite for that office; but <u>time</u>, the enemy of man, has much impaired his mental faculties. When Jay resigned Cushing was the eldest justice, & I fear that the promotion of the latter will form a precedent for making Chief Justices from the eldest Judge, tho' other candidates may be much better qualified.

I know nothing of judge Chase, but from your letter. Is he the man mentioned by the satirical writer of <u>The Times</u>.[1] He gives him a bad character—
    "Flit not around me thus pernicious elf,
    "Whose love of country terminates in self—
    "Back to the gloomy shades detested sprite,
    "Mangler of rhetoric, enemy of right—
    "Curst of thy father, scum of all that's base,
    "Thy sight is odious, & thy name is Chase."

I think these two appointments do not encrease the respectability or dignity of the judiciary.

It seems to me that many of the officers who were first appointed under the authority of the federal government were men of superior talents to those of their sucessors. Jefferson, the first secretary of State was succeeded by Edmund Randolph — In point of abilities what a striking contrast in favor of the former? Hamilton the secretary of the treasury is succeeded by Wolcott. The first was a prodigy of Genius & of strict undeviating integrity. The last is an honest man, but his talents are immensely beneath those of his predecessor. Not less striking is the contrast between Jay & Cushing as Chief Justices. . . .

ALbS (DLC, William Plumer Papers). Addressed "Philadelphia."

1. William Plumer may be referring to Peter Markoe, who had written a popular political satire entitled *The Times, A Poem*, published in Philadelphia in 1788. The poem satirized political leaders of the Confederation era, but there is no reference to Samuel Chase. Although Markoe had died in 1792, the verse repeated by Plumer could have been written by Markoe some time during the Revolutionary War. On September 8, 1800, the last two lines were published in the Philadelphia *Aurora* and attributed to "a wit" writing at the time of the war. *DAB* entry for Peter Markoe; Peter Markoe, *The Times, A Poem* (Philadelphia: Prichard and Hall, 1788); Peter Markoe, *The Times, A Poem*, 2d ed. (Philadelphia: William Spotswood, 1788).

Columbian Centinel
February 19, 1796   Philadelphia, Pennsylvania

. . . "I am told, that the Hon. Judge CUSHING, who has been appointed Chief Justice of the United States, has declined accepting the appointment, but acts *pro tem*, until another is appointed — We do not learn, however, that he declines serving as associate judge[.] . . . "

(Boston) March 2, 1796. Date and place are those of the news item. A reading has been supplied in brackets because type did not imprint. The quotation marks have been reproduced as they appear in the newspaper; they probably indicate that this article was taken from a letter. This supposition is strengthened by an item which appeared in the *Massachusetts Mercury* (Boston) on March 1, 1796. The latter item paraphrased the contents of part of a letter from a congressman to a resident of Springfield, Massachusetts; the information is exactly the same as, and the wording is virtually identical to, the text of the *Columbian Centinel* article. Another paraphrase appeared in *Claypoole's American Daily Advertiser* (Philadelphia), March 3, 1796.

The *Columbian Centinel* item also appeared in the *New-Hampshire Gazette* (Portsmouth), March 5, 1796, and in the *Connecticut Journal* (New Haven), March 10, 1796. A similar article appeared in the *Federal Orrery* (Boston), March 3, 1796.

Abigail Adams to John Adams
February 21, 1796   Quincy, Massachusetts

. . . I am very sorry that Judge Cushing has refused his appointment. Chace is not a man from all I have heard, who will make mr Jays place good

"How can a judge enforce that Law gainst some poor Elf
"Which conscience tells him, he hath broke himself,
the fountain of Justice should be as pure as virgin innocence[.] the Laws can
neither be administerd or respected if the minister of them is not unspotted._
. . .

ARS (MHi, Adams Manuscript Trust). The page has been torn, and, consequently, a reading has
been supplied in brackets.

Henry Sherburne to Benjamin Bourne ⸺⸺⸺⸺
February 23, 1796 Newport, Rhode Island

. . . It is generally thought that Neighbour Cushing gave a Clear proof of his
Understanding when he refused the Chief Justiceship. . . .

ARS (RHi, Peck Collection). Addressed "Philadelphia."

James Madison to James Monroe ⸺⸺⸺⸺
February 26, 1796 Philadelphia, Pennsylvania

. . . On the exclusion of Jnọ Rutledge, Cushing was made Chief Justice, but
has declined it & no successor is yet nominated. Chase is appointed to the
vacancy produced by Mʳ Blair's resignation. There is still a vacancy resulting
from Jay's translation to the Govᵗ of N. York to be filled. On these several
appointments, you will make your own comments. they are to a man of the
treaty party.[1] . . .

ARS (DLC, James Madison Papers).
   1. The phrase "they are to a man of the treaty party" is in code which has been deciphered
above.

Samuel Johnston to James Iredell ⸺⸺⸺⸺
February 27, 1796 Williamston, North Carolina

. . . I am sorry that Mʳ Cushing refused the office of Chief Justice, as I dont
know whether a less exceptionable character can be obtained without passing
                                              would
over Mʳ W⸺⸺[1] which ˄ perhaps be a measure which could not be easily
reconciled to strict propriety, I have no personal acquaintance with Mʳ Chase,
but am not impressed with a very favorable opinion of his moral Character
whatever his professional Abilities may be. . . .

ARS (Nc-Ar, Charles E. Johnson Collection). Addressed "Philadelphia." Endorsed "Ans^d."
1. James Wilson.

Thomas Jefferson to James Monroe ───────────────
March 2, 1796 [Albemarle County, Virginia?]

. . . the appointment of J. Rutledge to be C. J. seems to have been intended merely to establish a precedent against the descent of that office by seniority, and to keep five mouths always gaping for one sugar plumb: for it was immediately negatived by the very votes which so implicitly concur with the will of the executive. I may consign the appointment of Chace to the bench to your own knolege of him & reflections.[1] . . .

AR (DLC, James Monroe Papers). Place suggested by evidence in letter and by reference to contemporary letters in the Thomas Jefferson Papers, DLC.
1. On March 21, 1796, Thomas Jefferson again wrote to James Monroe mentioning the appointments of Associate Justice Samuel Chase and Chief Justice Oliver Ellsworth. James Monroe Papers, DLC.

Letter from a Member of Congress ───────────────
State Gazette of North-Carolina
[March 3, 1796] [Philadelphia, Pennsylvania]

. . . "Judge Cushing has resigned, or rather declined the acceptance of his appointment, as Chief Justice of the United States; this morning Oliver Ellsworth, of Connecticut, was nominated to the Senate by the President to fill the vacancy."

(Edenton) March 24, 1796. Date derived from reference to nomination of Oliver Ellsworth "this morning"; place from location of capital.

James Iredell to Hannah Iredell ───────────────
March 3-4, 1796 Philadelphia, Pennsylvania

[*March 3.*] The Circuits are not yet arranged, as we have hitherto waited for the vacancy of the office of Chief Justice being filled up, which is not yet done_ The Court will probably sit three or four days longer. Mr Cushing was able to come out yesterday, but Mr Chase is laid up with something of the Gout_ . . .
[*March 4.*] I this moment have read in a News-Paper, that Mr Elsworth is nominated our Chief Justice,[1] in consequence of which I think it not unlikely

that Wilson will resign. But this is only my own conjecture, and therefore I wish you not to mention it.

AR[S?] (Nc-Ar, Charles E. Johnson Collection). Addressed "Edenton   North Carolina." This document is damaged where James Iredell's signature should be. Below this appears the passage reproduced here under date of March 4, 1796.

1. James Iredell may have read about Oliver Ellsworth's nomination in the *Aurora* (Philadelphia), which reported the news on March 4, 1796. The same notice appeared in the *Columbian Museum* (Savannah) on March 22.

John Adams mentioned Ellsworth's nomination in a letter to Abigail Adams on March 3, 1796. Adams Manuscript Trust, MHi.

Jonathan Trumbull to John Trumbull ─────────────────────
March 4, 1796   Philadelphia, Pennsylvania

... Our M‹Elsworth has been taken from our Corps to fill the Seat of Chief Justice on the federal Bench — in room of M‹ Rutledge /dementated/ — a great Loss this to the Senate! — but a valuable acquisition to the Court — an acquisition which has been much needed — ...

ARS (Ct, Hubbard Collection). Addressed "To the Care of the American Minister   In London." Sent in the "Ship Manchester   Via Liverpool." Stamped "LIVERPOOL   SHIP." Endorsed "Rec‹ Paris May 13th and ans‹ 14th."

John Trumbull (1756-1843), brother of Jonathan Trumbull, was a distinguished early American painter. John Trumbull went to London with John Jay in May, 1794, as Jay's private secretary for the negotiations that led to the Jay Treaty. Following the negotiations, Trumbull remained in Europe, pursuing artistic and business ventures; he also served as one of the commissioners for Article VII of the Jay Treaty. *DAB*.

John Adams to Abigail Adams ─────────────────────
March 5, 1796   Philadelphia, Pennsylvania

... yesterday M‹ Elsworth's Nomination was consented to as Chief Justice, by which we loose the clearest head and most dilligent hand we had.[1] It will give a Stability to the Government however, to place a Man of his Courage Constancy fortitude and Capacity in that situation. The Nomination of M‹Chase had given occasion to uncharitable Reflections and M‹ Wilsons ardent Speculations had given offence to some, and his too frequent affectation of Popularity to others. ₐ Though Elsworth has the Stiffness of Connecticutt;[2] ₐ though His Air and Gait[3] are not elegant;[4] ₐ though He can not enter a Room nor retire from it with the Ease and Grace of a Courtier: yet his Understanding is as sound, his Information as good and his heart as Steady as any Man can boast. ...

ARS (MHi, Adams Manuscript Trust).
1. John Adams refers to the loss to the Senate.
2. John Adams seems to have written a period and then altered it to a semicolon.

3. Originally, John Adams wrote either an "l" or the ascender for a "t" and then altered it to be an "i."

4. John Adams seems to have written a period and then altered it to a semicolon.

Joshua Coit to Elias Perkins
March 5, 1796 Philadelphia, Pennsylvania

... I think it will give you pleasure to be informed that MʳEllsworth is C Justice of the U. S. _ ¹ he will take his Seat on the Bench _ to day I fancy or Monday as he does not go to the Senate any more _ ...

ARS (CtNlHi, Perkins Collection). Addressed "New London Connecticut." Postmarked "5 MR."

1. Joshua Coit also wrote a letter to his brother David Coit on March 5, announcing Oliver Ellsworth's appointment and when Ellsworth would attend Court (Joshua Coit Papers, MBNEH). Another member of the House of Representatives, Roger Griswold, wrote two letters from Philadelphia to Connecticut to announce the appointment of Ellsworth as chief justice. He sent one to his wife Fanny on March 4 (Griswold Papers, CtY) and one to his brother Matthew Griswold on March 5 (William Griswold Lane Collection, CtY). Abraham Baldwin, in a letter to Joel Barlow on December 3, 1796, also mentioned the appointment of their friend to be chief justice. Abraham Baldwin Papers, CtY.

Jeremiah Smith to William Plumer
March 5, 1796 Philadelphia, Pennsylvania

... I write merely to inform you that yesterday Mʳ Ellsworth was appointed Chief Justice of the United States _ ¹ The vote was unanimous in Senate except Mason of Virginia who is a very ill natured & sour man as well as politician. _ I presume no appointment in the U. S. has been more wise or judicious than this: He is a very able lawyer a very learned man a very great Politican & a very honest man in short he is every thing one would desire. _ I know this will give you much pleasure as you are a sincere well wisher to good Government & especially to a good judiciary; A thing which we know the Value of by the want of it[.] I hope he will accept. _

Connecticut can not send his equal into the Senate _ He was the life & soul of that body & they will severely feel his loss _ He was a man of investigation & uncommon Industry _ Nothing passed without his examination. _ I believe his enemies placed as much Confidence in him as his friends, if this is not an improper expression _

I intend this morning to hear the doings of the judiciary still in session[.] I think it probable they will rise on Monday & that this day will be spent in delivering the opinion of the Court on causes which have been argued²

...

I have just recᵈ your letter of 19 Febʸ from Dover _

Judge Blair resigned from old age & indisposition _ He was a good man & universally beloved _ ...

ARS (Nh, Plumer Papers).

1. In a letter to Jeremiah Smith on March 15, William Plumer mentioned that he had just heard of Oliver Ellsworth's appointment as chief justice. William Plumer Papers, DLC.

2. The passage that follows was written by Jeremiah Smith after he had already signed this letter; the passage follows the signature.

Letter from a Member of Congress
Connecticut Journal
March 5, 1796   Philadelphia, Pennsylvania

... "On Thursday of this Week, Mr. ELLSWORTH was nominated by the President to be Chief Justice of the United States— Yesterday the same was ratified by the Senate."

(New Haven) March 10, 1796. Date and place are those of the letter. Addressed "to his Friend in this City"; i.e., New Haven, Connecticut.

Reprinted in the *American Mercury* (Hartford), March 14, 1796, and in the *Newport Mercury* (Newport, Rhode Island), March 15, 1796. Several Philadelphia newspapers published reports of Oliver Ellsworth's appointment. The *Aurora* printed one on March 5. On the same day, the *Philadelphia Minerva* also published a report which was reprinted in the *New-Jersey State Gazette* (Trenton) on March 8. On March 5 the *Philadelphia Gazette* printed an item, which also appeared in the *Maryland Gazette* (Annapolis) on March 10. The *American Mercury* (Hartford) on March 7 incorrectly noted that the Senate had approved the appointment of Ellsworth on "Tuesday last" rather than Friday last. Different notices appeared in the *Boston Gazette* and the *Connecticut Courant* (Hartford), both on March 14, in the *Richmond and Manchester Advertiser* (Richmond, Virginia) on March 16, and in the *Rutland Herald* (Rutland, Vermont) on March 28.

Oliver Ellsworth to Oliver Wolcott, Sr.
March 8, 1796   Philadelphia, Pennsylvania

... It is, Sir, my duty to acquaint you[1] that I have, with some hesitation, accepted an appointment in the Judiciary of the United States, which of course vacates my seat in the Senate.— This step I hope will not be regarded as disrespectful to a State which I have so long had the honor to serve, and whose interests must forever remain precious to my heart. ...

AR[S] (CtHi, Oliver Wolcott Jr. Papers). Signature clipped. Endorsed "Rec^d March 26.— 1796 Acknow^d. 29."

1. Following the death of Connecticut Governor Samuel Huntington in January, 1796, Oliver Wolcott, Sr., became acting governor. In May, 1796, Wolcott was elected governor and held the post until his death in December, 1797. *DAB.*

Senate Record of Resignation of Oliver Ellsworth
March 8-9, 1796

Tuesday, March 8th 1796.

The Vice President communicated a letter from the Honourable Oliver Ellsworth, in which he states that he hath accepted the appointment of Chief Justice of the United States, which of course vacates his seat in the Senate, which letter was read.

Ordered, that it lie on file. . . .

Wednesday, March 9th 1796.

. . .

On motion, by Mr Trumbull,

Ordered, that the Vice President be requested to notify the Executive of the State of Connecticut, that the Honourable Oliver Ellsworth hath accepted the appointment of Chief Justice of the United States, and that his seat in the Senate is of course vacated.[1] . . .

D (DNA, RG 46, Legislative Journal).

1. A transcript of the proceedings of the Senate on March 8 and 9, 1796, was attested to by Samuel A. Otis, secretary to the Senate, and forwarded to Oliver Wolcott, Sr., governor of Connecticut. Oliver Wolcott Sr. Papers, CtHi.

Jeremiah Smith to William Plumer
March 9, 1796 Philadelphia, Pennsylvania

. . . I have just been attending the supreme Court of the U. S. & have with much pleasure heard the Commission of Oliver Ellsworth as chief Justice read & heard him take the Oath of Office _ . . .

ARS (Nh, Plumer Papers).

James Iredell to Hannah Iredell
March 11, 1796 Philadelphia, Pennsylvania

. . . The Supreme Court is yet sitting, and we shall not be able to finish half the business, so that I expect [we'll?] we shall be here 3 or 4 weeks in August.[1]
. . .

ARS (Nc-Ar, Charles E. Johnson Collection). Addressed "Edenton North Carolina." Postmarked "11 MR."

1. After the Supreme Court had adjourned until August, James Iredell wrote to Hannah Iredell on March 18 and repeated his prediction of a long August term. Charles E. Johnson Collection, Nc-Ar.

Oliver Wolcott, Sr., to Jonathan Trumbull
March 14, 1796 Litchfield, Connecticut

. . . Your letter of the 9th instant announcing the appointment of Mr Ellsworth to the office of chief Justice of the U States, and the consequent Vancancy of his Seat in the Senate, has been duly recd _ [1]

. . .

M! Ellsworth, appointment will be very satisfactory to all who are <u>willing</u> to be pleased— if our country shall be preserved from anarchy and confusion, it must be by men of his Character— ...

ACS (CtHi, Oliver Wolcott Sr. Papers).
1. Jonathan Trumbull had informed Oliver Wolcott, Sr., of Oliver Ellsworth's appointment in a letter dated March 9, 1796. Oliver Wolcott Jr. Papers, CtHi.

Oliver Wolcott, Sr., to Oliver Wolcott, Jr. —————————
March 21, 1796   Litchfield, Connecticut

. . . The established principles and abilities of Mr. Ellsworth render his appointment proper.[1] ...

Pr (Printed in Gibbs, *Memoirs of the Administrations of Washington and John Adams,* 1:322-23).
1. Oliver Wolcott, Sr., was responding to a letter from Oliver Wolcott, Jr., dated "March 1796" announcing the appointment of Oliver Ellsworth. Oliver Wolcott Jr. Papers, CtHi.

James Iredell to Helen Tredwell ——————————————
March 25, 1796   Philadelphia, Pennsylvania

. . . The kind expectations of my Friends that I might be appointed Chief Justice were too flattering. Whatever other chance I might have had, there could have been no propriety in passing by Judge Wilson to come at me— The Gentleman appointed I believe will fill the office extremely well. He is a Man of an excellent understanding, and a Man of business. . . .

ARS (Nc-Ar, Charles E. Johnson Collection). Addressed "Samuel Tredwell Esq' Edenton, North Carolina." Postmarked "25   MR."

Peleg Coffin, Jr., to Dwight Foster ——————————————
March 28, 1796   Nantucket, Massachusetts

. . . I am highly pleased with the Appointment of our Worthy friend. O: Ellsworth, he will do the highest honor to his Office, altho I consider ~~him~~ _{it} a great Loss to the Senate it is no less a gain to the Bench, and is very good.— ...

ARS (MB, Ch. F 3.13). Addressed "Philadelphia." Postmarked by hand "Nantucket March 29." Endorsed "Rec⁴ Phil* Ap! 13. 1796."
Peleg Coffin, Jr. (1756-1805), a native of Nantucket, Massachusetts, had previously served in the Third Congress (1793-1795) and in 1796 was a state senator from Nantucket. *BDAC;* Alexander Starbuck, *The History of Nantucket* (Rutland, Vt.: Charles E. Tuttle, 1969), p. 640.
Dwight Foster (1757-1823), a lawyer and Massachusetts congressman. A native of Brookfield, Massachusetts, Foster served in the House of Representatives from 1793 to 1800, when he resigned to become a senator (1800-1803). *BDAC.*

John Adams to Abigail Adams ─────────────────────
March 29, 1796 Philadelphia, Pennsylvania

... The Appointment of the C. J. was a wise Measure._ My Mind is quite at ease on that subject_ ...

ARS (MHi, Adams Manuscript Trust).

Oliver Wolcott, Sr., to Oliver Ellsworth ─────────────
March 29, 1796 Litchfield, Connecticut

... I have been duly honoured with your letter of the 8: instant giving information of your having accepted an Office in the Judiciary, and of the consequent Vacancy of your Seat in Congress, as a Senator from this State

I doubt not but that the State would Very reluctantly part with your Services, under their immediate appointment, ₍but₎ ~~unless~~ upon the Conviction that they will be rendered more extensively useful, by your discharging the duties of the Very important Office to which you are appointed_

...

Accept Sir, my sincere wishes that your present appointment may be as agreable to yourself, as I doubt not it will be useful and honourable to your Country_ ...

ADfS (CtHi, Oliver Wolcott Jr. Papers).

William Plumer to Jeremiah Smith ──────────────────
March 31, 1796 Epping, New Hampshire

... I have rec^d your's of the 5th & 9th announcing the nomination, appointment, & acceptance of Oliver Ellsworth as Chief Justice of the United States. I am pleased with the character you give him, & rejoice at his appointment. The office is important. In that court questions of the greatest magnitude, not only as it respects the national character, but the lives, liberty, & property of individuals, must ultimately be decided. A good Judiciary is highly useful, as we feel from the want of it in this State. ...

ALbS (DLC, William Plumer Papers). Addressed "Philadelphia."

Arthur Iredell to James Iredell ───────────────────
April 5, 1796 "near Lewes," Sussex County, England

... I had heard of Mr Rutledge's Appoint^t & Rejection; but Things are so oddly stated in Newspapers that I fancied the Speech, which displaced him, had operated with M^rW: in his Favor_ Such <u>Anodynes</u> are very common in Europe_; but, I find, you trust more to Nature_ M^rCushing may be a very worthy Man __; and yet I do not feel the Force of your Arguments __ In short, till the Chair shall be actually filled up, I shall continue to think as I have done __ . . .

ARS (Nc-Ar, Charles E. Johnson Collection). Addressed "Philadelphia   N America." Sent "By New York   Packet." "Philadelphia" has been crossed out and "Edenton   N^th Carlina" written above.

Henry Tazewell to James Monroe ──────────────
May 19, 1796   Philadelphia, Pennsylvania

. . . Blair of Virginia has resigned his office as a Judge and Chase of Maryland has succeeded him. Rutledge of S° Carolina who had been appointed Chief Justice of the US. in the place of Mr Jay, in the recess of the Senate, had accepted & acted, was refused by the Senate, and Ellsworth appointed in his place & confirmed by the Senate __ [1] So that you will discover, that every officer S° of the Potowmack has been succeeded by men north of that Line. In fact, Iredell of N° Carolina & yourself are now the only officers of ye Gov^t S° of Potowmack who hold emminent stations __ [2] . . .

ARS (DLC, James Monroe Papers). Addressed "Paris."
  1. Two members of the House of Representatives wrote circular letters to their constituents in which they mentioned the turnover in Court personnel: Samuel J. Cabell of Virginia and Robert Goodloe Harper of South Carolina. Noble E. Cunningham, Jr., ed., *Circular Letters of Congressmen to Their Constituents, 1789-1829*, 3 vols. (Chapel Hill: University of North Carolina Press, 1978), 1:39-50.
  2. James Monroe held the post of minister plenipotentiary to France.

Cyrus Griffin to George Washington ──────────────
May 23, 1796   Richmond, Virginia

Can I hope for pardon sir if once more I take the liberty to experience your well known goodness and Indulgence.

upon the resignation of Mr Blair I think it was generally expected that if a Judge was nominated from Virginia the prsent district Judge[1] would have the preference, unless indeed Mr Marshall[2] or Mr Washington[3] from their uncommon legal Talents.

I did not solicit because I thought it unseemly to do so for a man already upon the Bench; it would shew a greediness of disposition not characteristic with the office, and a diffidence that the chief magistrate had forgotten me; but the appointments being made from other states, and as they are Gentlemen of the best abilities in the Law the union are extremely happy and thankful to have the Supreme Court thus ably completed. And yet it has been now hinted to me that perhaps some objections might lay against my character if it should be in contemplation to appoint another Judge from Virginia when a vacancy shall arrive.

would there, sir, be any objection to my <u>moral</u> Character? Indeed I am not sensible of it myself. I do not game. I have not speculated to the amount of one shilling in my life; and I am temperate & retired, confining myself to Books, my Family, and the duties of my station.

would there be any objection to my political character? I do not believe there is a more orderly Citizen in the United States. always a sincere friend, and advocate for the prsent Constitution; a real well wisher and defender of the administration of government_ particularly in the late Treaty with England.

perhaps I have not Industry for the labour of a Judge? the Gentlemen of the Bar will not say so. I hold it impossible for any man to be more assiduous in the stated and special District and the Circuit Courts than I am. I have not lost one day since my Family were brought from new york unless by unavoidable necessity_ and I do a great deal of business out of Court; the district is very extensive and myself always upon the spot.

Then it would be for the want of Talents to exercise that very important Employment. I hope to Heaven that is the only objection, for I had rather be thought honest and attentive than a man of the most splendid Intellect. however I have determined many Causes of great importance in my Court from which there has not been a single appeal but in two cases to establish points of practice, and two others upon the Jurisdiction of the Court; none upon the merits of a question; the lawyers being perfectly satisfied with the reasons of the Judge. In the circuit Court indeed I gave my opinion that payment of British Debts into the loan office of the state should be considered as Valid and here m.r Iredell and myself had the misfortune to differ from a very learned and virtuous Judge, mr Jay, whom we both revere.[4] I gave my opinion also in another great question the Carriage Tax, and was unlucky enough to differ from Judge Wilson.[5] I thought the Tax one of the best that could be laid, but it appeared to me not to be done in a Constitutional manner. most of the Bar were of the same opinion. I was sworn to determine according to the best of my Judgment; but I constantly paid the Tax myself and advised others to do it also. upon both of these two important qustions I have the honor of according in opinion with a late amiable and able Judge.[6]

I should hope, sir, that no misrepresentations have been made to you relative to me. I have long known that a Genleman once high in your Confidence was not a friend of mine, that confidence is deservedly withdrawn, and his conduct shews that I never had occasion to lament his want of friendship.[7] other Gentlemen also who stood high in estimation professed a great deal have towards me, but having changed their principles, possibly they may changed their attachments. a Family rising into Consequence and who possess very considerable merit I hope are not Enemies of mine, tho early in the Confederation and upon the purest public principle I gave my voice in Congress to recall their relations from the Courts of Europe. this occasioned great bitterness against me in the elder names.[8] Some reports were ~~hinted~~ also hinted to me_

That I was not active enough in condemning a vessel belonging to a m.r Sinclair and said to be fitting out as a privateer. the case came before the Court upon the day appointed by the District Attorney, 24 witnesses were sup[œ?]ned on the part of the U. States, 22 of them appeared and were sworn, but their Testimony was not sufficient and the Jury acquitted the vessel without hesitation. as a material witness was absent the attorney obtained a new Trial and after a special Court lately the cause is dismissed unless good reasons can be given at the June Court to reinstate the business.[9] I was fully as active as a Judge ought to be.

another report was circulated that I was determined to condemn all prizes brought into this district by armed vessels of the above description or fitted in our ports. nothing under the sun was ever more false. there lives not a Judge upon Earth of more discretion in his office. my opinion upon any qustion was never known until given Judicially.

It was said also that I was an advocate for mr Genet. The only thing I ever said was, upon that subject, "that a man of mr Genet's understanding could hardly have acted so absurdly and unwarrantably unless he had been thus instructed by his nation, and if his nation had thus instructed him he was bound to obey." when the Instructions were published the points then agitated turned out such as I supposed them.[10]

Another matter has been mentioned that I admitted to bail a man charged with opposing the militia draught to be sent against the Insurgents;[11] the Truth is that no witness appeared against him, and I admitted the man to bail in a large amount to be prsent at the next succeeding Cout; the prisoner appeared, and the posecution was dismissed by the attorney.

a late affair also; a young man by the name of Goosely in the Town of York was surrendred upon my warrant for stealing Bank Bills [ef?] from the Postoffice. agreeable to the promises of the assistant postmaster, upon the surrender by the young man's friends when he might have escaped, upon his delivering up all the money, and upon his making a candid discovery of the particulars of that wicked Transaction, I thought it perfectly right to bail him with good security in the sum of 20,000 dollars.[12]

I beg leave to mention another matter also; some little time ago it was stated to me by Colonel Newton of Norfolk "That he had good grounds to believe certain British agents were purchasing Horses in this Country for the military use of that Government, to be sent against our Allies the French in the West Indies, and that vessels were getting ready to transport the said Horses." I wrote him for answer that the law of Congress pointed out the mode of proceeding, and that in the first Instance it was consistent with my station as Judge not to interfere. Mr Oster the french Consul has also written to me upon the subject by way of memorial.

I ought to mention also that I had the imprudence to write to you sir concerning my son John in Europe. poor Fellow! having no Fortune to give him, he being very anxious to be introduced to the public under the present administration, and being convinced myself that he was a young man of an active mind, sensible, and honorable in his demeanor I did venture to write in his behalf, but the letter was hardly gone before I repented and [saw?] the impropriety.

Thus sir I have taken the freedom to say somewhat relative to myself, only as a sort of exculpation if any person whatever has unkindly traduced me, and I defy any man to prove the contrary of what I have now the honor to assert. I know my Innocence and can challenge with Confidence.

That I have faults, that I have follies and deficiencies I do not deny— but I owe to you a thousand obligations, and no man breathing is possessed of a more feeling heart.

"Truth and candour will always estimate the conduct of public men" and well knowing that I have never said one syllable derogatory to your personal or political character I am with a grateful mind & the most profound respect sir

    Your very obedient servant

Cyrus Griffin

Richmond
   May 23ᵈ 1796—

ARS (DLC, George Washington Papers).

1. Cyrus Griffin was himself "the prsent district Judge."
2. John Marshall.
3. Bushrod Washington.
4. The case referred to is *Ware v. Hylton.*
5. The case was *United States v. Hylton.*
6. Possibly a reference to John Blair, formerly associate justice of the Supreme Court.
7. The references are to Edmund Randolph.
8. As a member of the Continental Congress, Cyrus Griffin had incurred the enmity of the Lee family by favoring the recall of Arthur Lee and the other American commissioners from France. Cyrus Griffin to Burgess Ball, [August 10, 1779?], and Cyrus Griffin to Benjamin Franklin, September, 1779, in Edmund C. Burnett, ed., *Letters of Members of the Continental Congress,* 8 vols. (Washington, D.C.: Carnegie Institution of Washington, 1921-1936), 4:360n, 463-64.
9. Captain John Sinclair (1755-1820) of Smithfield, Virginia, was suspected of outfitting a privateer (the *Unicorn*) in the summer of 1794 in violation of "An Act prohibiting for a limited time the Exportation of Arms and Ammunition, and encouraging the Importation of the same." *Stat.,* 1:369. In July, 1794, Governor Henry Lee sent the state militia, under the command of John Marshall, to seize the vessel and search Sinclair's house. Proceedings to libel the ship were initiated in the United States District Court for Virginia, which had admiralty jurisdiction. A preliminary hearing was held in September, 1794; on November 6, 1794, with Cyrus Griffin as presiding judge, a jury acquitted the vessel. The government appealed the case to the United States Circuit Court for the district of Virginia, and on June 8, 1795, with James Wilson presiding, the decision was reversed and a new trial was ordered to be held in the district court. Records as to the final disposition of this case in the district court are missing. *PJM,* 2:273-79; Claude O. Lanciano, Jr., *Legends of Lands End* (n.p., 1971), pp. 23-63, particularly pp. 48-49, 61; CCD Virginia, Order Book No. 1, pp. 464, 541, Vi; DC Virginia, Index to Record Books, Vi.
10. Upon his arrival in Charleston on April 8, 1793, Edmund Charles Genet, the newly appointed minister to the United States from the French Republic, began to equip privateers to capture British merchant ships and to implement French plans for operations in Louisiana, Florida, and Canada. When the government ordered that the French-equipped privateers be barred from American ports, Genet disregarded the orders and even threatened to make an appeal for public

support. Ultimately President Washington asked that Genet be recalled. By February, 1794, a new minister, Jean Antoine Joseph, Baron Fauchet, had arrived with orders to send Genet back to France for trial. Genet asked for and received asylum in the United States, married a daughter of George Clinton, and settled in rural New York. His instructions from the French government were published in 1793: *The Correspondence between citizen Genet, minister of the French Republic, to the United States of North America, and the officers of the Federal government: to which are prefixed the Instructions from the constituted authorities of France to the said minister. All from authentic documents* (Philadelphia: Benjamin Franklin Bache, 1793). *DAB;* John C. Miller, *The Federalist Era, 1789-1801* (New York: Harper & Row, Harper Colophon Books, 1963), pp. 132, 136-39.

11. Associate Justice James Wilson certified on August 4, 1794, that the situation in western Pennsylvania was beyond the control of United States marshals or the courts, which then allowed President Washington to call out state militias to put down the Whiskey Rebellion. The Virginia militia was ordered to proceed to Pennsylvania on September 4, 1794. Miller, *Federalist Era,* pp. 157-58n; *PJM,* 2:281.

12. John Goosley of Yorktown was indicted on a felony charge and arraigned on May 27, 1796, at the United States Circuit Court for the district of Virginia, before judges James Iredell and Cyrus Griffin. The case was dismissed when witnesses from Goosley's home county swore he was not guilty. CCD Virginia, Order Book No. 2, May 27, 1796, Vi.

George Washington to Cyrus Griffin ─────────────────────
June 8, 1796 Philadelphia, Pennsylvania

Cyrus Griffin Esq[r]

Philad[a] 8th June 1796_

Sir,

I am sorry, that, without being accused, you should think it necessary to go into a lengthy justification of your conduct and principles._

What the entire design of your letter of the 23[d] Ul[to] may be, I am at a loss, to conceive; and, pressed as I have been, and still am, on all sides, in the discharge of my public functions, I have no leisure to enquire._ If the object of it (among other things) is to intimate, that you have been overlooked in some recent appointments, I can only say, that nominations are made from the view[1] I am able to take of the cases which come before me;_ in doing which, I have often, if not always, where the appointments are not of a local nature, found it necessary to combine a variety of considerations_ none of which, however, have originated from a desire to serve a friend or relation;[2] or a wish to oblige this or that man or set of men; but from the best information I can obtain (where I have no personal Knowledge) of the fitness of characters to offices._

That I may have erred, and in many instancies made injudicious nominations, is highly probable:_ wonderful indeed would it be, if the case was otherwise; but numerous, and chagreening as disappointments may have been to individuals (and abundant they are), I can defy malignancy itself to ascribe partiality, or interested motives to any of my nominations;_ or omissions, to prejudice or dislike._ I have naught, therefore, on this score, to reproach myself with._

For the attachment you have professed for my person and administration, I pray you to accept my best thanks, and the assurances of the esteem & regard with which I am — Sir —

Your Most Ob.[1] Ser.[2]

G.Washington

Lb (DLC, George Washington Papers); ADfS (DLC, George Washington Papers).
  1. In draft, "best view."
  2. The "on" is written over "ve."

George Thatcher to Oliver Wolcott, Jr. —————————————
June 13, 1796   Boston, Massachusetts

[*Thatcher writes to recommend John Tucker for the office of supervisor of the revenue for Massachusetts.*] M.[r] Tucker was appointed Clerk to the Supreme Court of the United States at the first organization of the federal Government — but finding the compensation very small he was obliged to resigne — ...

ARS (CtHi, Oliver Wolcott Jr. Papers). Addressed "Philadelphia." Postmarked "BOSTON 17 IV." Endorsed "rec.[d] June 23.[d] — too late   to be transmitted to the   Prsident. OW."
  George Thatcher (1754-1824) was a congressman from Massachusetts, who represented the district of Maine. Thatcher graduated from Harvard in 1776, read law with Shearjashub Bourne, and moved to Maine, where he took over the law practice of James Sullivan. Thatcher served in the Confederation Congress and in 1789 was elected to the First Congress. He remained in Congress until 1801. *DAB.*

Cyrus Griffin to George Washington ————————————————
July 4, 1796   Williamsburg, Virginia

Sir

Being engaged upon duty at the Circuit and District Courts held in the City of Richmond I had not an opportunity of sooner acknowleging the honor of your letter.[1]

I am particularly uneasy and depressed to have taken one moment from the immense labour of your public functions or to have incured your displeasure in the remotest degree. We understood that Congress were to adjourn on the 20.th of May; I thought you would do me the favor to read the letter at some more leisure period; nor had I the least claim to receive an answer but what should arise from your extreme Goodness to every description of persons. Indeed Sir, I did not mean to intimate that I had been over looked in any recent appointments, but meant to obviate some objections to me that possibly might have come to your Information, in case that another Judg[e] of the Supreme Court should be nominated from Virginia, and upon supposition that Gentlemen of better Talents, from their lucrative practice at the Bar, would not think proper to accept such appointment.

I have taken the liberty to write to you three or four letters since your Benevolence was [shewn?] to me, in one of which I expressed a wish that my destination had been fixed to a diplomatic employment—[2] the wish was a most improper one as those employmen[ts] were so much better arranged, and I did wrong in fatiguing you with letters unnecessarily. repentance never reaches to restitution, but I will promise most faithfully never more to encroach upon your valua[ble] hours, [the?] only compensation in my power to make.

Most eagerly do I thank you for those kind assurances of esteem and regard; and 'tho I am destitute of the great advantages of the mind which other Gentlemen possess, yet very honestly may I take the liberty to profess the sentiments of my heart— that purest veneration, and most respectful attachment with which I shall always remain sir

Your obedient and obliged   humble servant

C Griffin

pardon me when I take the freedom to congratulate with you upon the return of this day,—[3] and that I most fervently hope many years hence you may in health preside over the Councils of our happy Country.

W^{ms}burg
July 4th 1796

ARS (DLC, George Washington Papers).
    1. See George Washington to Cyrus Griffin, June 8, 1796.
    2. Cyrus Griffin had asked for a diplomatic appointment in his letter to George Washington of July 10, 1789 (q.v.); see also, Cyrus Griffin to George Washington, August 14, 1789, and May 23, 1796.
    3. Cyrus Griffin was writing this on July 4, the anniversary of independence.

James Iredell to Hannah Iredell ——————————————
July 29, 1796   Head of Elk, Maryland

. . . From Mr Chase's account I have reason to fear a long Session. . . .

ARS (Nc-Ar, Charles E. Johnson Collection). Addressed "Edenton,   North Carolina." Head of Elk, Maryland, is now Elkton, Maryland.

James Iredell to Hannah Iredell ——————————————
August 3, 1796   Philadelphia, Pennsylvania

. . . We have a vast deal of business to do, but as the court meets punctually at 9 every morning I hope we shall dispatch more in proportion than usual—.
I am afraid however it will take us at least 3 or $_\wedge^{4}$ weeks. Every one of the Judges was here on Saturday— . . .

ARS (Nc-Ar, Charles E. Johnson Collection). James Iredell began this letter on August 1, 1796. Addressed "Edenton,   North Carolina." Sent "By favor of   M͏ʳ DeNar."

James Iredell to Hannah Iredell ————————————
August 5, 1796 Philadelphia, Pennsylvania

. . . so busily have we been engaged that I can scarcely command an hour for myself except in the evening when I never attempt to write if I can help it. It is impossible for me to say when I can get away, but it is pretty well ascertained that I am to go no Circuit this fall.[1] . . .

ARS (Nc-Ar, Charles E. Johnson Collection). James Iredell began this letter on August 3, 1796. Addressed "Edenton,   North Carolina." Postmarked "5   AV."

1. James Iredell, in a letter written to Hannah Iredell on August 12, confirmed that he would not have to ride circuit in the fall. Charles E. Johnson Collection, Nc-Ar.

James Iredell to Hannah Iredell ————————————
August 12, 1796 Philadelphia, Pennsylvania

. . . I have now every reason to hope that our Court will end to day or tomorrow[1] . . .

ARS (Nc-Ar, Charles E. Johnson Collection). Addressed "Edenton,   North Carolina." Postmarked "12   AV."

1. The Court adjourned on August 12, 1796.

James Iredell to Hannah Iredell ————————————
February 9, 1797 Philadelphia, Pennsylvania

. . . The Chief Justice has been sick the whole Court, and tho' better is still unable to attend. . . .

ARS (Nc-Ar, Charles E. Johnson Collection).

"Massachusitensis" to Thomas Russell ————————————
Columbian Centinel
February 11, 1797 Boston, Massachusetts

[*"Massachusitensis" nominates William Cushing to be governor of Massachusetts.*] He is of an age to give dignity to the office, but unsuitable to the fatigues of his present station under the Federal government, for that reason he declined the Chief Justiceship of the United States. . . .

(Boston) February 11, 1797. Date and place are those of the newspaper.

Jeremiah Smith to William Plumer ————————————
February 13, 1797   Philadelphia, Pennsylvania

. . . The supreme Court have been one week in session   They have little Business before them — No Cause of importance has been heard tho Mʳ Marshal & MʳPierpoint Edwards as well as MʳDexter in addition to the eminent lawyers of this City attend[_] It is said the Court will rise today — ¹ The Chief Justice has been so ill that he could not attend — He is said however to be in no danger — His life is eminently important to this Country — . . .

ARS (Nh, Plumer Papers).
  1. The Court did adjourn February 13.

Cephus Smith, Jr., to Jacob Wagner ————————————
July 15, 1797   Rutland, Vermont

Rutland, Vermont, July 15 1797.

Sir

This acknowledges the receiᵗ of yours of the 15ᵗʰ of March last¹ annexing an Order of the Supreme Court of the United States made at their session in February last relative to the return of Writs of Error — ²

I have not been furnished with a form of a Writ of Error — if my Predecessor was, he has lost it — I shall probably want to make use of one soon —

I am sir with sentiments of respect   your most obedient servant

Cephus Smith Junʳ
Clk of the District & Circuit
Cᵗ Vermont District —

To the Clerk of the Supreme
Court of the United States

ARS (DNA, RG 267, Records of the Office of the Clerk). Addressed "Philadelphia   32. Moraⁿ Alley." Jacob Wagner resided at 32 Moravian Alley. Cornelius William Stafford, *The Philadelphia Directory, for 1797* (Philadelphia: William W. Woodward, 1797). This letter has been endorsed as "recᵈ 2 Augᵗ 97."
  1. Letter not found.
  2. See "Fine Minutes," February 13, 1797.

James Iredell to Hannah Iredell ————————————
August 11, 1797   Philadelphia, Pennsylvania

. . . All the Judges are here but Wilson who unfortunately is in a manner absconding from his creditors — his Wife with him — the rest of the Family here! What a situation! It is supposed his object is to wait until he can make a more

favorable adjustment of his affairs than he could in a state of arrest__ Our
Court will not last longer than next week . . .

ARS (Nc-Ar, Charles E. Johnson Collection). Addressed "Edenton,   North Carolina." Postmarked "BALT-AUG-13."

Frederick Wolcott to Oliver Wolcott, Jr. ——————————
January 23, 1798   Hartford, Connecticut

. . . Mr Ellsworth will not go to Philadelphia till some time the next week.__
He is considerably unwell, & I understand quite hypocondriac. . . .

ARS (CtHi, Oliver Wolcott Jr. Papers).
   Frederick Wolcott (1767-1837), younger brother of Oliver Wolcott, Jr., had studied law after
graduating from Yale. Frederick Wolcott held the positions of clerk of the Court of Common
Pleas and clerk of the Superior Court for Litchfield County. He was also judge of the Litchfield
probate district. Dexter, *Graduates of Yale College*, 4:519-20.

Oliver Ellsworth to William Cushing ——————————
February 4, 1798   New Haven, Connecticut

. . . I am at length thus far on my way to Philadelphia. Want of health prevented my leaving home sooner, & yet requires that my movements should
be gentle & cautious. I hope to be with you the forepart of next week. You
will be so good as to make my apology with my respects to our brethren.__
. . .

ARS (MHi, Robert Treat Paine Papers). Addressed "Philadelphia." Sent to Cushing "At M^r
Stalls   North 3^d Street   about N° 20."

William Paterson to Euphemia Paterson ——————————
February 5, 1798   Philadelphia, Pennsylvania

. . . The Chief Justice has not yet come on, and it uncertain, whether he will
be here, as he has not been well for some time. Judge Wilson is in North
Carolina, and in such a bad state of health as to render it unsafe for him to
travel. The other judges are here, and to-day court was opened. I can form
no opinion as to the length of time we shall sit; but, I hope, we shall rise in
the course of three weeks at furthest. . . .

ARS (NjR, William Paterson Papers). Addressed "New Brunswick." Marked "Fav^d by Honble
Mr Kirkpatrick."

James Iredell to Hannah Iredell ————————————————
February 5 and 8, 1798   Philadelphia, Pennsylvania

[*February 5:*] Our Court is to begin to day, but we have barely a <u>quorum</u> consisting of the Judges Cushing, Paterson, Chase, and myself: the Chief Justice being unfortunately in very bad health, and we have now no reason to expect he can attend. . . .

[*February 8:*] Our Court has been very busily employed since Monday, being in Court every day from ten till three. Unluckily, the Chief Justice is in such bad health, that he has not been able to come on, nor is now expected. . . .

ARS (Nc-Ar, Charles E. Johnson Collection). Addressed "Edenton, North Carolina." Postmarked "8   FE."

Harrison Gray Otis to Sally Otis ————————————————
February 18, 1798   [Philadelphia, Pennsylvania]

. . . Mrs Wilson left this place yesterday for North Carolina in quest of her unfortunate Husband who is I am told greatly dejected and afraid to make his appearance here. She was accompanied by Judge Iredell— Wislon[1] left this city a few days since to escape from his creditors but managed with so little address that he has got himself arrested at New Castle in Delaware where he will probably be imprisoned— . . .

ARS (MHi, Harrison Gray Otis Papers). Addressed "Boston." Postmarked "19   FE."
    Harrison Gray Otis (1765-1848), a Boston lawyer, had served in the Massachusetts House of Representatives in 1796, the same year that he was appointed United States attorney for the district of Massachusetts. Otis resigned his office as district attorney at the end of 1796 and entered the Fifth Congress as a federalist on March 4, 1797. He served in Congress through March 3, 1801. In February of that same year, he was again appointed United States attorney for the district of Massachusetts. He was a second cousin of Hannah Gray, who had married James Wilson in 1793. Samuel A. Otis, secretary of the United States Senate, was Harrison G. Otis's father. *BDAC;* Marcus D. Raymond, *Gray Genealogy* (Tarrytown, N.Y., 1887), p. 192; *DAB.*
    Sally (Foster) Otis (1770-1836) was the wife of Harrison Gray Otis. *DAB* entry for Harrison G. Otis.
    1. Harrison G. Otis meant to write "Wilson."

John Rutledge, Jr., to Edward Rutledge ————————————————
February 25, 1798   Philadelphia, Pennsylvania

. . . Judge Wilson has not [retur?]ned yet from his southern circuit— heretofore it has been supposed by his Creditors that he was not tangible during the sitting of the Court, but this doctrine is over-ruled,[1] & he has not been able to make his appearance at the Court held this month— His poor Wife gives it out that he is sick in Carolina, & I am often asked if my Letters say whether Wilson is getting better__ His family, which is large, are supported by the needle work of his wife & daughters, & the practice of his Son which, I understand, is not extensive__ ...

ARS (PHi, Dreer Collection).

John Rutledge, Jr. (1766-1819), son of the former chief justice, a lawyer and planter, represented South Carolina in Congress from 1797 to 1803. Previously he had served in the South Carolina House of Representatives from 1792 until his election to Congress. *BDAC;* Edgar, *Biographical Directory of the South Carolina House of Representatives,* 1:238-47.

1. Beginning in the fall of 1796, James Wilson lived in constant fear of arrest because of angry creditors. After attending the February 1797 term of the Supreme Court, he went into hiding in Bethlehem, Pennsylvania. Smith, *James Wilson,* pp. 383-84. He was not present at the August 1797 term, and James Iredell, writing to his wife, Hannah Iredell, on August 11 (q.v.) commented that Wilson was "absconding from his creditors." By September a creditor had caught up with Wilson, and Wilson had been imprisoned in Burlington, New Jersey (entry of September 3, 1797, Diary of Thomas Shippen, Shippen Family Papers, DLC; James Wilson to Bird Wilson, September 6, 1797, James Wilson Papers, PHi). After Wilson extricated himself from jail, he took the opportunity of riding the Southern Circuit in the fall of 1797 to flee further away from his creditors and to get his southern investments in order. In April, 1798, however, Pierce Butler, one of Wilson's creditors, caught up with him. Wilson again was arrested and spent two months in jail in Edenton, North Carolina. Smith, *James Wilson,* pp. 385-86; November 8, 1797, Minutes, CCD Georgia, RG 21, GEpFAR.

Abigail Adams to Hannah Cushing ————————————
March 9, 1798   Philadelphia, Pennsylvania

... The Chief Justice I have seen since you left us, and engaged him to dine with us the next day. but he sent an apology as being too unwell. he is upon the whole better than when he came. ...

ACS (MHi, Adams Manuscript Trust).

Hannah Phillips (ca. 1754-1834) had married William Cushing, a distant cousin, in 1774. *DAB* entry for William Cushing; Clifford K. Shipton, *Sibley's Harvard Graduates,* vol. 13, *1751-1755* (Boston: Massachusetts Historical Society, 1965), pp. 26, 29-30.

Samuel Johnston to James Iredell ————————————
July 28, 1798   Williamston, North Carolina

... I feel very much for Judge Wilson. I hear that he has been ill, what upon earth will become of him and that unfortunate lady who has attached herself to his fortunes, he discovers to[1] disposition to resign his Office, surely, if his feelings are not rendered altogether callous, by his misfortunes, he will not suffer himself to be disgraced by a conviction on an impeachment. ...

ARS (Nc-Ar, Charles E. Johnson Collection). Originally addressed "Philadelphia." When this letter reached Philadelphia, James Iredell already had left the city and it was readdressed "Edenton.   North Carolina." Postmarked "PHI   15   AU."

1. Samuel Johnston probably meant to write "no."

Philadelphia Gazette ————————————————————————————
August 4, 1798   Philadelphia, Pennsylvania

On Monday next, the Supreme Court of the United States will commence its session, at the City Hall in this city.

(Philadelphia) August 4, 1798. Date and place are those of the newspaper.

Slight variants of this article appeared in the *Commercial Advertiser* (New York), August 7, 1798, and in the *City Gazette* (Charleston), August 25, 1798. The *Daily Advertiser* (New York), August 8, 1795, noted that the Court had commenced on Monday.

James Iredell to Hannah Iredell ————————————————————————
August 6 and 9, 1798   Philadelphia, Pennsylvania

[*August 6:*] I find there is a good deal of important business depending, so that I despair of getting away as soon as I had hoped— I shall however as soon as possible. All the Judges are in town except Judge Wilson; and all tolerably well— tho' M⸢r⸣ Chase has been very ill again, and still has something of the sciatica. . . .

[*August 9:*] There being some appearances of the Yellow Fever in [Water-street,][1] between the Bridge and Walnut Street, the lawyers agreed to continue most of the Causes, and our Court broke up yesterday. . . .

ARS (Nc-Ar, Charles E. Johnson Collection). Addressed "Edenton,   North Carolina."

1. James Iredell's letter has been damaged at this point. The reading in brackets comes from *MJI*, 2:534.

William Cushing to Charles Cushing ——————————————————————
August 14, 1798   Newark, New Jersey

. . . Our Court at Philadelphia began Monday the 6⸢th⸣ & Ended Wednesday the
                                                                    fever[1]   again
8⸢th⸣ Inst⸢t⸣, being shortened by the breaking out of the Yellow ⌃ arising ⌃ as it is said, from barrels of putrid coffee, & nursed[2] by a bad air & dirty narrow Streets. . . .

ARS (MHi, William Cushing Papers). Addressed "Boston."

1. In a letter dated October 8, 1798, Hannah Cushing told Abigail Adams of the Court's adjournment because of yellow fever. Adams Manuscript Trust, MHi.

2. The "ed" is written over "ing."

Thomas Iredell to James Iredell ————————————————————————
August 17, 1798   Edenton, North Carolina

. . . I am sorry to say Judge Wilson is by no means well, he takes ~~a great deal~~ too little exercise.— . . .

ARS (Nc-Ar, Charles E. Johnson Collection). Addressed "Edenton NC." Originally addressed "Richmond." Postmarked "RICHMOND, SEPT [1?] 1798."

Thomas Iredell (b. 1761), James Iredell's younger brother, studied law under him and became an attorney in Edenton, North Carolina. Thomas Iredell was also a clerk and master in the Court of Equity for the Edenton district. *PJI*, 1:72n; James Iredell, *Laws of the State of North-Carolina* (Edenton: Hodge & Wills, 1791), see list of names of subscribers at the end of the volume (unpaginated).

James Iredell to [Sarah?] Gray ——————————————————
August 25, 1798   Edenton, North Carolina

. . . At the desire of your dear and unfortunate Sister, Mrs Wilson, who is in good health but extreme affliction, I have the pain to acquaint you that Judge Wilson unfortunately died here on the night of the 21. Inst__. a few hours after my arrival.[1] Tho' he had been at times in very bad health, evidently occasioned by distress of mind owing to his pecuniary difficulties, yet the Illness of which he died was of short duration, tho' very sharp, and the greater part of the ~~delirium~~ ^time^ he was in a state of delirium during which he would not suffer many things to be done for him which were advised, and might possibly have restored him. . . .

ADf (Nc-Ar, Charles E. Johnson Collection). Marked "Substance of a Letter to Miss Gray."

"Miss Gray," identified by James Iredell as the sister of Hannah (Gray) Wilson (wife of James Wilson) was probably Sarah Gray (baptized 1772, died 1830). Sarah Gray married Joseph Hall in 1808. Hannah (Gray) Wilson had two other sisters: Harriet, who probably had died young, and Lucy, who apparently had married in 1797. *Records of the Church of Brattle Square, Boston* (Boston: Benevolent Fraternity of Churches, 1902), p. 188; American Antiquarian Society, *Index of Deaths in Massachusetts;* Raymond, *Gray Genealogy,* p. 192; Boston Record Commissioners, *Report of the Record Commissioners,* 39 vols. (Boston: Municipal Printing Office, 1876-1909), vol. 30, *Boston Marriages, 1752-1809* (1903), pp. 250, 178.

1. News of James Wilson's death spread quickly. References to it appeared in a letter from William Miller to Oliver Wolcott, Jr., on September 7, 1798 (Oliver Wolcott Jr. Papers, CtHi), and in one from William White to James Iredell on September 8, 1798 (Charles E. Johnson Collection, Nc-Ar).

Hannah Wilson to Bird Wilson ——————————————————
September 1, 1798   Edenton, North Carolina

. . . The shock my dear Bird which you must all have felt by the death of your dear[1] papa, affects me sensibly . . . his mind had been in such a state for the last six months, harassed and perplexed, that it was more than he could possibly bear, and brought on a violent nervous fever. . . .

ARS (PHi, James Wilson Papers). Addressed "274 High Street Philadelphia."

Hannah Gray (1774-1808) married James Wilson in 1793. Her second husband, whom she married in 1802, was Thomas Bartlett. Lawrence Park, comp., *Gilbert Stuart: An Illustrated Descriptive List of his Works,* 4 vols. (New York: William Edwin Rudge, 1926), 1:140.

Bird Wilson (1777-1859), son of Associate Justice James Wilson, studied law and was admitted to the Philadelphia bar in 1797. Bird Wilson later achieved fame as an Episcopal clergyman and professor of theology. He also edited his father's writings. *DAB*.

1. Hannah Wilson wrote "papa" and then erased it and wrote "dear."

Timothy Pickering to John Adams —————————————
September 7, 1798   Trenton, New Jersey

. . . Last evening I received the inclosed letter from Doctor Rush, desiring his brother[1] might be mentioned to you for the vacant seat on the Bench of the Supreme Court.[2] . . .

ARS (MHi, Adams Manuscript Trust); APcS (MHi, Timothy Pickering Papers).

1. Jacob Rush (1747-1820), brother of Benjamin Rush, was the chief judge of Pennsylvania's Third Judicial District. Jacob Rush, a graduate of the College of New Jersey (later Princeton), was admitted to the Philadelphia bar in 1769 and in 1773 gained admission to the bar of the Supreme Court of the province. He served as a secretary first to John Hancock and then to Charles Thomson in the Continental Congress. In 1784 Rush became an associate justice of Pennsylvania's Supreme Court, a position he held for seven years. In 1791 Governor Thomas Mifflin, for political reasons, failed to reappoint Rush to a seat on the state Supreme Court; Rush instead was appointed to the state district court. McLachlan, *Princetonians*, 1:525-30.

2. Benjamin Rush's letter dated September 5, 1798, has not been found; the date of Rush's letter is mentioned in John Adams to Timothy Pickering, Miscellaneous Letters, RG 59, DNA. Benjamin Rush (1746-1813), a prominent Philadelphia physician and patriot, had known John Adams for over twenty years. In 1797 Adams appointed Rush treasurer of the United States Mint. *DAB*.

Jacob Rush to Benjamin Rush —————————————
September 8, 1798   Reading, Pennsylvania

. . . The Death of Judge Wilson was to me an unwelcome & unexpected Event— I fear he hastned it by some unjustifiable Means. His Constitution was too good to have sunk in so short a Time, under the Weight of mere Intemperance. What a miserable Termination to such distinguished Abilities, and what a dark Cloud overcast ~~th~~ the last Days of a Life that had

once ~~been~~ with uncommon Lustre— (been shone marked)

I thank you for your kind[1] Efforts to have Me appointed his Successor—[2]

But all is in vain— even if it would be suitable and agreeable to me — There are some Men around Col. Pickering who will leave no Stone unturned to prevent it— Do you not apprehend Mr Peters[3] will accept of it? I should think he would accept it gladly_ and that Mr Sitgreaves[4] also will be thought of_ Remember, "'tis from high Life, high Characters are drawn"_[5] One thing I am sure of. Peters would <u>resign</u> rather than sit as inferiour to me in a Court of Justice. I have good Reason to believe, he is extremely opposed to the Idea of my being ~~the first~~ elected the first Magistrate of Pennsyvania; and my immediate Elevation over ‸him on the Bench would be still more painful. Perhaps Lewis will look for the Office_ and if he [*word inked out*] does not, he will push his Friend Peters._

    . . .

I cannot help thinking you had better withdraw the Application, from a Conviction it will never suceed_ and from an opinion the Office is attended with so much Labour & Expence as to be no Way desireable. I have been told the Expence incurred in the Duties of the Office, occassioned by travelling and being from Home one Half the year, amount to at least Half ~~of~~ the Salary. To use a culinary Figure, I fear it will be jumping out of the pan into the Fire; nor do I feel any Inclination at <u>my</u> Time of Life, [to?] double my bodily Labours, which are [at?] present quite sufficient. . . .

ARS (PPL, Benjamin Rush Papers). Addressed "Philad^a." Postmarked by hand "Rea^g Sept 9 1798."

1. Originally Jacob Rush wrote "kindly" but then erased the "ly."

2. See Timothy Pickering to John Adams, September 7, 1798.

3. Richard Peters (1744-1828) graduated from the College of Philadelphia (later the University of Pennsylvania) in 1761 and was admitted to the Pennsylvania bar in 1763. Peters began a successful law practice and in 1768 served as a commissioner to the Indian conference at Fort Stanwix. In 1771 he became register of admiralty and held that position until 1776. During the Revolutionary War, Peters served on the Continental Congress's Board of War and later was elected to a term at the Confederation Congress. In 1792 Peters was appointed United States judge for the district of Pennsylvania and he remained on the bench until his death. *DAB.*

4. Samuel Sitgreaves (1764-1827) graduated from the University of Pennsylvania and received his degree in 1780. Sitgreaves then studied law and was admitted to the Court of Common Pleas at Philadelphia (September, 1783). He was a member not only of Pennsylvania's convention to ratify the Constitution but also of that state's constitutional convention (1790). Sitgreaves was admitted as a counsellor to the bar of the Supreme Court of the United States on February 3, 1796. He served in Congress from 1795 to 1798. In August, 1798, he was appointed to fill a vacancy as a commissioner under the provisions of Article VI of the Jay Treaty; President Adams formally appointed him in December, 1798. The commission's deliberations terminated in July, 1799, when the American commissioners withdrew. Subsequently, Sitreaves left for London at the beginning of 1800 to aid Rufus King in the negotiations intended to resolve problems in the execution of Article VI. *MBBP,* p. 311; *Catalogue of the Trustees, Officers, and Graduates of the Departments of Arts and Science and of the Honorary Graduates of the University of Pennsylvania, 1749-1880* (Philadelphia: Society of the Alumni, 1880), p. 31; *BDAC;* Moore, *International Adjudications,* 3:18, 233-68, 350; *SEJ,* 1:296-97; *ASP, Foreign Relations,* 2:385.

5. This quotation (with different punctuation: " 'Tis from high Life high Characters are drawn") comes from Alexander Pope's *Epistles to Several Persons (Moral Essays),* Epistle 1, To Sir Richard Temple, Lord Viscount Cobham, line 87 in the Yale 1951 edition. The poem was first published in 1734. Alexander Pope, *The Poems of Alexander Pope,* vol. 3, part 2, *Epistles to Several Persons (Moral Essays),* ed. F. W. Bateson (New Haven: Yale University Press, 1951), pp. 15, 20.

Russell's Gazette ————————————————————————
September 10, 1798   Boston, Massachusetts

DIED.

At Edenton, on the 22d[1] ult. the Honorable JAMES WILLSON, one of the
Associate Judges of the Federal Court of the United States.[2] The Judge, with
his lady, had resided in that place near eight months, in a very private manner.
A few days previous to his death, he was taken with symptoms of the fever,
so prevalent there at this season of the year. From his refusing medical assistance, the fever increased with great rapidity, and put a period to his existence,
on the fourth day of its progress. He has left a disconsolate widow at a distance
from her relations, and in an unhappy climate to lament his loss. His remains,
attended by the most respectable inhabitants, was next day committed to the
earth.

(Boston) September 10, 1798. Date and place are from the newspaper.
   Reprinted in the *New-Hampshire Gazette* (Portsmouth), September 11, 1798.
   1. James Wilson died on August 21, not August 22; see "Appointments to the Bench," under
"James Wilson: Appointment as Associate Justice in 1789," James Iredell to Timothy Pickering,
August 25, 1798.
   2. Other newspapers printed briefer notices of James Wilson's death. *Commercial Advertiser* (New
York), September 10; *Philadelphia Gazette,* September 12; *Independent Chronicle* (Boston), Septem-
ber 17; *Georgia Gazette* (Savannah), September 20.

Benjamin Rush to John Adams ————————————————————
September 14, 1798   "Two miles from" Philadelphia, Pennsylvania

. . . My Brother in a letter which[1] I have just received from him declines the
appointment I solicited for him in my letter to you a few days ago.[2] He gives
                                          as a candidate
several reasons for not wishing to be considered ‸ for it _ The chief One is _
a belief that it will be acceptable to Judge Peters, and that his claims for past
Services, and from his present Office entitle him to it. Had I believed with
my Brother, that our friend Mr Peters would accept of the appointment, I
should not have taken the step that I did in favor of my ~~favor~~ Brother. Added
to other considerations, his experience in the business of our federal Courts
                                          to
should entitle him to a preference of ‸ any man in Pennsylvania. _ . . .

ARS (MHi, Adams Manuscript Trust). Marked as "[Encl. 19 Sept 1798];" this letter was enclosed
in a letter from Timothy Pickering to John Adams on that date.
   1. The "w" is written over "fr."
   2. For a reference to Benjamin Rush's letter supporting his brother, Jacob Rush, for a seat on
the Court, see Timothy Pickering to John Adams, September 7, 1798; for Jacob Rush's letter to
Benjamin Rush, see September 8, 1798.

Daily Advertiser ————————————————————————————
September 14, 1798   New York, New York

The Hon JAMES WILSON, Esq. one of the Associate Judges of the Supreme Court of the United States, died at Edenton, N. Carolina, last month. He was highly distinguished for his literary and legal abilities; and during the late war, and in the formation and adoption of our present constitution, rendered essential services to his country. His name is enrolled among her worthies.

(New York) September 14, 1798. The date and place are those of the newspaper.

Samuel Sitgreaves to James McHenry ————————————————
September 16, 1798   Easton, Pennsylvania

. . . I have heard that my old Friend & Master, M.̣ Wilson is dead at Newbern, N Carol.ạ_ [1] I would not be deemed importunate_ nor unthankful for the recent Proof of confidence which I have received from the Executive_ [2] [*letters inked out*] But a Man is naturally ambitious to acquire the Honors of his own Profession_ and my own particular Wishes have for some time past pointed to a Seat in the Supreme Court of the United States for their ultimate Gratification_ I am persuaded that I am essentially indebted to your good Offices for my late appointment, and I trust You will believe that I have had the proper Sensibility of my Obligation_ Will you, if it should not interfere with better Views, think of me again_ I hope I do not overrate my own Abilities in aspiring to the Bench_ But of this You are a much better Judge than I can be_ . . .

ARS (DLC, James McHenry Papers).
    1. James Wilson died at Edenton, North Carolina.
    2. The temporary appointment of Samuel Sitgreaves to be one of the commissioners appointed to hear British debt cases under Article VI of the Jay Treaty was made in August, 1798. Moore, *International Adjudications,* p. 18; *SEJ,* 1:297.

Samuel Sitgreaves to Timothy Pickering ————————————————
September 16, 1798   Easton, Pennsylvania

. . . I have heard that my old Friend & Master, M.̣ Wilson, is dead at Newbern, N Carolina_ [1] I would not be deemed importunate_ or insensible of the recent Proof which I have received of the Confidence of the Executive [2] But a Man's Ambition naturally points to the appropriate Honors of his own Profession; and I will avow that a Seat in the Supreme Court of the United States has been the favorite and ultimate Object of my Wishes_ I will not say more than thus respectfully to intimate the Direction of my own Hopes, founded perhaps on too partial an Estimate of my own Capacity._ . . .

ARS (MHi, Adams Manuscript Trust). Marked as "[Encl. 19 Sept. 1798]." This letter was enclosed in a letter from Timothy Pickering to John Adams of September 19, 1798.

1. James Wilson died at Edenton, North Carolina.

2. See note to Samuel Sitgreaves to James McHenry, September 16, 1798.

Timothy Pickering to Benjamin Rush
September 19, 1798 Trenton, New Jersey

. . . Your letter expressing your earnest desire that your brother might be appointed to fill the vacant seat on the Bench of the supreme court I forwarded immediately to the President.[1] Your letter of the 14th mentioning your Brothers declining the appointment I shall forward by this days mail. But it may not be improper to add, that I do not think the place will be offered to Judge Peters; and if it were to be offered, I am pretty sure he would not accept of it. I believe no employment in the gift of government would have any influence to separate him, for a considerable part of every year, from his family. In a pecuniary point of view, I suppose his present office better. ___ I do not know the Presidents ideas on the subject: but as there is not a necessity for it, should suppose that he would not instantly make the appointment. If time be allowed, characters eminently qualified, not now thought of, may present. . . .

ARS (PHi, Gratz Collection); APcS (MHi, Timothy Pickering Papers). Addressed "Philadelphia." Postmarked by hand "Trenton 19 Sep."

1. See Timothy Pickering to John Adams, September 7, 1798.

Timothy Pickering to Samuel Sitgreaves
September 19, 1798 Trenton, New Jersey

Trenton   Sept. 19. 1798

Dear Sir,

Last evening I received your letter of the 16th and this day shall forward it to the President, your own expressions appearing to me the fittest to make known to him your wishes. I do not know to what point he directs his views to find a successor to Judge Wilson whose death was communicated to me early by Judge Iredell; and his letter I immediately transmitted to the President.

I am with great respect   and esteem, dear sir,   your obt servant

Timothy Pickering

Samuel Sitgreaves Esqr

APcS (MHi, Timothy Pickering Papers).

Theodore Sedgwick to John Adams ——————————
September 25, 1798   Stockbridge, Massachusetts

Stockbridge   25ᵗʰ Septᵣ 1798.

Sir,

By the death of Judge Willson there is a vacancy on the bench of the supreme court. Whether I may be deemed competent to supply that vacancy, or whether it may be thought proper to appoint another Judge, from this State, I am ignorant. _ [1] Pardon, Sir, my thus suggesting a wish _ I should not have done it, but from a fear, that my friends, will compel me, again, to serve in the house of Representatives. The sacrafices which I have made, and which are exacted of me, are more than the just claims of a numerous family will authorise. I would have prefered ‸ a station wholly private to any other; but this the friends of the government, will not permit, withou[t] (what is impossible,) an absolute denial on my part_ An office, incompatible with a Legislative appointment, is the only mean of my escape._ Again I pray you, Sir, pardon this address, which I fear will be thought improp[er] or presumptuous. and believe me to be, with great esteem & sincere personal attachment,

   Sir,   your most obedᵗ Servᵗ

Theodore Sedgwick

The President

ARS (MHi, Adams Manuscript Trust).

1. For Theodore Sedgwick's legal background, see note to Theodore Sedgwick to John Jay, September 23, 1789.

Theodore Sedgwick (1746-1813) by Charles Balthazar Julien Févret de Saint-Mémin (1770-1852). Engraving, 1801. Courtesy National Portrait Gallery, Smithsonian Institution.

Robert Troup to Rufus King ——————————————————
October 2, 1798   New York, New York

           lately
... Judge Wilson ˄ died in North Carolina in the hands of the sheriff— a victim to misfortune & liquor? ...

ARS (NHi, Rufus King Papers).
   Robert Troup (1757-1832), an Albany lawyer, had studied law with both John Jay and William Paterson. In 1796 he was appointed United States judge for the district of New York. *DAB.*

Bushrod Washington to George Washington ——————————
October 19, 1798   Richmond, Virginia

... Upon my return to this place I met with a Commission from the President of the United States appointing me one of the Judges of the Supreme Court. This appointment I have accepted, and was induced thereto by the strongest motives.

I was very unwilling to abandon a profession, to which I was much attached, and to the study of which I had devoted the greatest part of my life. A situation which permits me to pursue it, and to improve the Knowledge which I have acquired in this science, without endangering my sight (already considerably injured) could not fail to be agreable to me.

Independent of this consideration, I could not upon a small piece of poor land in Westmoreland have paid debts which I owe, & supported my family.

Knowing the wish you had, that I should be a Candidate for Congress, I have felt much uneasiness lest my acceptance of this appointment should be disagreable to you. The desire of attempting to serve my country in that line had also created in myself an anxiety for success in the election, altho' I foresaw the extreme inconvenience which would result from it, in my private affairs, I was however willing to make the sacrifice. I trust that this candid statement of my situation will be an apology with you for having relinquished my first intention, and I flatter myself that my services will not be less useful to my Country in the office which I now hold, than they would have been in the legislative counsels.— ...

ARS (DLC, George Washington Papers).

George Washington to Bushrod Washington ——————————
October 24, 1798   Mount Vernon, Fairfax County, Virginia

Your letter of the 19ᵗʰ instant came duly to hand.— I think you were perfectly
                                            Judge
right in accepting the appointment of Associate ˄ — Not only for the reasons you have mentioned, but on every other account.— ...

ARS (ViMtV). Addressed to Bushrod Washington "In the Southern Circuit." Postmarked by hand "Alex 26 Oct^r."

James Iredell to William Cushing ————————————
October 28, 1798   Edenton, North Carolina

. . . Our unfortunate Friend Judge Wilson died the very night of my arrival from Philadelphia (the 21 August) and was speechless when I arrived. He had been for some time in ill health, but his last illness was but of a few days duration, and his death was undoubtedly owing to the extreme agony of his mind. . . . I have been much concerned in not hearing of an appointment to supply his place, as it was of great moment the Southern Circuit should not fall through _.[1] I informed Mr Pickering of the vacancy as early as possible, and at the same time of the impracticability of my attending it, which I would have done if I could rather than it should have fallen through. _ [2] . . .

ARS (MHi, Robert Treat Paine Papers). Addressed "Baltimore,   Maryland." Marked as "Recommended to the   care of the Honorable   Judge Chase." Endorsed inaccurately as "Oct^o 25."

1. Three days after James Iredell wrote this letter, the *State Gazette of North-Carolina*, which was published in Edenton, noted the appointment of Bushrod Washington. The first newspaper to carry a notice of the appointment was the *Federalist* (Trenton) of October 8, 1798. Other newspapers also noted it: *Claypoole's American Daily Advertiser* (Philadelphia), October 15; *Oracle of the Day* (Portsmouth, New Hampshire), October 27; and the *Georgia Gazette* (Savannah), November 8.

2. See "Appointments to the Bench," under "James Wilson: Appointment as Associate Justice in 1789," James Iredell to Timothy Pickering, August 25, 1798.

William Cushing to James Iredell ————————————
November 9, 1798   Baltimore, Maryland

. . . You have heard that Mr. Bushrod Washington is appointed to the bench, and I am told he has gone on for the Southern Circuit, and hope it is so. . . .

Pr (Printed in *MJI,* 2:539-40).

Cyrus Griffin to John Adams ————————————
November 10, 1798   Williamsburg, Virginia

. . . May I take the freedom, illustrious Sir, to mention that if consistent with the maxims of your wise Administration, I could wish most fervently to change my Situation upon the Bench, and would willingly take some other respectable employment. _ Indeed, Sir, I am the very oldest civil Officer under the general Government; that is, I have served more years than any other man, from early in the year 1778 to the present period, and sometimes in very high Stations, at the expence of all the property I possessed; and now with a large

family & nothing but a small Salary to maintain them, and even one fourth of that Salary at least I am obliged to spend in Public houses & other charges necessarily attending the duties of my Office at the stated & special Courts, the business of the District being probably more than any three Courts in the Union, & the Supreme Judges tell me, that the business of the Circuit Court for Virginia is considerably more than all the Union together. Nor have I omitted a single Court since my return to this Country from the Seat of Government at New York; no man can be more attentive to the requisites of his Station, and surely no person can be more federal, or a more strenuous advocate for the Administration _ & though at first view it seems to bear a little hard, and is certainly a great discouragement for men to be active and faithful in discharging their respective duties if they are always to remain as they set out _ and surely a laudable ambition to be promoted, & a parental anxiety about the better welfare of a man's family can never be considered as reprehensible in a virtuous Republic like ours; yet Sir I am very ready to confess that in point of Law Talents, if talents are the only criterion, that I am not equal to many other Gentlemen, a Marshall or a Washington for instance, tho' my Education has been a more systematical one; and thus knowing my inferiority in this respect whatever appointments you may think proper to make will always be highly satisfactory to me, & to every good federal Character _
                                                              my
yet this consideration of diffidence in ˄ Law talents will operate as an additional reason to pray you, Sir, for a change of my position if convenient & consistent with your arrangements in future. . . .

ARS (MHi, Adams Manuscript Trust).

James Iredell to Timothy Pickering
December 1, 1798 Edenton, North Carolina

. . . I wrote, the first opportunity, to inform you of Judge Wilson's death, but never have heard if the letter reached you _ [1] I am convinced some accident must have prevented the receipt of my letter or your answer _ I had great pleasure in hearing of M<u>r</u> Washington's appointment, and flatter myself he went on in time, at least to attend the Georgia and North Carolina Courts, which were the most important _. . . .

ARS (MHi, Timothy Pickering Papers). Endorsed "rec<u>d</u> 11."
1. See "Appointments to the Bench," under "James Wilson: Appointment as Associate Justice in 1789," August 25, 1798.

Aurora
December 21, 1798 Philadelphia, Pennsylvania

The tories know the *road* that leads to *profit,* and travel that way most diligently: *King, Ellsworth, Smith of South Carolina, Murray, Sitgreaves, Smith* of

New-Hampshire,[1] and a score more of members of congress, by preaching up executive infallibility, have got into good warm births, and Dana, Harper, Sewall, Craik, Rutledge and *little Otis*,[2] are now opening their mouths for the fruit of executive favor.

(Philadelphia) December 21, 1798. Date and place are from the newspaper.

1. Rufus King, senator from New York (July 16, 1789-May 23, 1796), resigned when appointed minister plenipotentiary to Great Britain. *BDAC,* pp. 56, 1167.

Oliver Ellsworth, senator from Connecticut (March 4, 1789-March 8, 1796), resigned after being appointed chief justice of the United States Supreme Court. *BDAC.*

William L. Smith, congressman from South Carolina (March 4, 1789-July 10, 1797), resigned when appointed minister plenipotentiary to Portugal. *BDAC.*

William Vans Murray, congressman from Maryland (March 4, 1791-March 3, 1797), resigned after being appointed minister resident to the United Netherlands. *BDAC.*

Samuel Sitgreaves, congressman from Pennsylvania (March 4, 1795-December 20, 1798), resigned after the Senate confirmed his appointment as a commissioner for carrying into effect Article VI of the Jay Treaty. *BDAC,* pp. 59, 1607; SEJ, 1:296-97.

Jeremiah Smith, congressman from New Hampshire (March 4, 1791-July 26, 1797), resigned after being appointed United States attorney for the district of New Hampshire. *BDAC.*

2. Samuel W. Dana, congressman from Connecticut (January 3, 1797-May 10, 1810). *BDAC.*

Robert G. Harper, congressman from South Carolina (February 9, 1795-March 3, 1801). *BDAC,* pp. 54, 1010.

Samuel Sewall, congressman from Massachusetts (December 7, 1796-January 10, 1800). *BDAC.*

William Craik, congressman from Maryland (December 5, 1796-March 3, 1801). *BDAC.*

John Rutledge, Jr., congressman from South Carolina (March 4, 1797-March 3, 1803). *BDAC.*

Harrison Gray Otis, congressman from Massachusetts (March 4, 1797-March 3, 1801). *BDAC.*

Aurora —————————————————————————————————————

January 16, 1799   Philadelphia, Pennsylvania

DISSENT of the undersigned, members of the House of Representatives, of the Commonwealth of Pennsylvania, from the address to the President of the United States, adopted by said House.[1]

. . .

We do not consider it matter of high approbation, uninformed as we are of the motives of the executive, that the great share of official powers, held by the natives of two of the eastern States (before unequal and preponderant) was so increased by the President, that finally out of five executive and judiciary departments, the heads of four were natives of Massachusetts, and Connecticut, leaving to the citizens of all the rest of the eastern, middle, and southern States, but a single one of those highly influential and weighty offices.[2] Too well informed, that not one native of Pennsylvania is in any of these stations, nor in the diplomatic foreign missions, and not having even the vacated place of associate Judge of the Supreme Court filled again from Pennsylvania, we may be permitted, on the footing of honest pride of native attachment, without arraigning the authority or purity of the executive, to lament, that so important a state should have so small a participation in the administration of the Federal Government.

. . .

For these, as well as other considerations, we the undersigned conceive it to be our duty to dissent from the high and *unqualified* address of the house of representatives of the commonwealth of Pennsylvania, to the President of the United States.

NATHAN BOILEAU   DANIEL ROSE
P. FRAILY   CHS. SHOEMAKER
JOHN COOLBAUGH   SIMON SNYDER
JOHN CUNNINGHAM   DANIEL UDREE
FRED. CONRAD   ISAAC WARRELL
MANUEL ERYE   ISSAC WEAVER jr
GEORGE INGELS   JACOB FALLMER
AARON LYLE   J HARTZELL
JOHN M'DOWELL   ABRAHAM HORN
THOS M'WHORTER   JAMES HARRIS
WILLIAM PENROSE   JOSEPH HUSTON.

(Philadelphia) January 16, 1799. Date and place are those of the headline.

This article had been published in an imperfect form by the *Aurora* on January 15.

1. President John Adams addressed the members of the House of Representatives and the Senate on December 8, 1798, at the beginning of the third session of the Fifth Congress. Adams's address dealt largely with foreign affairs, particularly the threatening state of relations between the United States and France. *HRJ,* 5th Cong., pp. 401-4. On December 21, 1798, the Pennsylvania House of Representatives presented John Adams with an address pledging their cooperation with the federal government "in averting all foreign influence and detecting domestic intrigue." The address was published in the *Aurora* (Philadelphia) on December 24, 1798.

2. The information given in this article about the numbers and residences of members of the executive departments is incorrect. There were six executive departments in January, 1799. They were headed by Secretary of State Timothy Pickering, born in Massachusetts but a citizen of Pennsylvania; Secretary of the Treasury Oliver Wolcott, Jr., of Connecticut; Secretary of War James McHenry of Maryland; Attorney General Charles Lee of Virginia; Postmaster General Joseph Habersham of Georgia; and Secretary of the Navy Benjamin Stoddert of Maryland. Oliver Ellsworth of Connecticut was chief justice of the Supreme Court. *BDAC,* p. 13.

Bushrod Washington to William A. Washington ──────────
January 19, 1799   Walnut Farm, Westmoreland County, Virginia

. . . I leave home tomorrow . . . I feel the greatest anxiety to call & see you, but it is impossible, & yet get to Phil^a in time. I know You will excuse me; since the necessity of being at the Supreme Court & prepared to take my seat at the beginning of the Session is indespensible. . . .

ARS (NjMoNP). Addressed "Haywood." Walnut Farm was the home of Bushrod Washington's brother, Corbin Washington. John Walter Wayland, *The Washingtons and Their Homes* (Staunton, Va.: McClure Press, 1944), pp. 125, 318, 330.

William Augustine Washington (1757-1810) and Bushrod Washington were cousins. Their fathers were stepbrothers. Reginald Buchanan Henry, comp., *Genealogies of the Families of the American Presidents* (Rutland, Vt.: Tuttle, 1935), pp. 1, 27, 75.

Samuel Chase to James Iredell ————————————————
March 17, 1799 Baltimore, Maryland

... For five weeks after you left Me[1] I was [*letters inked out*] confined to my Bed-Chamber, and three to my Bed. for some Days I was very ill. I was so very weak, that I could not walk across my Room without assistance. it is 14 Days, this Day, since I came below Stairs, and I have been only able, this last Week, to go in a close Carriage into the City for Exercise. I have not the least Hope of being able to travel in time to attend the Circuit Court at New York, on the 1st day of next Month. a Relapse would be fatal. my Cough is still bad and the Spitting continues. my Lungs are so very weak, that I cannot bear the least any but very gentle Exercise.[2] ...

ARS (NcD, James Iredell Sr. and Jr. Papers). Addressed to James Iredell at "Mrs Yorks No 2d Street No 62 Philadelphia."
  1. James Iredell had been passing through on his way to attend the Court in Philadelphia.
  2. Samuel Chase wrote a similar letter to William Paterson, also on March 17, 1799. Miscellaneous Manuscripts Collection, NHi.

Thomas B. Adams to William Cranch ————————————————
July 15, 1799 Philadelphia, Pennsylvania

... On the removal of the Seat of Government to the City, the Office of Clerk of the Sup: Court of U. S. will most probably become vacant, as the present incumbent, Mr Sam: Bayard, has since his return from England taken up his abode, chiefly at New York, with a design, as I hear & believe, of continuing there altogether. He will of course resign the Office of Clerk and as some one must be appointed in his stead, who resides either on the spot or near it, I should be very glad to assist you in making interest for the appointment, should you think it worth an application. The convenience of your situation, suggested the idea to me, and I mention it thus early, because I think that interest is making for the office by a person here, who though a friend of mine & a brother chip,[1] has not in my opinion, pretentions equal to yours. The appointment rests with the Judges, & I am persuaded an application from you would meet success— Judges Cushing, Ellsworth & Chase, would be those to whom I would take the liberty of addressing myself in your behalf, if you will give me leave— The Supreme Court will sit here next month, Yellow fever a part. The duties of the Clerkship are by no means arduous & they are entirely professional— The Records must be at the seat of Government, and though the emoluments are inconsiderable, it serves as an introduction to other business— At all events there can be no harm in applying for it, & that seasonably. I wish it were in my power to hold up a more seducing prospect for your hopes, but I am a perfect nulity in point of influence respecting appointments— indeed I rejoyce, generally speaking, that I am. Write me your own notions of this matter ...

ARS (OCHP, William Cranch Papers). Endorsed "Ans^d 25th_   rec^d 24_." William Cranch's answering letter not found.

Thomas Boylston Adams (1772-1832), son of President John Adams, had been a fledgling lawyer in Philadelphia before leaving to join his brother John Quincy Adams in Holland in 1794. Thomas Boylston Adams remained in Europe until January, 1799, when he returned to America and joined his family in Philadelphia. He and William Cranch were first cousins. Mitchell, *New Letters of Abigail Adams,* pp. 21, 39, 210-11; Charles W. Akers, *Abigail Adams: An American Woman* (Boston: Little, Brown, 1980), pp. 133-34.

William Cranch (1769-1855), nephew of President John Adams, had been admitted to the Massachusetts bar in 1790. In 1794 Cranch went to the District of Columbia as the lawyer for the North American Land Company, promoted by his cousin and brother-in-law, James Greenleaf. The land speculating company was a disastrous failure, and Cranch needed a post to recover from his financial difficulties. In 1800 John Adams appointed him a commissioner of public buildings for the District of Columbia and in February, 1801, appointed him to the bench of the United States Circuit Court for the District of Columbia. For the rest of his life, Cranch served on the bench, where his career was distinguished. He acted as reporter for the Supreme Court of the United States from 1802 until his replacement by Henry Wheaton at the February 1816 term. *DAB,* entries for William Cranch and Henry Wheaton; Mitchell, *New Letters of Abigail Adams,* pp. 85n, 86n, 211-12.

1. "A person of the same trade or calling." *Lexicon Balatronicum: A Dictionary of Buckish Slang, University Wit, and Pickpocket Eloquence* (1811; reprint ed., Northfield, Ill.: Digest Books, 1971).

Samuel Johnston to Hannah Iredell —————————————————
July 27, 1799 Hermitage, New Hanover County, North Carolina

. . . I was very much concerned to learn, from Mr Iredell's letters, which came
                                                                          I
by the last Post, that he was so much indisposed ~~he~~ ᶺ fear his Zeal for the Service will induce him to expose himself more than he ought. . . .

ARS (Nc-Ar, Charles E. Johnson Collection). Addressed "Edenton."

Thomas B. Adams to William Cranch —————————————————
July 30, 1799 Philadelphia, Pennsylvania

. . . I am happy to find that the suggestion I made was acceptable to you;[1] I shall of course mention the matter to such of the Judges as I know and probably in the course of a few days, should the Supreme Court be held in the City as usual. A direct application on your part to Judge Cushing, would not be amiss, and I have little doubt but you will obtain the appointment without difficulty_ The emoluments are but ten dollars per day during the Session of the Court_ a very trifling affair, but sufficient to compensate the labor of the Office, which is very little.

ARS (OCHP, William Cranch Papers). Addressed "Georgetown   Ptmk"; i.e., on the Potomac River. Endorsed "rec^d Augt 2^d_." Postmarked "PHI   30   JL."

1. In a letter dated July 15, 1799 (q.v.), Thomas B. Adams had suggested that William Cranch consider applying for appointment as the clerk of the Supreme Court.

Philadelphia Gazette ————————————————————————
August 5, 1799   Philadelphia, Pennsylvania

The August term of the Supreme Court of the United States commenced its sitting this day. We are sorry to learn, that Judge Iredell by an indisposition, will not be able to come on to this city.

(Philadelphia) August 5, 1799. Date and place are those of the headline.

This item also appeared in the *Federal Gazette* (Baltimore), August 7, 1799, and in *Russell's Gazette* (Boston), August 15, 1799.

A brief notice about the Court's sitting was printed in the *Newport Mercury* (Newport, Rhode Island), August 20, 1799.

Hannah Wilson to James Iredell ————————————————————
August 7, 1799   Spring Hill, Philadelphia County, Pennsylvania

. . . On Monday we passed the day at D[r] White's,[1] I mentioned to them that the Court opened on that day, and that you was in Philadelphia, Betsy[2] told me that M[r] Patterson had received a letter from you[3] and that you was prevented comeing by indisposition; knowing your punctuality I was afraid you was very sick, but I was relieved from great anxiety by your letter which I received last evening;[4] every individual of the family felt the disappointment.
. . .

ARS (Nc-Ar, Charles E. Johnson Collection). Addressed "Edenton   North Carolina." Postmarked "PHI   8   AU." Spring Hill, the country estate of Samuel Breck, Hannah Wilson's host, was located in what was then Lower Dublin Township of Philadelphia County. Today it is within the city limits of Philadelphia. S. F. Hotchkin, *The Bristol Pike* (Philadelphia: George W. Jacobs, 1893), pp. 206-10; Thomas F. Gordon, *A Gazetteer of the State of Pennsylvania* (1832; reprint ed., New Orleans: Polyanthos, 1975), p. 145; Samuel Breck, *Genealogy of the Breck Family* (Omaha: Rees Publishing, 1889), pp. 40-42, 206.

1. William White (1748-1836) was the Episcopal bishop of Pennsylvania and rector of Christ Church in Philadelphia. White and James Wilson had become close friends in Philadelphia in the 1760s, and following Wilson's death, White became one of the administrators of his estate. White had received his doctorate in divinity from the University of Pennsylvania in 1782. *DAB;* Smith, *James Wilson,* pp. 28-29, 390; Bird Wilson, *Memoir of the Life of the Right Reverend William White, D.D., Bishop of the Protestant Episcopal Church in the State of Pennsylvania* (Philadelphia: James Kay, Jr., & Brother, 1839), p. 73.

2. Probably Elizabeth White (1776-1831), daughter of William White. Thomas Harrison Montgomery, *Descendants of Colonel Thomas White* (n.p., 1879), p. 26.

3. Letter not found.

4. Letter not found.

Thomas B. Adams to Abigail Adams ——————————————————
August 10, 1799   Philadelphia, Pennsylvania

. . . The Supreme Court of the U. S. adjourned this day— Little business was done, because there was little to do— . . .

ARS (MHi, Adams Manuscript Trust). This excerpt is a short postscript appended to a letter begun on August 1, 1799.

Bushrod Washington to James Iredell ——————————
August 20, 1799   Alexandria, District of Columbia

. . . Upon my arrival at Baltimore about the first of the month, I heard from Judge Chace, with great concern that you were too much indisposed to attend the supreme Court. The fatigue to which you had been exposed during the Circuit[1] was well calculated to produce this consequence, and you would have acted imprudently I think to venture upon so long a Journey in your then state of health. It will afford me very sincere pleasure to hear of your recovery.

Judge Cushing was seized upon the road by an indisposition so severe as to prevent his proceeding. Fortunately, there was no business brought on which involved any question of importance or difficulty, & the term was consequently short. I went from and returned to Baltimore with our brother Chace, whose excellent flow of spirits & good sense rendered pleasant a Journey which would otherwise have been fatiguing & disagreable. . . .

ARS (Nc-Ar, Charles E. Johnson Collection). Addressed "Edenton   North Carolina." Postmarked "ALEX. VA   AUG   26." Endorsed "Ans^d." James Iredell's answering letter not found.

1. James Iredell's circuit riding the previous spring had been especially arduous because of the trial in Pennsylvania of John Fries and the Northampton Insurgents. Francis Wharton, *State Trials of the United States During the Administrations of Washington and Adams* (Philadelphia: Carey and Hart, 1849), pp. 458-648. The increasing emotional strain on Iredell during the course of the trial is apparent in his letters to his wife Hannah on May 2, May 11, May 16, and May 19, 1799. Charles E. Johnson Collection, Nc-Ar.

Oliver Ellsworth to William Cushing ——————————
August 24, 1799   Windsor, Connecticut

. . . I was favoured with your letter at Philadelphia,[1] and, with the rest of your Brethren, regretted very much that you failed of reaching us. And we all agreed that it never would do for you to think of travelling without Mrs Cushing. . . .

ARS (MHi, Robert Treat Paine Papers). Addressed "Scituate   near Boston." Postmarked "HARTFORD   AUG   27."

1. Letter not found.

James Iredell to [Sarah (Dolbeare)?] Gray ——————————
September 6, 1799   Edenton, North Carolina

. . . I was . . . unluckily taken sick myself about the time my duty called me to Philadelphia, and prevented (much to my regret) going there, but I have been
for a considerable time ~~quite~~ entirely recovered _. . . .

ADfS (Nc-Ar, Charles E. Johnson Collection). Marked "Copy of a Letter to Mᵣˢ Gray."

The "Mᵣˢ Gray" that James Iredell refers to probably is Sarah (Dolbeare) Gray (1746-1811), Hannah (Gray) Wilson's mother. Sarah Dolbeare married Ellis Gray in 1770. Edward Doubleday Harris, "The Dolbeares of Boston," in *A Few Facts Relating to the Origin and History of John Dolbeare of Boston and some of his descendants,* ed. Arthur Dimon Osborne (New Haven, 1893), p. 6; Raymond, *Gray Genealogy,* p. 192; *Boston Marriages,* 30:330.

Thomas B. Adams to William Cranch ——————————
September 24, 1799   Germantown, Pennsylvania

. . . Your favor of the 19ᵗʰ inst.[1] is before me, with the enclosure for Judge Cushing,[2] which I shall forward with my next letters to Quincy, with request to have it sent on. The terms & expressions of your application, strike me as perfectly apt & proper. Judge Cushing, was taken ill on his journey to Philadelphia, and returned home, but the Court met & dispatched business as usual. I waited on the Chief Justice and mentioned to him what I had heard, of the intended resignation of Mᵣ Bayard, of the Clerkship of the Supreme Court, on the removal of Government to the federal City, & at the same time named you as a competent, well qualified & convenient Successor to the Office, requesting his influence to promote your appointment. He received the application with flattering deference and promised to lay it before his colleagues, so that if priority of intercession should have an influence on pretentions of equal degree, your's should claim its rank, which I presume is unquestionably the first: I thought further interference on my part superfluous; nevertheless if occasion should offer, I will follow up the affair yet further, for I am desirous you should obtain this appointment, though its advantages & emoluments may be remote. There is no doubt in my mind that Bayard will resign after the next term, in February. . . .

ARS (OCHP, William Cranch Papers). Addressed "Georgetown   Ptmk." Postmarked "PHI 25   SE." Endorsed "recᵈ Octʳ 1ˢᵗ   Ansᵈ Novʳ 15ᵗʰ." William Cranch's answering letter not found.

1. Letter not found.
2. Enclosure not found.

Newport Mercury ————————————————————
October 28, 1799   Halifax, North Carolina

On the 20th inst. departed this life, at Edenton, after a few days illness, the Hon. John[1] Iredell, Esq; one of the associate Justices of the Supreme Court of the United States.

He was born in the city of Bristol, of respectable Irish parents, and came to this country at an early age. At the commencement of the revolutionary war he held a lucrative and important office under the crown in this state,[2] but a warm and decided friend to the rights and liberties of America, he espoused her cause with ardour, and devoted his best services to her interest.— At a gloomy and perilous period of the war he was appointed Attorney-General of the state, the duties of which office he executed with no less fidelity to the state than honour and reputation to himself.

On the formation of the Federal Constitution, he was chosen member of the Convention of this state, of 1789, and was one of the most able and eloquent advocates for its adoption, soon after North-Carolina became a member of the union, he was appointed to the important office he held at the time of his death. His ability and virtue, his impartiality and humanity as a Judge, made him no less revered than esteemed and beloved in every state of the union— in his death, therefore, the United States may deplore the loss of one of her most faithful and upright servants, and the state of North-Carolina of one of her brightest ornaments.

In the domestic and social virtues, he had but few equals and no superior. The kind and affectionate husband, the tender and indulgent parent, the generous and humane master, the sincere and benevolent friend, the virtuous and honest man, were happily combined in his character, and will induce all those who had the pleasure of his acquaintance to lament his death as a public misfortune.

(Newport, Rhode Island) December 10, 1799. Date and place are those of the headline.

Reprinted in the *Virginia Argus* (Richmond) on November 12, 1799. This paper noted that the article had come from the *North-Carolina Journal* which was published in Halifax.

1. In the *Virginia Argus* (Richmond), November 12, 1799, this appears as "JAMES."

2. James Iredell had held the office of collector of the port in Edenton, North Carolina, from 1774 to 1776. *DAB*.

North-Carolina Minerva —————————————————————————————
October 29, 1799   Raleigh, North Carolina

Died at Edenton, on the 20th inst. after an illness of 36 hours, The Hon. JAMES IREDELL, one of the Associate Justices of the Supreme Court of the United States. North Carolina and her Sister States, have great cause to regret the loss of this most valuable man.

(Raleigh) October 29, 1799. Date and place are those of the headline.

This article also appeared in *Claypoole's American Daily Advertiser* (Philadelphia), November 11, 1799. The *Aurora* (Philadelphia) on November 12 printed a shortened version which also appeared in the *Connecticut Courant* (Hartford) on November 18.

Other newspapers printed slightly different reports. On November 7 the *City Gazette* (Charleston) reported that Iredell had died "after three days illness" from a case of "yellow fever." The *Federal Gazette* (Baltimore) on November 8 and the *Commercial Advertiser* (New York) on November 12 both printed brief articles that could have been based on the *North-Carolina Minerva* article, but the *Commercial Advertiser* stated that Iredell had died "after an illness of 37 hours." The *Daily Advertiser* (New York) on November 13 printed a similar article to that which had appeared in the *Commercial Advertiser;* it also appeared in the *Providence Journal* on November 20, 1799.

Augusta Herald ———————————————————————————
   October 29, 1799   Raleigh, North Carolina

Died, at Edenton, in this state, on Sunday the 20th instant, after a very short illness, that valuable and highly respected citizen, the Honorable *James Iredell,* one of the Associate Judges of the United States. His memory will long be held dear by those who knew him best, on account of the many and eminent services rendered to this state; and his philanthrophy and suavity of manners, had procured him friends amongst some of the wisest and best men in every part of the Union, who will deeply regret his loss.

(Augusta, Georgia) November 13, 1799. Date and place are those of the headline.

Samuel Johnston to Arthur Iredell ————————————————————
   October 30, 1799   Edenton, North Carolina

~~The painful task of announcing~~ It is with the greatest concern and
           that
affliction ᐱ I have to perform the most painful task of announcing to you the death of my dearest friend, your Brother Judge Iredell, he expired after a few days illness on Sunday the 20ᵗʰ of this month at his [*letters inked out*] House in this Town, ~~notwithstanding the~~ [~~prescription of our most Useful P?~~] [*word inked out*] ~~he was attended~~ [to?] I happened to be here [*letters inked out*] with my family on a Visit every thing was done for him that the utmost tenderness &
           Physician
affection could suggest, the ~~Doctor~~ ᐱ at the time he was taken ill was attending
        then   they
two of his Children who were ᐱ dangerously ill, ~~but~~ have since recovered, but are still very weak & low, ~~poor things~~ when I tell you that he was the best of husbands and a most tender and ~~affectionate~~ [*letters inked out*] indulgent parent I need not add that his family is unconsoleable for their loss, no man could be more loved and esteemed not only by his family & friends but by the Citizens of thes¹ ~~Countr~~ United States in general, by whom his loss will be
           a tender
most sincerely lamented and most justly, he was ~~a good~~ ᐱ Husband & Father, a faithful friend, an able & upright Judge and a steady Patriot. . . .

ADf (NcU, Hayes Collection). Noted by Samuel Johnston that he "sent two Copies_ one V͟i͟a N. York, the other Philadelphia" to "The Reverend Mʳ Arthur Iredell of Glynde in the County of Sussex."
   1 Samuel Johnston originally wrote "this." He crossed out the "s" and left the "i" to be read as an "e."

"A Friend to Justice" to John Adams ————————————
November 8, 1799 Fredericksburg, Virginia

M.ʳ Adam

I have just read in the papers the death of Judge Iredall. That his place may be properly supplied is an important object with the Executive and the people. I as one of these take the liberty of recommending Major Francis T Brooke[1] of Fredericksburgh. The character of this gentleman is hardly to be surpassed, as it combines great talents & learning with unshaken integrity & patriotism __ Ch.ˢ Lee can vouch for this, but perhaps more substantially Judge Washington

a friend to Justice

Fredsbg 8ᵗʰ Nov.ʳ 99

ARS (MHi, Adams Manuscript Trust). Addressed "Philadelphia." Postmarked "FRED.ᴳ VA NOV   10."

1. Francis Taliaferro Brooke (1763-1851) served in the Revolutionary War and then studied law with his older brother Robert Brooke, who later was a governor and attorney general of Virginia. Francis Brooke was licensed as a lawyer in 1788. The next year, he was practicing law in northwestern Virginia, in present-day Morgantown, West Virginia, and was also the state's attorney for that district. Brooke represented Essex County in the Virginia House of Delegates in 1794 and 1795 and in the state Senate from 1800 to 1804. He became a judge of the Virginia General Court in 1804 and, seven years later, of the Virginia Court of Appeals. William R. Shands, "Francis Taliaferro Brooke," *Proceedings of the Virginia State Bar Association* 39 (1928): 407-21; Swem and Williams, *A Register of the General Assembly of Virginia, 1776-1918, and of the Constitutional Conventions,* p. 351; *DAB.*

John Steele to John Haywood ————————————————————
November 13, 1799 Philadelphia, Pennsylvania

. . . The death of that good, and amiable man Judge Iredell has made a vacancy in one of our important offices. I have reason to think my opinion might have some influence in the appointment of a Successor. Judge Grimke[1] of South Carolina, M.ʳ Rawle,[2] M.ʳ Lewis and Judge Rush of Pennsylv.ª, and a number to the Eastward have been mentioned. Can I with justice to the United States, and to individuals recommend Alfred Moore? Will he appear with reputation out of N.º Carolina? I am extremely anxious that all appointments which I may have any agency in bringing about should be f[illed?] with men possessing dignity of character and talent to be useful in their public stations, and ornamental members of society. Although M.ʳ Moore may never know it, I have concluded to mention him to the President. I never had intercourse enough with him to be considered an acquaintance, much less a friend, w[hi]ch I very much lament. His public & private character however I have always respected, and that for[3] ~~may~~ the present occasion is enough. Say nothing of this. __ You will perhaps hear more of it. . . .

ARS (NcU, Ernest Haywood Collection). Marked "Private." Readings have been supplied in brackets because of damage to the document.

John Steele (1764-1815), a North Carolina federalist, served in Congress from 1789 to 1793. In 1796 President Washington appointed him comptroller of the treasury, a position he held until 1802. *DAB*.

1. John Faucheraud Grimké (1752-1819) was associate judge of the South Carolina Court of Common Pleas and General Sessions. Grimké had been educated in England, where he was admitted to the Middle Temple in 1769 and graduated from Cambridge in 1774. Grimké returned to South Carolina in 1775 and fought in the Revolutionary War. A member of the South Carolina House of Representatives (1782-1790), he served as speaker in the 1785-1786 session. During the 1780s, Grimké served on a commission to revise the state laws and later wrote several legal studies. He supported adoption of the Constitution at the state convention in 1788. Grimké's judicial career began in 1783 when he was appointed to the Court of Common Pleas and General Sessions. In 1799 he became senior associate judge and served on the bench until his death in 1819. Bailey and Cooper, *Biographical Directory of the South Carolina House of Representatives*, 3:290-92.

2. William Rawle (1759-1836), of Philadelphia, had studied law with John Tabor Kempe in New York City during the Revolutionary War and in 1781 enrolled in the Middle Temple in England. Rawle returned to Philadelphia and in 1783 was admitted to the bar there. In 1791 Rawle was appointed United States attorney for the district of Pennsylvania and held that office for eight years. *DAB*.

3. John Steele seems to have squeezed the word "for" between the words "that" and "may" after crossing the latter out.

John Steele to John Haywood

November 21, 1799 [Philadelphia, Pennsylvania]

. . . I hinted at the Gentleman who might probably be [th]e Successor of our friend Judge Iredell.[1] S[ince] that letter I had a good opp.[y] of conversing on the subject at Head quarters, and stated exactly what kind of man he was when I left the State. If he is the same man still he is without doubt to be appointed. How is this to be ascertained? I replied only by postponeing the appointment, and conversing with some of the most respectable of the Representatives from the State when they arrive. Upon this footing it was left, open however to any change that circumstances might dictate. Are any of the Rep.[vs] personally his enemies? Or does he still stand so well that all would be pleased to see him distinguished? Let me have your opinion on this subject if you please, and in the m[e]an time keep the affair in reserve. . . .

ARS (NcU, Ernest Haywood Collection). Place determined by evidence in letter and contemporary letters of John Steele (Ernest Haywood Collection, NcU). Readings have been supplied in brackets because of damage to the document.

1. The "Gentleman" referred to by John Steele was Alfred Moore. See John Steele to John Haywood, November 13, 1799.

Thomas B. Adams to William Cranch ——————————————
November 25, 1799 Philadelphia, Pennsylvania

... I received with much pleasure a few days ago, your favor of the 15th instant[1] and shall not be inattentive to those parts of its contents which relate to the subject of your application for the clerkship of the Supreme Court of the U. S. and will be careful to give you seasonable notice whether your personal attendance here in February would be likely to conduce to the success of your plan. The indisposition of Judge Cushing, we hope, will not prevent his attendance at the next session, and your letter of application to him, having been transmitted by a sure conveyance, will have prepared his mind, for such fresh representations, on that subject, as it may be expedient to make when he comes here. I know not whether Judge Ellsworth communicated my application of last Summer to his Associates, but your letter to Judge Cushing is, I apprehend, the first written intercession on that subject. The interest of Judge Chase, would be serviceable, if you can secure it, and I promise my mite of representation, in your behalf, with him, if he should be here in February. Bayard will resign the Office, unless he has altered his purpose since the summer. ...

ARS (OCHP, William Cranch Papers). Addressed "Georgetown   Ptmk." Postmarked "PHI 26   NO."
  1. Letter not found.

John Steele to John Haywood ——————————————————
November 30, 1799 Philadelphia, Pennsylvania

... The moment that a successor to Iredell is fixed upon, I will let you hear from me. Moore I still think and hope will be the man. I wish I knew whether it would[1] an agreeable distinction to him; but this cannot be as I am not upon terms with him that would authorize me to hint at the thing. I once asked him previous to the election of Ashe to his late office whether he would consent to serve as a Senator,[2] and he treated me (as I thought) so cavillierly that I could not avoid feeling hurt and offended. I afterwards voted for him, because I could not conceive that he intended to doubt the sincerity of my professions, or to be otherwise uncivil to me. Not long ago I had his son appointed a captain[3] without being requested by any one to do so, and for no other reason that somebody had mentioned the young man in the spring of 1798 as a candidate for military employment[4] and perceiving that Davie[5] had not placed him on the list which he prepared and recommended. Within a few days past it has come to my knowledge incidentally that when[6] the Commission was sent to Captain Moore, both his father and himself wrote letters of thanks to Davie as the author of that unexpected distinction. The truth is, I assure you, that he had not the slightest agency in procuring it. This is in confidence and I only mention it to shew you that altho. I respect M.ʳ Moore very highly he does not know it, and perhaps considers it not worth knowing. . . .

ARS (NcU, Ernest Haywood Collection).

1. Presumably, John Steele meant to write "would be."
2. Samuel Ashe had been elected governor of North Carolina in 1795 and served until 1798. In 1795 Alfred Moore was defeated in his bid to become a United States senator. *DAB* entries for Samuel Ashe and Alfred Moore.
3. Probably Maurice Moore, who was appointed captain of the Sixth Infantry Regiment of the United States Army on May 14, 1799. Francis B. Heitman, comp., *Historical Register and Dictionary of the United States Army*, 2 vols. (1903; reprint ed., Urbana: University of Illinois Press, 1965). The information on Maurice Moore in this register probably represents two men of that name, one the brother and one the son of Alfred Moore (Marilu B. Smallwood, *Some Colonial and Revolutionary Families of North Carolina*, vol. 2 (Gainesville, Fla., 1969), p. 311). The appointment of Maurice Moore as a captain in the United States Army was confirmed by the Senate on April 9, 1800. *SEJ,* 1:343, 348.
4. The word "employment" is written over a partly erased "promotion."
5. William R. Davie, governor of North Carolina.
6. The word "when" seems to have been written over a partly erased "upon."

Aurora ——————————————————————————————
December 3, 1799   Philadelphia, Pennsylvania

Although the grass has not yet had time for growing over the grave of the late judge Iredell, it is said, (and believed) that Mr. Jerey Smith of New-Hampshire,[1] Mr. Ames of Massachusetts,[2] Mr. Bourne of Rhode-Island,[3] Mr. Benson of New-York,[4] and Mr. Harper of Baltimore,[5] had generously offered their services for the federal bench. . . .

(Philadelphia) December 3, 1799. Date and place are from the newspaper headline.

This article also appeared in the *American* (Baltimore), December 6, 1799.

1. Jeremiah Smith (1759-1842) attended first Harvard and then Queen's College (now Rutgers), from which he graduated in 1780. After studying law, he was admitted to the bar at Amherst, Hillsborough County, New Hampshire, in 1786 and opened a law practice in Peterborough, New Hampshire. Two years later he took a seat in the New Hampshire House of Representatives where he remained until his election as a congressman in 1790. He resigned his congressional duties in 1797 for an appointment as United States attorney for the district of New Hampshire, a position he held until 1800. In that year Smith became judge of probate for Rockingham County, New Hampshire. On the recommendation of John Marshall, President Adams appointed Smith as a circuit court judge on February 20, 1801, under the Judiciary Act of 1801. This position was abolished by the repeal of the 1801 act in April, 1802. Smith went on to serve in a number of distinguished posts: chief justice of New Hampshire's Superior Court of Judicature, 1802-1809; governor of New Hampshire, 1809-1810; and chief justice of New Hampshire's Supreme Judicial Court (successor to the Superior Court of Judicature), 1813-1816. *BDAC; DAB.*
2. Fisher Ames, who retired from the House of Representatives in 1797, had begun his career as a lawyer. After his graduation from Harvard in 1774, Ames taught in local schools and read deeply in the classics until 1778, when he was accepted as a law student in the office of William Tudor. Following his admission to the bar in 1781, Ames established a successful law practice in his native Dedham, Massachusetts. *DAB;* "Record-Book of the Suffolk [County] Bar," *Proceedings of the Massachusetts Historical Society* 19 (1881-1882): 152-53.

Fisher Ames (1758-1808) by John
Trumbull (1756-1843). Oil on
wood, 1792. Courtesy Yale University Art Gallery.

3. Benjamin Bourne graduated from Harvard in 1775 and soon joined the war effort. He read
law with James K. Varnum, his future brother-in-law, and then opened a law office in Providence.
Bourne was elected to the Rhode Island General Assembly in 1779 and in September of that year
was appointed to a committee to revise the military laws of Rhode Island. During the 1780s, he
held several judicial appointments. In 1782 he became a justice of the Inferior Court of Common
Pleas and in 1784 of the Superior Court. He was also a justice of the peace (1785-1789). In
1786 he served on a commission to examine the revision of state laws. Bourne campaigned for
adoption of the Constitution in Rhode Island and served in the House of Representatives from
1790 to 1796 when he succeeded Henry Marchant as United States judge for the district of Rhode
Island. Helen Bourne Joy Lee, *The Bourne Genealogy* (Chester, Conn.: Pequot Press, 1972), pp.
59-60.

4. Egbert Benson had graduated from King's College (later Columbia) in 1765, read law with
John Morin Scott, and was admitted to the bar in 1769. Benson was attorney general of New
York from 1777 to 1787. During those years he also served in the state Assembly, in the Confederation Congress, and as a delegate to the Annapolis Convention. Benson served in Congress
from 1789 to 1793 before being appointed a judge of the New York Supreme Court of Judicature
in 1794. His service on the state bench ended in 1801, when President Adams appointed him
chief judge of the United States Circuit Court of the Second Circuit. Following repeal of the
Judiciary Act of 1801—which had established this court—Benson retired from public life. *DAB.*

5. Robert Goodloe Harper (1765-1825) graduated from the College of New Jersey (later
Princeton) in 1785. Harper then moved to Charleston, South Carolina, read law, and was admitted
to the bar in 1786. He served in the state House of Representatives from 1794 to 1795. He was
elected a congressman from South Carolina and served from 1795 to 1801. In 1799 Harper
moved his law practice to Baltimore. Two years later he married Catherine Carroll, daughter of
Charles Carroll of Carrollton. Harper became one of Baltimore's leading lawyers and later represented Maryland in the Senate. *DAB;* Edgar, *Biographical Directory of the South Carolina House of
Representatives,* 1:240-44; *Federal Gazette* (Baltimore), August 3, 1799.

Timothy Pickering to Oliver Ellsworth ————————————
January 6, 1800   Philadelphia, Pennsylvania

. . . Alfred Moore of North Carolina is appointed to fill the seat on the bench of the Supreme Court, vacant by the death of Judge Iredell.[1] . . .

APcS (MHi, Timothy Pickering Papers). Marked as "triplicate."
   1. Several newspapers reported the appointment of Alfred Moore. One item appeared in the *North-Carolina Minerva* (Raleigh) on December 17, 1799, and in the *Augusta Herald* (Augusta, Georgia) on January 15, 1800. Another was printed in the *Universal Gazette* (Philadelphia) on January 16, 1800, and in the *United States Oracle* (Portsmouth, New Hampshire) on February 15, 1800. The *Columbian Centinel* (Boston) on March 5, 1800, published a report that also appeared in the *New-Hampshire Gazette* (Portsmouth) on March 12 and in the *Connecticut Journal* (New Haven) on March 13. Different items were printed in the *Providence Gazette* (Providence) on March 15, in the *Newport Mercury* (Newport, Rhode Island) on March 18, and in the *Federalist* (Trenton) on March 24.

Timothy Pickering to Oliver Ellsworth, William R. Davie, and William Vans Murray ————————————
January 20, 1800   Philadelphia, Pennsylvania

. . . Alfred Moore Esq[r] of North-Carolina accepts his commission as one of the associate judges of the supreme court.[1]

C (DNA, RG 59, Despatches).
   Oliver Ellsworth, William R. Davie, and William Vans Murray were envoys extraordinary and ministers plenipotentiary to the French Republic empowered to negotiate a treaty settling all controversies between the two countries. *SEJ,* 1:317, 326, 327.
   1. On January 21, 1800, the *North-Carolina Minerva* (Raleigh) published a brief report that Alfred Moore had accepted the appointment as associate justice.

William Cranch to Abigail Adams ————————————
January 28, 1800   Georgetown, District of Columbia

. . . [I hope?] M[r] Bayard will continue in his determination [to re]sign the office of Clerk of the supreme court, and that the Judges may think proper to give me the place.— It is such an one as would suit with my abilities & Education & would seem to be a small something on which I could place a little dependence.— The supreme Court will set on the 3[d] of february when I suppose the subject will be agitated. Your son[1] was so good as to mention the subject to the Chief Justice in August last, who promised to communicate the application to the other Judges, but I suspect it was neglected. I wrote to Judge Cushing, but as I am unacquainted with either of the other Judges, I have made no further application. M[r] Martin[2] the Att[y] Gen[l] of this state promised

me his influence with Judges Washington, Chase & Iredell, but I imagine he
is so full of other affairs that he has said nothing on the subject.＿ I shall write
again to my negociator T. B. A. & tell him how anxious I am to obtain the
office＿ that it would make me a new man, and by affording me an idea of
independence, would ˄again expand my faculties & give vigour to my mind.＿ ...

ARS (MHi, Adams Manuscript Trust). Addressed "Philadelphia." Incorrectly endorsed "Jan^{ry},
29th 1800." Readings have been supplied in brackets because of damage to the document.
　　1. Thomas B. Adams.
　　2. Luther Martin (1748-1826) was born in New Jersey and graduated from the College of
New Jersey (later Princeton) in 1766. Martin's first position after college was as a schoolteacher
on Maryland's Eastern Shore, where he had the opportunity to read law at the home of Solomon
Wright. He also briefly studied law with Samuel Wilson and then moved to Virginia's Eastern
Shore, where he was admitted to the bar in 1771. Martin then moved back to Maryland, to
Somerset County where he established a lucrative practice. In 1778 Maryland's governor, Thomas
Johnson, appointed Martin attorney general. Martin served in that post for twenty-seven years,
resigning in 1805. *DAB;* Clarkson and Jett, *Luther Martin,* pp. 11, 23-26.

William Cranch to Thomas B. Adams ————————————
January 30, 1800   Georgetown, District of Columbia

... I suppose this session of the supreme Court will decide the point whether
Mr Bayard will resign his office of Clerk and whether I shall be appointed to
succeed him. It is an object which has occupied my thoughts and absorbed my
wishes, ever since you first suggested to me the Idea. Whenever I have felt
the heartake, the hope of obtaining this little unenvied place, has cast a beam
of light on my desponding mind. And if I should obtain it, the hope that it
might hereafter aford me some considerable assistence in educating my children & providing for their wants would reinvigorate my abilities, reanimate
my faculties, & expand the powers of my mind. I fear that Mr Bayard will have
repented of his determination to resign. But if he has not, I must beg your
attention to it, and will thank you to remind Judge Cushing of my applica-
tion＿ and of the application which you made in my behalf to the Chief Justice
in August last. Are you acquainted with Mr Bayard, and can you find out
whether he has not some friend to whom he wishes to transfer the office＿ If
he has, it will be extremely difficult to manage the business, as he will not
resign, ~~himself~~, untill he has an assurance[1] of his friend being appointed. The
great point is to ascertain whether he really intends to resign or not, and then
whether he has not some friend who will stand in my way. If you can see the
other Judges on the business, I should be obliged to you＿ and inform me as
early as possible whether it will be of any service for me to be in Philad^a＿ if
it should, I will be there if possible before the session closes.＿ ...

ADfS (OCHP, William Cranch Papers). Marked "Copy to T. B Adams. Jany 29th 1800＿."
William Cranch seems to have changed the date from January 30 on the draft to January 29 on

the recipient's copy. When Thomas B. Adams acknowledged the receipt of this letter in a letter to William Cranch dated February 15, 1800 (q.v.), Adams made reference to a letter of the "29th ult?."

1. The "r" is written over an "a."

William Paterson to Euphemia Paterson
February 2, 1800 Philadelphia, Pennsylvania

...Judge Moor of North Carolina will not be on. Judges Chase and Washington have not arrived;[1] but it is said, that they are on the way. Perhaps, they will be in during the day. Four judges are requisite to constitute the court, and more than that number will not be here. The business will occupy at least two weeks_ ...

ARS (NjR, William Paterson Papers).

1. On February 4, 1800, John Rutherfurd wrote to Robert Morris, the district court judge for New Jersey, that Edward Tilghman had reported from Philadelphia that only William Cushing and William Paterson had arrived for the February term of the Supreme Court. William Paterson Papers, NjR.

Thomas B. Adams to William Cranch
February 3, 1800 Philadelphia, Pennsylvania

... I spoke with Judge Cushing yesterday on the subject of your application for the clerkship of the Supreme Court, and he suggested the utility & propriety of your addressing Judge Patterson by letter; communicating your wish to be appointed to the Office after the present occupant shall resign_ your residence on the spot to which Government will soon be transferred_ your professional pretentions & for character you have Judge Cushings leave to refer to him. The Judge says that the next session of the Supreme Court will be held here, but he thinks and can say pretty confidently that Mr Bayard will resign after this session. This is the day on which the Court should meet, but it is doubtful whether there be a Quorum present_ The Judges however will be in town all the week and if you will enclose a letter under cover to me for Judge Patterson I will take care it be delivered. ...

ARS (OCHP, William Cranch Papers). Addressed "City of Washington Ptmk." Postmarked "PHI   4   FE." Endorsed "Ansd feb. 9th." William Cranch's answering letter not found.

Philadelphia Gazette
February 3, 1800 Philadelphia, Pennsylvania

The Hon, Judge CHASE very narrowly escaped being drowned, a few days ago, in crossing the Susquehanna. He was taken from the river almost lifeless. Mr. Chase was on his way to this City.

(Philadelphia) February 3, 1800. The date and place are those of the news item.

This article also appeared in the *City Gazette* (Charleston), February 13, 1800, and in the *Rutland Herald* (Rutland, Vermont), February 24, 1800. A variant appeared in the *Massachusetts Mercury* (Boston), February 11, 1800.

Samuel Chase to Hannah Chase
February 4, 1800   Havre de Grace, Maryland

. . . It has pleased God once more to save Me from the most imminent Danger of sudden Death. my Son also in his great Exertions to save Me fell in three times and was in very great Danger. a young Officer of the Name of Alexander was the chief Instrument. he tied a Leather Strap round my leg, and my Son held Me the whole time, by my Coat near my Neck, I beleive about five Minutes. I once exerted myself so far as to get my Breast on the Ice, but it broke. I was perfectly collected, but quite exhausted, I relied only on the protection of my god, and he saved Me. I am was concerned to see my son in such Danger, but he would not save himself without saving Me. a Negroe Fellow (called Ben) was the only Person besides Mr Alexander, who gave any assistance. there were two french gentlemen, who were so frightened they ran ashore.— the other Negroes were also so alarmed that they did not assist, but running up all together but my Son called and stopped them, as all would have broke in and probably all perished. when I was haled[1] out I got on the Baggage Sledge, and was drawn ashore by two Negroes.— again all would have come to the Sledge but my Son prevented them. I was brought in Arms of all to the House. I immediately was rubbed dry and put into Bed between Blankets. I fell in before Sun-rise— At 10 oClock Sammy[2] wrote Tommy,[3] and Capt Barney sent to the post office; by Neglect of the post Deputy Post Master [he?] it was not sent. after 12 oClock Capt Ketty was so kind (with Mr Pleasants) to call to see Me. I was then in a little perspirabal,[4] which came on with Difficulty. My Head was rubbed all over with Brandy. I took a little burnt,[5] and drunk [Whey?] and Tea. I was afraid to sit up to write, and sent You a Message by Capt Ketty. in the Morning I set up to have my the Bed [made and?] yesterday Morning I got up and shaved, and I cannot discover that I have taken Cold, and I think I am as well as if the accident had not happened. for fear You should think I was hazardous I will give You the particulars.— We got here on Fryday about 4 o'Clock. Capt Barney said the Ice would not bear. and could not easily be cut. on Saturday afternoon some Persons crossed on the Ice. on Sunday before Day light one of the Negroes came into my Room. and desired me to get up, that the passengers were going over, that the Ice had been tried and would bear a Waggon and horses. when I came down I asked Capt Barney, who said the Ice had been tried, & there was no Danger.— two Negroes went before Me with the Baggage on a sleigh. I followed directly on the Track. Sammy went about ten feet on my right Hand.

the other Passengers followed. Myself and Son carried a long Boat-Hook. about 150 Yards from the shore, (in about fifteen feet Water) one of my feet broke in, I stepped forward with the other foot, and both broke in. I sent the Boat-Hook, & across, which prevented my sinking. Sammy immediately ran up, and caught hold of my Cloaths, and fell in. _ he got out and lay on the Side of the Hole, and held Me and broke in twice afterwards. _ I was heavily cloathed. my Fur Coat was very heavy when it got wet. _ I must inform You of our Circumstance. I had just offered up a prayer to god to protect Me from the Danger, when I instantly fell in. You know I have often mentioned Instances of the special Intraposition[6] of providence in my favor, among several, last December in Annapolis. I believe I was saved by his special favor. and I feel myself most grateful, and shall now have cause to remember and to give Thanks. _

Sammy wrote Tommy on yesterday, & I hope it got safe and made You easy. _ In the afternoon Judge Washington got here, & immediately passed in the Mail Boat. _ I will pass when I can go in the large Boat. the people are now breaking over, and the passengers are preparing to go over[.] I shall stay, at least until the Boat returns, and be satisfied I ~~will~~ will not go until there is no possible Risque. . . .

ARS (PHi, Dreer Collection). Samuel Chase misdated this letter as January instead of February. When he wrote it, he was "At Captain Barneys," a tavern at Havre de Grace, Maryland, on the west bank of the Susquehanna River. *PGW, Diary,* 6:204.

Hannah Kitty Giles (1756-1848) married Samuel Chase in 1784. She was his second wife. *DAR Lineages* 110 (1914): 94.

1. "To draw or pull." *OED.*

2. Samuel Chase, Jr. (1773-1841), son of Samuel Chase. Papenfuse, et al., *Biographical Dictionary of the Maryland Legislature,* entry for Samuel Chase.

3. Thomas Chase (1774-1826), son of Samuel Chase. Ibid.

4. Samuel Chase, who was thawing out from his fall in the icy river, means here that "in a little" time, as he warmed up, he was perspirable, or able to perspire.

5. I.e., burnt brandy.

6. I.e., interposition.

Thomas B. Adams to William Cranch ———————————
February 15 and 17, 1800   Philadelphia, Pennsylvania

[*February 15.*] Since the date of my last to you, I have received your favors of the 29ᵗʰ ultᵒ and 4ᵗʰ currᵗ _ the latter enclosing letters for the Judges of the Sup: Court,[1] four of which, I immediately caused to be delivered, to the judges present. My Mother's suggestion was better than mine, and I am glad you observed it. The same Gentleman who procured, or was at least greatly instrumental in procuring the appointment of Mʳ Bayard, knowing of his intention to resign, was desirous of patronizing another young man & actually interested himself in favor of his appointment as Bayard's Sucessor _ [2] When I spoke to Bayard myself, asking a Categorical answer, do you or do you not

intend to resign the Office after this term? He answered, that such had been
his intention, but that, Judge Patterson, had advised him to retain, until it
should appear whether any & what provision should be made for the Clerkship
in reforming the judiciary system;[3] at the same time he told me of the application made in favor of Mr. Caldwell, whom I understand he recommended as
his Sucessor when he communicated his positive intention to resign.

From the interest, which Judge Cushing has taken in your favor and from
the applications that have been repeatedly made to Judges Chase & Patterson
in person & in writing— supposing Judge Washington only to be indifferent
between the two Candidates, and I think there can be no doubt you will Succeed in obtaining the Appointment.

. . .

[*February 17:*][4] Bayard will hang on most probably until after the next Term,
and if any provision should be made for the Ofice to make it more lucrative,
he may keep it in spite of us. I will forward your letter to Judge Moore so
that we may have the benefit of his vote, in case of a division among the rest.

. . .

ARS (OCHP, William Cranch Papers). Addressed "George town   Ptmk." Postmarked "PHI
18 FE."

1. For William Cranch's letter of "29th ulto," see his letter to Thomas B. Adams of January 30,
1800. William Cranch's letter of February 4, 1800, has not been found; neither have the letters
to the justices.

2. The "Gentleman" referred to is probably Elias Boudinot. In 1789 William Bradford, Jr.,
Boudinot's son-in-law and Samuel Bayard's former law partner, had written Elias Boudinot about
procuring a clerkship for Bayard with either the federal district or circuit court for Pennsylvania.
In 1790 Samuel Bayard married Boudinot's niece, Martha Pintard. There is no direct evidence,
however, that Boudinot promoted Bayard for clerk of the Supreme Court in 1791. Bayard and
Boudinot maintained a close relationship; they corresponded regularly during Bayard's years
abroad. In 1799 Boudinot was aware of Bayard's career plans and advised him about the desirability of becoming a master in chancery in Westchester County, New York. Boudinot was equally
close to Elias B. Caldwell. He had raised Caldwell from childhood after the death of Caldwell's
parents. Boudinot naturally would have been interested in promoting Caldwell's career, and given
Boudinot's close connection with Bayard, he would have been in a position to do so. Although
there is no direct evidence that Boudinot solicited the clerkship for Caldwell, he did serve as one
of the sureties when Caldwell assumed the position. See headnote to "The Clerks and their Record;" Boudinot, *Life and Public Services, Addresses, and Letters of Elias Boudinot,* 2:151; see "Fine
Minutes," August 15, 1800.

3. As early as 1798 two judiciary bills had been introduced in the Senate. One relieved the
justices of circuit duty, and the other provided for an increase in the number of justices with two
justices assigned to each circuit. Neither bill was voted on in the House of Representatives. Nothing further happened until after President Adams's speech to Congress in December, 1799, urging
judicial reform. Both the Senate and the House appointed committees and a bill was introduced
in the House by Robert Goodloe Harper in March, 1800. Although final action was postponed
until the next session and substantial revisions were made, this bill eventually became the Judiciary
Act of 1801. George Lee Haskins and Herbert A. Johnson, *Foundations of Power: John Marshall,
1801-15,* vol. 2 of *The Oliver Wendell Holmes Devise History of the Supreme Court of the United States,*
Part One by George Lee Haskins (New York: Macmillan, 1981), pp. 122-26; *Annals,* 7:548-50,
556, 558-59, 561-64; 10:15, 196-97, 623; *Stat.,* 2:89.

4. This was written as a postscript to the February 15 letter.

Elias Boudinot (1740-1821) by Charles Balthazar Julien Févret de Saint-Mémin (1770-1852). Engraving, 1798. Courtesy National Portrait Gallery, Smithsonian Institution.

Thomas B. Adams to John Quincy Adams ——————
February 25, 1800 Philadelphia, Pennsylvania

... Nothing of a very interesting nature has occurred in our public affairs, since I wrote you last. The Supreme Court of the United States held its ordinary session here since the beginning of this month, but little business was done. The new Judge appointed in the room of Iredell, deceased, is a M^r. Moore of North Carolina,[1] but he has not yet taken a seat on the bench. ...

ARS (MHi, Adams Manuscript Trust). Addressed "Berlin." Endorsed "25. May rec^d" and "28 May. Ans^d."
    1. John Rutherfurd on February 4, 1800, also reported the appointment of Alfred Moore to Robert Morris, United States judge for the district of New Jersey. Robert Morris Papers, NjR.

Elias B. Caldwell to William Gaston ——————
February 28, 1800 Burlington, New Jersey

[*Caldwell reminds Gaston of their past friendship and notes that he has heard that Gaston was licensed to practice law and is doing so quite successfully.*] I am still trudging on, anxiously waiting for some little harvest after so much toil— I am in hopes however, to get license this Spring, and for that purpose am going to Baltimore, at which place or at Washington, I expect to take up my residence and begin my career—
I will inform you of the circumstance which lead[1] to this determination, at the same time crave your assistance in the completion of my project—

M.r Bayard the present Clerk of the Sup. Court of the UStates, not wishing to follow the Court to Washington, has signified his intention of resigning, & promised me his influence for the vacancy_ The appointment was to have been made in Feb.y Term last, but was put off to August Term for a fuller Court. The appoint.t is made by the Judges of the Court; you would therefore greatly oblige me by speaking to Judge Moore of your State in my behalf, or procuring some of your friends who are acquainted with him to interfere. As the appointment will be of great consequence to me, I shall rely on your friendship, and hope you will exert your influence in my favor. I would write to Guion[2] likewise on the subject, but am at present busily engaged preparing for my departure, but request you to remember me to him, and I doubt not he will readily give any assistance in his power_

I would thank you to answer this letter as soon as possible,[3] directing to Baltimore, and inform me what can be done further, and what hopes from Judge Moore, and how far I may depend upon him_ . . .

ARS (NcU, William Gaston Papers). Addressed "Newbern   North-Carolina." Handwritten postmark reads "Burlington 1.st March 1800." Endorsed "March 25.th 1800."

William Gaston (1778-1844) had been Elias Boudinot Caldwell's classmate at the College of New Jersey (later Princeton). Gaston was practicing law in North Carolina. On November 17, 1800, he began service in his first public office as a state senator from Craven County, North Carolina. *DAB; Princeton University, General Catalogue of Princeton University, 1746-1906* (Princeton: Princeton University Press, 1908), p. 110; Cheney, *North Carolina Government*, p. 240.

1. Elias B. Caldwell first wrote "led" and then wrote an "a" over the "d" and added another "d."

2. Isaac Lee Guion (1776-1815) had been a classmate of Elias Boudinot Caldwell and William Gaston at the College of New Jersey (later Princeton). At the time of his death, Guion was the state solicitor for the district of New Bern, North Carolina. Theresa Hall Bristol, "Purdy, Guion, Beecher and Thomas Family Notes," *New York Genealogical and Biographical Record* 51 (1920): 26; Princeton, *Catalogue*, p. 110; Lois Smathers Neal, comp., *Abstracts of Vital Records from Raleigh, North Carolina, Newspapers, 1799-1819*, vol. 1 (Spartanburg, S.C.: Reprint Co., 1979).

3. According to a letter from Elias B. Caldwell to William Gaston on May 12, 1800 (q.v.), Gaston responded on March 27, 1800. Letter not found.

Letter from an Anonymous Correspondent to the Editor ———
Aurora
April 30, 1800   New York, New York

[*The anonymous correspondent supports George Clinton[1] to replace John Jay as governor of New York.*] We expect to be able to put Mr. Jay in the way for a Federal office, it is understood that his old station of Chief Justice would be given him as a *make peace* but Jay wishes to be Vice President or President. . . .

(Philadelphia) May 2, 1800. Date and place are those of the letter.

1. George Clinton (1739-1812), a leading New York anti-federalist, had been governor of New York from 1777 to 1795. In 1792 Clinton had defeated John Jay for the office of governor in a close and bitterly contested election. Three years later, in order to avoid an embarrassing defeat, Clinton declined to run. In 1800 he was elected to his seventh term as governor. *DAB.*

Elias B. Caldwell to William Gaston ─────────────
May 12, 1800   Baltimore, Maryland

... I received your friendly letter of the 27th March,[1] and sincerely thank you for the interest you take in my welfare, and attention to the business contained in my last. In freely stating to you my situation & relying on your friendship, I consulted my own feelings, and am happy to find as I expected, that neither time nor situation has been able to obliterate the remembrance of our past enjoyments & youthful friendships.

I would thank you to inform me if Judge Moore will probably give me his interest, and when he comes on to the Supreme Court write to me by him. I grow more anxious every day to get in some situation where I may be independent, my situation in this place is very disagreeable[.] ...

                                                             April Term
I was admitted into the fraternity of lawyers in this place in ˄ ~~September~~, but have not yet been able to make any use of my priviledge ─ ...

ARS (NcU, William Gaston Papers). Addressed "Newbern ─ North Carolina." Postmarked "BALTᴱ Mᴰ MAY 12." Endorsed "May 26th 1800."
    1. Letter not found.

Alfred Moore to William Gaston ──────────────
May [26?], 1800   [North Carolina?]

... A few days before I began my Journey to Savannah I received a letter from you respecting Mr Caldwell's appointment to the Clerkship of the Supreme federal Court ─[1] I thought I had left an answer to that letter, to be delivered to you when you should arrive at Wilmington ─ on Enquiry I find my intended letter was either not written or has been lost ─

How far Mr Caldwell is qualified for such an office is not known to me ─ As a man of Sense & learning & virtue I esteem him very much & am glad to find that you who know him much better than myself entertain such esteem & affection for him ─ I forget whether you mention'd anything of his [word inked out] knowledge of the law; your Judgment will have weight, with me at least ─

If I shall have the pleasure to see you at Raleigh we will if you please talk the matter over ─ ...

ARS (NcU, William Gaston Papers). Place suggested by evidence in letter and by the fact that Alfred Moore had completed the South Carolina circuit in early May and was to begin the North Carolina circuit in early June. This letter is addressed "Wilmington"; endorsed "May 27th 1800." The date of this letter can be read as "20" or "26." The endorsement indicates that Gaston received it on May 27. The May 26 dating has been adopted because Moore should have been in North Carolina preparatory to the opening of the federal circuit court in Raleigh, and the letter could have arrived at Wilmington in one day.
    1. Letter not found.

Jeremiah Condy to Samuel Hodgdon
July 28, 1800   Georgetown, District of Columbia

. . . The Candidates I understand for the appointment of Clerk of the Supreme
Court of the U. States are Mess.ʳˢ Crainch & Caldwell — of the latter you know
more than myself — the former is a relation of M.ʳˢ Adams — and a Brother in
law to Mʳ Greenleaf who married lately Miss Allen —[1] he founds his expectations of success on his family interest — he is an attorney at Law and resides
in Washington — . . .

ARS (DNA, RG 94, Hodgdon-Pickering Papers). Addressed "Philadelphia." Postmarked
"GEOR.ᴺ PT.ᴷ JUL 28." Endorsed "Rec.ᵈ 1.ˢᵗ Aug.ᵗ"

Jeremiah Condy was admitted to the Philadelphia bar in June, 1799, and practiced law there
through 1802. *MBBP*, p. 258; Cornelius William Stafford, *The Philadelphia Directory, for 1800*
(Philadelphia: William W. Woodward, 1800); Cornelius William Stafford, *The Philadelphia Directory, for 1801* (Philadelphia: William W. Woodward, 1801); James Robinson, *The Philadelphia
Directory, City and County Register, For 1802* (Philadelphia: William W. Woodward, 1802).

1. Ann Penn Allen (born 1772), second wife of James Greenleaf, whom he married on April
26, 1800. James Edward Greenleaf, comp., *Genealogy of the Greenleaf Family,* (Boston: Frank Wood,
1896), p. 217.

Aurora
August 8, 1800   Philadelphia, Pennsylvania

JUDGE CHASE

One of the Judges of the Supreme Court of the United States, now *waiting
for his honor in this city*. Absenting himself from his public (paid for) duty, and
thereby preventing the court for *ten days* at least, if not the entire term, from
proceeding on the important business before them, at the heavy and oppressive
expence of the parties litigant, their counsel and others, and to the great dis-
credit of the judiciary; and this too at a time when he knows the *chief Justice*
is absent by *appointment of the President* on a foreign embassy, and that himself,
Judge Chase, has been recently attending public meetings of the people of
Maryland, and haranguing them on the propriety of keeping in office *such men*
as President *Adams* and *himself.*[1] From such men good Lord deliver us!

(Philadelphia) August 8, 1800. Date and place are those of the newspaper.

1. During the election of 1800, Samuel Chase actively campaigned for John Adams in Maryland. In late July, Chase spoke at election canvasses in Annapolis and Elk Ridge. Haw, et al.,
Stormy Patriot, p. 208; Edward G. Roddy, "Maryland and the Presidential Election of 1800," *Maryland Historical Magazine* 56 (1961): 257.

Thomas B. Adams may have read this article in the *Aurora*. He wrote his cousin, William Smith
Shaw, on the day the account appeared: "The Sup. Court are waiting for the Hon'ble Judge Chase,
who is said to be too much engaged in Electioneering, to be able to attend." Thomas B. Adams
to William S. Shaw, August 8, 1800, *Proceedings of the American Antiquarian Society,* New Series, 27
(April 1917): 120-22.

For a different explanation of Chase's absence, see the *Philadelphia Gazette* under date of August 12, 1800, and William Paterson to William Cushing, August 19, 1800.

Aurora —————————————————————————————————
August 9, 1800 Philadelphia, Pennsylvania

It must be extremely gratifying to the lovers of justice to know, that the Supreme Court of the United States was to hold its session here on Monday last; but that owing to the absence of *Judge Elsworth* who is on a *foreign mission*, of *Judge, Chase* who is *electioneering* in Maryland, and of Judge Cushing who is sick, no business has, as yet been done, for want of a quorum.[1] The suspension of the business of the highest court of judicature in the United States, to allow a *Chief Justice* to add NINE THOUSAND DOLLARS a year to his salary,[2] and to permit *Chase* to make electioneering harangues in favor of Mr. *Adams,* is a mere bagatelle. The people must heartily desire the re-election of a President, who could take one judge from the bench for one purpose, and permit another to crusade through Maryland for a second. It certainly comports with the spirit and intention of the Supreme Court of the United States, that there should be an aptitude in the judges which should fit them either for ministers plenipotentiary, or for electioneerers as may seem meet to the chief magistrate. What a becoming spectacle to see *Chase* mounted on a stump, with a face like a full moon, vociferating in favor of the present President, and the Supreme Court adjourning from day to day, and the business of the nation hung up, until Chase shall have disgorged himself!! *O tempora! O mores!*

(Philadelphia) August 9, 1800. Date and place are those of the headline.
 This article also appeared in the *Virginia Argus* (Richmond) on August 19, 1800, and in the *Albany Register* on August 29.
 1. The Court did in fact convene on August 9.
 2. "An Act to ascertain the compensation of public Ministers," passed on May 10, 1800, specified that any minister plenipotentiary should not be allowed more than $9,000 per annum for services and expenses. *Stat.,* 2:78. Questions of salary and extrajudicial activity by the justices will be considered in the last volume of this series.

Aurora —————————————————————————————————
August 11, 1800 Philadelphia, Pennsylvania

JUDGES OF THE COURTS OF THE
UNITED STATES

Are they, or are they not necessary? In the present state of things such a question forces itself upon us; for if they are necessary, we should naturally expect to meet with them in their proper places, and executing their constitutional and legal functions_ The Supreme Court of the United States ought at this moment to be in session;[1] but where are the Judges who compose this Court? One is on an embassy to France, another is on an embassy to the people of Maryland, endeavouring to negociate a treaty of amity with them for Mr. Adams_ The former derives *nine thousand dollars a year independently of his out-fit and his salary* as Chief Justice, for this service, what the other is to receive as his reward, is no more public, than was the *flour speculation* at the moment of its conception_ [2] Some sop[3] for such a cur must be intended; for great cravings must be satisfied by some means or other_ Such a creature must not be told as children often tell each other when they ask favours, "we'll *chase* you with it"_ The wages of sin must be paid, or the service expires_ and desertion at a critical moment might prove fatal.

The *President* is at BRAINTREE *superintending the faithful execution of the laws, Chief Justice Ellsworth* is in PARIS, negociating a treaty which no man in the United States could do but himself, *Judge Chase,* like an itinerant mountebank, is displaying electioneering tricks in Maryland, and the Supreme Court of the United States, and those who are looking for Justice from it, are taking a nap in Philadelphia until JUDGE CHASE shall have concluded his gambols!! Hail Columbia happy land!

(Philadelphia) August 11, 1800. Date and place are those of the newspaper.
   The first paragraph of this article was reprinted in the *Virginia Argus* (Richmond), August 22, 1800.
   1. The Court had sat on August 9 and did meet on August 11.
   2. For Samuel Chase's involvement in the flour scandal, see "Appointments to the Bench," headnote to "Samuel Chase: Appointment as Associate Justice in 1796."
   3. The *Virginia Argus* (Richmond) of August 22, 1800, has this as "stop."

Philadelphia Gazette ————————————————————————————
August 12, 1800   Philadelphia, Pennsylvania

On Saturday last, the Supreme Court of the United States commenced its session in this city. The indisposition of Judge Chase prevented the Court from proceeding to business on the first day of the term. Several important causes will be heard and determined in the course of the present week. . . . Judge Cushing (owing to indisposition) has not attended.

   . . .

The Hon. Judge Chase, who arrived in town yesterday, attended this day.[1]

(Philadelphia) August 12, 1800. Date and place are from the headline.
   Also printed in *Federal Gazette* (Baltimore), August 14, 1800. The *Gazette of the United States* (Philadelphia) published this article on August 12, 1800, but did not include the last, incorrect sentence. The *United States Oracle* (Portsmouth, New Hampshire) on August 30 published the same version that had appeared in the *Gazette of the United States.* The *Massachusetts Mercury* (Boston) published a summary of this article on August 19, which also was printed in the *Providence Gazette*

on August 23. The *Virginia Argus* (Richmond) on August 22 published a summary of this article; but in condensing the information, the publisher left out the phrase "on the first day of the term" and thereby created the impression that the Court had adjourned without proceeding to its business on Saturday, August 9, rather than on Monday, August 4.

1. The *Philadelphia Gazette* reports here that Samuel Chase arrived in Philadelphia on August 11. This is inaccurate. He sat with the Court on Saturday, August 9. According to William Paterson's letter to William Cushing on August 19 (q.v.), Chase arrived in Philadelphia on Saturday, August 9.

Claypoole's American Daily Advertiser ———————————————
August 14, 1800 Philadelphia, Pennsylvania

The following Judges of the Supreme Court of the United States are now in this city:
Hon. William Paterson, _ from New Jersey,
    Samuel Chase,   Maryland,
    Bushrod Washington,   Virginia,
    Alfred Moore,   N. Carolina. . . .

(Philadelphia) August 14, 1800. Date and place from the headline.
This news also appeared in the *City Gazette* (Charleston) on August 28.

Thomas B. Adams to William Cranch ———————————————
August 15, 1800 Philadelphia, Pennsylvania

. . . Your favor of the 11ᵗʰ inst. which has this moment come to hand,[1] found me with pen in hand; on the very threshold of writing to you, for the purpose of offering you my very sincere & hearty congratulations upon the success of your Competitor Mr. Caldwell, who has obtained the appointment of Clerk to the Supreme Court of the U. S. _ This exordium may appear singular to you, the more so, when you hear, that I never relaxed in my efforts to procure this Office for you, and that since the sitting of the Court, at this time, I interceded, as before, with some of the Judges in your behalf _ I addressed a letter on the subject, to the new Judge, enclosing that which you wrote for him last winter, wherein I explained the circumstances under which your application came forward, & requesting him to consider you still, a candidate for the Office.

All would not do _ Ellsworth is in France, or on the high seas _ Cushing is old _ infirm _ unable to travel _ & consequently not here. Your advocates, except Judge Chase, were, I believe, all absent, no wonder then, that the original crying, unforgiven & <u>forgivless</u> sin of being a new Englandman, blasted all your hopes and withered your pretentions _ The patronage of Judge Patterson & the unwearied efforts of the young man's friends, added to the recommendation of the present incumbent, irresistibly inducted this Clerk in to the living. Now for a confirmation of my premisses —

That situation must be desperate indeed, which offers to the disappointed, no ray of consolation — Such is not your case. "Out of the bitter came forth sweet," and again "Our very wishes, give us not our wants."

I congratulated you upon the success of your rival. Why? For this plain reason, that your station at the Bar, free to practise in the Sup: Court of the United States, will be much more conducive to your interest in the course of a short time, than the emolument derived from the Clerkship. I know the fact, that a single fee of Counsel in a cause of any magnitude in that Court, is worth more than the Clerks salary for a twelvemonth. The Clerk of the Court is precluded practise in his own Court. The dignity of the Office, is not much.

The next Session of the Court will be held at Washington, and the business will center, chiefly, with the distinguished professional gentlemen of that vicinity. It has rarely happened, that any but Philadelphia lawyers have been retained, in causes, to be managed before this Court — I know but one or two who intend pursuing the practice after the removal to Washington & I infer upon the whole, that your being on the spot & entitled to take business in that Court, will redound more to your advantage, than the gratification of our wishes as to the clerkship would have done.

Now, am not I a comforter? To bear disappointment with fortitude — is well — but to derive consolation from it — is far better. . . .

ARS (OCHP, William Cranch Papers). Addressed "City Washington." Postmarked "PHI   15 AU."

1. Letter not found.

Gazette of the United States ——————————————————
August 16, 1800   Philadelphia, Pennsylvania

. . . On Saturday[1] the 9th inst. the Supreme Court of the United States, commenced its session for August Term — the quorum consists of their honors Judge Patterson, Jud[ge] Chase, Judge Washington and Judge Moo[re.]

Judge Patterson being the oldest associate by commission, presides.

The list of causes was called over on Saturday and several were marked for argument on Monday.

Monday the 11th, The court met pursuant to adjournment. . . .

. . . The Court rose yesterday.

(Philadelphia) August 16, 1800. Date and place are those of newspaper.

The *Daily Advertiser* (New York) reprinted this on August 20, 1800, but omitted the sentence stating that William Paterson presided.

1. In the newspaper, an "n" appears instead of a "u."

Claypoole's American Daily Advertiser —————————
August 18, 1800   Philadelphia, Pennsylvania

On Friday last the Supreme Court of the United States rose, after a session of one week, during which time they heard and determined sundry causes of great importance. . . .

At the close of the term, SAMUEL BAYARD, Esq. Clerk of the Court, resigned his office, declining to attend the future sessions, which are to be held in the city of Washington.

ELIAS B. CALDWELL, Esq. of New Jersey, has been appointed Clerk of the Court. He will reside and keep his office in Georgetown, state of Maryland.[1]

(Philadelphia) August 18, 1800. Date and place are from headline.

    This article also appeared in the *Daily Advertiser* (New York), August 20, 1800. On August 16 the *Philadelphia Gazette* published an article containing similar information which also appeared in the *City Gazette* (Charleston) on September 3. A variant appeared in the *Massachusetts Mercury* (Boston) on August 26.

    1. Other newspapers mentioning the appointment of Elias B. Caldwell as clerk include the *Gazette of the United States* (Philadelphia) on August 18, 1800; the *Federal Gazette* (Baltimore) on August 21, 1800; and the *Columbian Centinel* (Boston) on August 27, 1800.

William Paterson to William Cushing —————————
August 19, 1800   New Brunswick, New Jersey

. . . Judge Chase, being indisposed, did not arrive at Philad[a] till saturday, the 9[h] of the month, when we made a court, and went through the business by friday afternoon of the following week. Your letter reached me at Philad[a] — [1]
. . .

ARS (MHi, Robert Treat Paine Papers).

    1. William Cushing's letter to William Paterson not found.

Elias B. Caldwell to William Gaston —————————
September 18, 1800   Georgetown, District of Columbia

. . . With great pleasure I rec[d] your letter of the 1st Inst.;[1] I had just returned from Phil[a] & New Jersey, and intended soon to write but your anticipation proves your friendship & wishes for my success — . . .

The emoluments of my office are small, yet with my practice, I hope I shall be able to live along; being an entire stranger here I must trust to my exertions, and the assurances I have received from a few in this place, give me some hopes of success . . .

ARS (NcU, William Gaston Papers). Addressed "Newbern   North Carolina." Postmarked "GEOR[N] PT[K]   SEP   18." Endorsed "Received Oct. 2nd 1800."

    1. Letter not found.

Oliver Ellsworth to David Ellsworth ──────────────
October 10, 1800   Le Havre, France

... "I know you will be much disappointed at my not returning this fall; but
the gravel and the gout in my kidneys, which constantly afflict me, forbid my
undertaking a voyage in a cold and boisterous season of the year. I hope that
by going to a mild climate in the South of France to spend the winter, and
by being freed from the anxiety and perplexity of business, which has much
increased my complaint, that I shall be able by the opening of the Spring to
return without hazard.[1] ... "

Pr (Printed in William Garrott Brown, *The Life of Oliver Ellsworth* (New York: Macmillan, 1905),
pp. 302-3).
   David Ellsworth (1741-1821) of Windsor, Connecticut, was the brother of Oliver Ellsworth.
DAR Lineage Book 17 (1896): 15.
   1. On the same day that Oliver Ellsworth wrote to his brother David, he also wrote to George
Cabot about his poor health and travel plans. Stephen Strong Collection, MNF.

Oliver Ellsworth to Oliver Wolcott, Jr. ──────────────
October 16, 1800   Le Havre, France

... Sufferings at sea, and by a winter's journey thro' Spain, gave me an ob-
stinate gravel, which by wounding the kidnies, has drawn & fixed my wan-
dering gout to those parts. My pains are constant, and at times excruciating;
they do not permit me to embark for America at this late season of the year,
nor if there, would they permit me to discharge my official duties. I have
therefore, sent my resignation of the office of Chief Justice; and shall, after
spending a few weeks in England, retire for winter quarters to the south of
France.[1] ...

ARS (CtHi, Oliver Wolcott Jr. Papers).
   1. On the same day that Oliver Ellsworth wrote to Oliver Wolcott, Jr., he also wrote to Timothy Pickering reporting on his health, resignation, and travel plans. Timothy Pickering Papers,
MHi.

"A Pennsylvanian" to the Members of the Legislature of the State of Pennsylvania ──────────────
Aurora
October 29, 1800   Philadelphia, Pennsylvania

... There cannot be a doubt of the public sentiment of Pennsylvania being
more unanimous for Mr. Jefferson, than for any other heretofore, but gen.
Washington. If we have a fair just chance to vote as we have done heretofore,
or if the legisl[a]ture votes prudently, we shall choose electors for Mr. Jefferson

beyond a doubt. Good men in our legislature surely will not prevent our having some share in the federal executive government; for, unless we get a share in electing the president, we shall continue to have none.

We have no federal supreme judge, no federal secretary or head of a department, no federal foreign minister, no federal attorney general, no federal military general officer, no share in the federal or president's council.

General Washington, appointed Mr. Pickering (who had become a Citizen of Pennsylvania) General Wayne, and Judge Wilson.[1] But Mr. Adams, when Mr. Wilson and General Wayne died, put in a Judge and a General from another state; and he removed Mr. Pickering and supplied his place from another state also. _[2] Pennsylvania is now reduced to have no office of power or weight in the Executive Department, or in the Law and Judiciary Department, or in the Public Councils. It is easy to see, that, if Mr. Adams and Mr. Pinckney's[3] friends hold the power longer, this rich, agricultural, manufacturing, commercial, industrious, and honest state, will be kept in the same deprived si[t]uation.

Massachusetts and Connecticut keep to themselves the great powers of the government.[4] They have President, speaker of the representatives, temporary speaker of the senate, a majority of trustees of the sinking fund, secretaries of the treasury and war, chief justice, first associate judge, ambassadors to Britain, Spain, and Prussia, and first ambassador to France.[5] . . .

(Philadelphia) October 29, 1800. Date and place are from the newspaper issue. Readings have been supplied in brackets because type did not imprint.

1. Timothy Pickering received several appointments during the Washington administration. Pickering first was appointed postmaster general on November 7, 1791. Then he was appointed to be an Indian commissioner on March 2, 1793, and reappointed to the office of postmaster general on December 11, 1794. In 1795 Pickering was appointed to two cabinet posts: on January 2, the Senate confirmed Pickering as secretary of war and on December 10, as secretary of state. General Anthony Wayne was appointed major general of the United States Army on April 11, 1792, and James Wilson was appointed an associate justice of the Supreme Court on September 26, 1789. SEJ, 1:88, 136, 165, 169, 193, 119, 29.

2. James Wilson was replaced by Bushrod Washington of Virginia. After Anthony Wayne's death in 1796, Brigadier General James Wilkinson of Kentucky became the ranking officer of the United States Army (but he did not become major general). John Marshall of Virginia replaced Timothy Pickering as secretary of state. SEJ, 1:296-97, 353-54; DAB entry for James Wilkinson.

3. Charles Cotesworth Pinckney, federalist candidate for vice president in 1800.

4. On November 8, 1800, the Columbian Centinel (Boston) tried to refute the charge of partiality to New Englanders in John Adams's appointments by listing appointments that had been made in both the Washington and Adams administrations (including those to the Supreme Court). A similar list appeared on November 11, 1800, in the Federalist (Trenton) which noted that Virginia had been particularly favored in the number of appointees drawn from that state.

5. President John Adams of Massachusetts, Speaker of the House Theodore Sedgwick of Massachusetts, President Pro Tempore of the Senate Uriah Tracy of Connecticut, Secretary of the Treasury Oliver Wolcott, Jr., of Connecticut, Secretary of War Samuel Dexter of Massachusetts, Chief Justice Oliver Ellsworth of Connecticut, and senior Associate Justice William Cushing of Massachusetts. The five commissioners of the sinking fund by virtue of their offices were Uriah Tracy of Connecticut (president pro tempore of the Senate), Oliver Ellsworth of Connecticut (chief justice of the Supreme Court), Oliver Wolcott, Jr., of Connecticut (secretary of the treasury), John

Marshall of Virginia (secretary of state), and Charles Lee of Virginia (attorney general). *BDAC*, pp. 13, 61. The ambassador to Great Britain was Rufus King, who had been born in the district of Maine, raised and educated in Massachusetts, but had resided in New York since the 1780s; the ambassador to Spain was David Humphreys of Connecticut; and the ambassador to the King of Prussia was the president's son, John Quincy Adams of Massachusetts. *DAB* entry for Rufus King; *SEJ*, 1:209, 310, 240. No ambassador to France was appointed during the Adams administration, but two special missions consisting of three envoys each were appointed. The last of the two missions, whose negotiations had been completed in October, 1800, was headed by Chief Justice Oliver Ellsworth of Connecticut. Miller, *Federalist Era*, pp. 205-6, 245-46; Henry Flanders, *The Lives and Times of The Chief Justices of the Supreme Court of the United States*, 2 vols. (New York: James Cockcroft, 1875), 2:255-57.

James Hillhouse to Stephen Twining ————————————————
December 16, 1800 Washington, District of Columbia

... Mr Elsworth has not returned on account of ill health__ To my great sorrow he has resigned the office of Chief Justice of the United States __ [1] who will succeed him is not yet known. . . .

Tr (CtY, Hillhouse Family Papers).

James Hillhouse (1754-1832), a New Haven attorney, represented Connecticut in the Senate from 1796 to 1810. Hillhouse had previously served in the House of Representatives from 1791 until his election to the Senate to replace Oliver Ellsworth. *DAB*.

Stephen Twining (1767-1832) was a lawyer in New Haven and also served as city tax collector. Franklin Bowditch Dexter, *Biographical Sketches of the Graduates of Yale College*, vol. 5 (New York: Henry Holt, 1911), p. 173.

1. In a letter of December 17 to James Kent, Jonas Platt also mentioned the resignation of Oliver Ellsworth. James Kent Papers, DLC.

Theodore Sedgwick to Alexander Hamilton ————————————
December 17, 1800 Washington, District of Columbia

[*Sedgwick informs Hamilton of some of the contents of the convention with France negotiated by Oliver Ellsworth. It is evident that Sedgwick is not pleased with the results.*] After this information it will be needless to add that the mind as well as body of Mr Ellsworth are rendered feeble by disease. He has resigned as Ch. Jus^e
. . .

ARS (DLC, Alexander Hamilton Papers). Addressed "New York." Postmarked "WASH-CITY DEC [17]."

Theodore Sedgwick to Caleb Strong ————————————————
December 17, 1800 Washington, District of Columbia

... the mind as well as body of Mr Ellsworth are debilitated by disease. He has resigned as Ch. Justice __ I know not who will succeed but I hope Patterson. __ . . .

AR[S] (MHi, Caleb Strong Papers). Signature clipped. Addressed "Northampton   Mass[ᵗˢ?]."
Postmarked "WASH-CITY   DEC   17."

James Gunn to Alexander Hamilton ─────────────────
December 18, 1800 Washington, District of Columbia

... The President this day nominated M.ʳ Jay Cheif Justice— M.ʳ Elsworth resigned.— M.ʳ Jay having once declined the office of Cheif Judge it is no compliment to re-appoint him to that office, nor was it decent to wound the feelings of Judge Patterson.— Either Judge Patterson, or Gen.ˡ Pinckney[1] ought
to have been appointed, But both those worthies are your friends.—[2] ...

ARS (DLC, Alexander Hamilton Papers). Addressed "New York." Postmarked "GEORᴺ PTᴷ
DEC   18."

1. Charles Cotesworth Pinckney.
2. John Adams had cause to mistrust Alexander Hamilton as well as Hamilton's friends. Before
the election of Adams as president in 1796, Hamilton tried to get Thomas Pinckney, the federalist
candidate for vice president, elected as president in place of Adams. At the end of Adams's administration, Adams realized that three of his cabinet officers—Timothy Pickering, James McHenry,
and Oliver Wolcott, Jr.—were following Hamilton's directions rather than his own. In May, 1800,
Adams dismissed Pickering and forced McHenry to resign; Wolcott resigned in December, 1800.
Hamilton sought to deprive Adams of the presidency again in 1800 by a similar stratagem as in
1796, but used Charles Cotesworth Pinckney instead of his brother Thomas Pinckney. Finally,
Hamilton published a "Letter from Alexander Hamilton, Concerning the Public Conduct and
Character of John Adams, Esq. President of the United States," maintaining the unfitness of Adams
to be president. Extracts of the pamphlet were published toward the end of October, 1800, in
the Philadelphia *Aurora* and the New London *Bee* and a copyrighted edition of the whole pamphlet
was available for sale by October 24, 1800. *PAH*, 24:483n, 477; 25:109n, 169-85.

John Marshall to Charles C. Pinckney ─────────────
December 18, 1800 Washington, District of Columbia

... M.ʳ Ellsworth has resigned his seat as chief justice & M.ʳ Jay has been nominated in his place.[1] Shoud he as is most probable decline the office I fear the
President will nominate the senior Judge ~~to that office.~~ ...

ARS (DLC, Charles C. Pinckney Papers).
1. James Hillhouse also mentioned John Jay's nomination in a letter to Simeon Baldwin on
December 19, 1800. Printed in Simeon E. Baldwin, *The Life and Letters of Simeon Baldwin* (New
Haven: Tuttle, Morehouse, & Taylor, 1919), pp. 424-25.

William Cooper to John Jay ────────────────────
December 19, 1800 Washington, District of Columbia

... You are nominated and will this day no doubt be approved Cheife Justice
of the United States. in the Place of O Elsworth Resignned— ...

ARS (N, No. 13682). Addressed "albany." Postmarked "WASH-CITY   DEC   19."
    William Cooper (1754-1809), first judge of Otsego County, New York, served as a congress-man (1795-1797, 1799-1801). *DAB*.

Thomas Jefferson to James Madison ————————————
December 19, 1800 Washington, District of Columbia

. . . Elsworth remains in France for his health. he has resigned his office of C. J. putting these two things together we cannot misconstrue his views. he must have had great confidence in m̄r A's continuance to risk ~~the~~ such a certainty as he held. Jay was yesterday nominated Chief Justice.[1] we were afraid of something worse. . . .

AR (DLC, James Madison Papers). Addressed "Orange."
    1. In a letter also dated December 19, 1800, Abraham Baldwin informed Joel Barlow of John Jay's appointment to replace Oliver Ellsworth. Abraham Baldwin Papers, CtY.

Thomas B. Adams to Abigail Adams ————————————
December 20, 1800 Philadelphia, Pennsylvania

. . . I understood that chief Justice Ellsworth had sent home his resignation of his seat on the Bench which leaves a vacancy to be filled. I presume that M͞r Patterson of New Jersey will be promoted to the highest seat, as Judge Cushing the senior judge is understood to have once declined it. Not knowing what consideration will govern the president in supplying the place at this time, I venture to suggest that some young or middle-aged man, for many obvious reasons would be, in my opinion, most eligible— I have thought of M͞r Dexter[1] & M͞r Ingersoll or M͞r E— Tilghman,[2] but whether either of these latter gentlemen would accept the office, if offered to them— I know not— It is thought M͞r Tilghman would, but I am pretty sure M͞r Ingersoll would not— Lewis I have sometimes thought aspired to a seat, but I doubt the validity of his pretentions— If the old rule of locality is to have its weight, Connecticutt may perhaps be looked to for a character, but I think the President will obey the dictates of his own opinion in this instance, without regard to the narrow principle which has heretofore prevailed with respect to such appointments, & which I know was never approved by him— Judge Cushing will not be likely to retain his place much longer, as his age & infirmities must bear him down and M͞r Dexter is the man I should wish to see as the representative Judge of Massachusetts— But my opinions are worth very little on this subject and are only offered for their humble share of consideration— . . .

ARS (MHi, Adams Manuscript Trust).
    1. Samuel Dexter (1761-1816), John Adams's secretary of war and soon to be secretary of the treasury, was born in Boston and graduated from Harvard in 1781. Dexter read law with Levi

Lincoln in Worcester and was admitted to the Worcester County bar in 1784. In 1788 Dexter established a practice in Charlestown, Massachusetts, and was also elected to the state House of Representatives. Dexter served in Congress from 1793 to 1795, in the Senate from December 2, 1799, to June, 1800, and in President Adams's cabinet from June, 1800. He remained secretary of the treasury for a short time in the administration of Thomas Jefferson before returning to Massachusetts to practice law. *DAB; BDAC.*

2. Edward Tilghman (1751-1815) was a leader of the Philadelphia bar for over a quarter of a century. Born into a prominent Maryland family, Tilghman graduated from the College of Philadelphia (later the University of Pennsylvania) in 1767 and then studied law at the Middle Temple in England where he was admitted to study in 1772. After his return to Philadelphia, he was admitted to the bar in 1774. Tilghman never held public office, and he declined an offer to be chief justice of the Pennsylvania Supreme Court in 1806. *DAB.*

Henry Glen to John Jay ——————————————————
December 20, 1800 Washington, District of Columbia

. . . On Thursday last the President sent up to the Senate A nomination for you to be the Chief Justice of the United States in the Room of Judge Ellsworth Resigned, yesterday the Senate took up the nomination And have appinted you the Chief Justice . . .

ARS (NNC, John Jay Papers).
Henry Glen (1739-1814) was clerk of Schenectady County, New York, from 1767 to 1809 and a congressman from 1793 to 1801. *BDAC.*

Richard D. Spaight to John G. Blount ——————————————
December 22, 1800 Washington, District of Columbia

. . . Jn° Jay has been nominated by the President Chief-Justice of the U. S. Vice O. Elsworth resigned, and the Senate has confirmed the appointment. Quere,[1] is there no man in the U. S. fit for this appointment but Jn° Jay, that we must re-appoint a man who has before held it & given it up? . . .

ARS (Nc-Ar, John Gray Blount Papers). Addressed "Washington   N° Carolina." Postmarked "WASH-CITY   DEC   23."
Richard Dobbs Spaight (1758-1802) began his public career in the North Carolina House of Commons in 1781. Spaight also served in the Confederation Congress and the Constitutional Convention where he supported the adoption of the Constitution. He was elected governor of North Carolina in 1792 and served three terms. In 1798 Spaight was elected to fill a vacant seat in the Fifth Congress and remained in the House of Representatives until March, 1801. *DAB; BDAC.*
John Gray Blount (1752-1833), a justice of the peace for Beaufort County, North Carolina, commissioner for the port of Bath, and postmaster of the town of Washington, was a member of North Carolina's leading mercantile family. Earlier Blount had represented Beaufort County in the North Carolina House of Commons (1782-1793) and in the state Senate (1791, 1793, 1795). While his political career was confined to local offices, John Gray Blount was often consulted on national affairs. Alice Barnwell Keith, ed., *The John Gray Blount Papers,* vol. 1 (Raleigh: North Carolina Department of Archives and History, 1952), pp. xv, xxi-xxiv.
1. I.e., query.

Letter from an Anonymous Correspondent to the Editor ————
Daily Advertiser
December 22, 1800 Washington, District of Columbia

"Judge Ellsworth having resigned the office of chief justice of the U. States,
governor Jay has been n[o]minated to fill the vacancy.[1] It is not known
whether he accepts the office. . . . "

(New York) December 31, 1800. Date and place are those of the letter. A reading has been
supplied in brackets because type did not imprint.

    1. The nomination of John Jay to replace Oliver Ellsworth was noted also in an anonymous
letter from Washington, D.C., dated December 22, 1800, and printed in the *Boston Gazette* on
January 5, 1801. Another letter formed the basis for an article in the *Philadelphia Gazette* on December 24, 1800, which appeared elsewhere (sometimes with minor textual variation), such as in
the *Massachusetts Mercury* (Boston) on January 2, 1801. Another report, with some variations, was
printed in the *Commercial Advertiser* (New York), December 24, 1800, and in the *United States
Oracle* (Portsmouth, New Hampshire), January 3, 1801. Other notices appeared in the *Newport
Mercury* (Newport, Rhode Island), December 30, 1800; the *Times* (Charleston), January 3, 1801;
the *City Gazette* (Charleston), January 10, 1801; and the *Raleigh Register* (Raleigh, North Carolina),
January 13, 1801.

    Senate confirmation of Jay as chief justice appeared in a letter from Washington, D.C., dated
December 23, 1800, and published in the *Columbian Centinel* (Boston), January 3, 1801. The
Columbian Centinel article, or a slight variant of it, appeared also in the *United States Oracle* (Portsmouth, New Hampshire) and in the *Philadelphia Gazette,* both on January 10, 1801. The *Museum*
(Georgetown, District of Columbia), December 31, 1800, mentioned the confirmation. A brief
notice also appeared in the *Universal Gazette* (Washington, District of Columbia) on January 1,
1801. A similar notice was published in the *United States Oracle* (Portsmouth, New Hampshire)
on January 10 and in the *Georgia Gazette* (Savannah) on January 22.

Museum ————
December 22, 1800 Georgetown, District of Columbia

We understand that Chief-Justice Ellsworth, being in a bad state of health
and having gone to England from whence he proposes to return to the South
of France, has resigned his office. A new appointment may therefore be expected soon to take place.

(Georgetown, District of Columbia) December 22, 1800. Date and place are those of the headline.

    Oliver Ellsworth's resignation also was noted briefly in *Poulson's American Daily Advertiser* (Phil-
adelphia) on December 23, 1800, in the *Massachusetts Mercury* (Boston) on December 30, 1800,
and in the *Times* (Charleston) on January 3, 1801. These articles are virtually identical.

John Adams to Thomas B. Adams ————
December 23, 1800 Washington, District of Columbia

. . . I have appointed Mr Jay Chief Justice. He may refuse. if he should, I shall
follow the Line of Judges most probably and then there will be a vacancy. I

Jared Ingersoll (1749-1822) by
Charles Willson Peale (1741-
1827). Oil on canvas, 1820. Courtesy Independence National Historical Park.

wish to know if Mr Ingersoll would accept an appointment as one of the assistant Justices of the Sup[ream?]^1 Court. . . .

ARS (MHi, Adams Papers); ALb (MHi, Adams Manuscript Trust), signed "your father." Marked
"Confidential." Addressed "Philadelphia." Postmarked "WASH-CITY   DEC   24." Endorsed
"27th [Dec^r] Rec^d 28th [Dec^r] Ans^d."
 1. In letterbook, "superior."

Abigail Adams to Thomas B. Adams
December 25, 1800 Washington, District of Columbia

. . . The president has appointed mr Jay chief Justice if he refuses as I fear he
will, mr Cushing will be offered it, but if he declines, then mr patterson will
be appointed — I know it to be the intention of the president to appoint mr
Ingersoll a Judge if a vacancy offers — this is in confidence, your opinion is
so correct and judicious upon all those subjects in̲ᵘᵖᵒⁿ which you offer it, that I
have great confidence in it, and so has the president . . .

ARS (MHi, Adams Manuscript Trust).

Oliver Wolcott, Jr., to Alexander Hamilton ─────────────
December 25, 1800   Washington, District of Columbia

. . . M.ʳ Ellsworths health is I fear destroyed― he has resigned his office & the
President has sported a nomination of M.ʳ Jay, who will n[ot] accept the ap-
pointment― . . .

ARS (DLC, Alexander Hamilton Papers). Marked "(Private)." Reading supplied in brackets because of damage to the document.

Thomas Jefferson to James Madison ─────────────────
December 26, 1800   [Washington, District of Columbia]

. . . All the votes are now come in except Vermont & Kentuckey, and there
is no doubt that the result is a perfect parity between the two republican characters. the Feds appear determined to prevent an election, & ⌄ᵗᵒ pass a bill giving the government to m̄r Jay, appointed Chief justice, or to Marshall as Sec.ʸ
of state.[1] . . .

AR (DLC, James Madison Papers); APc (DLC, Thomas Jefferson Papers). Contemporary letters
in the Thomas Jefferson Papers in the Library of Congress indicate that Jefferson was in Washington, D.C.
    1. Thomas Jefferson implies that John Jay and John Marshall had been appointed to office as
part of a federalist effort to circumvent the election of Jefferson or Aaron Burr. Jefferson repeated
this implication in a letter to Tench Coxe on December 31, 1800: "the Federalists . . . propose to
prevent an election in Congress, & to transfer the government by an act to the C. J. (Jay) or
Secretary of state or to let it devolve on the Pres. pro tem. of the Senate till next December"
(Thomas Jefferson Papers, DLC). On January 7, 1801, the *Aurora,* a republican newspaper published in Philadelphia, printed the same contention: "We shall just state, that A BILL similar to
the *infamous bill* of JAMES ROSS . . . is now contemplated to be brought into Congress. The intention of this bill is, by stratagem to place the *Chief Justice* of the United States in the Presidential
Chair― JOHN JAY was recommended in the spirit and body of this plan―."
    The "infamous" Ross bill, introduced by Senator James Ross of Pennsylvania on February 14,
1800, evolved from a bitter dispute between Pennsylvania republicans and federalists over the
method of choosing that state's presidential electors. The Ross bill ("A Bill Prescribing the mode
of deciding disputed elections of President and Vice President of the United States") provided
for the formation of a "Grand Committee" consisting of six congressmen and six senators and
chaired by the chief justice (or, in his absence, the next senior justice able to attend). Once all
the electors' votes had been opened and counted by the president of the Senate (as specified in
Article II, section 1, of the Constitution), the committee would be sworn in. Its task would be to
ascertain the validity of all certificates and other documents transmitted by the electors along with
any petitions challenging these votes. The committee also could examine the constitutional qualifications of the electors and of the candidates for office. The committee then would make a final
report to the Senate and House of Representatives "stating the number of *legal* votes for each
person, and the number of votes which have been rejected" that would constitute "a final and
conclusive determination of the admissibility, or inadmissibility, of the votes given by the Electors
for President and Vice-President." Richard Buel, Jr., *Securing the Revolution: Ideology in American
Politics, 1789-1815* (Ithaca: Cornell University Press, 1972), pp. 208-9; RG 46, DNA.
    The Ross bill never became law and died in the House on May 10, 1800. *Annals,* 10:713.
There is no evidence to suggest that Ross or anyone else attempted to resurrect this bill after this

date. There was, however, a resolution introduced on January 21, 1801, by Congressman John Rutledge, Jr., of South Carolina, that "a committee be appointed on the part of this House, jointly with a committee on the part of the Senate, to ascertain and report a mode of examining the votes for President and Vice President." *Annals,* 10:916. This resolution may have prompted the following report in the *Aurora* of February 3: "The renewal of *Ross's* project in the senate of last session, by *Rutledge,* in the house of representatives in the present, is another feature of the desperate designs of that faction which has never tired of intrigues, or of the most fatal and ruinous measures."

There is no evidence that the Rutledge resolution was intended to elevate the chief justice to the office of president, as the *Aurora* implied in its article of January 7, cited above. Most correspondents in December, 1800, and January, 1801, assumed that, if the House could not agree on a president, then the president of the Senate pro tempore would take over, under authorization of "An Act relative to the Election of a President and Vice President of the United States, and declaring the Officer who shall act as President in case of Vacancies in the offices both of President and Vice President." *Stat.,* 1:239-41; Gouverneur Morris to Alexander Hamilton, December 19, 1800, Alexander Hamilton Papers, DLC; Abigail Adams to Thomas B. Adams, January 3, 1801, Adams Manuscript Trust, MHi; Timothy Pickering to Rufus King, January 5, 1801, Rufus King Papers, NHi; Alexander Hamilton to Gouverneur Morris, January 9, 1801, Alexander Hamilton Papers, DLC. This statute of March 1, 1792, had been passed according to provision of the Constitution in Article II, section 1, which stated that "the Congress may by Law provide for the Case of Removal, Death, Resignation or Inability, both of the President and Vice President, declaring what Officer shall then act as President." *ROC,* 1:313. Contemporaries do not seem to have queried the applicability of this statute—meant to provide a successor in the case of removal, death, resignation, or inability—to the succession crisis that would ensue if the House could not agree on a president. Some individuals (including Thomas Jefferson in this letter to James Madison of December 26, 1800, and also in Jefferson's letter to Tench Coxe of December 31, 1800, quoted above) suggested that, in order to thwart the election of a republican, the federalists would provide by law for a different succession, possibly including the secretary of state, chief justice, or other officials (James Monroe to Thomas Jefferson, January 6, 1801, Thomas Jefferson Papers, DLC; Albert Gallatin to Hannah Gallatin, January 15, 1801, Albert Gallatin Papers, NHi; James Monroe to Thomas Jefferson, January 18, 1801, Thomas Jefferson Papers, DLC; John Adams to Elbridge Gerry, February 7, 1801, Adams Manuscript Trust, MHi; Thomas Jefferson to James Monroe, February 15, 1801, Thomas Jefferson Papers, DLC). The *Aurora* of January 10, 1801, linked this federalist strategy with passage of a bill similar to the Ross bill, "which should put into the hands of the *Senate* the power of chusing a *President* under certain circumstances."

Timothy Pickering to Rufus King
December 27, 1800   Easton, Pennsylvania

... There is a news-paper report that Judge Ellsworth is about to resign: I should be gratified to see our friend Sitgreaves on the Bench. If Judge Ellsworth contemplated a resignation, when at Paris, I hope he may have mentioned it to M.ʳ S.[1] & thus he may be authorized to recommend the latter to the P.[2] ...

ARS (NHi, Rufus King Papers).

1. Samuel Sitgreaves of Pennsylvania. Sitgreaves had been one ot the American members of the commission to settle British debt controversies under Article VI of the Jay Treaty. Dissatisfied with the proceedings of the board, the American commissioners withdrew from it on July 31, 1799, and the work of the commission stopped. Negotiations with the British were undertaken to facilitate the execution of Article VI. Sitgreaves was sent to London in early 1800 to aid Rufus

King, the American ambassador to England, in these negotiations. Moore, *International Adjudications*, pp. 233-77, 350; *ASP, Foreign Relations*, 2:383-85.

2. President Adams.

Thomas B. Adams to John Adams ————————————
December 28, 1800   Philadelphia, Pennsylvania

... I have received your affectionate & confidential favors of the 17ᵗʰ & 23ᵈ instᵗˢ¹ and have conferred with Mʳ Ingersoll on the subject of their contents, so far as they concerned himself. He observed, that his communication with me, on the subject of his resignation of the office he now holds under government, was intended merely to afford an opportunity for filling the vacancy, which would thereby be created, with such a character as you might think proper to select, and that in conformity to your wish he would continue his functions, until it should be signified to him, that a suitable successor had been found.² I ventured, in confidence, to show him your letter of the 23ᵈ, and he requested time, 'till Monday, to consider the subject, when he would give me an answer. This I will communicate, when received. Should this gentleman, whom I have always considered one of the strictly virtuous, independent & honest men of our Country, consent to accept the contingent proposal, which has been made to him, at this time, I shall view it as no common sacrifice of private feeling, domestic & retired habits, and pecuniary benefit, to an imperious conviction, that an upright judiciary is the only bulwark that can oppose & restrain the impetuous torrent of division & disorganization with which this Continent is threatened. He has a stake in the common weal, and cannot be indifferent as to its protection, from wild theories, and no less extravagant practice. I hope he may come in.

The justice & the policy of appointing Mʳ Jay, cannot be doubted, and no gentleman of reflection, will feel a spirit of competition in opposition to it. I had been so habituated to the idea of his fixed determination, to seek retirement from public life, that his pretentions did not occur to me, when contemplating this subject. Since however he has been appointed, without consultation, and the possibility of his declining to accept, yet exists, I am glad that the contingent offer has been made to Mʳ Ingersoll — I have some expectations now, that he will not refuse to be considered a candidate, should a vacancy occur — ...

ARS (MHi, Adams Manuscript Trust). Addressed "Washington."

1. The letter of December 17, 1800, has not been found.

2. Jared Ingersoll was United States attorney for the district of Pennsylvania.

Oliver Wolcott, Jr., to Timothy Pickering ——————
December 28, 1800   Washington, District of Columbia

... I enclose you a Letter which I lately rec^d from our friend Chief Justice Ellsworth,[1] who I am concerned to hear is in a very reduced state of health. you will perceive by the papers, that he has resigned his Office, and that the President has nominated Mr Jay. If it were not difficult in these strange times, to predict any thing we might suppose it impossible, that Mr Jay should resume a station more arduous, than that which he has declined on account of advanced age.[2] The nomination ^is here considered as having been made in one of those "sportive" humours for which our Chief is distinguished. ...

ARS (MHi, Timothy Pickering Papers); ADfS (CtHi, Oliver Wolcott Jr. Papers). Marked "(Private)." Endorsed "rec^d Jany 1801."

1. The letter referred to may have been a copy or the original of Oliver Ellsworth to Oliver Wolcott, Jr., October 16, 1800 (q.v.).

2. John Jay, who had been governor of New York, declined to run for a third term in November, 1800. Frank Monaghan, *John Jay* (New York: Bobbs-Merrill, 1935), p. 424.

Samuel Sewall to Theodore Sedgwick ——————————
December 29, 1800   Marblehead, Massachusetts

... I am pleased at the prospect of Mr Patterson as succeeding to the place of Chief Justice: and I wish M^rCushing would have a successor appointed during this administration __ The Judiciary is now almost the only security left us __ and it is at all times the most important branch[1] of the federal Gov^t __ ...

ARS (MHi, Theodore Sedgwick Papers).

Samuel Sewall (1757-1814), a lawyer in Marblehead, Massachusetts, served in Congress from December 7, 1796, until his resignation on January 10, 1800. In 1801 Sewall became an associate judge of the Supreme Judicial Court of Massachusetts and was chief justice of that court in 1813 and 1814. *BDAC.*

1. The "c" is written over an "h."

Thomas B. Adams to Abigail Adams ——————————
December 30, 1800   Philadelphia, Pennsylvania

... I talked with Mr Ingersoll to-day on the subject of the proposal, which has been mentioned to him at my father's request. It is confidential business, but I presume you are in the secret, and as I am now writing to you, to save time, I shall mention what passed between us, respecting it.

He has not fully formed a resolution, what answer to give, and his greatest difficulty arises from the uncertainty whether any change will take place in the

Judiciary system, during this Session. If that were certain, he would not scruple to give an affirmative answer, but said he, "with my habits of life, to be six months in the year absent from my family, I know of nothing scarcely that could induce the sacrifice." He requested me however to defer a decisive answer to my fathers letter [a few?] days longer_ ... Mᵣ Ingersoll will be at Washington in February at the Supreme Court_ ...

ARS (MHi, Adams Manuscript Trust). Addressed "Washington."

Robert Troup to Rufus King ⸻
December 31, 1800 New York, New York

... Mʳ Jay has been nominated to succeed Mʳ Ellsworth as Chief Justice; but no one believes he will accept the appointment. In his late resignation of all further pretentions to the government he states his fixed determination to devote the remainder of his life to retirement. ...

... I have for some time past consoled myself with the idea that Mʳ Ellsworth would form a rallying point for us. This idea however has vanished with his resignation of the office of Chief Justice. We fear he is lost to public life for ever! What destinies await us must be left to that supreme governor who directs all things according to his sovereign pleasure. ...

ARS (NHi, Rufus King Papers).

Abigail Adams to Thomas B. Adams ⸻
January 3, 1801 Washington, District of Columbia

... I presume mr Ingersol, will not be hurried for his decicion, no answer has yet come from mr Jay; your Father will write to you I trust ...

ALS (MHi, Adams Manuscript Trust).

Timothy Pickering to Oliver Wolcott, Jr. ⸻
January 3, 1801 Philadelphia, Pennsylvania

       it
... I consider ^ impossible that Mʳ Jay should consent to take the office of Chief Justice: and it is deeply to be regretted that the P. will so often sport in serious things. ...

ARS (CtHi, Oliver Wolcott Jr. Papers). Timothy Pickering misdated this letter as "Janʸ 3. 1800."

Timothy Pickering to Rufus King ───────────────────────
January 5, 1801   Philadelphia, Pennsylvania

... The president has nominated M͏ͬ Jay to be Chief Justice in the room of Judge Ellsworth. The Senate of course ratified the nomination: but the P. as well as every body else must know that M͏ͬ Jay will not accept the office. He formally announced to the Legislature of New York his determination to retire from public life, on account of his advanced age and <u>infirmities</u>. Under such circumstances, nobody but M͏ͬ A. would have made the nomination without consulting M͏ͬ Jay._ ...

As M͏ͬ Jay will certainly refuse the Chief-Justiceship, I presume Judge Patterson will be appointed: and his vacancy, I am disposed to think, will be filled either from N. York or Pennsylvania. If from the former, perhaps by Judge Laurance.[1] ...

ARS (NHi, Rufus King Papers).
   1. John Laurance (1750-1810) read law in the office of New York's provincial lieutenant governor Cadwallader Colden and in 1772 gained admission to the New York bar. In 1777 Laurance was appointed judge advocate general on George Washington's staff and served in that position until June, 1782. Laurance was a member of the Confederation Congress and the First and Second Congresses. On May 6, 1794, he was named United States judge for the district of New York, a post he resigned in November, 1796, upon his election to the Senate. Laurance remained in the Senate until August, 1800. *DAB.*

Elias Boudinot to Elisha Boudinot ────────────────────
January 7, 1801   Philadelphia, Pennsylvania

... I take it for granted that M͏ͬ Jay will refuse the Chief Justiceship_ who will succeed him I know not, but I wish he would accept it_ M͏ͬ Adams could not accept it, as he is totally unable to perform the labours of a Post_ If the Judiciary should be altered, perhaps it might be more eligible for him, but I doubt his accepting of it_ ...

ARS (NjP, Thorne Boudinot Collection). Addressed "New Ark." Postmarked "PHI   7   JAN."

Aurora ──────────────────────────────────────
January 8, 1801   Philadelphia, Pennsylvania

John Jay after having thro' decay of age become incompetent to discharge the duties of Governor, has been appointed to the *sinecure* of *Chief Justice* of the United States.

─────────────

That the *Chief Justiceship* is a sinecure needs no other evidence, than that in one case the duties were *discharged* by one person who resided at the same time in England; and by another during a year's residence in France.[1]

(Philadelphia) January 8, 1801. Date and place are from headline.

The first paragraph of this article appeared in the *Massachusetts Mercury* (Boston), January 16, 1801.

1. A reference to Chief Justice John Jay's service in England as envoy extraordinary and Chief Justice Oliver Ellsworth's in France in the same capacity.

Thomas B. Adams to John Adams —————————————————
January 9, 1801   Philadelphia, Pennsylvania

... I have heard nothing further from M: Ingersoll and suppose he is waiting to hear what answer M: Jay gives and what fate attends the new judiciary Bill. I will be careful to give you his definitive answer, in season— He will be at Washington in February— ...

ARS (MHi, Adams Manuscript Trust). Endorsed "Ans^d 2^d time Jan. 16. 1801." No answering letter discussing the Jared Ingersoll appointment has been found.

John Jay to Peter Augustus Jay —————————————————
January 12, 1801   Albany, New York

... as to my new appointment, I have declined accepting it—[1] I postpone Details on this Subject until we meet, which I hope will as you expect, be in the course of this month. ...

ARS (CtY, Jay Family Papers). Endorsed "rec^d 15 Jan."

1. Newspapers reported in several different versions the fact that John Jay had declined appointment as chief justice. A very brief article appeared in the *Philadelphia Gazette* on January 12, 1801, which also was printed in the *United States Oracle* (Portsmouth, New Hampshire) on January 24. *Poulson's American Daily Advertiser* (Philadelphia) noted the declination on January 13, 1801. The *Washington Federalist* (Georgetown, District of Columbia) published a report on January 13, 1801, which also appeared in the *Philadelphia Gazette* on January 16 and in the *Times* (Charleston) on January 26. The *Museum* (Georgetown, District of Columbia) printed a brief report on January 14. The *National Intelligencer* (Washington, District of Columbia) noted Jay's declination on January 14 and this was reprinted in the Boston *Independent Chronicle* on January 26. The *Columbian Centinel* (Boston) printed a report on January 21, and this report also appeared in the *Newport Mercury* (Newport, Rhode Island) on January 27. A different article appeared in the *American Mercury* (Hartford) on January 22.

Samuel A. Otis to John Adams —————————————————
January 13, 1801   Washington, District of Columbia

Washington   Jany 13th 1801

Sir

There being a probability of at least one vacancy on the Bench of the supreme Court, M^rRead of S^oCarolina[1] hath requested me to mention him as a

Candidate for the office of Judge. His Lady entertains such apprehensions from a Southern climate as have induced his determination in favor of a more Northern residence. The important stations in which M{r}Read hath been placed added to his law knowledge & experience may entitle him to consideration; more especially as he seems to have been sacrificed for his support of Government.

I do not recollect any appointments in that quarter interfe[a?]ring with this application, and presume this would be satisfactory to a respectable & influential part of the Southern Country. In any event your goodness will excuse my zeal in behalf of a friend, & believe me

    With unabating esteem & respect   Sir   Your most obed{t} &   Most humble Ser{t}

                                              Sam A Otis

The President of the UStates

ARS (MHi, Adams Manuscript Trust).
    1. Jacob Read.

Richard D. Spaight to John G. Blount ——————————
January 13, 1801   Washington, District of Columbia

. . . The Anglo-federalists will try all in their power to prevent the election of Mr Jefferson, they say they prefer Mr Burr, but they dont speak truth, it is their wish if they Can to prevent ~~any person,~~ _either of those gentlemen_ from being President, & to provide by law, that in case of NO election taking place, the Chief-Justice shall administer the Government, untill a new election takes place, and it is for this purpose that the Essex Junto have perswaded Mr Adams to nominate Mr Jay—[1] But I am Certain that he knew not[2] their schemes, when he made the nomination, and that in fact he was pursuing measures dictated or advised by A. Hamilton his most bitter enemy.[3] I hope & Trust in God that we shall defeat all their diabolical schemes, & that by their attempt, they will only consign themselves to eternal infamy here, & Damnation in the world to Come. . . .

ARS (Nc-AR, John Gray Blount Papers). Addressed "Washington   N{o} Carolina."
    1. See note to Thomas Jefferson to James Madison, December 26, 1800.
    2. The "n" is written over "th."
    3. For the enmity between John Adams and Alexander Hamilton, see note to James Gunn to Alexander Hamilton, December 18, 1800.

Thomas B. Adams to John Quincy Adams ——————————
January 15, 1801   Philadelphia, Pennsylvania

. . . Judge Patterson will most probably be chief Justice of the US, as Mr Jay to whom it was offered declines it. . . .

ARS (MHi, Adams Manuscript Trust).

Uriah Tracy to James McHenry ───────────────────
January 15, 1801   Washington, District of Columbia

. . . Gov.̣ Jay has refused the Office of Chief Justice, who will have it now is
uncertain._ . . .

ARS (DLC, James McHenry Papers).

Robert Troup to Rufus King ───────────────────
January 15, 1801   New York, New York

[*Troup expresses his sadness on John Jay's retiring from public life.*] We all however
agree that it is time for him to retire_ For several years past his energies have
been on the decline._ He has been appointed to succeed Chief Justice Elsworth but he has declined his appointment & is bent on his retirement. . . .

ARS (NHi, Rufus King Papers). Endorsed "Rc.ᵈ feb 28.ᵗʰ"

Jonas Platt to James Kent ───────────────────
January 16, 1801   Washington, District of Columbia

. . . Judge Benson . . . ought to be placed on the Bench of Sup. Court in the
Place of Judge Patterson who ought to be Chief Justice; but the President
seems determined to outrage the patient attachm.ᵗ of his friends; and there is
very little Hope that he will ever again do any act that shall be consoling to
his Party. . . .

ARS (DLC, James Kent Papers). Addressed "Albany." Postmarked "[WASH-]CITY   JAN   16."
    Jonas Platt (1769-1834), a lawyer, had been county clerk of Herkimer County, New York
(1791-1798). In 1798 he became clerk of Oneida County and served there until 1802, during
which time he also represented New York in the Sixth Congress (1799-1801). *BDAC.*
    James Kent (1763-1847), later famous for his *Commentaries on American Law.* Kent's legal career
began in 1781 when he was apprenticed to Egbert Benson, then New York's attorney general.
Admitted to the bar in 1785, Kent began his practice in Poughkeepsie, where he had the opportunity to meet federalist leaders at the New York convention to consider the Constitution.
Kent was master in Chancery (1796-1798) and recorder of New York City (1797-1798). He
served as a judge of the New York Supreme Court of Judicature from 1798 to 1814, the last ten
years as the court's chief judge. In 1814 Kent became chancellor of the New York Court of
Chancery. *DAB.*

John Drayton to John Jay ───────────────────
January 19, 1801   Charleston, South Carolina

. . . Your intention of retiring to private life, I suppose cannot be easily carried
into execution, by your re-appointment to the Chief Justiceship of the United
States. I myself am particularly gratified at it: as, in performing the duties of

that Station, I flatter myself, I shall have the pleasure of seeing you in this country. Believe me my Dear Sir, You will be received by none in it, with greater friendship, than by myself: and I hope I shall have the pleasure of seeing you, as soon after your arrival as possible. . . .

ARS (NNC, John Jay Papers).
  John Drayton (1766-1822) was governor of South Carolina. Drayton may have met John Jay during a trip to the northern states in the early 1790s, because in 1794 he sent Jay a copy of his book, titled *Letters written during a Tour through the Northern and Eastern States of America. DAB;* Henry P. Johnston, ed., *The Correspondence and Public Papers of John Jay,* 4 vols. (New York: G. P. Putnam's Sons, 1890-1893), 4:127-28.

Benjamin Stoddert to John Adams ————————————
January 19, 1801 Washington, District of Columbia

19. January 1801

Sir
  The bad weather prevented my doing myself the honor of calling this morning, to mention, at the request of some members of Congress_ that the Judiciary bill would be taken up in the House of Representatives tomorrow_ & be passed upon.
  As the bill proposes a reduction of the Judges to five_ and as there are already five Judges in commission, it is suggested that there might be more difficulty in appointing a chief Justice without taking him from the present Judges, after the passage of this bill even by one Branch of the Legislature, than before.[1]
  I have the honor to be with the highest respect & esteem sir Y^r most obed. Servt

Ben. Stoddert

ARS (MHi, Adams Manuscript Trust).
  Benjamin Stoddert (1751-1813), a Georgetown merchant, was the secretary of the navy. *DAB.*
  1. "A bill to provide for the more convenient organization of the courts of the United States" had its first reading in the House of Representatives on December 19, 1800. It had its third reading and passed in the House on January 20, 1801. *HRJ,* 3:743, 767-68. The bill was enacted on February 13, 1801. Section 3 provided "That from and after the next vacancy that shall happen in the said court, it shall consist of five justices only; that is to say, of one chief justice, and four associate justices." *Stat.,* 2:89.

Elias Boudinot to John Adams ————————————
January 20, 1801 Philadelphia, Pennsylvania

. . . Being just returned from New Jersey, will you excuse the liberty I take in mentioning to you, that I found the Gent^n of the Law there, are exceedingly anxious, relative to a report that is prevailing, that the Office of Chief Justice of the united States may possibly be filled by our present Chief Magistrate[1] after the month of march next— I am authorized to say, that it would give them the highest pleasure, and raise their drooping confidence in the future government of the united States.— This being an entirely independant Office, and not subject to the changes incident to other Offices of Government, might not be unworthy of the attention of one who had previously filled the presidental Chair— This hope is on condition that the new Judiciary Bill, shall change the present itinary state of that important Office by rendering it stationary & of course more respectable. I have taken the liberty barely to hint this, as the sincere wishes of the Gentlemen of the Bar in New Jersey— ...

ARS (MHi, Adams Manuscript Trust). Marked "private."
  1. John Adams.

Jonathan Dayton to William Paterson —————————
January 20, 1801   Washington, District of Columbia

Washington   Jan.ʸ 20.ᵗʰ 1801
Dear sir,

With grief, astonishment & almost indignation, I hasten to inform you, that, contrary to the hopes & expectations of us all, the President has this morning nominated Gen.ˡ Marshall, the present Sec.ʸ of State, for the office of Chief Justice of the U. States.[1] The eyes of all parties had been turned upon you, whose pretensions he knew were, in every respect the best, & who, he could not be ignorant, would have been the most acceptable to our country. Painful as it would be for the Senate to reject a man of such respectable talents & standing as M.ʳMarshall unquestionably is, I am convinced nevertheless that they would do it, if they could be assured that thereby <u>you</u> would be called to fill it, & <u>he</u> brought upon the bench as a Junior Judge. Instead of this, it is feared that the rejection of this might induce the nomination of some other character more improper, & more disgusting. I shall however consult my colleague M.ʳSchureman[2] & sound the Federal Members upon the propriety of making a stand here. The nominations & whole conduct of M.ʳ Adams during the present session have manifested such debility or derangement of intellect, that I am convinced, in common with the most Federal of our Members, that another four years Administration in his hands would have exposed us to destruction.[3]

Excuse my warmth & believe me to be with the
sincerest respect & esteem   Your very hum. serv.ᵗ

Jona: Dayton

Judge Paterson—

ARS (NjR, William Paterson Papers).
   After eight years in the House of Representatives (1791-1799)—the last four of which he was speaker of the House—Jonathan Dayton (1760-1824), a New Jersey federalist, was elected to the Senate. Dayton served there until 1805. Richard A. Harrison, *Princetonians*, 3:31-41.

1. Congressman David Stone of North Carolina noted in a January 24 letter to Samuel Johnston that John Adams had nominated John Marshall. Hayes Collection, NcU.

Although John Marshall's nomination occurred on January 20, the *Museum* (Georgetown, District of Columbia) on January 19, 1801, published a notice of it, which also appeared in the *Gazette of the United States* (Philadelphia) on January 22 and in the *Columbian Museum* (Savannah) on February 6. The *Washington Federalist* (Georgetown, District of Columbia) reported the nomination on January 21, and this report appeared in the *Philadelphia Gazette* on January 26. The *National Intelligencer* (Washington, District of Columbia) on January 21 carried a brief story, which was reprinted in the *Raleigh Register* (Raleigh, North Carolina) on February 3.

The *Philadelphia Gazette* seems to have had a difficult time verifying the fact that the nomination had occurred. Basing its story on a letter received from Washington, it first reported the nomination on January 21. (This article appeared with minor variations as far north as Portsmouth, New Hampshire, in the *United States Oracle* on January 31.) Doubting its own story of January 21, the *Philadelphia Gazette* retracted it on January 22. (The retraction appeared in the New Haven *Connecticut Journal* on January 29.) Finally, on January 23, the *Philadelphia Gazette* printed the correct news and gave the exact date of Marshall's nomination. (This last story appeared also in the New York *Commercial Advertiser* of January 27.)

Other newspapers which published notices of Marshall's nomination include the *Aurora* (Philadelphia) on January 22, the *Times* (Charleston) on January 30, and the *Boston Gazette* on February 2.

2. James Schureman (1756-1824), a New Jersey federalist, sat in the Senate from March 4, 1799, to February 16, 1801, when he resigned. Schureman previously had served two terms in the House of Representatives in the First and Fifth Congresses (1789-1791, 1797-1799). *BDAC.*

3. One of Jonathan Dayton's colleagues, Jonas Platt of New York, expressed similar widely held sentiments about John Adams's insensitivity in making appointments without first consulting with other federalists. Jonas Platt to James Kent, January 16, 1801, James Kent Papers, DLC.

Thomas B. Adams to John Adams ───────────────────
January 22, 1801   Philadelphia, Pennsylvania

. . . It has been said in the papers of the morning that L. H. Stockton has been nominated as Secretary at War, and Gen¹ Marshall Chief Justice _ The latter is contradicted this evening, and I think Richard Stockton must be the person nominated for the other office _ [1] . . .

ARS (MHi, Adams Manuscript Trust). Addressed "City of Washington." Endorsed "ans^d 27th."

1. On January 14, 1801, President Adams nominated Lucius Horatio Stockton of New Jersey to be secretary of war, but he withdrew the nomination on January 29 at Stockton's request. *SEJ,* 1:368, 375.

James McHenry to Oliver Wolcott, Jr. ───────────────
January 22, 1801   Baltimore, Maryland

. . . I know not what you think of the late nomination of Mr Jay to be chief justice, so immediately after he had publickly declared it to be his intention to spend the remainder of his life as a private citizen. The nomination excited the idea, that Mr Adams considered such declarations were always made without sincerity, and meant to be disregarded. It pleased me, of course, to see Mr Jay act a consistent, and I think a sincere part, in refusing an appointment, thus unseasonably, if not, under the existing circumstances, indecorously offered.

Mʳ Adams it strikes me has committed another blunder, but, it is true one not altogether so rare, I mean, in rewarding new friends and neglecting old ones. Here it was expected, by every body, that he would have named Mʳ Patterson, to the vacant seat on the bench, except by Mʳ _____,[1] who thought he should have been appointed; and by me, who thought the President should have appointed himself. . . .

ARS (CtHi, Oliver Wolcott Jr. Papers).
    1. It is not known to whom James McHenry was referring.

Abigail Adams to Thomas B. Adams ——————————
January 25, 1801   Washington, District of Columbia

. . . It is laughable to hear the offices which even the federilist are for placing the president in. one wants to make him Ambassador, an other Chief Justice_ and an other Goveneur_ comforting things be sure_ Farmer Adams if Farmer he can be upon his own System, would be enviable to any thing in the power of the Country to give or grant, no more elective offices for me_ I think too highly of the Rank and Station in which I have been placed ever to give my consent to a secondary and subordinate Station; looking upon myself in this sense, one and indivisible to degrade ourselves, to descend voluntarily, and by choice, from the highest to a lower Rank, to quit the care of a Nation, for that of a State_ those who will submit to it, must possess more of Humity[1] than falls to my Lot_ yet can I in a private and retired life practise all the oeconomy to which I know I must be called, and feel no degradation or mortification but for my Country_ . . .

ARS (MHi, Adams Manuscript Trust). Endorsed "30ᵗʰ [Janʸ] Recᵈ" and "1ˢᵗ Febʸ ansᵈ."
    1. I.e., humility.

William Paterson to Jonathan Dayton ——————————
January 25, 1801   New Brunswick, New Jersey

. . . Your letter of the 17ᵗʰ of this month[1] I had the honor of receiving to-day. With respect to the office of chief-justice, I have always considered myself as being out of the question. I long ago made up my mind on the subject, and have invariably and repeatedly declared, that if appointed to that office I would not accept. This opinion was the result of due deliberation. After this, if the president had put my name in nomination I should have considered it a complimental thing, a mere feather, which might tickle a vain mind, but which I neither wished nor wanted. Mʳ Marshall is a man of genius, of strong reasoning powers, and a sound, correct lawyer. His talents have at once the lustre and solidity of gold. I have no doubt, that he will discharge the duties of the office with ability and honor. But notwithstanding the nomination was unexpected, because the late president[2] laid it down for a rule, which I presumed the pres-

ent had adopted, not to select two judges from the ^same state. In casting about, therefore, for a chief-justice, I did not take Virginia into view, but supposed that a gentleman of another state would have been chosen. My eyes were naturally turned to Gen! Pickering, and I fully expected, that he would have been M! Ellsworth's successor.

. . .

Many things strange, passing strange, have turned up in the world of politics in the course of a few months. But you lay matters too seriously to heart. Why grieve and lament? Give me the easy chair of the jolly, laughing philosopher, Democritus,[3] and anybody for me shall be welcome to the gloomy tub[4] of weeping Heraclitus.[5] "Laugh where we can" is one of the best maxims to pass through life with ease and comfort. You will at least agree, that some things have been done, which "exceed all power of face."[6]

A sprain in my arm, which gives considerable pain, and a cold, which generally terminates in an inflammatory sore throat, will prevent my attendance at the next session of the court. . . .

ARS (PHi, Gratz Collection).

1. No letter of January 17 from Dayton to Paterson has been found. Paterson may have mistaken the date; he is clearly responding to the news first reported by Dayton in his letter to Paterson of January 20, 1801 (q.v.). Dayton could not have reported the news of Marshall's nomination until January 20, when President Adams submitted it to the Senate; see above, Jonathan Dayton to William Paterson, January 20, 1801.

2. George Washington.

3. Democritus (ca.460-ca.370 B.C.), a Greek philosopher who taught that happiness—the true end of life—could be attained in inner tranquility. He is sometimes known as the "laughing philosopher." *New Columbia Encyclopedia;* Paul Harvey, comp. and ed., *The Oxford Companion to English Literature,* 4th ed. rev. by Dorothy Eagle (New York: Oxford University Press, 1967).

4. "Applied contemptuously or jocularly to a pulpit." *OED.*

5. Heraclitus (ca.535-ca.475 B.C.), a Greek philosopher teaching that all things carry with them their opposites, including that death was potential in life. His melancholy view of life's fleeting character led to his being called the "weeping philosopher." *New Columbia Encyclopedia;* Harvey, comp. and ed., *Oxford Companion to English Literature,* 4th ed. rev. by Dorothy Eagle.

6. "Command of countenance, *esp.* with reference to freedom from indications of shame." *OED.*

John Adams to Elias Boudinot ——————————————
January 26, 1801 Washington, District of Columbia

. . . I have this morning, received your favor of the 20th The anxiety of the gentlemen of the law in New Jersey, to have the present P.[1] of the U S appointed chief Justice, after the third of March, is very flattering to me. Although neither pride nor vanity nor indolence would prevent me from accepting any situation, in which I could be useful, I know of none, for which I am fit. The office of Chief justice is too important for any man to hold of sixty five years of age, who has wholly neglected the study of the law for six & twenty years. I have already by the nomination of a gentleman in the full vigour of middle age— in the full habits of business & whose reading in the science is fresh in his head to this office, put it wholly out of my power & indeed it never was in my hopes or wishes

The remainder of my days will probably be spent in the labors of agriculture and the amusements of litterature in both of which I have always taken more delight, than in any public office of whatever rank. Far removed from all intrigues & out of the reach of all the the great and little passions, that agitate the world, although I take no resolutions nor make any promises, I hope to enjoy more tranquility, than has ever before been my lot.— ...

ALb (MHi, Adams Manuscript Trust).
    1. I.e., president.

James A. Bayard to Andrew Bayard ————————————
January 26, 1801   Washington, District of Columbia

... I see it denied in your paper that Mr Marshall was nominated Chief Justice of the US.[1] The fact is so & he will without doubt have the concurrence of
                                                                    first
the Senate, tho some hesitation was at ^ ~~present~~ expressed from a respect to the pretensions of Mr Paterson— ...

ARS (DLC, Bayard Family Papers).
    James Ashton Bayard (1767-1815), a Delaware attorney and first cousin of former Supreme Court clerk Samuel Bayard, served in Congress from 1797 to 1803. James A. Bayard later served in the Senate from 1804 to 1813. *BDAC.*
    Andrew Bayard (1762-1832), a Philadelphia merchant involved in insurance and banking activities, was a first cousin of Congressman James Ashton Bayard and a brother of Samuel Bayard, the former clerk of the Supreme Court. Harrison, *Princetonians,* 3:263-66.
    1. The confusion concerning the nomination of John Marshall as chief justice is discussed in a note to Jonathan Dayton to William Paterson, January 20, 1801.

Thomas Rodney Diary Entry ————————————————
January 26, 1801   [Kent County, Delaware?]

... Upon Elsworths Resignation, Jay, was again appointed Chief Justice of the U. States— but he <u>declines</u> accepting— Adams, probably made this appointment to affront the Democrats— & shews he is greatly Vexed, at being left out— ...

AD (DLC, Rodney Family Papers). Place suggested by reference to other entries in Thomas Rodney's diary around this date.

Aurora ———————————————————————
January 27, 1801   Philadelphia, Pennsylvania

It is understood that *Judge Cushing* is resolved to retire from the *federal bench,* and that Mr. DEXTER is to be made a JUDGE in his place!

(Philadelphia) January 27, 1801. Date and place from the headline.

Jonathan Dayton to William Paterson ———————————
January 28, 1801   Washington, District of Columbia

Washington   Jan.ʸ 28ᵗʰ 1801

Dear sir,

The nomination of Mr Marshall to supply the vacancy of Chief Justice occasioned by Mr Ellsworth's resignation, was yesterday approved unanimously by the Senate.[1]

The delay which has taken place was upon my motion for postponment, & was intended to afford an opportunity for ascertaining whether the President could be induced under ~~either~~ any circumstances whatever to nominate you. If we could have been satisfied of this, we should have taken measures to prevail on Mr Marshall to have hi[m]self declined the highest, for a lower seat, upon the bench, or in case of his refusal, have negatived him. This would have been a course of proceeding, painful indeed to the Federalists on account of their esteem for that gentleman & their respect for his talents, & to which nothing could have brought them, but their very strong attachment to you, & their very high sense of your superior title & pretensions. It must be gratifying to you to learn that all voices, with the exception of one only were united in favor of the conferring of this appointment upon you. The President alone was inflexible, & declared that he would never nominate you. Under these circumstances we thought it adviseable to confirm Mr Marshall, lest another not so well qualified, & more disgusting to the Bench, should be substituted, & because it appeared that this gentleman ~~had~~ was not privy to his own nomination, but had previously exerted his influence with the President in your behalf.

In this painful transaction, there was the most perfect understanding & concert among the Federal Members of the Senate, & the most perfect disposition on the part of the gentleman in question to promote our favorite object, which

only
has been defeated ˄ by the wild freak of a man, whose Administration, happily for this country, is soon to terminate.

With great respect & esteem   I am Dᵣsir your most obedᵗ

Jona: Dayton

Hoñble
Judge Paterson

ARS (NjR, William Paterson Papers). Addressed "New Brunswick." A reading has been supplied in brackets where page is torn.

1. John Quincy Adams received word of John Marshall's appointment in a letter from his mother, Abigail Adams, dated January 29, 1801, and in an undated letter from William Vans Murray (both in Adams Manuscript Trust, MHi). Thomas Rodney noted the appointment of Marshall, "an Old Tory," in his diary under date of February 25. Rodney Family Papers, DLC.

Newspapers also reported on the Senate's confirmation of John Marshall as chief justice. A January 29 report in the *Washington Federalist* (Georgetown, District of Columbia) also appeared in *Poulson's American Daily Advertiser* (Philadelphia) on February 4 and in the *City Gazette* (Charleston) on February 16. The *Museum* (Georgetown, District of Columbia) on January 30 printed a story that (with minor variation) was reprinted in the *Boston Gazette* on February 12 and in the *Georgia Gazette* (Savannah) on February 19. A notice in the *Aurora* (Philadelphia) on February 3 appeared with minor differences in the *United States Oracle* (Portsmouth, New Hampshire) on February 14. A variant was published in the *Massachusetts Mercury* (Boston) on February 10.

James Hillhouse to Simeon Baldwin ——————
January 31, 1801   Washington, District of Columbia

... We have appointed Mᵣ Marshall, Secretary of State, Chief Justice of the United States— I wish it had been Mᵣ Patterson, I think it a pitty that the feelings of so honorable and able a Judge should be wounded, as I have no doubt his will be by having a yonger man, and a yonger Lawyer, and not more eminent in that line, put over his head— ...

ARS (CtY, Baldwin Family Papers). Addressed "New Haven   Connecticut."

Jonathan Dayton to William Paterson ——————
February 1, 1801   Washington, District of Columbia

... Your letter of the 25ᵗʰ Ult. is received, & has given me peculiar pleasure in the assurance, that you feel neither resentment nor disgust at the appointment of MᵣMarshall. The dissatisfaction among the Members of Congress, in consequence of your being thus passed by, appeared to me universal, & this sensation probably derived greater strength from the apprehension, that it might drive you from your seat upon the bench, where all men of all parties were anxious that you should remain.

Influenced by this common sentiment, & irritated at the injury done to you, I wrote in a ~~style &~~ temper, more than usually warm. You have however reproved, or rather corrected me, in that gay, playful style and manner, which you understand so well how to employ, in order to bring back your friends to a good humor with themselves or with the world. . . .

ARS (NjR, William Paterson Papers).

John Marshall to William Paterson —————————————
February 2, 1801   Washington, District of Columbia

. . . I had this instant the pleasure of receiving your letter of the 26th of January.[1]

For your polite & friendly sentiments on the appointment with which I have been lately honord I pray you to accept my warm & sincere acknowledgements.

I regret much that you cannot attend this session of the supreme court & still more the cause which detains you from us.[2] I hope it will be of short duration & that the other members will be present. As yet however I have only seen Judge Cushing. . . .

ARS (NjR, William Paterson Papers). Addressed "New Brunswick   New Jersey." Postmarked "WASH-CITY   FEB   2."
 1. Letter not found.
 2. On February 17, 1801, the *North-Carolina Minerva* (Raleigh) printed a letter from "Washington, February 3." The letter reported that William Paterson was absent from the Court because of indisposition.

Richard Stockton to John Adams —————————————
February 2, 1801   Princeton, New Jersey

. . . I cannot close this letter without assuring you that your appointment of M[r] Marshal to be Chief Justice of the United States meets the entire approbation of all impartial men here who know what high qualifications are required in him who shall execute this office with dignity and advantage to the Nation. . . .

ARS (MHi, Adams Manuscript Trust).
 Richard Stockton (1764-1828), a lawyer and politician, had graduated from the College of New Jersey (later Princeton) in 1779. He studied law with his uncle, Elisha Boudinot, gained admission to the bar in 1784, and began an active law practice. He served in the Senate from November 12, 1796, to March 3, 1799. In January, 1801, President Adams offered him a position as circuit judge under the new judiciary act, but Stockton declined the offer. *DAB.*

Aurora ————————————————————————————
February 3, 1801   Philadelphia, Pennsylvania

[*After a brief mention that there may still be a plot by the federalists to overturn the election of a republican president,*[1] *this report continues.*] We cannot permit ourselves to believe that *John Marshall* has been called to the bench to foster such a plot— We cannot believe that it will be seriously attempted— Yet how can we account for the strange mutations which have passed before us— Marshall for a few weeks Secretary of State, ascends to the bench of the Chief Justice. . . .

(Philadelphia) February 3, 1801. Date and place are those of newspaper.
   1. See note to Thomas Jefferson to James Madison, December 26, 1800.

Gazette of the United States ————————————————————
February 6, 1801   Baltimore, Maryland

On Wednesday last the Supreme Court formed a quorum in a room appropriated for their sitting in the Capitol. The honorable John Marshall, late secretary of state, produced the diploma of his appointment as cheif justice. The usual oaths upon that occasion were administered to him. . . .

(Philadelphia) February 9, 1801. Date and place are from the headline.
   This article also appeared in the *Newport Mercury* (Newport, Rhode Island) on February 17, 1801, and in the *Times* (Charleston) on February 18, 1801.

Timothy Pickering to Rufus King ————————————————
February 7, 1801   Salem, Massachusetts

. . . M.r Marshall has been nominated, and I presume will be appointed Chief Justice. . . .

ARS (NHi, Rufus King Papers).

Charles Cotesworth Pinckney to Theodore Sedgwick ————————
February 12, 1801   Savannah, Georgia

. . . It gave me great pleasure to hear that my friend Gen.l Marshall had been appointed Chief Justice, I hope nothing will prevent his acceptance of that office. at a time when attempts are making to construe away the Energy of our Constitution, to unnerve our Government, & to overthrow that system by which we have risen to our present prosperity, it is all important that our supreme Judiciary should be filled by men of Elevated talents, sound federal principles, & unshaken firmness. . . .

ARS (MHi, Theodore Sedgwick Papers). Addressed "Washington." Postmarked "SAVAN-GA FEB 13."

Columbian Centinel ——————————————————————————————
February 14, 1801 Boston, Massachusetts

The assent of the Senate to the nomination of the Hon. Mr. MARSHAL to be Chief Justice of the *United States,* was UNANIMOUS. We expect the Jacobin jackals, at some future period, will deny having abused this gentleman also. . . .

(Boston) February 14, 1801. Date and place are those of the newspaper.

Henry Van Schaack to Theodore Sedgwick ————————————
February 17, 1801 Pittsfield, Massachusetts

. . . I am truly concerned that Patterson has not been nominated to be at the head of the Judiciary.— The public Voice proclaims him a great Law Character, besides his Law knowledge he possesses nerve— . . .

ARS (MHi, Theodore Sedgwick Papers). Addressed "Washington." Postmarked by hand "Pittsfield U. S. Feb. 18th."

 Before the revolution, Henry Van Schaack (1733-1823) had been a merchant in upstate New York. There Van Schaack had held public office as a postmaster and alderman in Albany. He also was a justice of the peace in his native Kinderhook. A loyalist during the Revolutionary War, Van Schaack was sent to Hartford, Connecticut. He later moved to Massachusetts and spent nearly twenty-three years in Pittsfield where he was active in local politics, supporting the federal Constitution and serving in the Massachusetts legislature. In 1807 he returned to New York. Edward A. Collier, *A History of Old Kinderhook* (New York: G. P. Putnam's Sons, 1914), pp. 406-9.

David Stone to Samuel Johnston ——————————————————
February 28, 1801 Washington, District of Columbia

. . . no one I believe doubted General Marshalls Talents honorably to discharge the duties of Chief Justice— nor has the hesitation on the part of the Senate to advise his appointment been explained. . . .

ARS (NcU, Hayes Collection).

 David Stone (1770-1818) graduated from the College of New Jersey (later Princeton) in 1788 and then studied law under William Richardson Davie. Stone gained admission to the bar in 1790. He served as member of the North Carolina House of Commons (1791-1794) and as judge of the Superior Court (1794-1798). Stone became a congressman in 1799 and was serving in that capacity at the time that he wrote this letter; on March 4, 1801, he took his seat in the Senate. *DAB; BDAC.*

John Marshall to Joseph Story ——————
1827

[*John Marshall recounts the offer of a seat on the Supreme Court in 1798.*]
I . . . received a letter from the secretary of state offering me the seat on the
bench of the supreme court which had become vacant by the death of Judge
Iredell;[1] but my preference for the bar still continued & I declined it. Our
brother Washington was intercepted in his way to Congress by this appointment.

. . .

On the resignation of Chief Justice Ellsworth I recommended Judge Patteson
as his successor. The President objected to him, and assigned as his ground of
objection that the feelings of Judge Cushing would be wounded by passing
him and selecting a junior member of the bench. I never heard him assign any
other objection to Judge Patteson, though it was afterwards suspected by many
that he was believed to be connected with the party which opposed the second
attempt at negotiation with France.[2] The President himself mentioned Mr Jay,
and he was nominated to the Senate. When I waited on the President with
Mr Jays letter declining the appointment he said thoughtfully "Who shall I
nominate now?" I replied that I could not tell, as I supposed that his objection
to Judge Patteson remained. He said in a decided tone "I shall not nominate
him." After a moments hesitation he said "I believe I must nominate you." I
                                                                          even
had never before heard my self named for the office and had not ~~my self~~
thought of it. I was pleased as well as surprized, and bowed in silence. Next
day I was nominated, and, although the nomination was suspended by the
                                                            when taken up
friends of Judge Patteson, it was I believe ͜ unanimously approved. I was un-
feignedly gratified at the appointment, and have had much reason to be so. I
soon received a very friendly letter from Judge Patteson congratulating me on
                    occasion
the ~~appointment~~ and expressing [*word missing*] hopes that I might long retain
office.
the ͜ I felt truely grateful for the real cordiality towards me which uniformly
marked his conduct. . . .

ARS (MiU-C). For an account of the origin of this manuscript, see John Stokes Adams, ed., *An
Autobiographical Sketch by John Marshall* (Ann Arbor: University of Michigan Press, 1937), pp. xi-
xxiii. A word is missing because the page is torn.

Joseph Story (1779-1845) became an associate justice of the Supreme Court in 1811. A friend
and colleague of John Marshall, Story requested in 1827 that Marshall send him some biographical
material that Story could use to accompany a book review he was writing of Marshall's *History of
the Colonies*. Marshall sent him a sixteen-page letter which includes these two extracts. *DAB* entry
for Joseph Story; Adams, *Autobiographical Sketch by John Marshall*, pp. xvi-xvii.

1. The vacancy on the bench of the Supreme Court was caused by the death of James Wilson,
not James Iredell. See "Appointments to the Bench," under "Bushrod Washington: Appointment
as Associate Justice in 1798," Timothy Pickering to John Marshall, two letters under September
20, 1798.

2. Alexander Hamilton and members of President Adams's own cabinet opposed sending a second mission to France to negotiate a new treaty in 1799. *PAH*, 23:545-47n. William Paterson was viewed as an ally of Alexander Hamilton; see James Gunn to Alexander Hamilton, December 18, 1800.

On September 20, 1803, the *Aurora* (Philadelphia) included a brief article about William Paterson and mentioned a "cause which raised all New England against him, and prevented his being appointed Chief Justice in the room of *Jay*." Referring to Paterson's opinion in the Circuit Court for the district of Pennsylvania in April, 1795, in the case of *Vanhorne's Lessee v. Dorrance* (*Dallas*, 2:304), the *Aurora* continued "*Judge Patterson's* offence against the tories was, his opinion on the *Connecticut claim* to lands which they invaded and occupied in this state. He decided against the *usurpation* and *violation of territory* by *Connecticut;* and Connecticut united all New England to prevent his being appointed Chief Justice_ afterwards they pretended to *forgive* him, but they only pretended." On September 28, 1803, the *Aurora* repeated its praise of Paterson's decision "though it lost him the succession to *Jay* on the bench." There is no evidence to confirm the *Aurora's* interpretation of why President Adams did not appoint Paterson chief justice. In fact letters written during January, 1801 (published above), indicate there was no opposition to Paterson's candidacy.

James Kent to Elizabeth Hamilton
December 20, 1832   New York, New York

. . . While the constitution was in its progress to maturity, some of his[1] friends had suggested in my hearing,[2] that the office of Chief Justice of the Supreme
   of the United States,
court ∧ would be one every way suited to the exercise of his discernment & judgment; & that he was well fitted for it by his accurate acquaintance with the general principles of jurisprudence. Of all this there could be no doubt,

Alexander Hamilton (1757-1804) by James Sharples (ca. 1751-1811). Pastel on paper, ca. 1796. Courtesy National Portrait Gallery, Smithsonian Institution.

but his versatile talents, adapted equally for the bench & the bar, the field,[3] && the Senate house & the Executive cabinet, were fortunately called to act in a more complicated, busy & responsible Station.[4] . . .

ARS (DLC, Alexander Hamilton Papers).

Elizabeth Schuyler (1757-1854) married Alexander Hamilton in 1780. *PJJ*, 2:545.

1. I.e., Alexander Hamilton's.

2. James Kent had met Alexander Hamilton in October, 1787. After meeting Hamilton, Kent arranged with Egbert Benson to publish copies of "The Federalist" essays in Poughkeepsie. Kent attended as a spectator the New York convention to consider the Constitution held in Poughkeepsie in 1788, where Hamilton was the principal defender of the Constitution. By 1789 the two men were close friends. William Kent, *Memoirs and Letters of James Kent, LL.D.* (Boston: Little, Brown, 1898), pp. 282-83, 301, 312-13; John Theodore Horton, *James Kent: A Study in Conservatism, 1763-1847* (1939; reprint ed., New York: Da Capo Press, 1969), pp. 56-57.

3. The "1" is written over a "d."

4. I.e., as secretary of the treasury.

Glossary of Legal Terms

The definitions appearing below have been drawn from three sources: Giles Jacob, *A New Law-Dictionary*, 10th ed. rev. and enl. by J. Morgan (London: W. Strahan and W. Woodfall, 1788); John Bouvier, *Bouvier's Law Dictionary*, rev. by Francis Rawle (Boston: Boston Book, 1897); and, Henry C. Black, *Black's Law Dictionary*, 4th ed. rev. (St. Paul, Minnesota: West Publishing, 1968). Context was the most important criterion in deciding which definitions to print. Only those meanings used in the text have been included. The contemporary eighteenth century definitions in Jacob have been preferred over those in Bouvier or Black, except where the latter contain clearer and more concise definitions with essentially the same meaning. In cases where a definition is carried forward from an earlier to a more recent dictionary, only the earlier source has been cited. Alternate spellings appearing in the text are in brackets after the preferred spelling.

Action on the case: A common law remedy generally to recover damages for an injury committed without force, or which results indirectly from the action of the defendant. Bouvier, s.v. "trespass on the case."

Administrator: A person appointed by the court to manage and distribute the estate of an intestate. Bouvier, Black.

Affidavit: A written statement sworn before a person having the authority to administer an oath. Jacob.

Affirm: 1) To confirm the judgment of a lower court; 2) to make a solemn religious declaration in the nature of an oath. Bouvier.

Alias subpoena: A second or further subpoena issued after the first has been sued out without effect. Jacob.

Alias summons: A second or further summons issued after the first has been sued out without effect. Jacob.

Amicable action: An action brought by the mutual consent of the parties. Black.

Answer: In equity, a written defense made by the defendant to the complainant's bill. Bouvier.

Appeal: The removal of a cause from a court of inferior to one of superior jurisdiction, for the purpose of review and retrial. Bouvier.

Appearance: The formal proceeding by which a defendant submits himself to the jurisdiction of the court. Bouvier.

Appellant: The party taking an appeal from one court to another. Black.

Assignment of errors: The written statement of the plaintiff-in-error alleging errors in the proceedings of the court below. Bouvier.

At bar: Before the court. Black.

Bill in equity: The initial pleading by the complainant in an equity suit, containing the names of the parties, a statement of facts, the allegations of wrongdoing, and a prayer for relief. Bouvier.

Capias or *capias ad respondendum:* That you take to answer (Lat.); a writ by which actions were frequently commenced and which commanded the sheriff to take the defendant, keep him safe, and produce his body in court on a certain day to answer the plaintiff. Black.

Case: See action on the case.

Certiorari: A writ issued by a superior to an inferior court, requiring the latter to send to the former some proceeding therein pending, or the record and proceedings in some case already terminated where the procedure is not according to the common law. Bouvier.

Chancery: A court of general equity jurisdiction. Bouvier.

Citation: A judicial writ commanding a person to appear on a certain day and do something therein specified, or show cause why he should not. Bouvier.

Commission: An instrument issued by a court or other competent tribunal to authorize a person to take depositions or perform any other action so specified within. Bouvier.

Common appearance: The filing of bail on the part of a defendant when served with an arrest warrant. Jacob, s.v. "appearance."

Common error: An error for which there are many precedents. Black, s.v. "error."

Complainant: A party asking for legal redress; a plaintiff in an equity suit. Bouvier, Black.

Complaint: In criminal law, the allegation made before a magistrate that a person has committed some specified offense. Bouvier.

Curia advisare vult: The court will advise (Lat.); an entry in the record indicating the continuance of a cause until a final judgment should be rendered. Bouvier, Black.

Declaration: A plaintiff's first pleading in an action at law, being a formal statement of the facts constituting the cause of action. Black.

Decree: The judicial decision of a case by a court of equity or admiralty. Bouvier.

Default: Nonperformance of a duty; nonappearance in court by a defendant or plaintiff on an assigned day; failure of any party to take a required step to advance his cause. Jacob, Bouvier, Black.

Defendant: The party sued in a personal action. Jacob.

Defendant-in-error: The party against whom a writ of error is sued out. Bouvier.

Demurrage: Payment for delay of a vessel beyond the time allowed for loading, unloading, or sailing. Bouvier.

Demurrer: In equity, an allegation by the defendant stating that even if the facts alleged in the pleading be true, they are insufficient for the complainant to proceed upon or to oblige the defendant to answer. Bouvier, Black.

Deposition: The written testimony of a witness, not in open court, in answer to interrogatories and intended to be used in a trial. Jacob, Bouvier.

Diminution (of the record): Incompleteness of the record of a case as sent from an inferior to a superior court. Bouvier.

Discharge (of a rule): To vacate. Bouvier.

Discontinuance: The interruption in proceedings occasioned by the plaintiff's failure to continue the suit from day to day until conclusion. Jacob. Bouvier.

Dismiss without prejudice: To dismiss, as of a bill of equity, without impairing the right of the complainant to sue again on the same cause of action. Black, s.v. "dismissal without prejudice."

Distringas: A writ commanding the sheriff to seize a defendant's goods and chattels, usually to compel an appearance in court. Bouvier, Black.

Enter: To formally place anything before the court, or upon the record, usually in writing. Black.

Equity: A branch of remedial justice by and through which relief is afforded suitors in the courts of equity. Originating in the Curia Regis, the great court in which the English king administered justice in person, equity overcame limitations in common law by permitting all persons having an interest in the case to be made parties, by framing pleadings so as to present the whole case, and by allowing a variety of remedies. Bouvier.

Eodem die: On that day (Lat.). Black.

Error: See writ of error.

Errors: See assignment of errors.

Ex officio: From office (Lat.); the power a person has, by virtue of the office, to do certain acts. Jacob, Black

Ex parte: Of the one part (Lat.); done by or for one party. Jacob, Black.

Exception: An objection made to a decision of the court in the course of a trial. In admiralty or equity, a formal written allegation that some pleading or proceeding in a cause is insufficient. In common law, a written statement of objections to the decision of the trial court upon a point of law is a bill of exceptions. Upon issuance of a writ of error, the bill of exceptions is filed with the appellate court and serves to place before the court information about the trial which could not be included in the record. Bouvier, Black.

Execution: A writ directing an officer to carry into effect the court's final judgment or decree. Bouvier.

Executor: A person appointed to carry into effect a last will and testament. Bouvier.

Exemplification: An official transcript of a document from public records, authenticated as a true copy. Black.

Exit or et exit: It goes forth (Lat.); a docket entry signifying the issue of process. Black.

Gaol, (goal): Jail; prison for temporary confinement. Black.

General jury, general traverse jury: See petit jury.

Habeas corpus: You have the body (Lat.); a writ directed to a person detaining another and commanding him to produce the body of the prisoner at a certain time and place. Bouvier.

In case: See action on the case.

In error: See writ of error.

In nullo est erratum: In nothing is there error (Lat.); a plea by which the defendant-in-error affirms there is no error in the record. Bouvier, Black.

Inhibition: A writ to forbid a judge from further proceeding in a cause depending before him. Jacob.

Injunction: A kind of prohibition generally issued by a court of equity to stay proceedings in courts at law. Jacob.

Interlocutory: Something intervening between the commencement and the end of a suit which decides some point or matter, but is not a final decision of the whole controversy. Black.

Interrogatories: A series of formal written questions used in the judicial examination of a party or a witness. Black.

Joinder or *joinder in error:* In proceedings on a writ of error, a denial of the errors alleged in the assignment of errors. Jacob.

Joinder in demurrer: The answer to a demurrer. Bouvier.

Judgment: The decision of the court on proceedings instituted therein. Bouvier.

Judgment nisi: A judgment which is to stand, unless the affected party appears and shows cause, or takes other appropriate measures to avoid it or cause its revocation. Black, s.v. "nisi.".

Lessee: A person who holds an estate by virtue of a lease. Bouvier, Black.

Letters patent: An instrument granted by the government to convey a right or authority to an individual. Bouvier.

Libel: In admiralty, the initial pleading on the part of the plaintiff, corresponding to the declaration, bill, or complaint. Bouvier, Black.

Mandamus: A high prerogative writ, usually issuing out of the highest court of general jurisdiction, directing any natural person, corporation, or inferior court to do a specific thing pertaining to their office or duty. Bouvier.

Moiety: The half of anything. Jacob.

Motion: An application to the court by a party, or his counsel, in order to obtain some rule or order of court. Jacob, Bouvier.

Narratio: A plaintiff's declaration, being a narrative of the facts relied upon. Bouvier, Black.

Non assumpsit: He did not undertake (Lat.); in personal actions, the defendant's plea that he did not promise that which is alleged. Jacob, Bouvier.

Non pros, non pros'd, or *non prosequitur:* He does not pursue (Lat.); the failure of the plaintiff to prosecute his action, or any part of it, within a certain time, and the judgment in such instance that the plaintiff pay costs. Bouvier, Black.

Order: A written direction of a court not included in a judgment. Bouvier.

Panel: The roll or piece of parchment, containing the names of jurors summoned to decide a case, which the sheriff must return to the court with the venire facias. Bouvier.

Per curiam: By the court (Lat.); a phrase often used to distinguish the opinion or decision of the court from that of a single judge. Bouvier.

Per querentes: For the plaintiffs (Lat.). Black, s.v. "querens."

Petit jury: A body of men sworn to declare the facts of a case as presented by the evidence. Bouvier, s.v. "jury."

Plaintiff: The party who brings a personal action. Black.

Plaintiff-in-error: The party who sues out a writ of error. Black.

Plea: That which either party alleges for himself in court. In common law, a pleading, especially the first pleading on the part of the defendant. In equity, a special answer arguing that the suit should be dismissed, delayed, or barred. Jacob, Bouvier, Black.

Pleadings: The formal allegations by the parties of their respective claims and defenses, for the judgment of the court. Black.

Precept: A writ directed to the sheriff commanding him to perform a specific act. Bouvier.

Process: A formal written command issued by authority of law; the means by which a defendant is compelled to appear in court. Bouvier, Black.

Proctor (procter): In admiralty, a person employed to manage a cause. Bouvier.

Prohibition: A writ issued to an inferior court commanding it to cease all proceedings in a cause, upon suggestion that jurisdiction is lacking. Bouvier.

Recognizance: An obligation of record, entered into before some court or authorized officer, with a condition to do some particular act. Bouvier.

Record: A written history of a suit from beginning to end, including the conclusion of law. Black.

Rejoin: To answer a plaintiff's replication. Black.

Rejoinder: The defendant's answer to the plaintiff's replication. Jacob.

Remand: To send a cause back to the same court from which it came for further action. Bouvier, s.v. "remanding a cause."

Replication: A reply made by the plaintiff to the defendant's plea, or in equity to the defendant's answer. Black.

Return: The act of a sheriff in delivering back to the court a writ, notice, or other paper which he was directed to serve or execute, with a brief account of his actions under the mandate; also, the indorsement made by the sheriff upon the writ or paper. Black.

Reverse: To vacate, set aside, or make void. Bouvier.

Rule: An order made by a court. Rules of court are either general or special: the former are the laws by which the practice of the court is governed;

the latter are special orders made in particular cases. Bouvier, s.v. "rule of court."

Seriatim: In a series (Lat.). Bouvier.

Service: The execution of a writ or process. Bouvier.

Shew cause or *show cause:* To appear as directed, and present the court with reasons why something should not be done by the court. Black.

Special jury: A jury selected with the assistance of the parties, usually to try matters of great importance; consisting of forty-eight freeholders from which each side strikes twelve names, and from the remainder the jury is selected. Jacob, Bouvier, s.v. "jury."

Special mandate: An order issued by an appellate court, upon the decision of an appeal or a writ of error, directing the lower court to take action on or make disposition of a case. Black.

Stay: The act of arresting a judicial proceeding by the order of a court. Black.

Subpoena: Under penalty (Lat.); a writ issued to call a witness to appear and testify in court. In equity, a writ for calling a defendant to appear and answer the complainant's bill. Jacob, Bouvier.

Suggestion: A statement, formally entered on the record, of some fact or circumstance which will materially affect the further proceedings in the cause, or which is necessary to be brought to the knowledge of the court in order for the proper disposition of the cause, but which, for some reason cannot be pleaded. Black.

Summons: A writ commanding the sheriff to notify a party to appear in court on a specified day to answer a complaint. Bouvier.

Supersedeas: A writ to stay proceedings at law. Jacob.

Sur: On. Black.

Surety: A person who binds himself to pay money or perform any other act for another. Bouvier.

Terre tenant: A person who has the actual possession of the land. Jacob.

Teste: The concluding clause of a writ beginning with the word "Witness ... " and including the date executed. Bouvier, s.v. "teste of a writ."

True verdict: The voluntary conclusion of the jury after deliberate consideration. Black.

Venire, venire facias, venire facias juratores: That you cause to come (Lat.); a judicial writ directed to the sheriff to cause a jury of the neighborhood to appear to try a suit at issue. Jacob, Black.

Venire de novo or *venire facias de novo:* A new writ of venire facias, awarded when the proper effect of the first has been frustrated, or the verdict has become void, or when a judgment is reversed. Bouvier.

Viva voce: With the living voice (Lat.); given orally in open court. Bouvier.

Warrant: A writ issued by an authorized officer, directing a sheriff, or other officer, to arrest a person therein named, charged with committing some offense, and to bring him before the proper judicial authorities. Bouvier.

Writ: A mandatory precept, issued by and in the name of the sovereign or state, commanding something to be done touching a suit or action. Jacob, Bouvier.

Writ of error: A writ issued out of a court of appellate jurisdiction, directed to the judges of a court of record in which final judgment has been given, commanding them to send the record to the appellate court in order that some alleged error in the proceedings may be corrected. Bouvier.

Writ of inquiry (enquiry) of damages: A writ issued to the sheriff upon a judgment by default commanding him to summon a jury to enquire what damages the plaintiff has sustained. Jacob.

Signs and Abbreviations

This list includes only those eighteenth-century signs and abbreviations that might not be recognized easily by the modern reader. The list begins with a presentation of signs and then continues with abbreviations. When an abbreviation appears in the text of this volume with the same letters but in different forms, we only record it once in this list; thus, the word "against" might be abbreviated as "agt" or "ag^t," but in this list only "agt" would be given. In general, all superior letters have been dropped to the baseline with only one exception ("an^d" for "answered"). Plural forms of these abbreviations also have been eliminated; so too have variants due to different capitalization.

9	A sign used at the end of a word to replace the letters "us" or "os" or "ost."
℮	A sign used at the end of a word to replace "is" or "es" or, more generally, any word ending.
℗	per
℗	Per
⊗	A reference mark, called an obelisk.

& ali(s)	and others		*affe*	affectionate
& als	and others		*affece*	affectionate
&c	et cetera		*affect*	affectionate
&ca	et cetera		*affecte*	affectionate
acknowd	acknowledged		*affectte*	affectionate
actn	action		*afft*	affidavit
adjd	adjourned		*afsd*	aforesaid
adjdt	adjournment		*aftwds*	afterwards
adjo	adjourned		*agreet*	agreement
adm	administrator		*agst*	against
admnor	administrator		*agt*	against
admnr	administrator		*amic*	amicable
admor	administrator		*an^d*	answered
admr	administrator		*Annapl*	Annapolis
af	affirmed		*Annaps*	Annapolis

app	appeal	*et als*	and others
appelts	appellants	*evg*	evening
argt	argument	*ex*	executor
att	attorney	*excors*	executors
atty	attorney	*exec*	executor
AV	August	*exon*	execution
chancy	chancery	*exor*	executor
Chs Town	Charleston	*exr*	executor
Congr	Congress	*favd*	favored
cir	circuit	*favr*	favor
circt	circuit	*feds*	federalists
cirt	circuit	*frd*	friend
cit	citation	*frm*	from
claimt	claimant	*G*	God
cler	clerk	*G.B.*	Great Britain
clk	clerk	*h*	humble
commissr	commissioner	*hb*	humble
comn	commission	*hble*	humble
complt	complainant	*hl*	humble
compts	compliments	*hle*	humble
cont	continued	*hond*	honored
contd	continued	*IA*	January
ct	court,	*inst*	instant
	circuit	*int*	instant
cty	county	*IV*	June, July
cur	court	*jud*	judgment
currt	current	*lee*	lessee
D	Dear	*ler*	letter
decd	deceased	*M.*	Massachusetts
def	defendant	*mands*	mandamus
defdt	defendant	*memor*	memorial
defend	defendant	*mo*	most, month,
defendt	defendant		motion
defets	defendants	*N.A.*	North America
deft	defendant	*narr*	narratio
deld	delivered	*non asst*	non assumpsit
depy	deputy	*non pro*	non prosequitur
dft	defendant	*ob*	obedient
do	ditto	*obet*	obedient
dr	dear	*obt*	obedient
dt	district	*oppy*	opportunity
dy	deputy	*oth*	other
eno	enough	*p*	president
et ali(s)	and others	*P.*	Pennsylvania

pact	packet		*sert*	servant
plff	plaintiff		*spl mand*	special mandate
plft	plaintiff		*ss*	scilicet (Lat.):
plts	plaintiffs			to wit
prohi	prohibit		*st*	servant
prohib	prohibition		*sunmnd*	summoned
prot	prothonotary		*sup*	supreme
provdd	provided		*supa*	subpoena
PTK	Potomac		*surg*	surviving
Ptmk	Potomac		*svt*	servant
qy	query		*tents*	tenants
r	received		*vy*	very
rd	received		*wch*	which
recog	recognizance		*wd*	would
rectble	returnable		*wh*	which
regd	regard		*whh*	which
repln	replication		*wod*	would
retble	returnable		*wt*	writ
sernt	servant			

Index

tion 1, 909n; Article I, section 6, 90, 90n; Article VI, clause 2, 71; Article VI, clause 3, 1; as authority for presidential appointment, 10, 50, 64, 74, 77, 78, 92, 96, 102, 113, 132, 135, 141, 145, 153; Eleventh Amendment, 303, 303n, 305, 305n, 453, 459, 460, 482, 512, 519 (*see also* Judiciary, federal: jurisdiction of Supreme Court; *Brailsford v. Georgia; Chisholm v. Georgia; Cutting v. South Carolina; Hollingsworth v. Virginia; Moultrie v. Georgia; Oswald v. New York; Vanstaphorst v. Maryland; Vassall v. Massachusetts*); ratification by Connecticut, 118, 119n, 693n, 778n; ratification by Maryland, 71, 108, 805; ratification by Massachusetts, 26, 602n, 603n, 626n, 628n, 641n, 642n, 646n, 649n, 671, 834n, 927n; ratification by New York, 692n, 816n, 930n; ratification by North Carolina, 63, 138, 649n, 672n, 681n, 698n, 878; ratification by Pennsylvania, 47, 606n, 611n, 616–17n, 619, 620n, 632n, 863n; ratification by Rhode Island, 182n, 733n, 764n, 837n, 884n; ratification by South Carolina, 17, 18n, 668n, 669n, 684n, 720n, 768n, 881n; ratification by Virginia, 54, 124, 150, 603n, 627n, 736n, 748n, 798n, 807n, 818n
Constitutional Convention, 17, 33, 47, 54, 85, 87n, 117; Committee of Detail, 17, 47, 118
Constitution (ship). See *Talbot v. Seaman*
Continental Association, 5
Continental Congress, 5–6, 46, 63n; journals used in Supreme Court, 264, 415–16
Continuance, 198, 202, 218, 231, 232, 243, 245, 246, 270, 273, 276, 281, 284, 285, 293, 296, 297, 305, 306, 308, 309, 316, 319, 323, 324, 325, 330, 350, 354, 357, 373, 374, 382, 383, 396, 399, 421, 426, 429, 434, 436, 437, 439, 442, 443, 444, 448, 449, 453, 454, 460, 463, 464, 465, 466, 471, 474
Conyngham, David H., 273, 427
Cooke, John, 283, 436
Cooke, Silas: congratulates James Iredell on Supreme Court appointment, 702; *id.*, *702n*; letter from, 702; solicits appointment as federal court clerk for North Carolina, 702
Cooke, William: *id.*, *739n*; suggested as associate justice, 738
Coolbaugh, John, 872
Cooper, Basil. See *Cooper v. Telfair*
Cooper, William: *id.*, *904n*; letter from, 903
Cooper v. Telfair: in Docket, 526; in Fine Minutes, 322, 323, 325; in Inventory of Case Papers, 586

Cope, Israel, 283, 436
Corbley, Ex parte. See *Ex parte Corbley*
Corbley, John. See *Ex parte Corbley*
Cornwallis, Lord, 62, 124, 148
Costs, 201, 227, 234, 241, 252, 261, 265, 266, 268, 272, 277, 278, 279, 280, 281, 282, 283, 288, 288–89, 290, 291, 295, 296, 297, 300, 309, 320, 322, 324, 325, 356, 378, 386, 393, 412, 416, 417, 419–20, 423, 430, 431, 432, 433, 434, 434–35, 435, 439–40, 440, 441, 443, 446–47, 447, 448, 454, 456, 463, 465, 474, 480–81, 481–82, 486, 487, 488, 492, 493, 496, 497, 498, 498–99, 499, 500, 501, 502, 504, 505, 506, 507, 508, 509, 510, 512, 513, 513–14, 514, 515, 516, 517, 518, 520, 521, 523, 524, 526, 527, 528, 530, 575–76, 579
Cotton, John, 24
Cotton, John B. See *Cotton v. Wallace*
Cotton, Josiah, 24, 26n
Cotton, Mary. *See* Cushing, Mary (Cotton)
Cotton v. Wallace: in Docket, 499; in Fine Minutes, 250, 266, 274, 278–79, 279; in Inventory of Case Papers, 587; in Original Minutes, 404, 417, 426, 427, 431–32, 432
Counsellors. *See* Supreme Court of the U.S., bar of
Course, Elizabeth. See *Course v. Stead*
Course v. Stead: in Docket, 527, 530; in Fine Minutes, 323, 330; in Inventory of Case Papers, 586; in Orders and Rules, 581
Courts, Bermuda: Court of Vice Admiralty, 166n
Courts, Connecticut: admission to bar in, 115, 198n, 285n, 298n, 693n; Court of Common Pleas, clerk of, 857n; New Haven, admission to bar in, 315n; New London County, assistant judge of, 832n; Vice Admiralty Court, judge of, 639n;
—Litchfield County: admission to bar in, 304n; judge of probate for, 857n;
—Superior Court: admission to bar of, 219, 374, 545, 553; clerk of, for Litchfield County, 857n; judge of, 117, 119n, 219, 374, 553, 553n, 612n, 693n, 831n;
—Supreme Court, 514; decree affirmed by Supreme Court of the U.S., 309, 463, 465, 515, 534; judge of, 117, 831n
Courts, Delaware: admiralty court, judge of, 653n; admission to bar in, 545, 616n; Kent County, admission to bar in, 185n; Sussex County, admission to bar in, 185n;
—Court of Common Pleas: admission to bar of, 615; judge of, 615;

James Iredell on Supreme Court appointment, 710–11, 711; *id.*, *711n*; letter from, 710–11, 711, 793–94, 809–10, 847–48; letter to, 699n, 879

Iredell, Francis, 60

Iredell, Hannah (Johnston), 60, 699n, 708, 720, 802–3; *id.*, *753n*; letter to, 753, 754, 755, 755n, 760, 771, 780, 803n, 831, 832, 836, 841–42, 845, 845n, 854, 855, 855n, 856–57, 858, 860, 874, 876n

Iredell, James, 49n, 649n, 662n, 698n, 701, 701n, 704n, 705, 705n, 753n, 755n, 861n, 878n, 881, 882–83; *biographical headnote*, *60–63*; as attorney general of North Carolina, 62, 137; as compiler of *Laws of the State of North-Carolina*, 62, 63, 150; as judge of Superior Court of North Carolina, 62, 708n; as king's attorney in North Carolina, 60–61, 62; character, 662; comments on appointment of John Rutledge as chief justice, 780; comments on appointment of Oliver Ellsworth, 846; comments on declination of William Cushing as chief justice, 836; comments on John Jay's resignation as chief justice, 760; death, 68, 139, 140, 321n, 327n, 877–78, 878, 879, 880, 883, 885, 891, 928, 928n; fights for ratification in North Carolina, 138; financial affairs, 698, 699n, 705; health, 316n, 317n, 743, 755, 874, 875, 876, 879; letter from, 52–53, 67, 171n, 182n, 654, 698, 700–701, 701n, 705, 706, 706–7, 707n, 732, 743, 743n, 753, 754, 755, 755n, 760, 771, 780, 783, 783n, 803n, 831, 832, 836, 841–42, 845, 845n, 846, 854, 855, 855n, 856–57, 858, 860, 861, 869, 870, 876, 876n; letter to, 64, 66–67, 648, 681, 688, 692–93, 694, 698, 699, 701–2, 702, 703, 704, 707, 708, 708–9, 709, 710–11, 711, 712, 714, 715n, 719–20, 735, 779, 783n, 793–94, 801, 802–3, 803n, 809–10, 825, 840, 847–48, 859, 860, 861n, 869, 873, 875, 876; on circuit, as commissioner in invalid pension claim of John Chandler, 222, 375; publishes *Proceedings and debates of the Convention of North-Carolina*, 649n; solicits appointment as Supreme Court justice, 654, 672; suggested as chief justice, 793–94, 809–10; suggested as Supreme Court justice, 648, 662; writes about illness of John Rutledge, 182n;

—as associate justice, 157, 858, 859n, 873n; absence from Court, 214n, 219n, 316n, 317n, 706, 743, 743n, 747, 875, 876; accepts appointment, 67, 698; and appoint-

ment of Supreme Court clerk, 886; appointment, 64, 692–93, 692, 693, 693n, 694, 697–98, 698, 699, 701–2, 701n, 702, 703, 704, 706, 707, 708, 708–9, 709, 710, 710–11, 711, 712, 714, 715n; attendance at Court, 182, 183, 186, 191, 192, 194, 196, 197, 198, 199, 200, 202, 203, 204, 205, 206, 207, 209, 210, 211, 212, 213, 214, 215, 216, 217, 218, 229, 230, 231, 232, 233, 234, 235, 236, 237, 238, 239, 240, 241, 242, 243, 244, 244–45, 245, 246, 247, 248, 249, 250, 251, 253, 255, 255n, 256, 257, 258, 259, 260, 261, 262, 263, 264, 265, 266, 267, 268, 269, 270, 271, 272, 273, 274, 275, 276, 277, 279, 280, 281, 283, 284, 285, 288, 290, 292, 293, 294, 295, 298, 299, 300, 301, 302, 303, 304, 307, 308, 309, 310, 311, 312, 314, 315, 340, 341, 342, 345, 346, 347, 348, 349, 350, 351, 352, 353, 354, 356, 357, 358, 359, 360, 361, 363, 364, 365, 366, 367, 368, 369, 370, 371, 372, 373, 380, 381, 382, 383, 384, 385, 386, 388, 389, 390, 391, 392, 393, 394, 395, 396, 398, 399, 400, 401, 402, 403, 404, 405, 406, 407, 408, 409, 410, 411, 412, 413, 414, 415, 416, 417, 418, 419, 420, 421, 422, 423, 426, 427, 428, 429, 430, 432, 433, 434, 436, 437, 438, 439, 440, 442, 443, 444, 445, 446, 450, 451, 452, 453, 455, 456, 457, 458, 459, 462, 463, 464, 466, 467, 468, 469, 470, 713, 716, 732, 747, 858; attire, 779; author of Original Minutes entry, 157, 355, 355n; circuit assignments, 52–53, 126, 695, 698, 703, 708, 754, 781n, 803, 803n, 855, 855n, 869, 870, 876, 876n; comments on appointment, 700–701, 705, 706, 706–7; comments on circuit duties, 52–53, 126, 700–701, 754, 760, 771, 781, 803, 869; comments on Court term, 753, 754, 755, 755n, 780, 783, 841, 845, 845n, 854, 855, 857, 858, 860; comments on Court vacancy, 831; comments on possible appointment as chief justice, 846; commission, 66, 67, 67n, 68n, 171n, 698, 706n; commission read, 182, 340; cover letter to commission, 66–67; grand jury charge of, 783n; joins in decision in *West v. Barnes*, 477; nomination, 64–65, 65n, 692–93, 693n; notifies Timothy Pickering of James Wilson's death, 52–53, 126, 866, 869, 870; oaths taken, 22–23, 68; on circuit, 2, 22–23, 852n; opinion on circuit

305n, 363, 364, 369, 370, 435, 453, 459, 460, 482, 512, 519, 582

Judiciary, state: comment on New Hampshire, 847; jurisdiction of, 71, 111, 112n, 767, 770n

Judiciary Act of 1789, 1, 23n, 36, 38, 40, 41, 51, 74, 77, 80, 85–86, 87n, 90, 118, 143, 146–47, 173n, 575, 576, 636, 639–40, 657, 661, 666, 734; and title of chief justice, 173n; plans for revision of, 40, 41, 76, 80, 146–47, 890, 890n; section 24, 227, 379, 499; section 35, 173n; section 5, 187n; section 7, 157, 175n; section 8, 682; section 9, 187n, 195n

Judiciary Act of 1801, 752n, 883n, 884n, 890, 890n, 911–12, 913, 914, 917, 917n, 918, 925n

"Junius": letter from, 713–14

Jurisdiction. *See* Judiciary, federal: jurisdiction of circuit court; Judiciary, federal: jurisdiction of Supreme Court; Judiciary, state: jurisdiction of; *Brailsford v. Georgia; Chisholm v. Georgia; Cutting v. South Carolina; Hollingsworth v. Virginia; Moultrie v. Georgia; Oswald v. New York; Vanstaphorst v. Maryland; Vassall v. Massachusetts*; and under individual courts

Jury, grand: charge to, at Circuit Court for the district of Connecticut, 783n; charge to, at Circuit Court for the district of Maryland, 109; charge to, in Massachusetts state court, 26; form of venire for, 571, 571n; presentment of, in Maryland state court, concerning Samuel Chase, 108; presentment of, in South Carolina state court, concerning John Rutledge, 816

Jury, petit: of District Court for the district of New York attends first session of Supreme Court, 688; of District Court for the district of Virginia, 850;

—in Supreme Court, 308, 464, 521; dismissed, 230, 246, 303, 381, 399, 438, 452, 458; excused, 231, 298, 382, 383, 455, 571n; form of venire for, 571, 571n; ordered summoned, 230, 381, 480, 488; summoned, 222, 230, 233, 246, 283–84, 291, 292, 298, 303, 375, 381, 382, 385, 399, 436, 442, 443, 452, 455, 458, 491–92, 493; verdict, 223, 234, 292, 376, 385, 386, 443, 492, 493

Jury, special: form of venire for, 570, 570n; in Supreme Court, 273, 274, 276, 427, 429

Jutan, John. See *Arcambal v. Wiseman; Wiseman v. Arcambal*

Kaighn, John, 273, 427

Keen, Reynold, 222, 223, 375, 493

Keese (Keep), John W.: admission to Supreme Court bar, 181, 340, 541, 694; *id., 181n*

Keith, Mary Randolph. *See* Marshall, Mary Randolph (Keith)

Kempe, John Tabor, 881n

Kennebec Proprietors, 25

Kent, James: and Alexander Hamilton, 930n; *id., 916n*; letter from, 929–30; letter to, 902n, 916, 919n

Keppele, Michael, 296, 439, 448, 511, 512

Ketland v. The Cassius: in Fine Minutes, 251, 253; in Original Minutes, 404–5, 407. See also *United States v. Peters*

Ketty, Captain, 888

Killen, William, 544–45

King, Mary (Alsop), 642n

King, Rufus, 871n; and John Tucker, 166n, 665, 665n; and possible appointment of Edmund Randolph as chief justice, 761; as minister plenipotentiary to Great Britain, 863n, 870, 871n, 901, 902n, 909–910n; comments on possible appointments to judiciary, 663; *id., 642n*; letter from, 663; letter to, 641–42, 652, 742, 781, 811–12, 868, 909, 909n, 912, 913, 916, 926; votes against Rutledge nomination, 99, 99n; votes for Ellsworth nomination, 121, 121n

King's College, 3, 7n, 165–66n, 544n, 621n, 884n. *See also* Columbia College

Kingsley (Kingley, Kinsley), Ebenezer. See *Kingsley v. Jenkins*

Kingsley v. Jenkins: in Docket, 487; in Fine Minutes, 202, 206, 211, 212, 213, 215, 227; in Formulary, 566n; in Inventory of Case Papers, 586; in Original Minut Kuhn, Peter, 273, 427

Kinkaid (Kincaid), Maria. See *Williamson v. Kinkaid*

Kinkaid, Williamson v. See *Williamson v. Kinkaid*

Kinley, William, 292, 443

Kinsey, J., 569

Kintzing, Abraham, 283, 436

Kirby, Ephraim, 219, 374; admission to Supreme Court bar, 218–19, 374, 553, 553n; *id., 218n, 658n*; letter to, 657, 696; solicits appointment as federal court clerk for Connecticut, 657, 658n; solicits appointment as Supreme Court clerk, 658n, 696

Kirkpatrick, Mr., 857n

Kirkpatrick, Andrew, 87n; admission to Supreme Court bar, 275, 428; *id., 275n*